SSSP

Springer
Series in
Social
Psychology

SSSP

Norman T. Feather

The Psychological Impact of Unemployment

Springer-Verlag New York Berlin Heidelberg
London Paris Tokyo Hong Kong

Norman T. Feather
Discipline of Psychology
School of Social Sciences
The Flinders University of South Australia
Bedford Park, South Australia 5042
Australia

With 10 Illustrations.

Library of Congress Cataloging-in-Publication Data
Feather, Norman T.
  The psychological impact of unemployment / Norman T. Feather.
    p.   cm.—(Springer series in social psychology)
  Includes bibliographical references.
  1. Unemployment—Psychological aspects. I. Title. II. Series
HD5708.F43   1989
331.13'7'019—dc20   89-19687

Printed on acid-free paper.

Typeset by Asco Trade Typesetting Ltd., Hong Kong.
Printed and bound by Edwards Brothers Incorporated, Ann Arbor, Michigan.
Printed in the United States of America.

9 8 7 6 5 4 3 2 1

ISBN 0-387-97027-4 Springer-Verlag New York Berlin Heidelberg
ISBN 3-540-97027-4 Springer-Verlag Berlin Heidelberg New York

Preface

This book is concerned with the psychological effects of unemployment. In writing it I had two main aims: (1) to describe theoretical approaches that are relevant to understanding unemployment effects; and (2) to present the results of studies from a program of research with which I have been closely involved over recent years.

In order to meet these aims I have organized the book into two main parts. I discuss background research and theoretical approaches in the first half of the book, beginning with research concerned with the psychological effects of unemployment during the Great Depression and continuing through to a discussion of more recent contributions. I have not attempted to review the literature in fine detail. Instead, I refer to some of the landmark studies and to the main theoretical ideas that have been developed. This discussion takes us through theoretical approaches that have emerged from the study of work, employment, and unemployment to a consideration of wider frameworks that can also be applied to further our understanding of unemployment effects.

A consistent theme throughout the book is that research into the psychological impact of unemployment can draw upon a range of theoretical ideas from psychology, depending upon the type of question that is asked. We are not limited to theories that specifically derive from the study of work, employment, and unemployment. The net can be spread more widely so as to gather in ideas from psychological research concerned with the self, stress and coping, expectancy-value theories of motivation, causal attributions, learned helplessness, self-efficacy, and life-span development, to cite some of the approaches that I discuss in the first half of the book.

The second half of the book describes a set of studies with which I have been associated over the past few years. Most of this research has been concerned with youth unemployment but more recently I have initiated studies of the psychological impact of unemployment in older age groups. In presenting these studies I have drawn freely from my previous publications, often verbatim. This book provides me with the opportunity to bring these studies together for the first time, showing how they interrelate and how there has been a development from relatively simple cross-sectional investigations to more complex longitudinal studies. The reader is thereby presented with a bird's-eye view of an extensive, evolving research program concerned with unemployment effects, a view that is not possible when studies are considered in isolation.

The studies cover a wide range of variables. The results inform us about affective reactions to unemployment; changes in causal attributions, values, and aspects of the self-concept; perceptions of time use; and the effects of financial stress, among other variables. In order to account for some of these effects one is inevitably drawn to the theories discussed in the first half of the book. Hence the two parts of the book are not separate halves; they stand together. Where possible, I have tried to relate findings from the research program to the theoretical ideas discussed in previous chapters and to recent findings from the literature.

I am grateful to the Australian Research Grants Scheme, the British Council Academic Links and Interchange Scheme, and to Flinders University for providing funds that enabled me to develop and complete the various studies described in this book.

I also wish to acknowledge the help of my colleagues and students at Flinders University who, over the years, have worked with me in the research program. I also wish to thank Carol McNally, Kay Guest, and Rosemary Kamenjarin who assisted in typing the manuscript—especially Carol McNally who took the major role with patience, thoughtfulness, good humor, and skill.

Adelaide, September 1989   Norman T. Feather

Contents

Contents

Chapter 1

Introduction and Overview

The principal aim of this book is to describe a set of studies concerned with the psychological impact of unemployment. This program of studies was initiated by the author in the late 1970s and the research has continued throughout the 1980s. This volume brings this set of investigations together for the first time and thereby provides an opportunity for examining the evolution of the research program, the variety of questions that have been asked, and the main findings that have been obtained.

Most of the studies have been concerned with the effects of unemployment among young people. More recently, however, we have also investigated unemployment among the middle-aged and some of the results from these studies will be described. Why focus on youth unemployment? The main reason is that a lot of current unemployment in Australia is concentrated among young people, with dramatic increases in teenage unemployment occurring during the 1970s and 1980s (Windschuttle, 1979). The Australian Bureau of Statistics tables show, for example, that in 1979 the unemployment rates for 15 to 19-year-old men and women in the labor force were 14.6% and 20.4% respectively, compared with rates of 2.4% and 4.2% for men and women in the 35–44 age range. In 1985 the respective male and female unemployment rates for the 15–19 age range were 19.3% and 17.1%, and for the 35–44 age range the unemployment rates were 4.4% and 5.3% for men and women respectively. The unemployment rates for teenage men and women in the late 1970s and through the 1980s contrast with average rates of around 4% during the 1960s and early 1970s. It is evident that youth unemployment is a very important social problem in Australia, as it is in many other countries. The cold statistics mask the social and economic waste that occurs as young people are denied jobs and they fail to capture the negative effects that unemployment can have on individual lives.

Research interest in the psychological impact of unemployment appears to follow rapid increases in unemployment rates. Thus, the 1930s and 1940s saw a spate of publications relating to the Great Depression (e.g., Bakke, 1933,

1940a, 1940b; Eisenberg & Lazarsfeld, 1938; Jahoda, Lazarsfeld, & Zeisel, 1933; Komarovsky, 1940; Pilgrim Trust, 1938) and the recent dramatic increases in unemployment have also been followed by renewed research interest in the effects of being without a job. The literature spans different countries, with contributions from research groups in the United Kingdom, Europe, North America, and Australia. This literature will be referred to throughout this volume but in selective fashion. My intention is not to present an encyclopedic compendium of unemployment research in the 1970s and 1980s, but to focus on my own research program, referring to other related studies where appropriate. This more restricted focus limits the range of topics to be addressed but it has the advantage of enabling discussion of research findings in somewhat more depth than can be achieved in an overall literature survey. As will be evident, it does not preclude the drawing out of wider implications or the necessary linking of results with theories and findings from other sources. The research program to be described is not an isolated set of studies but is firmly embedded in the mainstream of current investigations of the psychological impact of unemployment.

The main questions to be addressed are as follows:

1. What are the effects of unemployment on psychological well-being, on work values and work motivation, on a person's view of self, and on behaviors such as job-seeking?
2. How do these effects vary between individuals and groups and what factors may account for this variation?
3. How do people explain unemployment and how can these explanations be understood in terms of personal experience and underlying attitudes and values?
4. What kinds of psychological theories have been advanced to explain how people react to unemployment both subjectively in relation to cognition and affect and overtly in relation to coping behaviors such as job-seeking?

Not all of these questions are examined in the same detail and many of the answers that emerge are qualified ones. We are dealing with a complex and difficult topic that is not the sole province of the psychologist. Indeed, unemployment is a topic that cries out for multidisciplinary study with a need to consider psychological, economic, political, sociological, historical, and other social science perspectives. Psychological investigations can cover only part of the territory but nevertheless an important part.

The topic is not an easy one to investigate. One has to decide which variables to study, how to measure them, how to conduct the sampling, and how to design studies that go beyond description and that provide some clues about underlying cause-effect relations. Psychologists have studied a wide range of variables in their research on the impact of unemployment. These variables include measures of positive affect, experience of pleasure, negative affect, global and differentiated self-esteem, depressed mood, self-rated anxiety, depressive symptoms, guilt, physical illness, potential and diag-

nosed psychiatric illness, psychological distress, experience of strain, present life satisfaction, apathy, the structured and purposive use of time, stress
symptoms, and self-rated happiness. These variables relate to psychological
health and psychological well-being. Research has also been conducted into
how the unemployed explain their condition, attributional styles, external
locus of control, feelings of helplessness and controllability, confidence, employment commitment, the work ethic, work values, anger, measures of
psychosocial development, loneliness, boredom, changes in particular kinds
of behavior (e.g., watching TV, book-borrowing, going to sporting events),
the form and frequency of job-seeking, and other coping responses. There are
other variables that could be added to this list, but those included demonstrate the wide range of variables that have already been researched.

The scope of investigations extends all the way from major surveys with
large samples of respondents to more intensive investigations of small, specially selected groups of individuals who are interviewed in depth. Commonly
used psychological scales have been included in these surveys, as well as specially designed scales, specific items, and other kinds of measures that span
the range from the more subjective to the physiological (see Warr, 1987a, for
examples). Some researchers have used aggregate measures (e.g., Brenner,
1973, 1980; Dooley & Catalano, 1980, 1984a, 1984b, Dooley, Catalano, &
Rook, 1988). There are no recent studies, however, that have involved the
detailed examination of a specific community as in the classic Marienthal
study conducted in the early 1930s (Jahoda et al., 1933). However, the research styles that are adopted in current research clearly vary all the way from
individual-centered investigations that use quantification, interviews, and
questionnaires to research that takes account of social institutions, aggregate
forms of analyses, and the wider impact of unemployment on the family and
elsewhere (Elder & Caspi, 1988; Jahoda, 1988; Liem & Liem, 1988).

The degree of sophistication in sampling varies according to the resources
available. In some studies it has been possible to take carefully selected
national samples and to employ trained interviewers. In other cases researchers have relied on available samples that can be conveniently obtained
(e.g., school-leavers, people attending local employment offices, etc.). Longitudinal studies that follow up unemployed people over time are rare when
compared with cross-sectional studies that obtain information from various
groups (e.g., employed and unemployed) at one point in time.

When one selects samples it is obviously necessary to have a clear definition
of what unemployment means. This definition may vary from country to
country and in the same country at different times, depending upon government enactments. The research to be reported focuses on those unemployed people who are of working age and who are active job seekers. Hence
we exclude discouraged unemployed people who have given up looking for a
job and others who, for whatever reason (e.g., poor health, family responsibilities), are unemployed but not actively seeking a job. Definitions may or may
not take account of people who are seeking part-time employment or who are

already employed part-time but are looking for a full-time job. Jahoda (1982) prefers to avoid differences in legal definitions and instead takes a social-psychological position. She regards the unemployed as "all who have not got a job but would like to have one or who when they have no job are dependent on some financial support from whatever source for their livelihood" (p. 13).

These few comments indicate some of the conceptual issues involved in defining who is unemployed. To these we can add the problems of making contact with the unemployed in any sampling study, especially those who no longer bother to look for jobs because of discouraging experiences but who would still like to work. Official statistics usually mask an unknown level of hidden unemployment and they may also fail to cater for underemployment.

Most authors indicate the importance of distinguishing between employment and work conceived in more general terms. Warr (1987a) defines work as "an activity directed to valued goals beyond enjoyment of the activity itself" (p. 57). It can take place over a short time period and involve momentary exertion or it may be sustained over long periods of time and be linked to a network of social roles and institutions. Employment is work that involves a contractual relationship between an employer and an employee accompanied by a salary, a relationship in which there is an exchange of economic reward for labor and that involves rights and responsibilities. Warr (1987a) notes that most definitions of unemployment include the notion that an unemployed person must not only lack a job but also be seeking one. One would therefore exclude adults below the age of retirement who lack a job but who are not looking for one. For example, a woman may voluntarily give up her job to care for her children. Warr (1987a) calls people in this group the "nonemployed" and distinguishes them from the unemployed (see also Jahoda, 1982). It is clear that work can occur within employment, unemployment, and nonemployment. Work is the general concept and it can take different forms depending upon the presence or absence of an exchange agreement, a salary, an obligation to an employer, intention and choice, and so forth.

These various distinctions are important in the interests of conceptual clarity. They also suggest areas of research still to be pursued. For example, what are the effects of employment when compared with full-time unemployment, with continuous part-time unemployment, with intermittent casual employment, and with intentional nonemployment? Can the effects of unemployment be cushioned by work that does not involve an economic exchange? In what ways are the discouraged unemployed who have given up looking for employment different from those who are still seeking employment or from those who are nonemployed but active in other ways? What are the effects on a person of being underemployed, of working in a job for which the person is overqualified in terms of his or her skills or in which the person lacks motivation and interest? A detailed conceptual analysis of what is meant by work, employment, underemployment, unemployment, and nonemployment opens up questions such as these.

The research findings to be reported in this volume relate to employed and

unemployed groups and to schoolchildren who have not yet entered the workforce. As noted, the primary interest is in unemployment among young people. To what extent can these findings be generalized? Most authors agree
that the effects of unemployment may be somewhat different for different
groups and circumstances. For example, Jahoda (1982) notes that the results
of unemployment research look:

> . . . somewhat different for every individual affected, depending on a whole
> host of personal circumstances. Paraphrasing a famous formulation in the
> study of personality (Kluckhohn, Murray, & Schneider, 1955), in some re-
> spects every unemployed is like every other unemployed (i.e., without a
> job); in some respects every unemployed is like some other unemployed
> (e.g., with similar previous jobs); and in some respects every unemployed is
> like no other unemployed (i.e., a unique individual). All these "respects"
> raise legitimate issues. (p. 48)

Jahoda's comment indicates that research findings on unemployment are likely to reveal general effects that apply to all unemployed people, group effects
that relate to particular groups (e.g., school-leavers, women, middle-aged
men, managers), and unique effects that operate at the level of individuals.

These effects occur within a physical and social milieu that also requires
definition. For example, the effects may vary depending upon whether a person lives in a large city or a small country town; in a location with a sunny
climate or with a cold, wet climate; comes from a small family or a large
family; has a restricted social network or a large circle of friends; enjoys
sources of financial support or is without financial resources. Some of these
variables are externally imposed and largely outside of the control of the unemployed person. Nations, for example, vary in the economic support they
provide for unemployed people. At the time of writing this book, for example, unemployment benefits in Australia continue to be paid as long as there
is evidence that a person is seeking employment. Social welfare benefits for
the unemployed vary across countries, however, and some benefit schemes
are more generous than others, cushioning the financial effects of unemployment over longer time periods. These economic constraints impose conditions
that affect the livelihood of unemployed people and thereby limit what the
unemployed can do to ameliorate their situation.

Not to be ignored are the personal characteristics of the unemployed themselves and their role in the psychological impact that unemployment has.
Some individuals may cope better than others because they have different sets
of abilities, skills, attitudes, values, self-perceptions, or other personal resources that help them to survive under adverse conditions.

It should be clear, therefore, that a wide range of variables can be considered in the analysis of the psychological impact of unemployment. These
variables relate not only to the personal characteristics of the unemployed
that influence how they are able to cope with adversity but external conditions
as well that facilitate or restrict the adjustments that are possible. These personal and situational variables interact to influence psychological adjustment

and coping behaviors. Whether an unemployed person becomes depressed; changes his or her life-style; persists in looking for a job; explores alternative occupations; modifies his or her beliefs, attitudes, or values; withdraws from social contacts; suffers psychological distress and physical symptoms, or reacts in other ways to the condition of unemployment depends on both the person and the situation and the way they interact. This interaction is a two-way process. The situation can affect the person and the person can in turn influence or modify the environment.

The interactional form of analysis that I adopt sees the person as an active agent and not as passive point of contact of situational forces. The person both construes and interprets information from the environment and has the capacity to act on the environment so as to alter it. The environment in turn provides information and sets the context for action. This interactional perspective draws from the earlier contributions of Lewin (1936, 1938, 1951) and, in its general form, it is congruent with much current thinking about the person and the environment (e.g., Bandura, 1986; Feather, 1982c; Warr, 1987a).

This general framework does not constitute a fully developed theory but rather a perspective or metatheory within which particular theoretical formulations can be embedded. A number of such formulations will be referred to in the course of this volume, including the motivational approach termed expectancy-value (or expectancy-valence) theory used to analyze job-seeking behavior. A key point to be made throughout this book is that the study of the various psychological effects of unemployment should move beyond description to the formulation of hypotheses that are linked to theoretical models. There is now a vast literature that describes the psychological effects of unemployment. It is clearly impossible to account for all of these effects by using one all-embracing theory. What is needed is the application of theoretical models from different areas of psychology (e.g., motivation, coping behavior, developmental psychology) so as to bring some order into the wide array of findings and to generate new predictions that can be tested in further research. There is some indication that this kind of progress is starting to occur.

Jahoda (1982), in her recent discussion of employment and unemployment, also notes the need for theories in an area where many studies are atheoretical and occasionally yield contradictory findings (see also Jahoda, 1988). She indicates that some of the theories that have been applied are designed to provide explanations for different phenomena associated with employment and unemployment. Moreover, some theories are primarily individualistic in character and pay little attention to the effects of social institutions; other theories take more account of the "two-dimensional interaction between individual psychological processes and institutional arrangements that constrain or enable the conduct of daily life" (Jahoda, 1988, p. 19). As Jahoda (1982) notes:

> Every theory inevitably selects limited aspects out of the vast reservoir of behavior and experience and uses appropriate concepts, units of analysis and

methods within its restricted scope of convenience; the very appropriateness for one purpose makes it inappropriate for another. . . . This is as it must be if theoretical thought is to advance. . . . (p. 6)

In the chapters that follow we begin our discussion of the psychological impact of unemployment by first describing some of the main findings that have been obtained in research that is related to our own. As noted previously, this will not be an exhaustive, encyclopedic account but one that is directed toward abstracting some of the major results. It will be followed by a review of theoretical ideas that have been developed in attempts to understand the psychological effects of unemployment, along with a discussion of other current theoretical approaches that could also be applied. The initial chapters will therefore provide a framework or background of findings and ideas in terms in which the set of studies that we have conducted can be described and evaluated. The subsequent chapters will be concerned with details of this research program. In these chapters the single-group studies and cross-sectional studies will be presented first, followed by the more sophisticated longitudinal studies. I will conclude by presenting some general issues that emerge from the previous discussion and I will indicate some new directions that future research into the psychological impact of unemployment might take.

Chapter 2
Background Research

Interest in unemployment and associated issues is not a new development but spans the centuries. Some recent publications refer to the historical background and widen our perspective, reminding us that unemployment is not just a 20th-century phenomenon and that current attitudes towards the unemployed can be linked at least in part to previous attitudes towards the unemployed, the disadvantaged, and the poor and the way society dealt with these issues at the time. Thus, Garraty (1978) has presented an account of unemployment that looks at it from the perspective of history, economic thought, and public policy. In their analysis of the social-psychological effects of unemployment, Kelvin and Jarrett (1985) describe historical precursors of current attitudes. For example, in their interesting discussion of the Protestant work ethic (which they regard as largely a myth), they refer to a 14th-century English ordinance that made the distinction between "sturdy beggars," who were fit for work, and the "deserving poor," who were sick, old or incapacitated. The sturdy beggars were not to be given charity because there was a shortage of labor due to the devastation of the Black Death. Thus, work by the able-bodied was valued for rational, economic reasons rather than because of an ethic that work was good for the soul. Fryer and Payne (1986) note a *Bibliography of Unemployment and the Unemployed* (Taylor, 1909) that included nearly 800 books, articles, pamphlets, and other publications and that was prepared for a Royal Commission into the poor laws and the relief of distress from unemployment.

Detailed psychological research into the effects of unemployment is of more recent origin, however, and the literature has expanded over the last 60 years so that it is now a formidable one to consider. Fortunately, a number of excellent reviews of this research have been published in recent years (e.g., Fryer, 1988; Fryer & Payne, 1986; O'Brien, 1986; Warr, 1987a). What follows draws extensively from these reviews, abstracting some of the main findings and conclusions.

Studies of the Great Depression

It is tempting to dismiss studies of unemployment in the 1930s as of little relevance to the understanding of the psychological effects of present-day unemployment. These earlier studies were conducted in a different era when the standard of living was lower, life expectancy was shorter and health care less advanced, welfare schemes were more limited in scope, communication through the mass media was more restricted, less of the population stayed at school or went on to higher education, and many other social and economic differences existed in comparison with conditions in the 1980s. Moreover, the unemployed in the 1930s tended to come predominantly from those adult males who were in semiskilled and unskilled jobs. Today unemployment involves young people and women as well and spreads across low-, medium-, and high-status occupations. Finally, the methodology used in the 1930s' studies was often deficient, based on small samples and case material. There have been obvious improvements in methodology over the intervening years as large survey and quasi-experimental procedures have become available and more sophisticated techniques of statistical analysis have been developed.

Nevertheless, it would be incorrect to dismiss the 1930s' studies too lightly. Some of the studies have deservedly achieved the status of classic investigations that provide a richness of detail often missing in much current research. They allowed the unemployed to describe their lives and experiences using their own language and to highlight their own problems. Some of these earlier accounts have a deeply human impact, telling the story of unemployment from the point of view of those affected by it. They have been the source of important ideas about the functions of work and employment and about the economic and psychological factors that underlie the negative effects that unemployment can have.

A major source of ideas was the classic sociographic study of people living in the Austrian village of Marienthal, a village whose livelihood depended on a flax factory. This factory began to close down in 1929, thereby creating a period of prolonged unemployment for the inhabitants of Marienthal in the 1930s. A group of researchers led by Jahoda investigated the effects of this closure over a number of months, in research that involved close participation in the life of the Marienthal community (Jahoda et al., 1933). Though Lazarsfeld in his 1971 introduction to the Marienthal report indicates that an English translation was resisted for many years because certain aspects of the research were thought to be naive, the Marienthal study was unique for its time and still stands as an excellent example of what can be achieved by combining analysis of numerical data with detailed observations of life in a small community. Many different sorts of information were obtained that included the compilation of family files; the recording of detailed life histories; the use of time sheets outlining the way people spent their time; reports and complaints sent to the industrial commission; school essays on "What I want most of all," "What I want to be," and "What I want for Christmas"; a prize essay competition on "How I see my future"; family records of meals and what children took to school in their packed lunches the day before and the day after relief money was paid; other miscellaneous reports such as information about the Christmas presents children received, medical tests, performance at school, amount of money spent at different locations (e.g., tavern, butcher, barber, confectioner), and reports from various political clubs and other organizations; statistical data on accounts at the local cooperative store, loans from the public library, membership of clubs, election results, newspaper subscriptions, age distributions, births, deaths, and marriages, and migration figures and some household statistics.

Special projects were also launched that were of use to the community—projects such as distributing clothing, arranging courses that people could attend, organizing medical consultations and becoming active in various other functions. A valuable ethical lesson can be learned from the attitude the researchers took toward their role in the investigation. They were not in Marienthal merely as reporters or outside observers but as helpful participants in the community, fostering aid as well as obtaining information. The variety of data collected, together with immersion in the community, enabled the investigators to achieve a deeper understanding of events ". . . just as the true position of a distant object can be found only through triangulation, by looking at it from different sides and directions" (Lazarsfeld, 1971).

Jahoda (1979) has summarized some of the main findings from the Marienthal study:

> . . . the study showed that being unemployed is something very different from having leisure time. The unemployed decreased their attendance of clubs and voluntary organizations, their use of the free library, their reading habits. Their sense of time disintegrated, having nothing to do meant that they became less able to be punctual for meals or other arrangements. Budgeting, so much more necessary than before, was progressively abandoned. While family relations continued in established patterns longer than other relations and activities, there was some evidence that they, too, deteriorated and family quarrels increased. (p. 309)

In their original publication Jahoda et al. (1933) reported that their basic insight into the effects of unemployment was that it was followed by ". . . a diminution of expectation and activity, a disrupted sense of time, and a steady decline into apathy through a variety of stages and attitudes" (p. 2). They distinguished four different attitudes, the most common of which they called *resignation* with ". . . no plans, no relation to the future, no hopes, extreme restriction of all needs beyond the bare necessities, yet at the same time maintenance of the household, care of the children, and an overall feeling of relative well-being" (p. 53). This attitude was distinguished from one that they called *unbroken* where the unemployed showed ". . . maintenance of the household, care of the children, subjective well-being, activity, hopes and plans for the future, sustained vitality, and continued attempts to find employment" (p. 53).

Two remaining attitude groups were also distinguished, both of which were called *broken*. One attitude described people who were *in despair*. Though they kept their households in order and looked after their children they experienced ". . . despair, depression, hopelessness, a feeling of the futility of all efforts, and therefore no further attempts to find work or to ameliorate the situation; instead, constant comparisons of the present with a better past" (p. 53). The final attitude, however, was associated with a disordered household. It was called *apathetic* and Jahoda et al. characterized it as involving

> . . . complete passivity, the absence of any effort. Home and children are dirty and neglected, the mental outlook is not desperate but simply indifferent. . . . Family life begins to disintegrate. . . . Nobody plans for a more distant future, not even for the days and hours immediately ahead. (p. 54)

The four attitudes were correlated with level of income. Jahoda (1982) reported that the average income per consumer unit in each of the four attitude categories was 34 schillings per month for the unbroken category, 30 schillings for the resigned category, 25 schillings for the despair category, and 19 schillings for the apathetic category. They noted that the psychological deterioration that accompanied a shift from resigned and unbroken attitudes on the one hand to despairing and apathetic attitudes on the other ran ". . . parallel to the narrowing of economic resources and the wear and tear on personal belongings. At the end of this process lies ruin and despair" (p. 87). Indeed, throughout the report of the Marienthal study we find reference to the negative effects of financial hardship on family lives and the limits that low levels of income impose on what an unemployed person can do and on how a family can cope. The consequences of unemployment were seen to be closely intertwined with the consequences of poverty.

In her later writings Jahoda (1982, 1988) referred to categories of experience that the unemployed person has lost and the consequences of this loss for psychological well-being and adjustment. Thus, the sudden onset of unemployment destroys a person's habitual time structure for the waking day, undermines the sense of purpose in life, reduces social contacts, results in a loss of status and identity, and removes the regular activities that were part of a person's daily life when employed. There was plenty of evidence in the Marienthal study for these effects, especially in regard to deterioration in the use of time among the unemployed men, reduction in activity, and a developing hopelessness and lack of purpose.

During the 1930s Jahoda conducted another sociographic study in South Wales in the Eastern Valley of Monmouthshire. She became associated with a small group of Quakers who started a Subsistence Production Society with the intention of organizing and financing a cooperative enterprise enabling unemployed miners to produce goods and services for their own subsistence. A detailed report of this study has only recently appeared (Jahoda, 1987), more than 50 years after the study was conducted, though the findings have been referred to previously (Jahoda, 1982, pp. 31–32). Jahoda (1987) indicates that the normal attitude among the unemployed was one of resignation. She goes on to comment that:

> The fact that nothing worse than resignation was found in the Eastern Valley, while in Marienthal despair and complete apathy were discovered, may have been mainly because of the size and permanence of the unemployment allowance in Wales. The resignation manifested itself in an almost complete cessation of any capacity to make an effort. (p. 13)

Note, however, that even in Marienthal only 7% of families were classified as "in despair" or "apathetic," using the categories that were described previously (Jahoda et al., 1933, p. 56). The dominant attitude in Marienthal was also resignation, with 70% of the families placed in this class (Jahoda et al., 1933, p. 56). There are therefore similarities in the findings from the Marienthal and Eastern Valley studies and convergence in the framework of ideas used to interpret these findings (see Fryer, 1987, for a fuller discussion). Both studies provided rich information about the experience of unemployment in different communities and they were interpreted with a deep awareness of the impact that economic, social, psychological, and historical factors can have on individual lives.

Another major set of studies concerned with the effects of unemployment in the 1930s was conducted by Bakke (1933, 1940a, 1940b). In his works we again find descriptions based upon personal contact with individuals and the use of other kinds of information that were assembled to build up a detailed picture of the unemployed condition. For example, in *The Unemployed Man*, Bakke (1933) presents the results of a study conducted with unemployed working-class families in Greenwich, a borough of London. It was Bakke's intention:

> to take lodgings with a working-class family, to share their life insofar as it was possible to do so, to join in their activities or loaf on the streets or at factory gates as the occasion might require, to go with them to clubs and churches and "pubs", to join the hunt for a job, and during the whole process find out all I could of the causes and consequences and adjustments involved in unemployment among the men and women who were unemployed. (p. xiv)

He used five main sources of information: (1) interviews with workers, particularly those who were unemployed; (2) interviews with other members of the community; (3) time diaries kept by a number of unemployed men; (4) personal observations of the life circumstances of the unemployed while living among them; and (5) statistical information relating to school attendance, marriage, health, unemployment, visits to the employment exchange, church activity, and other activities of interest.

In *The Unemployed Man*, Bakke (1933) discussed the work environment in which his families lived and drew out a number of features of this environment that he thought shaped the worker's orientations toward work in important ways. Some of these features have been emphasized by O'Brien

(1985, 1986) in his recent analysis of Bakke's contributions. Two deserve special mention: insecurity and external control. Male workers felt insecure because of the development of new machinery, fear that young workers would be dismissed if their wages or unemployment insurance became too high, fear that women might displace them in their jobs, uncertainty about the effects of migrating labor, and concerns about restricted job opportunities because of older men holding on to their jobs even when they were on pensions. They developed feelings that their destinies were controlled by others. These "others" were seen for the most part to be remote, impersonal, and unknown. Feelings of external control were seen by Bakke to have important consequences, one of which was the development of a generalized attitude that one is not really responsible for one's fate. There was also a tendency for the workers to attach indiscriminate blame attributed to people belonging to this other world and to be suspicious of any plan for cooperation between the worker and the employer. According to Bakke (1933), the others were seen and accepted as the "masters," having special qualifications that justified their power. The men themselves were seen to experience a measure of hopelessness and to assign to luck an important role in determining whether or not they had employment. Thus:

> The worker sees all about him experienced and skilled men with no work to do. If he is in work, he feels lucky. If he is out of work, he is the victim of hard luck. He can see little relation between worth and consequences. (p. 14)

Luck may be seen as another component of a generalized attitude that events are controlled by outside forces. Bakke (1933) also noted that the workers in his study had few alternative ways of life available to them:

> His course is well laid out for him and he has to walk in it, if only for the lack of financial resources which make alternative choices on a large scale possible. . . . If the ways out are few, planning soon ceases. Ambition comes swiftly to an end. (pp. 13–14)

Bakke (1933) recognized that there were differences between unskilled and skilled workers in the incentives that were available and the attitudes that were developed on the job. As O'Brien (1986) has noted, an important contribution of Bakke (1933) is his emphasis on the effects of past job experiences and the shaping influence that the context of work has on job satisfaction, feelings of security, and more generalized attitudes of control and responsibility.

In the case of the unskilled worker:

> The experience of having his destiny controlled from another world has left him, naturally enough, with a reduced sense of responsibility for his fortunes, and more especially for his misfortunes which. . . he is prone to lay at the door of the "masters". . . . The lack of choice which characterizes his life has produced little training in alternative planning. . . . The belief that luck occupies a large place in the determination of his fortunes is a further check to planning. . . . The experience of exploitation is sufficiently frequent and

> forceful to make him suspicious of any action on the part of the master which
> might reduce his standard of living. (pp. 32–33)

The major satisfaction from work is the immediate reward of wage. "From wages to dole is not such a long journey for these men. If their wages are close to what the dole would be, there is greater temptation to secure the latter as long as possible" (p. 27). In contrast, the more-skilled workers have greater satisfaction in their jobs beyond the mere reward of money. They have greater chances of promotion, more security, and more opportunities to acquire status. Thus, for both unskilled and skilled workers, ". . . the conditioning power of the job soon makes its influence felt" (p. 33).

Bakke (1933) also indicated that the workers that he studied displayed personal foresight. The workers joined "slate" clubs or informal savings associations that enabled them to save for the future; they tried to plan for their children's future; some might take out private insurance against misfortune or join a protective association such as a trade union; others might join clubs and lodges in an attempt to extend the range of influential contacts who might help them in adversity. Bakke (1933) described various factors that influenced the development of foresight and recognized that these factors varied depending upon the nature of the work environment and the rewards that it offered. Thus:

> The long arm of income, as it places people almost automatically within certain fields of possible achievement, is a factor constantly to be reckoned with. Income, steadiness of income, skill, education, all of these are the high fences which surround the fields. (p. 45)

Bakke (1933) found that the unemployed men in his Greenwich study became discouraged, decreased their social activities, and suffered from feelings of insecurity and diminished self-confidence. They continued to respect the law and did not become involved in organized political protests. Unemployment insurance moderated some of the effects of unemployment, helping to reduce starvation and ill health. However, according to Bakke (1933), it did not relieve ". . . the mental and moral fatigue and discouragement which result from having no job. It cannot supply the loss of status and the sense of self-respect which vanish with the job" (p. 251). Bakke noted that the unemployed workers were not idle and that most continued to seek employment. They tried to fill their time in meaningful ways, though what they could do was limited by their low levels of income.

Similar findings were obtained by Bakke (1940a, 1940b) in a subsequent study of unemployed workers in New Haven, Connecticut. Again one finds a wealth of detail in descriptions of how the unemployed coped with being jobless and an awareness of the shaping effects of the work environment on general beliefs and attitudes. Note that Jahoda (1982, 1987) also recognized the influence of previous experience on how the miners in the Eastern Valley of Monmouthshire reacted to the social experiment conducted by the Subsistence Production Society. Jahoda (1982) argued that:

. . . these unemployed miners were steeped in the traditions of capitalism
that had for generations split them from the bosses and induced them to fight
against often brutal exploitation. These long-established habits of thought
made them wonder whether they had involved themselves through membership in the Quaker scheme in a subtler form of exploitation and led them
to distrust the Quaker organisers, though their gentle manner was in sharp
contrast to the treatment they had previously experienced from the mine-
owners. (p. 32)

I have focused on the work of two of the major contributors to research on
the psychological impact of unemployment in the 1930s because the studies by
Jahoda and her associates and by Bakke share important features. As Fryer
and Payne (1986) indicate, these studies were essentially descriptive and they
involved close investigation of communities in well-specified geographical
locations. Moreover, interpretations of the findings that were obtained recognized the effects of limited incomes and poverty and the fact that the unemployed workers came to unemployment with preestablished frames of mind,
capacities, and skills that were a product of their previous experience, involving past employment and other socializing influences on their lives.

The findings that emerged from the pioneer work of Jahoda et al. (1933)
and Bakke (1933) were supported by other studies in the 1930s. One can
note, for example, research by the Pilgrim Trust (1938) that set out to study
the effects of long-term unemployment in six towns (Deptford; Leicester;
Liverpool; Blackburn; Crook, County Durham; and Rhondda), selected so
as to encompass two prosperous towns, two with a mixture of employment and
unemployment, and two that were especially depressed economically. This
study involved a sample of over 1,000 men and women; the researchers
collected data on a wide range of variables (age, previous occupation, family
size, income, employment record, appearance, health, attitudes, leisure activities, and so forth). The Pilgrim Trust study drew attention to the negative
effects of poverty as a cause of anxiety and, in some cases, physical deterioration. With good management, families without children could live at a reasonable level on unemployment assistance. Even in those cases, however, existence was at the same "dead level" without much possibility of variation.
Families with children were much worse off and the parents (especially the
wives) bore much of the burden in order to provide reasonably adequate
food and clothing for their children. The researchers found evidence of anxiety, restlessness, and nervousness among the unemployed as well as depression, hopelessness, apathy, and feelings of loneliness and isolation. These
psychological states were seen to be part of a vicious cycle, with increasing
negative affective reactions making a person more unfit for work.

We also find reference in the report of the Pilgrim Trust (1938) study to the
disruptive effects on unemployed people of a lack of structure and purpose in
their lives. Thus:

Work provides for most people the pattern within which their lives are lived
and when this pattern is lost they have thrown on them a responsibility

which, in the case of most unemployed men, their working lives in no way qualified them to bear—the responsibility for organizing their own existence. They fall in ultimately with some new makeshift pattern. (p. 149)

Again we see recognition of the fact that the nature of a person's past working life may not foster attitudes of personal control and responsibility or coping skills that would enable the person to come to terms with unemployment and reduced economic circumstances.

The Carnegie Trust (1943) study of unemployed youth also produced findings that were similar to some already mentioned. The young people in this study were not idle and tried to fill their days with various activities. Their attempts were limited by lack of money and sometimes poor health. They found it difficult to establish regular routines and to maintain their self-respect.

Other studies of the time referred to negative expectations of failure and other emotional reactions among unemployed people (Israeli, 1935) and to the effects of length of unemployment on changes in attitude (e.g., Beales & Lambert, 1934; Zawadski & Lazarsfeld, 1935). Over 100 studies of the psychological effects of unemployment during the 1930s were reviewed by Eisenberg and Lazarsfeld (1938). These authors concluded that unemployment tends to make people more emotionally unstable, that morale was lower following unemployment, and that the unemployed pass through a series of psychological stages in their response to unemployment, moving from initial shock through phases of optimism and pessimism to a state of fatalism or resignation as length of unemployment increases. Eisenberg and Lazarsfeld (1938) also discussed studies that were concerned with the effects of unemployment on families, children, and youth. Given the focus in the present book on youth unemployment, it is of some interest to note their conclusions.

They reported studies that showed that lack of employment opportunities may have the following negative effects among the young: alienation and drifting about, irritability leading to family tension, prostitution and criminality, diminished motivation, a loss of ambition, and the development of hopelessness and feelings of superfluousness. They concluded as follows:

In general we obtain the same effects upon the personality of unemployed youth as upon that of unemployed adults, but because of the greater suceptibility of youth and because they are going through a transition period between childhood and maturity these effects are probably more lasting. (p. 383)

Note that Eisenberg and Lazarsfeld (1938) provided no real evidence to support the latter conjecture. Long-term effects of the Great Depression, however, have been investigated by Elder and his associates (Elder, 1974, 1978; Elder & Caspi, 1988; Liker & Elder, 1983), using longitudinal data from men and women who experienced the Great Depression as children or adolescents. The results of these studies are too complex to summarize but they do reveal the effects of low incomes and family attitudes on subsequent achievement and psychological functioning. Unemployment had an effect on the family and the way it functioned. The wife often had to take a greater role in generating family income (where possible) and in deciding on how income was to be used; the unemployed husband felt inadequate and experienced a decrease in self-respect and self-confidence, and there was a concomitant increase in family strain (see also Komarovsky, 1940). Children born into these families therefore lived through conditions of strain, insecurity, and economic deprivation and it is not surprising that they were affected by the experience. The young people tended to attribute greater value to job security and income and there was some evidence that their subsequent attainment was related to motivational factors such as need for achievement and aspiration levels, despite disadvantages in the children's education. O'Brien (1986) sees these studies as showing that "economic deprivation during the Depression and subsequent persistent economic hardship had significant long-term effects on educational achievement and psychological functioning of unmarried women and children" (p. 207). The effects of economic disadvantage were mediated by changes in family attitudes, family relationships, and family role structures. Elder and Caspi (1988) have recently presented two micromodels that specify how a drastic economic loss influences children's development. Their first model deals with how family relationships are affected by a shift in the family economy from capital to labor-intensive operations. Their second model involves the effects of alterations in family relationships on children's social and personality development.

According to Eisenberg and Lazarsfeld (1938), studies of young unemployed people in the 1930s also showed that their behavior and attitudes were affected because of the general lack of jobs and the depressed economic climate. Young people were thought to be more likely to move into "blind-alley jobs" with no future; the bad economic situation and the undermining of morale was thought to lead some unemployed youth increasingly to employ fraudulent means in their efforts to get the dole; other young people continued with their education rather than leaving school. Negative attitudes toward legal and economic institutions were found to develop in some cases. Attitudes within the family between young unemployed people and their parents varied depending upon the previous condition of the home (e.g., whether it was generally supportive or nonsupportive) and the psychological and economic resources available to the family.

The Eisenberg and Lazarsfeld (1938) review of the effects of unemployment in the 1930s has been very influential and is widely cited, especially in regard to their conclusion about successive attitude stages that were assumed to be associated with increasing length of unemployment. Less recognized is the fact that their conclusions were often qualified and that they did recognize the role of individual differences in personality and the effects of predisposing factors such as economic and social status, age, gender, and economic resources on how people coped with the unemployed condition. Often ignored also is their final point that:

> . . . the greatest need in this field of investigation is an effort to lay out a
> network of interlocking theoretical problems so that whoever has the regret-
> table opportunity to study unemployed people can see what information is
> most needed and where his contribution could do the most toward improving
> our very deficient knowledge of the psychological effects of unemployment.
> (p. 385)

Thus, over 50 years ago, there was explicit recognition of the need to link
findings from unemployment studies to theoretical ideas. The accumulation
of descriptive information was seen as useful and important and a necessary
step toward developing theoretical ideas.

More Recent Studies

After a spate of publications relating to the effects of unemployment during
the Depression years, there was a decline in research on unemployment as
employment levels rose. That is not to say that useful work was not going on.
The 1960s and 1970s saw the publication of case studies, quantitative research,
and some reviews (e.g., Cobb & Kasl, 1977; Daniel, 1974; Harrison, 1976;
Hill, 1977, 1978; Marsden & Duff, 1975; Sinfield, 1968, 1970; Tiffany,
Cowan, & Tiffany, 1970; Wedderburn, 1964); Jahoda (1979) published her
comparative study of the impact of unemployment in the 1930s and 1970s;
and Garraty's (1978) important historical account of unemployment
appeared. New projects were started and some began to come to fruition.

The increase in unemployment levels from about 1975 onwards has also
been followed by a rise in the number of publications concerned with unemployment effects. The literature is now very extensive, encompassing not only
contributions from psychologists but from other social scientists as well.
Rather than attempting to review this literature in detail, I will again refer to
reviews that have recently appeared (e.g., Fryer, 1988; Fryer & Payne, 1986;
O'Brien, 1986; Warr, 1987a), drawing out some of the main conclusions.
Apart from these general reviews, there are other more specific sources of
information that relate to particular countries. I described the Australian
literature on unemployment effects in 1985 (Feather, 1985c) and that review
will be a further source for the summary that follows. Warr, Jackson, and
Banks (1988) recently reviewed British studies of the effects of unemployment on health. European studies have been reported in a collection of
papers edited by Schwefel, Svensson, and Zöllner (1987) on unemployment,
social vulnerability, and health in Europe. Finally a special issue of the
Journal of Social Issues in 1988 contained a set of papers from American,
British, and European contributors on the psychological effects of unemployment (Dooley & Catalano, 1988). So there is a wealth of recent material to
draw on and one must inevitably be selective.

Just before the sudden spate of publications in the 1980s and on the basis of
the fairly limited range of studies in the 1970s, Jahoda (1979) commented that

"even though the evidence is sparse and not systematic, what there is presents apparently much the same impact of unemployment as in the earlier period, even repeating the occasional exception to the general picture of apathy and resignation" (p. 310). Warr's (1987a) recent summary also emphasizes the negative effects of unemployment over a wide range of variables, though he is careful to indicate that there are individual and group differences in these effects still to be explained. Thus, "unemployment is in general seen to impair mental health, although this effect is not universal; indeed a small minority of people show gains in mental health after losing their job" (p. 207).

My own reading of the psychological literature leads me to a similar conclusion. Negative effects of various kinds predominate but people vary in their ability to cope depending both on context and their own personal resources. The pattern of results is often confusing with differences that are not easy to explain. The problems investigated cover a wide spectrum and it would be naive to expect that one can make sense of all the findings in terms of one set of integrative theoretical principles. It seems much more likely that future progress in the different areas of unemployment research will come from the application of middle-range theories from different fields of psychology such as human motivation, developmental psychology, social psychology, and organizational research. Thus, there is a need to differentiate the field in order to make theoretical sense of the parts; to carve up the pie and to concentrate on each segment separately. It may be possible to forge some links between the parts in the future. This is more likely to occur if investigations are pursued with a vision that is both focused on the topic and sideways looking, in the hope that one can build routes to and from adjacent areas. And one has to be constantly aware of the fact that research on unemployment is multivariate research and that the effects that occur depend upon a host of variables that combine and interact in many different ways.

Let us now turn to some of the findings. Both O'Brien (1986) and Warr (1987a) have reviewed aggregate time-series studies that examine overall data about diagnosed illness, suicides. and mortality collected from communities or nations over a long period of time and that relate these variables to economic indicators. For example, Brenner (1973) found that admissions to New York State public mental hospitals between 1914 and 1967 were positively related to the state's manufacturing employment index when lagged relationships were examined. As the employment index decreased, the number of people admitted to mental hospitals increased. This research has stimulated a lot of comment and criticism on methodological grounds (e.g., Eyer, 1977; Kasl, 1982; Warr, 1985) but detailed discussion of the points that have been raised (e.g., the types of hospital used, the size of the time lag, differences between admissions and readmissions, the nature of the samples) and the range of other related studies that have appeared is beyond the scope of the present report.

We can note, however, that relationships between economic indicators and psychiatric admissions when found permit at least two alternative interpretations. An economic downturn may for various reasons provoke new illness or it may uncover previous illness that was contained or held in check under the previous conditions of low stress. According to Warr (1987a, p. 200), it is not possible to make a clear choice between these two interpretations on the basis of existing data (Dooley & Catalano, 1984a). Warr (1987a) also notes that one cannot infer processes at the individual level from aggregate-level findings. Some studies have attempted to link information from the aggregate and individual levels of enquiry. In a survey of Los Angeles households Catalano and Dooley (1983) found that aggregate-level variations in employment rate were significantly associated with individual-level measures of both general distress and physical illness and injuries in the subsequent two months (see also Dooley & Catalano, 1984a). These relationships varied, however, depending on the nature of the respondents (e.g., the working population versus retirees, housewives, and students; middle-class respondents versus others). Catalano and Dooley (1983) also found that changes in stressors defined by individual-level reports of recently experienced undesirable job and financial events predicted distress but that the local unemployment rate had its own additional influence on distress. Thus changes in the local economic climate were shown ". . . to influence level of affective well-being, whether or not people have themselves experienced negative job events" (Warr, 1987a, p. 201). Dooley et al. (1988) also found evidence that aggregate unemployment adversely affected all principal wage earners in the community, not just those who were personally unemployed. The effects of personal unemployment indicated elevated symptoms in the four different groups that Dooley et al. (1988) investigated but there was no evidence to support the hypothesis that aggregate unemployment interacts with personal unemployment experience in its effect on psychological distress.

What do we conclude from these various findings? Dooley and Catalano (1984a) argue that an increased unemployment rate may affect mental health partly because of its direct effects on individuals via job loss but also because it has more extended consequences that affect a wide range of people in subtle and gradual ways and not only those who lose their jobs. For example:

> the spouses and children of job-losers may pay a price in conflict or abuse. Workers dislocated from one job may find reemployment in another but at a psychological cost of relocation or of retraining and may well slip down the status ladder. People who have not themselves lost a job may suffer anxiety anticipating job loss and may remain in unsatisfactory working conditions because no alternate jobs can be found. (p. 396)

In addition, organized labor may find its bargaining position undermined and cuts in government revenues may be translated into cuts in social services. Thus, ". . . an economic indicator such as unemployment rate can be understood as reflecting adverse changes throughout the population" (p. 396).

Studies of the impact of unemployment at the individual level have shown a range of negative effects. A lot of the recent research has been conducted at the MRC/SSRC Social and Applied Psychology Unit at the University of Sheffield by Warr and his associates. Other evidence comes from North American and European studies and from our own research program at Flinders University in South Australia. Warr has published a number of useful summaries (Warr, 1984a, 1984c, 1987a, 1987b) and other reviews that cover individual reactions to unemployment have been presented by Banks and Ullah (1988), Bartley (1987), Damstrup (1987), DeFrank and Ivancevich (1986), Feather (1985c), Fraser (1981), Fryer (1988), Fryer and Payne (1986), Furnham (1985), Hartley and Fryer (1984), Hayes and Nutman (1981), Jahoda (1979, 1981, 1982), Kasl (1979), O'Brien (1986), Schaufeli (1988b), and Warr et al. (1988). These reviews deal with a number of variables and they encompass both cross-sectional and longitudinal investigations. For example, O'Brien (1986) provides tabular summaries of cross-sectional and longitudinal investigations up to 1985 that were concerned with the consequences of adult and youth unemployment and Fryer and Payne (1986) and Fryer (1988) summarize the effects of unemployment on such variables as affective reactions (such as feelings of happiness, positive and negative affect, and experience of pleasure and strain), self-esteem, measures of minor psychiatric morbidity, depression, anxiety, hopelessness, cognitive difficulties, physical health, mortality, suicide, and parasuicide. Warr's (1987a) summary covers effects on mental health (conceived in terms of psychological well-being, subjective feelings of competence, subjective autonomy, level of aspiration, and integrated functioning), diagnosed illnesses such as neurotic and psychotic disorders, physical health, and family processes.

Most recent reviews recognize that the psychological impact of unemployment varies considerably depending upon the people who are unemployed and the circumstances under which they live. In some cases negative effects on mental and physical health may be slight, in other cases much more severe. Among the important variables that influence the outcome are length of unemployment, age, gender, ethnic background, social class, employment commitment, financial strain, prior job experience, and social support (Fryer, 1988; Fryer & Payne, 1986; O'Brien, 1986, Warr, 1987a; Warr et al., 1988). For example, the Sheffield studies show that middle-aged unemployed men experience greater distress than younger or older men, partly because they have greater financial strain relating to family commitments, and that people who are personally strongly committed to being in paid employment experience more psychological distress when they are unemployed than do those with lower employment commitment.

The conclusions that emerge from these summaries vary somewhat but there is general acceptance that unemployment has negative effects on individuals. Thus, Warr (1987a) concludes:

> . . . the findings presented . . . leave no doubt that unemployment has substantial harmful effects upon many individuals and their families. Furthermore, the consequences are likely in practice to be more serious than is revealed in most survey investigations. Survey researchers typically have difficulty in obtaining access to unemployed people. . . . It is not known

whether unemployed people who decline to take part differ substantially from those who do, but it seems very likely that they will in general be of poorer mental health. . . . Particularly low levels of affective well-being and unusually large impairments in subjective competence, aspiration, and autonomy are expected to discourage acceptance of an invitation to be interviewed. (p. 207)

Fryer and Payne (1986) conclude that:

. . . for many unemployed people their economic, social, and psychological well-being deteriorates. For a small number of people the deterioration is so bad that they commit or attempt suicide, but among that large majority whose experience is generally worsened by job loss there is still a wide range of reactions, partly because of wide variations in economic and social circumstances but also because of wide individual differences in the ability to cope with economic, social, and psychological pressures. (p. 259)

O'Brien (1986) is rather more qualified in his conclusions. In his review of cross-sectional studies with adults he notes that the results suggest that:

. . . unemployment is associated with short-term dissatisfaction but not necessarily with changes in relatively stable states of anxiety and stress. Long-term adjustments are likely to be related in a complex way to economic changes, orientations to work, time unemployed, prior work status and the activities undertaken in unemployment. (p. 220)

His conclusions concerning longitudinal studies and studies of the effects of youth unemployment are similarly qualified. Negative effects are recognized but there is awareness of the overall complexity of determining the causal antecedents of reactions to unemployment and of the need for carefully conducted, systematic research.

As one would expect, the studies conducted in the 1970s and 1980s sample a wider range of methods when compared with the 1930s research. The procedures cover both qualitative and quantitative approaches (Fryer, 1988). Some of them have involved survey designs with questionnaires and interviews targeted to defined populations (e.g., adults, teenagers, black and white unemployed). Psychological scales with known test characteristics have also been included to measure such variables as psychological well-being, life satisfaction, proneness to psychiatric disorder, positive and negative affect, positive and negative self-esteem, depressive symptoms, anxiety, work values, cognitive difficulties, external locus of control, and causal attributions. Physiological measures involving biochemical analysis of blood and urine samples have been employed in American studies of the effects of job termination (Cobb & Kasl, 1977). Questionnaires have been constructed to assess health changes and behavior changes following job loss. Structured interviewing, depth interviewing, personal document analysis, time budget analysis, psychiatric diagnosis, ethnographic procedures, and epidemiological methods have all been used. There has been increasing awareness of the need to strengthen inferences either by including specially selected control groups (e.g., employed samples) in studies or by applying techniques of multivariate analysis (e.g., covariance analysis, multiple regression, path analysis) to achieve statistical control of variables such as social class, education, and income. In recent years, there has been increasing use of longitudinal designs in which samples of unemployed people are followed up over varying time periods. These prospective studies also permit stronger inferences about cause and effect, enabling one to rule out alternative interpretations of obtained relations that are always possible in cross-sectional investigations conducted at one point in time.

Despite these methodological advances, however, there is still an over reliance on measures that depend upon verbal report. Unemployed people who complete questionnaires may distort their answers in the direction of presenting what they believe are appropriate responses in relation to their own goals and those of the researcher. In some cases, they may not even be in possession of the information that is requested. The clear implication is that research should be designed so as to include multiple measures of variables, going beyond verbal reports to include behavioral measures, observations by others, physiological measures where appropriate, unobtrusive measures, and other kinds of assessment. Inferences can then be on a firmer basis and not qualified by overreliance on a particular method. The Marienthal study (Jahoda et al., 1972) still provides a model of how triangulation can be achieved by the use of different methods, including methods that are unobtrusive (Webb, Campbell, Schwartz, & Sechrest, 1966).

While large survey investigations can yield a lot of valuable information about unemployment effects, they need to be supplemented by more intensive, in-depth studies of unemployed individuals in their daily lives. The averages that come out of the statistical analysis of large data banks are impersonal and far removed from the life experiences of the unemployed themselves. Recent publications have given more attention to the fine detail of the unemployment experience (e.g., Fagin & Little, 1984; Fineman, 1987; Fryer & Ullah, 1987) and some of these published accounts remind one of the sociographic work of the 1930s. (e.g., Bakke, 1933; Jahoda et al., 1933) in the pictures they present of unemployed individuals, their families, their concerns, and how they cope with their daily existence.

One can also note in the recent literature a greater concern with cultural and group differences in how people react to unemployment (e.g., Feather, 1985c, 1989b; Fryer, 1988; O'Brien, 1986; Warr, 1987a), more awareness of the negative effects of income loss and diminished economic resources following unemployment (e.g., Fraser, 1981; Jahoda, 1988; Kelvin & Jarrett, 1985; Kessler, Turner, & House, 1988; O'Brien, 1986; Sinfield, 1981; Warr, 1987a), a move toward considering the individual as an active coping agent rather than as a passive object acted upon by external forces (e.g., Fryer, 1988; Fryer & Payne, 1984, 1986), more concern with the wider impact of unemployment beyond the individual so as to include the family and other people (e.g., Elder & Caspi, 1988; Liem & Liem, 1988; McKee & Bell, 1986), and an increasing interest in applying theoretical models to the analysis of unemployment effects. It is this latter development that we turn to in the next chapter.

Chapter 3

Theoretical Approaches from the Study of Work, Employment, and Unemployment

In this chapter I discuss theoretical ideas that have emerged from the study of the psychological impact of unemployment both from the 1930s and from the more recent literature. As will become evident, some of these approaches are not restricted to the conceptual analysis of unemployment effects; they also develop theoretical ideas about the nature and functions of work and employment. In the next chapter I will consider theoretical approaches that are more general in their focus but that are also useful for understanding aspects of the unemployment experience. The two chapters therefore differ in the scope of the theories to be discussed. This chapter looks at theories that have emerged from the study of work, employment, and unemployment and that have particular relevance to the analysis of adjustment and psychological well-being. The next chapter extends the discussion by considering other approaches that have a wider application beyond the employment/unemployment area but that are also relevant for research into unemployment effects.

We should note that some of the theories to be described in the two chapters are at a relatively low level of conceptual analysis and formal presentation while others are more fully developed. Furthermore, the theories are keyed to different aspects of the unemployment experience. We will examine theories that are relevant to health issues—for example, to the effects of unemployment on mental health and psychological well-being; theories that relate to the cognitive world of the unemployed person, particularly in relation to the self-concept and individual belief systems; theories that are more concerned with understanding the actual behavior of the unemployed, such as looking for a job; theories that enable some understanding of age-related differences in reactions to unemployment; and other approaches that draw from the psychology of stress and coping, personality theory, social psychology, or other fields of psychology.

It will be evident from this survey that there have been several attempts to move beyond concrete, descriptive accounts of the experience of unemployment to more abstract, theoretical interpretations. This kind of development is a natural one as investigators try to make sense out of research findings, linking them to wider frameworks. The various approaches to be discussed differ in their metatheoretical perspectives. Some are oriented more toward the person, with an emphasis on basic needs and other person variables that are related to satisfactory health and adjustment; some are more concerned with features of the environment and their role in relation to health and adjustment. These differences, however, tend to be relative ones. Most theoretical discussions of unemployment effects recognize the importance of considering both person variables and environmental variables in the conceptual analysis.

We therefore have a congeries of ideas, some old and some new, some close to description and some at higher levels of abstraction, some specific and some more general in their application. In these two chapters I will move from ideas that have been with us for some time to more recent contributions and I will draw attention to other theories and concepts from psychology that could be usefully applied in future research relating to the psychological impact of unemployment.

Stage Theories

The notion that people move through successive stages in their responses to unemployment as their unemployment continues is a legacy of the 1930s. Its origins have been traced by Kelvin and Jarrett (1985), Fryer (1985), and Fryer & Payne (1986). These authors have described different stage models and the evidence on which they were based. This evidence largely consisted of autobiographies, memoirs, and case histories and interviews that came from structured research (e.g., Beales & Lambert, 1934; Jahoda et al., 1933; Zawadski & Lazarsfeld, 1935). Hence the evidence involved what people wrote or said. In rare cases subjects were interviewed on more than one occasion (e.g., in a case study by Bakke, 1933). The idea of stages was discussed in the influential review of unemployment effects by Eisenberg and Lazarsfeld (1938) and has persisted in discussions of unemployment ever since. In the 1970s both Harrison (1976) and Hill (1978) described stage models, drawing both on the 1930s' statements and, in the latter case, on planned cross-sectional studies in which there was systematic sampling of unemployed subjects with different periods of unemployment. The reference to stages has continued into the 1980s (e.g., Hayes & Nutman, 1981) but it is only in recent years that the notion of stages in reactions to unemployment has been subjected to critical scrutiny.

Let us return to the 1930s. I have already described the distinction made by the Marienthal investigators between the different kinds of attitude (unbroken, resigned, in despair, apathetic) that they found in their unemployed community and the relationship between these attitudes and income level. Beales and Lambert (1934) referred to a pattern of change from optimism to pessimism to fatalism that was assumed to reflect a progressive decline in the reactions of the unemployed with increasing length of unemployment. Their proposed sequence was based upon analysis of essays or "memoirs" from the unemployed submitted to the *Listener,* an English magazine. Similar material from a Polish essay competition formed the basis for a more differentiated stage model proposed by Zawadski and Lazarsfeld (1935). They listed six stages that were assumed to reflect the typical course of changes in moods with increasing length of unemployment. Thus:

> (1) As reaction to dismissal, there comes generally a feeling of injury; some-times fear and distress; sometimes an impulse toward revenge; hatred; in-dignation; fury. (2) Thereafter comes a stage of numbness and apathy which is gradually (3) replaced by calming down and an increase in steadiness bring-ing one to a relative mental balance. This mental stage is characterized by a resumption of activity; the unemployed become calm as they see that things go along somehow, and adapt themselves to circumstances; they trust in God, fate, or in their own ability, and try to believe that the situation will improve very soon. (4) But this hope becomes constantly weaker, when they see the futility of effort. (5) When the situation becomes harder, the old savings and new sources exhausted, then comes the hopelessness which ex-presses itself at first in attacks of fear, for instance, fear of winter and of homelessness, which culminates in distress, the expression of which is the thought of and attempt at suicide. (6) After these outbreaks usually comes either sober acquiescence or dumb apathy, and then the alternation between hope and hopelessness, activity and passivity, according to the momentary changes in the material situation. (p. 235)

The most influential 1930s statement of stages came from the Eisenberg and Lazarsfeld (1938) review. They concluded that:

> We find that all writers who have described the course of unemployment seem to agree on the following points. First there is shock, which is followed by an active hunt for a job, during which the individual is still optimistic and unresigned; he still maintains an unbroken attitude. Second, when all efforts fail, the individual becomes pessimistic, anxious, and suffers active distress; this is the most crucial state of all. And third, the individual becomes fatalis-tic and adapts himself to his new state but with a narrower scope. He now has a broken attitude. (p. 378)

The next qualifying part of their conclusion has been given less emphasis in subsequent commentaries but it is nevertheless very important:

> Of course there are large individual differences, but one would expect that the various types of attitudes maintained are more a function of the stage of unemployment than anything else, though there is no doubt that they are also a function of the other predisposing factors that have been discussed above. It would seem instructive to map the course of events for those beginning unemployment with differing attitudes. It may be that all have the same course, except that the unbroken take a longer time before becoming broken than those who begin as distressed or broken individuals.(p. 378)

Thus, as noted previously, Eisenberg and Lazarsfeld (1938) recognized that reactions to unemployment were moderated by individual differences and by other factors, limiting the generalizations that they made.

Jahoda's (1979) conclusion in the late 1970s about findings from the 1930s' research echoes the Eisenberg and Lazarsfeld (1938) statement. She writes that these early studies

> . . . do establish at least the temporal priority of unemployment to the decay of self-esteem and morale. This process is not a smooth curve. More often the onset of unemployment produces an immediate shock effect which is followed by a period of almost constructive adaptation in which some enjoy their free time and may engage in active job search; but deterioration follows quickly with boredom and declining self-respect ending in despair or fatalistic apathy. (p. 310)

She also emphasized the individual and group differences that occur in the unemployment experience.

Harrison's (1976) discussion draws heavily upon the Eisenberg and Lazarsfeld (1938) conclusion. He recognized a sequence that moves from initial shock through optimism to pessimism, and finally to fatalism. He also indicated that ". . . prolonged unemployment brings many people face to face with acute personal dilemmas and fundamental questions about their identity and value to society" (p. 340). Harrison (1976) believed that some kinds of people would be less likely to suffer from being without a job than would others. Those less likely to suffer would be those who had adequate financial resources enabling them to cope with the situation, those for whom the unemployed role was somehow legitimate (e.g., a solo father-housekeeper), older men who were close to retirement, and those whose aspirations and expectations were low to begin with. He also argued on the basis of Bakke's (1933) Greenwich study that prolonged unemployment would be especially stressful for those who were ambitious and previously successful.

The stage models so far described are basically rather similar and the summary version presented by Eisenberg and Lazarsfeld (1938) distills the shift from initial optimism towards pessimism, resignation, and fatalistic attitudes, a shift that was assumed to occur as length of unemployment increases. Hill (1977, 1978) has taken a somewhat different approach by treating the effects of unemployment as conceptually and experientially similar to bereavement. The loss of a job is seen to be followed by reactions that are similar to those that occur in bereavement. Thus one would expect to find such reactions as denial, anger, grief, and depression with a gradual movement towards some acceptance and recovery from the loss. In the case of unemployment the strength of the reactions would depend in part on how strongly a person was identified with the lost job, stronger identification being associated with stronger reactions just as reactions to bereavement are related to the strength of the attachment.

Other stage models have been described by Fineman (1983, pp. 8–12) as applied to white collar unemployment. Most of these models resemble those that we have already described, involving a movement from initial shock through to a degree of final acceptance. Some of these models derive from the life crisis model proposed by Fink (1967). In other cases the stages are derived from observations of unemployed managers and professionals (e.g., Powell & Driscoll, 1973). Fineman (1983) comments that these various models attempt to take account of the time dimension by showing that responses can vary considerably over time. However, he believes that it is ". . . unclear whether the unemployed *experience* moving in and out of phases, or whether the phases represent mere labels of convenience for the observer/investigator. Furthermore, it is possible that phases may loop, or be cyclical, rather than linear" (p. 11). He also indicates that there may be considerable variability between individuals in their responses over time and that these differences ". . . may be as (or more) important for understanding the impact of unemployment than a search for similarities and invariant patterns" (p. 11).

The various stage models that have been presented can be seen as descriptions of changes that may occur over time as individuals react to their unemployed condition. They do not have the status of explanations because they do not provide information about the mechanisms or processes that might underlie the assumed changes. They also tend to gloss over the marked individual differences that occur in how people cope with unemployment. Their very simplicity may lead them to be too readily accepted so that people come to believe that there is a general pattern of reactions to unemployment and thereby develop a misleading stereotype of the behavior of the unemployed.

These general points are reiterated in other discussions of stage models of unemployment. Thus Kelvin and Jarrett (1985) state that:

> The description of stages does not itself provide an explanation of the effects of unemployment; at most it is merely the first step towards it, and that only if the description is sufficiently accurate. A general model may simply not be able to achieve the necessary accuracy, because its very generality obscures essential differences—differences due to levels of skill, age, regional traditions and experiences, ethnic background and hostilities, and so forth. (p. 26)

Kelvin and Jarrett are willing to accept that prolonged unemployment may, in the majority of cases, lead to resignation and apathy but they call for detailed studies of the processes that determine change in reactions, especially transitions between stages and developments within them (see also Fryer, 1985).

We should note that there is a long history in psychology of attempts to formulate stage theories that assume sequential changes that occur with development. The stages may refer to cognitive development, personality development, or the development of other capacities such as moral judgment. Freud, Piaget, and Kohlberg have all been identified with this search for generality and for the processes that determine stage transitions. These developmental approaches have been subject to much controversy. Criticisms of them have questioned whether individuals do in fact move through a uniform set of stages in their development. These criticisms note that there is a lot of variability in behavior, that individuals may revert to earlier stages or jump stages, that most theories place the final stage in adolescence or early adulthood and neglect changes in middle and old age, that there are discontinuities as well as continuities in development, that different functions seem to mature at different rates, and that the detailed explication of the processes assumed to determine transitions tend to be neglected. Bandura (1986, pp. 483–485) mentions most of these criticisms in his recent discussion of stage theories. He argues from a social cognitive framework that one achieves a better understanding of thought and action by close examination of the conditions of social learning and the nature of the immediate situation along with information about such variables as perceived self-efficacy, short- or long-term goals, and the nature of feedback. Stage theories have been resolutely defended, however, by some of their advocates—especially by Kohlberg (1984).

These debates are beyond the scope of the present discussion but some of the criticisms of developmental stage theories are relevant to stage theories of unemployment effects. For example, do some unemployed people move straight from optimism to apathy? Do some revert back to optimism, having experienced pessimism? In terms of the bereavement analogue, do all unemployed people ultimately adjust or recover, even if they have not found employment? Why do some people seem to cope better than others? What causes the variability that one finds in the way people respond to unemployment? Does the past experience of individuals in employment influence how they react to their unemployed condition? To what extent are their reactions affected by positive and negative features of the immediate situation such as the presence or absence of social support or the availability or absence of financial resources that one can fall back on in the absence of a regular income? The literature on the stages of reactions to unemployment provide few answers to questions such as these and the descriptive accounts are largely based upon selected evidence of the 1930s, which is not a sufficient basis for far-reaching generalizations. Note also that the findings that come from longitudinal studies conducted in the 1980s continue to demonstrate a high level of variability among individuals in the way they respond to unemployment. This variability makes it difficult to fix upon a normative set of stages that move toward some ultimate reaction to unemployment such as fatalism or apathy. These more recent studies have not been explicitly designed to test particular stage models, however, and hence the evidence is only indirect.

Recent evidence from other areas does not lead one to be optimistic about the validity of a stage theory of unemployment effects. There are related formulations about how people cope with negative events in their lives that are relevant to possible general stages in reactions to unemployment—events such as bereavement, physical injury, illness, or other trauma. Some of these models have been reviewed by Silver and Wortman (1980)—see also Lazarus and Folkman for other examples (1984, pp. 143–148). The Silver and Wortman review includes incentive-disengagement theory (Klinger, 1975, 1977), reactance theory (Wortman & Brehm, 1975), learned helplessness theory (Abramson, Seligman, & Teasdale, 1978; Seligman, 1975), reactions to physical injury and illness (Shontz, 1975), and the analysis of the coping process by Lazarus (e.g., Lazarus & Folkman, 1984; Lazarus & Launier, 1978).

Silver and Wortman (1980) also discuss other stage approaches that relate to questions such as how terminally ill patients react to their illness (Kubler-Ross, 1969) and how people cope with bereavement (e.g., Glick, Weiss, & Parkes, 1974; Hansson, Stroebe, & Stroebe, 1988; Parkes & Weiss, 1983). They pose a number of questions which they seek to answer by referring to the empirical literature: (1) Is there a general pattern or consensual response to undesirable life events? Silver and Wortman (1980) conclude that the evidence suggests that there is little consensus and that there is a great deal of variability across life crises; (2) Do people go through stages of emotional reactions in response to an undesirable life event? Silver and Wortman (1980) conclude that the limited data that are available do not appear to clearly fit a stage model of emotional response following life crises and that the extreme pattern of variability in response does not support the notion of stages; (3) Do people accept or recover following an undesirable life event? Silver and Wortman (1980) conclude that a substantial minority of people continue to experience distress for much longer than expected and some may continue to reexperience the crisis for the rest of their lives (see also Lehman, Wortman, & Williams, 1987).

Silver and Wortman (1980) conclude that the models that they review cannot account for the variety of responses that occur when individuals experience aversive outcomes. They argue that a better understanding of reactions to stressful events might follow closer investigation of the role of perceived social support, the opportunity for ventilation or free expression of feelings, the ability to find meaning in the crisis, and whether or not individuals have had experience with other stressors that might confer some immunity. They describe some of the evidence relating to each of these factors. Note that the four factors that they discuss are of obvious relevance to the unemployment experience and that at least one of them, the role of social support, has been investigated in recent studies of unemployment effects (e.g., Ullah, Banks, & Warr, 1985). If one analyzed individual statements from unemployed people, one would doubtless find that some attempt to cope with the situation by finding meaning in the crisis, just as victims of illness or other trauma may strive to understand and find some purpose in the negative events that they are living through (e.g., Taylor, 1983). Finally, a person's past experience of moving in and out of employment or having continuous employment in a particular occupation should influence how the individual adjusts to a current period of unemployment. The "first time" unemployed person would have to develop coping skills that those with a history of previous employment and unemployment may already have in their repertoires.

The literature of the 1980s demonstrates a much greater awareness of the many factors that influence how individuals cope with stress in their lives. In recent years, there has been a veritable explosion of research and publication in the areas of stress, coping, and health—a literature that is too extensive to review here (see Lazarus & Folkman, 1984; Taylor, 1986). Kessler, Price, and Wortman (1985) have recently reviewed contributions that are concerned with social factors in psychopathology, especially in relation to stress, social support, and coping processes. Like Silver and Wortman (1980), they are critical of stage theories that attempt to account for how people react to negative events in their lives. Their concluding remarks indicate that there is some convergence in the literature on a common conception of the stress process and on a common research design. This conception has at its center:

> . . . the notion that stress exposure sets off a *process of adaptation*. It recognizes that this process unfolds over time, and it acknowledges that this process is modified by structural factors as well as by personal dispositions and vulnerabilities. There is growing recognition that the analysis of this process requires longitudinal methods. Also, it is becoming increasingly clear that experimental interventions are required to unravel the parts of this process that link stress and health. (p. 565)

Stage theories have therefore been overtaken by new developments in the field that move one away from analyses in terms of general and oversimplified stages towards detailed investigations of the coping process itself.

Jahoda's Functional Approach

This theoretical approach was developed by Jahoda (1979, 1981, 1982; see also Jahoda & Rush, 1980). Jahoda recognizes that paid employment has both manifest and latent functions as far as its benefits to the individual are concerned. The most important manifest function of paid employment is to provide a wage, and any deprivation in this aspect of employment can have negative consequences for a person's standard of living with multiplier effects elsewhere (e.g., on psychological well-being, the family, and many other aspects of daily life). There is hardly need to comment on the dire effects of poverty. One can take findings from the Marienthal study as an example. I noted previously that an important finding from this study was that variation in the amount of income available during unemployment was associated with different attitudes and behaviors (broken and unbroken) among the unemployed (Jahoda et al., 1933). Indeed, a major emphasis in the Marienthal report was on the effects of financial hardship. Jahoda (1982) considers that while the unemployed of the 1930s suffered absolute deprivation, in many cases close to poverty, the experience of the 1970s and 1980s is more one of relative deprivation as far as reduced income is concerned because of the greater access of the unemployed to welfare schemes when compared with the situation during the Great Depression. On this basis she believes that psychological responses to unemployment in the 1970s and 1980s ". . . can with greater confidence than in the past be attributed to the absence of a job not just to restricted finances" (p. 58).

What aspects of a job are so important to a person's psychological well-being that loss of them has negative consequences as far as adjustment is concerned? Jahoda (1982) conceives of paid employment as having a number of latent functions as well as enabling a person to earn a salary (a manifest function). As an institution, employment provides certain broad categories of experience that are:

> . . . enforced on the overwhelming majority of those who participate in it: the imposition of a time structure, the enlargement of the scope of social activities into areas less emotionally charged than family life, participation in a collective purpose and effort, the assignment by virtue of employment of status and identity, and required regular activity. These categories of experience . . . follow necessarily from the structural forms of modern employment. (p. 59)

Jahoda (1982) then draws the link between loss of these categories of experience and psychological well-being: "To the extent that these categories of experience have become a psychological requirement in modern life, the unemployed will suffer from their absence unless through their own deliberate efforts they have found alternative ways of satisfying these requirements" (p. 59). She recognizes that there are: ". . . other institutions that enforce one or more of these categories on their participants; but none of them combines them all with as compelling a reason as earning one's living" (p. 59). Thus, one finds in the institution of paid employment both the provision of a source of income and the availability of categories of experience that are important to the individual. The loss of a job involves deprivation of both the manifest and latent benefits; hence one can expect to find that, in the large majority of cases, unemployment has negative consequences.

Although Jahoda's ideas refer to the functions of employment and the categories of experience that employment offers, she also takes account of personal needs and ways of satisfying these needs through varying institutional arrangements. She notes, for example, that in societies where employment as an institution does not exist, the psychological functions of employment are met in other ways by rituals and religious and community practices that bring people together and provide them with activities, clear identities, and shared purposes. She also calls upon Freud's (1930) ideas to support her assumption that the functions of employment are related to basic human needs by citing his aphorism that work is man's strongest tie to reality. Unemployment therefore weakens a person's contact with reality and affects the person's ability to gratify certain basic human needs, given the Freudian assumption that the development of the ego and the control of the id require that the pleasure principle and the reality principle work together. Thus, one finds in the reality of employment a means of satisfying deeper human motivations. From these and other considerations Jahoda (1982) concludes that ". . . the psychological needs met by employment are probably deeper and more enduring than the institutional arrangements to which we have become accustomed as satisfying them" (p. 61).

It should be clear that Jahoda's discussion of employment and unemployment is intricate and qualified. Her functional approach provides a framework of ideas, however, rather than a well-developed theory, and it suggests questions to be answered. For example, how much of each category of experience (time structure, activity, status, etc.) is necessary to determine psychological well-being on the job? Can the amount of each category that is necessary in a particular instance be quantified? Can the absence of one category be compensated for by enhancement of other categories? Can one have too much of a particular category (e.g., structure and routine) so that psychological well-being is negatively affected by overabundance? Does the amount of each category that a person prefers depend upon the strength of the underlying human need that corresponds to the category? What determines these needs? Are all of the categories of experience present in every job or do they vary considerably in their profile from job to job , as one might expect? What does it mean to say that employment "enforces" the categories? Might it not also be reasonable to say that the individual can generate the categories in some instances? How far is it possible to compensate for deficiencies in the categories within employment by participating in activities outside of employment, as in various forms of leisure or other organised pursuits? The answer to questions such as these depends upon a more detailed theoretical statement that goes beyond a listing of manifest and latent functions in relation to social institutions.

Some recent discussions of Jahoda's functional approach characterize it as reflecting a metatheory in which the person is seen as a passive object, at the mercy of social institutions and external forces. As counterpoint, these discussions encourage an alternative view of the person as an active and autonomous agent who copes with situations, construes information, shapes new modes of reaction, and generally is the origin of actions rather than the pawn, having some measure of personal control over events and outcomes (e.g., Fryer, 1986; Fryer & Payne, 1986; Hartley & Fryer, 1984). I consider this interpretation of Jahoda's position to be an oversimplification. At times she does appear to overemphasize the effects of social institutions at the expense of individual choice, particularly in the statement that the objective consequences of employment override "individual differences in feelings, thoughts, motivation, and purposes" (Jahoda & Rush, 1980, p. 10) and in her use of terms such as "imposes" and "enforces" when she describes employment as a social institution. But it is surely going too far to conclude that Jahoda's deprivation approach " . . . is not only a negative diminishing view of people, not only identifies psychology with the industrial-political *status quo,* but also throws into darkness and distorts the theoretical framework potentially available to researchers in the field" (Hartley & Fryer, 1984, pp. 17–18). Jahoda (1982) does recognize that the individual has a need to understand the world so as " . . . to make sense of events, to see through the baffling diversity of appearances to the underlying meaning of it all" (p. 69), and a need " . . . for some degree of personal control over one's immediate environment" (p. 70). She displays a sensitive and humane attitude toward the individual and recognizes that employment as well as unemployment can have negative effects on people. Thus, she writes (Jahoda, 1981) that: "Time structure can be rigid, contact with supervisors unpleasant, the purposes clear or unacceptable, the status too low, and the activity boring and exhausting" (p. 189). And she does consider ways in which employment can be humanized (Jahoda, 1982, pp. 62–82).

Her approach draws our attention to the kinds of experiences that employment provides, how these relate to human needs, and what the consequences may be when the individual is deprived of these experiences. That she recognizes both the influence of the social environment and the effects of human needs on psychological adjustment is evident in her statement (Jahoda, 1982) that:

> It is the privilege and the obligation of social psychology to avoid the extremes of biological or social determinism by studying the actual interplay between individual needs and available social structures, keeping in mind the possibility that either one may change gradually or suddenly. (p. 84)

Although, as I have noted, Jahoda's (1979, 1981, 1982, 1988) theoretical orientation towards the analysis of the psychological impact of unemployment has been subject to some criticism, her critics also convey considerable respect for her contributions to the literature (Fryer, 1986; Fryer & Payne, 1986; Hartley & Fryer, 1984). Fryer (1986) calls Jahoda's theory a "deprivation theory" because it assumes that people who are no longer employed are deprived of the desirable categories of experience that employment provides. He notes several merits of Jahoda's theory, which include the following: (1) It leads one to expect that there will be a variety of reactions to unemployment, depending on how well each of the categories of experience listed by Jahoda can be satisfied outside of employment; (2) It enables suggestions about how one might alleviate some of the effects of unemployment, depending on which of the categories of experience are most deprived; (3) It helps one to understand why some people may not suffer the deleterious consequences of unemployment (e.g., the "idle-rich" or people from nonindustrialized or different cultures who may have different ways of obtaining the categories of experience that Jahoda lists); and (4) It links the study of the psychological effects of unemployment to the wider psychological literature on the effects of loss.

At the same time Fryer (1986) believes that Jahoda's approach can be criticized on theoretical, pragmatic, and empirical grounds. For example, it may be difficult to measure categories of experience in a way that is independent of the measurement of psychological well-being; it may be difficult to disentangle different causes of psychological distress because the negative well-being experienced by some unemployed individuals may reflect the present conditions of their lives, as well as the categories of experience that they have lost by virtue of the fact that they are now unemployed. Fryer (1986) also believes that the theory is presently unfalsifiable because it can always be argued that those unemployed individuals who are not suffering psychological distress have been able to find other activities that satisfy the categories of experience listed by Jahoda.

These various criticisms raise important issues even though in places they tend to oversimplify Jahoda's own position (Jahoda, 1982, 1987, 1988). Jahoda's analysis includes many qualifications and allows for a lot of complexity in the way people respond to employment and unemployment. She is aware of how some people can cope with unemployment in productive ways, how they can also be frustrated by the negative quality of their experiences in employment, how they strive to achieve some personal control over their daily activities, and how they seek to understand and give meaning to the events that they experience. She paints a complex picture that incorporates the variations that can occur in individual responses and that provides a wealth of substantive information. Her theoretical ideas are general ones that concern the person and the social environment. Jahoda's functional approach is an important contribution to the literature and, until recently, it has been the main theoretical position available for analyzing unemployment effects. It has been influential not only as a basis for the development of related theoretical approaches but also as a counterpoint for alternative viewpoints.

Job Content and Locus of Control

One of the useful contributions made by O'Brien (1986) in his review of the areas of work and unemployment is his observation that current discussions have neglected the early contributions of Bakke (1933, 1940a, 1940b) and have given much more attention to the views of Jahoda (1979, 1981, 1982), already discussed in this chapter. Bakke did not present a formal theory but he did draw attention to certain key variables that ought to be considered when interpreting how people react to unemployment. One of the variables is the content of work. Workers who become unemployed have already been shaped by the content of the work that they were required to perform in their previous employment. As O'Brien (1986) points out:

> Semi-skilled and unskilled manual workers had experienced jobs that did not use their skills, gave little opportunity to control task processes and provided minimal income. These jobs had "damaged" them and produced orientations that explained much of their behavior in a state of employment. Thus, many of the behavioral deficits that Jahoda attributes to unemployment may not be attributable to the loss of the job activities, but to past job experience. (p. 246)

A careful reading of Jahoda would reveal that she is aware of the shaping effects of past job experiences on personal beliefs and attitudes (e.g., on attitudes toward employers and the nature of the job, on a person's sense of control and autonomy). Nevertheless, she does give much more attention to what people lose when they become unemployed and to the underlying needs that having a job helps to satisfy. Bakke's emphasis on how people are shaped by their previous job experiences does introduce another dimension to the discussion that has been somewhat neglected in the analysis of the psychological impact of unemployment. As noted in the previous chapter, Bakke (1933) described how unskilled workers in his Greenwich study developed feelings of insecurity in their jobs and beliefs that their fate was controlled by others, as well as other beliefs that distinguished them from workers from more skilled occupations. He also drew attention to the profound effects on unemployed people of the loss of income that came with unemployment and how the fear of poverty could shape their personal beliefs and attitudes.

Some of O'Brien's (1986) own research has been concerned with generalized beliefs about internal versus external locus of control (O'Brien, 1984). The concept of locus of control permeates many areas of psychology. Rotter (1966) defined locus of control as a generalized expectancy that concerns the extent to which reinforcements are under internal or external control. People with an external locus of control believe that reinforcements are largely determined by other people, social structures, fate, and luck, whereas those with an internal locus of control put more emphasis on personal initiative, ability, and effort as the major source of reinforcements. Bakke's (1933) descriptions are obviously related to the concept of locus of control, in that the workers and unemployed people that he studied were shaped in the direction of external control beliefs by their specific experiences in employment and unemployment (see also Kohn & Schooler, 1983).

O'Brien (1984) argues, however, that the dichotomy between internals and externals is oversimplified and that it is also necessary to take account of people who are intermediate in control. These he calls the "realists" because they have the ability to discriminate between those situations that are amenable to control and those that are not. O'Brien (1986) reminds us that, although the unemployed workers in Bakke's (1933) study accurately perceived that there was a lot of external constraint in their lives, they were also personally controlled in situations where they could use their skills, effort, and foresight. Hence they were realists. As O'Brien (1986) indicates, their unemployment ". . . had not ruined their capacity for self-reliance but, instead, had delimited the number of life situations where personal control was possible" (p. 245). This emphasis is an important corrective to simplified views that unemployed people are necessarily externally controlled and that they are passive victims of social forces without scope for initiative and personal agency.

Finally, O'Brien (1988) also argues that work not only may shape beliefs about personal control but it may also develop capabilities that relate to intimacy and task performance. A match between personal characteristics and job structures may foster psychological growth and determine higher levels of adjustment.

Agency Theory

An emphasis on personal agency also appears in Fryer's (1986) discussion of the unemployed (see also Fryer, 1988; Fryer & Payne, 1986; Hartley & Fryer, 1984). His presentation cannot be described as a formally stated theory but rather as an assumptive starting point that sets out how one conceives of the person. In this approach, the person is presented as active and striving, making decisions, initiating new activities, trying to influence events, planning for the future, guided by values and purposes, organizing and structuring information, and attempting to have some control over events and outcomes. Thus, the person is proactive rather than reactive—an active agent who shapes and plans activities and searches for meaning across a wide time frame of events. Fryer (1986) acknowledges the past contributions of Miller, Galanter, and Pribram (1960) and Harré and Secord (1972) in promoting the importance of plans and the structure of behavior. One could extend these references by noting that there is widespread agreement in many areas of current psychology that psychological theories should acknowledge that the person is an active agent and not a passive object. This kind of emphasis occurs, for example, in theories concerned with the analysis of action, coping behavior, and the self. I will describe some of these approaches subsequently.

Fryer (1986) argues that the agentic features of individuals can be blocked and undercut both in the workplace and under conditions of unemployment. The frustration of agency is assumed to have negative consequences for individuals as far as their psychological well-being is concerned. It should be noted that agency theory is presented by Fryer as a counterpoint to Jahoda's (1979, 1981, 1982) functional or deprivation approach, which he sees as representing the person as much more passive. In a sense, agency theory is really a metatheory rather than a developed theory. It directs us toward taking a particular view of the person as an active, goal-directed agent. As noted, many theories do that already, and in a more formalized way. Nevertheless, Fryer's emphasis is an important corrective to discussions of the effects of unemployment that ignore the resourcefulness, planfulness, and constructive ways of coping that many people display in their adjustment to negative life events. It is supported by qualitative studies that show proactive behaviors in small samples of unemployed people (e.g., Fryer, 1988; Fryer & McKenna, 1987; Fryer & Payne, 1984; McKenna & Fryer, 1984).

Warr's Vitamin Model

Warr's (1987a) vitamin model is a development of ideas that he presented in his earlier statements where he made a distinction between psychologically "good" and psychologically "bad" jobs and extended the distinction to encompass psychologically "good" and psychologically "bad" unemployment (e.g., Warr, 1983). Good jobs were considered to have less psychological threat and to provide more money, variety, goals, decision latitude, opportunities for the use or development of skill, security, interpersonal contact, and a more valued social position. Bad jobs were seen to involve these characteristics in reverse. Warr assumed that psychological well-being is enhanced by jobs that are defined as psychologically good in terms of the characteristics listed and diminished in jobs defined as psychologically bad. Similarly, unemployment can be psychologically good or bad depending upon the extent to which these characteristics are present or absent. "Good" and "bad" were seen as the poles of a continuum for each characteristic. Warr accepted that some of the characteristics may be desirable only up to a point. Past that point the characteristic (e.g., interpersonal contact) may become excessive and undesirable.

The more recent statements elaborate on these ideas (Warr, 1987a, 1987b). Warr now lists nine features of the environment that are assumed to relate to mental health. These features are as follows:

1. *Opportunity for control.* Environments vary in the opportunities they provide for a person to control activities and events. A person may have little decision latitude, for example, or considerable discretion as far as personal control is concerned.
2. *Opportunity for skill use.* Environments vary in the degree to which they provide opportunities for the exercise and development of competence and skill.
3. *Externally generated goals.* Environments vary in the extent to which they generate goals and task demands, enabling individuals to have a sense of purpose and to be actively motivated.
4. *Variety.* Environments vary in the degree to which they provide for varied and novel experiences.
5. *Environmental clarity.* Environments vary in the degree to which they are clear, providing feedback about the consequences of actions, some degree of predictability, and clear statements of role requirements and normative expectations about what is appropriate behavior.
6. *Availability of money.* Environments vary in the financial rewards that they offer, in the extent to which access to money is restricted.
7. *Physical security.* Environments vary in the physical security they offer, some environments affording more physical protection than others.
8. *Opportunity for interpersonal contact.* Environments vary in the amount of interpersonal contact they provide. Such contact with others is important because it meets needs for friendship, provides for the possibility of help and social support, enables a person to make social comparisons with others, and provides opportunities for goal attainment through interdependent effort.
9. *Valued social position.* Environments vary in the degree to which they enable individuals to achieve status and esteem, often by way of assuming roles that have value attached to them.

Warr (1987a, 1987b) considers that these nine environmental categories are all conducive to better mental health. The nine features overlap and are not independent. Thus, higher status positions are usually associated with larger incomes, and increased personal control may carry with it a greater opportunity for skill use. These features provide a useful set of categories for describing environments. One might develop shorter or longer lists of categories but Warr's list appears to be a fairly comprehensive one. Note that it overlaps with Jahoda's (1982) manifest and latent functions. Two of the latent functions (shared experiences and contacts with other people, personal status and identity) appear on Warr's list as environmental features 8 and 9 (interpersonal contact, valued social position). The other three latent functions (time structure, linking people to goals and purposes, and the enforcement of activity) are subsumed under the third environmental feature in Warr's list (externally generated goals). Both Warr and Jahoda include financial resources as an important feature. For Jahoda earning a living is taken as a manifest consequence of employment; for Warr the availability of money is another environmental feature. Warr (1987a) notes that the larger number of categories that he proposes may not be incompatible with Jahoda's (1981) perspective because she observes that ". . . the five broad categories do not cover all the available research on employment. There are other latent by-products" (p. 189). However, she does not elaborate on these.

How are these categories used to further our understanding of the psychological effects of employment and unemployment? Warr proposes a vitamin model, with mental health influenced by the environment in a manner that is analogous to the way vitamins affect physical health. Warr points out that vitamins are beneficial to physical health up to certain level, after which there is no further benefit from taking them. Vitamin deficiency, however, can impair physical health. Some of the environmental features are assumed to operate in the same way as far as mental health is concerned; the more the environment provides these features the more beneficial it is, up to a point. Their absence, however, tends to impair mental health. Warr (1987a) also notes that certain vitamins are harmful if taken in very large quantities; large doses can impair physical health. In an analogous way, very high levels for some environmental categories may lead to a decrement in mental health; the person has too much of a "good" thing. Warr (1987a) summarizes his position as follows:

> The model of environmental influences upon mental health which is being developed here thus parallels the operation of chemical vitamins in two ways. In all cases, low levels of an environmental feature are considered harmful, but increases beyond a certain level confer no further benefit. And environmental features, like vitamins, are viewed as being of two kinds in their effect at very high levels. Some are harmful (as vitamins A and D, yielding an additional decrement) and others have no additional impact (as vitamins C and E, yielding a constant effect). The generic account, identifying nine principal categories and specifying a non-linear impact upon mental health, will be referred to as the "vitamin model", and when necessary separate mention will be made of the "vitamin AD model" and the "vitamin CE" model. (pp. 10–11)

Warr's vitamin model is summarized in Figure 3.1, where the nonlinear relationships between mental health and environmental features are apparent. Warr indicates that there is plenty of evidence for the effects of low levels of

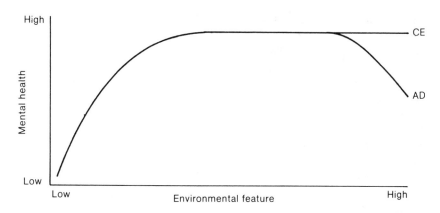

Figure 3.1. Schematic representation of two assumed relationships between environmental features and mental health. (CE is constant effect; AD is additional decrement.) (From Warr, P.B. (1987a), *Work, Unemployment, and Mental Health.* Copyright 1987 by Clarendon Press (Oxford University). Reprinted with permission.)

the employment features on mental health (the left-hand side of the curve), as in the findings from unemployment studies or from studies where different kinds of jobs are compared. Most empirical research, however, has looked for linear relationships between mental health and environmental features. Hence, evidence for the plateau in Figure 3.1 and for the downturn in the right-hand side of the curve is lacking. Warr recognizes that a conceptual underpinning for the plateau and for the downturn is necessary and he provides a number of arguments to support these assumptions (see Warr, 1987a, pp. 11–15). Thus, there are many settings that appear to have a broadly similar and positive impact on mental health, despite variation in environmental features. Mental health is sustained over a wide but unproblematic range, even though a specific environmental factor may vary. People have the capacity to adapt to a wide range of environmental conditions once the critical environmental features have reached a certain point. Problems of adaptation may arise again, however, if some of the environmental features reach very high levels.

Which of the environmental features belong to the CE or constant effect class and which to the AD or additional decrement class? Warr (1987a) proposes that six environmental features are analogous to vitamins A and D, producing a falling-off in mental health when they occur at very high levels. These features are externally generated goals, variety, environmental clarity, control, skill use, and interpersonal contact. For example, individuals may suffer overload as goals become exceptionally difficult or too numerous; too much variety in the environment may create problems in controlling attention efficiently; very high clarity may mean that everything is predictable and that there is no challenge or room for further control over the environment; unremitting demands for control or continuous use of high levels of skill may lead to overload; high levels of interpersonal contact may be associated with environments that are overcrowded and with excessive demands from other people. The remaining three environmental features (money, physical security, and valued social position) are proposed as analogues to vitamins C and E because there seems to be no good reason to expect that high levels in any one of these features will be problematic for mental health. Rather, once these features reach a certain point (on the left-hand side of the curve in Figure 3.1), their effects on mental health should level out.

Given Warr's emphasis on environmental features, it is relevant to ask how he incorporates the person into his approach. He refers to Gergen and Gergen's (1982) suggestion that any theory can be described as primarily situation-centered or person-centered and that, within each category, one can distinguish accounts that are "enabling" or "controlling." Warr sees his approach as "situation-enabling" because, while it proposes that environmental influences are very important, it also includes the assumption that people can mold these influences in various ways. They can construe and evaluate the information that flows from the environment and they have the capacity to make choices and select the environments that they want to enter. Thus, the person can influence the environment both cognitively and behaviorally. It is clear, therefore, that Warr allows for a reciprocal form of interaction between the person and the environment. Warr's discussion reminds one of other related proposals about person-situation interaction (e.g., Endler & Magnusson, 1976; Pervin & Lewis, 1978). Bandura (1986), however, points out that interactionism can take different forms. Warr's emphasis on some degree of reciprocity between person and environment resembles Bandura's (1986) approach, except that Bandura explicitly includes behavior as well as person and environment in his triadic model of reciprocal determinism. Warr's willingness to accept cognitive appraisal and evaluation as an important aspect of how individuals act on the environment is also compatible with much of the recent literature on stress and coping (e.g., Lazarus & Folkman, 1984).

How can the vitamin model be applied? Warr (1987a) lists seven possible applications:

1. The model permits one to describe and compare different kinds of jobs and groups of occupations in a comprehensive way, incorporating features that have been used by others in previous analyses of job characteristics.
2. The model can be applied to unemployment and used to describe and compare the situations in which unemployed people find themselves. Because the same features are proposed to be important both in employment and in unemployment, it also becomes possible to compare a person's unemployed situation with the same person's situation during employment.
3. The model can be used more generally beyond the description and comparison of jobs and unemployed situations to encompass other kinds of environment such as family settings, hospitalization, and leisure activities. It also allows one to compare different social groups in regard to the nine environmental features.

4. The model allows one to predict or interpret the effects of changing environments as when a person moves from employment to unemployment (or the reverse) or from employment to retirement.
5. The model implies that variations in the nine features between many kinds of jobs are of no psychological consequence for mental health because they fall in the middle range of the curve in Figure 3.1. The model implies that one should look instead for the effects of either very low levels of the environmental features or the effects of very high levels.
6. A related implication of the model is that one should plan research so that one can discover nonlinear effects between mental health and environmental features, if they are present. Thus, it would be prudent to identify at least three different ranges of environmental factors (low, moderate, high) and to test for nonlinear relationships.
7. The model implies the need for careful measurement of each of the nine environmental features. Warr (1987a) notes that there is plenty of scope for extensive development and standardization of new instruments. Warr also notes that by applying the model one should be able to identify environments that are harmful for mental health and to make recommendations about how these environments might be changed.

Warr (1987a) applies the vitamin model to a wide range of topics in his book *Work, Unemployment, and Mental Health*. Mental health is conceived as involving five main components: affective well-being, competence, autonomy, aspiration, and integrated functioning. The second, third, and fourth aspects (competence, autonomy, aspiration) cover aspects of mental health that relate to behavior and the environment. As is the case for the nine environmental features, these three components can be measured "objectively," as would happen if assessments of a person's status on each component were rated by outside observers, or "subjectively," as would occur if the assessments were in terms of the individual's own perceptions and evaluations. The five components of mental health are seen as usually interrelated but the fifth component (integrated functioning) is at a more macroscopic level than the others. Finally, mental health can be considered across a wide range of settings or for life in general or it can be assessed in relation to a particular context, as would be the case when job-related mental health was measured.

How is the vitamin model applied to the analysis of the psychological impact of unemployment? Warr (1987a, 1987b) sees unemployment as generally having negative effects on mental health. These negative effects can be related to decrements in one or more of the nine environmental features. Thus, in most cases, people who become unemployed have reduced opportunities for control in their lives. Their freedom to act in chosen ways becomes more limited. They may see themselves as at the mercy of environmental forces and develop feelings of hopelessness, helplessness, and depression. Their sense of personal worth might also suffer. The unemployed are also likely to suffer decreases in their opportunities to use the skills that they already possess and to develop new skills. Their environment also presents fewer goals and task demands and less encouragement of purposeful behavior. The sorts of routines that the unemployed were used to in their jobs are no longer present and they have a lot more time on their hands along with an absence of time-markers that help to break up the day or the week. They are confronted with the problem of how to structure their time. Added to this, their environment is likely to have a lower level of variety and their experience may become much more homogeneous than it was when they were in employment.

Environmental clarity, the fifth environmental feature identified by Warr, is also likely to be reduced when a person becomes unemployed. It becomes more difficult to judge the consequences of behavior and to predict the future. Life is more uncertain and anxiety-provoking and it is more difficult to decide on what are the appropriate decisions and actions. Unemployment also leads to a shortage of money, which becomes a focus for personal and family problems. The person may have to borrow money and then have to repay loans, often under adverse conditions such as high interest rates. Poverty bears down on the unemployed, with all of its negative psychological consequences. Social contacts may be reduced because of lack of money and additional expenditure may have to be incurred due to the fact that a person is unemployed (e.g., the need to spend extra money on transport or on postage or on suitable clothing when the unemployed person attends job interviews).

Unemployment may also introduce threats to physical security as when a person loses suitable accommodation because loan repayments cannot be met or when it becomes difficult for the unemployed person to pay for light or heating. The unemployed person is also likely to experience reduced opportunities for interpersonal contact. In some cases this may lead to feelings of loneliness and a felt lack of emotional support and encouragement. Both the amount of social contact and its diversity have to be considered, as well as the types of social encounter that are affected. Thus, contact with family members and casual meetings with others may increase in frequency while contact with former work colleagues and social forms of entertainment probably decrease. Finally, the unemployed person usually experiences a loss of valued social position. In most societies, being employed carries with it more status than being unemployed. The loss of the socially approved role that goes with employment may be accompanied by a loss in self-esteem and a change in one's social identity.

Warr (1987a, 1987b) cites evidence that supports the general prediction that transitions to lower levels for each of the nine environmental features would be expected to have negative effects on psychological well-being. Note that the extent of these effects would depend upon the amount of change in a given variable. For example, a shift to unemployment from a low-skilled and routine job with low wages would not be as dramatic as a shift from a highly skilled job with high wages, variety, and opportunities for control. One might even conceive of a shift from "bad" employment to "good" unemployment where "goodness" and "badness" are defined in relation to levels of the nine environmental features. Warr is aware of these possibilities and of the different experiences that different groups may have when they become unemployed. Thus, he discusses the psychological effects of unemployment for middle-aged men, teenagers, women, and the long-term unemployed (Warr, 1987a, 1987b). He also shows how the vitamin model can be applied to unemployed people who regain a job, where one would expect to find changes in some or all of the nine environmental features depending upon the nature of the job that is obtained (Warr, 1987a). He concludes that:

> The nine features vary widely within the settings of unemployment and within the settings of paid work; and differences between people in the magnitude of mental health changes following the transition between these environments are therefore to be expected. The vitamin model can be used conceptually and empirically to interpret these differential effects. (p. 235)

We should note that there are many related taxonomies in the literature that concern job characteristics and mental health (e.g., Hackman & Oldham, 1975, 1980; Jahoda, 1979, 1981, 1982; Karasek, 1979, 1981) and these are examined through the lens of the vitamin model. Warr also discusses ways of incorporating personal characteristics into his approach, especially in relation to interactions between persons and situations. In this regard he is more concerned with enduring personal characteristics such as demographic features, abilities, values, and baseline mental health and how they interact with defined job features than with more transient personal characteristics. Warr acknowledges that we need more conceptual analyses of the processes assumed to underlie the vitamin model and the effects of person-situation interactions. He is aware that relevant data concerning the nonlinear relationships assumed in the model (Figure 3.1) are very scarce because most investigations have relied on linear statistical procedures. But that would be a poor basis for abandoning the model.

One question that probably deserves more attention than it has received is why the nine environmental features are important aspects. As Warr (1987a, p. 288) indicates, vitamins are usually conceived as associated with basic physiological needs. Are the environmental features that he lists reflections of basic human needs? Warr concedes that this may be the case for some of them but development of that possibility would move one away from a situation-centered model to a person-centered model and he believes that such a shift is not appropriate at this stage. Nevertheless, the question remains a tantalizing one. Closer analysis of what individuals bring to situations would make the picture more complete. Nevertheless, a focus on environmental features may be more heuristic when one wants to implement procedures that promote better mental health. Situations may be more modifiable than people. It may be easier to change an aspect of a situation than to alter well-established needs, values, abilities, and modes of thought characteristic of individuals.

Chapter 4

Theoretical Approaches: Some Wider Frameworks

The theoretical ideas presented in the previous chapter were drawn from discussions that were specifically concerned with psychological aspects of work, employment, and unemployment. In this chapter we extend the analysis of the psychological impact of unemployment by discussing the relevance of more general theoretical approaches that are not specifically tied to the fields of employment and unemployment. Our discussion will be selective, with the main aim of indicating how each approach is relevant to the analysis of unemployment effects. Such an emphasis may have the positive effect of stimulating future research. As emphasized previously, there is a need to ground investigations of how people respond to unemployment within theoretical frameworks, moving beyond descriptive accounts to more abstract conceptual analyses.

Self-Concept Theory

In their recent account of unemployment and its social psychological effects Kelvin and Jarrett (1985) give a lot of attention to the self-concept in its various aspects. The self is a key concept in psychology with a long history that spans many years. Interest in the self-concept has increased in the 1970s and 1980s as researchers have considered such topics as self-presentation, self-awareness, self-schemata, self-perception, self-consistency, self-knowledge, self-efficacy, the construction of possible selves, the nature and structure of the self-concept, self-serving biases, the measurement of self-esteem, self-definition, self-handicapping strategies, self-monitoring, and self-deception. It would take us too far afield to discuss these various topics, though many of them are relevant to how unemployed people view themselves and how their self-concepts may influence what they do.

Rosenberg (1981), in a useful summary discussion of the self-concept from the viewpoint of sociological theory, notes that there have been two rather different emphases in the literature. In one approach the self is seen as a relatively stable, enduring feature of personality and as an object to which a stable set of meanings is attached. One might, for example, view oneself as a competent, good, and active person, as a loving parent, a diligent worker, and a member of various groups. A second approach focuses more on changing self-presentations that occur in the course of social interaction. The self is viewed as tied to roles and situations and thus has a transient nature depending upon the demands of the situation and the particular role that is being enacted. William James distinguished between these two concepts of self in his monumental work, *The Principles of Behavior* (James, 1890). He argued in favor of viewing the self-concept as an enduring disposition, on the assumption that there is a common core of selfhood that transcends situations. At the same time, James observed that people have many different social selves that vary from situation to situation and that relate to how they want to present themselves to other groups or individuals about whose opinions they care.

Both of these views of self have been influential in psychology and sociology. Rosenberg (1979) is closer to the Jamesian approach in his analysis of the self-concept as encompassing ". . . the totality of the individual's thoughts and feelings with reference to oneself as object" (p. 7). As such it is a complex and multidimensional entity with many different facets. It is also linked with stable, structural features within society such as statuses and roles, shared norms and values, groups and social categories. Rosenberg (1981) indicates, however, that the "situated" self has also received a lot of attention from psychologists and sociologists, especially from those who are interested in the processes of social interaction, communication, and role playing. Much of this interest in sociology can be traced to the early contributions of Mead (1934) on communication and the importance of taking the role of the other and Cooley (1902) with the concept of the looking-glass self. These processes determine a tendency to see ourselves as others see us.

The two approaches to the analysis of the self-concept are interrelated as Rosenberg (1979, 1981) recognizes. Indeed, his discussion draws out in detail how the individual's self-concept is shaped by social interaction, social identity, the social context, and social institutions. Wylie's (1979) detailed review of theory and research on the self-concept provides an important account of how the concept has been used in psychology and there have been other recent discussions that aim to show different approaches to the analysis of the self-concept (e.g., Greenwald & Pratkanis, 1984; Wells & Marwell, 1976). Most of these statements are beyond the scope of the present discussion, where our main concern is with the effects of unemployment on the self-concept. It is in this respect that Kelvin and Jarrett's (1985) discussion is relevant.

They observe that normally people do not devote a lot of their time to self-analysis. Indeed, if they are unduly preoccupied with self, we use the somewhat pejorative term "self-conscious" to describe their behavior. Most individuals take themselves for granted and learn to live with their self-concepts. However, situations and events may lead people to consciously focus on themselves—as when there is a dramatic change in one's life or something happens that is unexpected, unusual, or out of the ordinary. The recent literature on self-awareness specifies some of the conditions under which people pay more attention to themselves, though many of the experimental manipulations used in the related research (e.g., presence or absence of a mirror) seem somewhat contrived (e.g., Carver & Scheier, 1981; Duval & Wicklund, 1972; Fenigstein, Scheier, & Buss, 1975).

Kelvin and Jarrett (1985) observe that the situation of unemployment provides circumstances that would heighten the tendency for people to look at themselves as unusual objects. The central cognitive processes that involve complex structures are disrupted and behavior that has become second nature and automatic, like driving to work and arriving at one's workplace at a certain time, is no longer appropriate. New adaptations have to occur and the person becomes especially responsive to information about self that comes from self-observation and from the responses of others. In regard to the former source of information, the new circumstances that confront the unemployed person, the new behaviors and adjustments that become necessary, and the extent to which the adjustments are effective in meeting situational demands and immediate goals may force changes in the unemployed person's view of self. So too, the self-concept may be modified on the basis of how unemployed individuals perceive themselves to be seen by others—by family, friends, commentators in the mass media, politicians, and individuals and groups. On this basis, Kelvin and Jarrett (1985) argue that:

> . . . the literature on the effects of unemployment may be seen as a record of the conditions and processes which undermine the functional autonomy of one's previously taken-for-granted self-concept: the unemployed individual becomes once again exceptionally dependent on how he is seen, and perceives himself to be seen, by others. . . . Psychologically, as well as economically, unemployment is a condition of forced dependence, which makes the individual deeply vulnerable to others. . . . (pp. 49–50)

Much of their book is concerned with how unemployed individuals see themselves, are seen by others, see other people, and perceive themselves to be seen by others. Their discussion of how the unemployed see themselves considers what it is that the unemployed lose, drawing especially on the accounts given by Jahoda et al. (1933), Bakke (1933), Beales and Lambert (1934), Komarovsky (1940), Marsden and Duff (1975), and others. We have already described the kinds of deprivation that commonly occur and that involve changes in one's income, social relationships, family life, social roles, daily routines, goals and purposes, and so on. These changes would be expected to lead to more self-observation according to Kelvin and Jarrett (1985) and to increasingly negative views of self.

Their discussion of how the unemployed person is seen by others deals with family reactions to the unemployed person, attitudes of friends, and the perceptions of welfare officers, employers, and society (and public opinion).

Kelvin and Jarrett argue that society presents conflicting views of the unemployed. On the one hand they are seen as scroungers looking for welfare handouts; on the other hand, there is widespread sympathy for unemployed people because of the deprivations that they suffer. One finds a curious mix of these themes in the media and in the pronouncements of politicians. In particular, ". . . preoccupation with the scrounging few has distorted the system of providing for the great majority for whom there is genuine sympathy" (p. 100).

Kelvin and Jarrett (1985) also discuss the theme of the Protestant work ethic. As noted previously (Chapter 2), they view this ethic as a modern product and, having considered some counter evidence for the work ethic, they state that:

> . . . explanations in terms of the Protestant Ethic emerge as little more than an invention of twentieth-century social science, with unwarranted pretensions to an ancient lineage. The "ethic" which has been predominant and pervasive is not a work ethic but, for want of a better term, a *wealth ethic*. Wealth is (quite correctly) perceived as the basis of economic independence; *that* is the key issue, and has been so for centuries. (p. 104)

Thus, they assert that, for most people in jobs, work does not have a moral significance but functions as a means of earning a living. Nevertheless, explanations of unemployment in the mass media often refer to lack of effort on the part of the unemployed themselves, blaming the person rather than the situation. Kelvin and Jarrett (1985) point out that the very language used in the labels applied to the unemployed imply focus on the person, although terms such as "jobless" are more situational in their implications. The general point, however, is that an emphasis within society on the work ethic and other individualistic forms of explanation for being without a job are sources of information that affect the self-concepts of the unemployed. Whether the Protestant ethic is a myth or a reality, the fact that it is part of public opinion will influence how the unemployed see themselves (see also Kelvin, 1980).

How do the unemployed view others and how do they perceive themselves to be seen by others? Again mainly on the basis of autobiographical accounts and case histories (e.g., Bakke, 1933; Beales & Lambert, 1934; Briar, 1977; Gould & Kenyon, 1972; Hill, 1978; Marsden & Duff, 1975; Zawadski & Lazarsfeld, 1935), Kelvin and Jarrett (1985) abstract certain main themes. They observe that the unemployed tend to regard other people as not knowing how lucky they are in having a job and they see others as not understanding what it is like to be unemployed. The ascription of luck to others may help to reduce the unemployed person's feeling of personal responsibility for being unemployed; the attributed lack of understanding by others also may help unemployed people to reduce self-blame because the focus of blame is shifted outside of the self. The way the unemployed perceive their families will depend upon the quality of family relations before unemployment. A cohesive family may be brought closer together; a family already under stress may disintegrate more rapidly following unemployment. Unemployment may also sensitize the unemployed person to loyalty and disloyalty in friendships—more so than under normal circumstances. How loyal one's friends are becomes an important question for the unemployed when evaluating the nature of their friendships. Kelvin and Jarrett (1985) suggest that this heightened sensitivity to loyalty, and especially to disloyalty, may be a product of feeling vulnerable. This vulnerability also appears in the attitudes of the unemployed toward employers who may be seen as trying to exploit them by offering them lesser jobs or lower wages or, in other ways, attempting to take advantage of them. Employers and welfare officers are seen as having considerable power over their lives under conditions where the unemployed are dependent on their assistance and vulnerable to failure.

Finally, Kelvin and Jarrett (1985) discuss the relevance of the concept of stigma and stigmatization (Goffman, 1968) as influences on the self-concepts of the unemployed. They observe that the unemployed of the 1970s often have a sense of stigma, being very aware of their low social status and their second-class citizenship by virtue of the fact that they are unemployed. In the 1930s, however, there was less evidence of a sense of the stigma of unemployment. If there was a stigma, it was the stigma of poverty and the consequences that poverty had. In explaining these differences, Kelvin and Jarrett point to the very high levels of unemployment that were present in the 1930s and that were preceded by some 10 years of high unemployment. The 1970s saw the onset of a rise of unemployment following 20 years of so of high employment. A further difference between the 1930s and 1970s is the rise of concepts such as the Protestant ethic and stigma in the 1970s, spread by way of the mass media and often oversimplified journalistic accounts. These two factors (levels of unemployment and concepts) interact. For example, it is more difficult to attribute unemployment to lack of a work ethic when many people from all walks of life are without jobs than when unemployment levels are low and the economy is expanding. Stigmatization of the unemployed may depend upon some critical level of unemployment, neither too high nor too low but somewhere in between. Thus, the unemployed may not be seen as "scroungers" and "dole-bludgers" when there is widespread unemployment and a lot of people, including some who are personally known, are without jobs; in times of very low levels of unemployment the jobless may be seen as disadvantaged and as needing special help. Somewhere in the middle range of unemployment levels one might expect to find negative references to the unemployed in which the unemployed are discredited and their social identity diminished because they are unemployed.

Kelvin and Jarrett (1985, pp. 123–124) discuss these processes in relation to the psychology of social comparison and reference groups. Thus, at some critical level of unemployment, "the unemployed" becomes a negative reference group of inadequates, the hard-core unemployed, and the unemployable and ". . . the unemployed ordinary worker feels tainted by association; he believes that others associate him with these 'inadequates,' as indeed they often do" (p. 123). Self-concepts may then be affected in a negative direction; the unemployed person may come to internalize some of the negative views of others in perceiving and evaluating self.

Kelvin and Jarrett (1985) conclude their monograph by reiterating the point that how unemployed people perceive others is very much influenced by how these others are seen by the unemployed to regard them. These beliefs are partly based upon direct contact with others and partly by the mass media. Images of the unemployed conveyed by the mass media are often stereotyped and unhelpful and they are sometimes reinforced by oversimplified views of the unemployed that are communicated by psychologists and other specialists. Kelvin and Jarrett conclude that the unemployed:

> . . . are not a group of people but essentially an *economic category* . . . they are also an *administrative category*, because the great majority of the unemployed depend on others, and especially on the state, to support them . . . belonging to this economic-administrative category *seems* to be correlated with certain social and psychological characteristics and consequences. However, for a variety of reasons, the size of this category changes, up and down, over time; with size it changes in composition; and with changes in size and composition go changes in many of its social and psychological characteristics and implications. (p. 127)

Their analysis, though somewhat discursive in parts, nevertheless raises important and challenging observations about the social psychology of unemployment, widening the treatment of unemployment so as to encompass the social context and its effects on individual self-concepts.

I will conclude this discussion by noting two further developments in self theory that have relevance to the study of the psychological impact of unemployment. There are other possible developments that one could refer to and some of these will be mentioned later (e.g., self-efficacy, self-blame). For the present, however, the discussion will focus upon: (1) the measurement of the self-concept; and (2) self-discrepancy theory.

Recent contributions to the analysis to the self-concept have emphasized the multidimensional nature of self-conceptions. A person's knowledge about self includes a wide range of characteristics. For example, a young woman might see herself as a pleasant, successful, affiliative, and loyal person, as a responsible wife and mother, as a member of a political party, as an active tennis player, and so on. She might also be able to bring to mind knowledge of what she was like in the past and what she might be like in the hypothetical future in relation to possible events and outcomes. Her self-knowledge therefore involves different dimensions and it relates not only to the present but also to the past and future. This multifaceted approach to self-knowledge is characteristic of recent discussions of "possible selves" and it is involved in the development of new procedures for measuring self-esteem.

According to Markus and Nurius (1986) the type of self-knowledge that relates to possible selves:

> . . . pertains to how individuals think about their potential and about their future. Possible selves are the ideal selves that we would very much like to become. They are also the selves we could become, and the selves we are afraid of becoming. An individual's repertoire of possible selves can be viewed as the cognitive manifestation of enduring goals, aspirations, motives, fears, and threats. Possible selves provide the specific self-relevant form, meaning, organization, and direction to these dynamics. As such, they provide the essential link between the self-concept and motivation. (p. 954)

Markus and Nurius (1986) explore these ideas in detail, citing research evidence and relating the analysis of possible selves to other approaches to the self-concept. The analysis may be related to the study of unemployed people. What kinds of possible selves do unemployed people have? To what extent are the possible selves positive or negative? What are the implications of a positive or negative possible self for the behavior of the unemployed? These kinds of questions are suggested by an approach to the self concept that considers not only what the self is like now but also what other possible selves might be salient for the person.

A focus on multiple aspects of self also occurs in recent research on the measurement of the self-concept. A number of investigators have developed multidimensional measures of the self-concept (e.g., Byrne & Shavelson, 1987; Marsh & O'Neill, 1984) and have applied these measures in educational and other settings with positive advantage. For example, findings from the research indicate that it is useful to separate the academic self-concept from the general self-concept and from other specific facets and that it is also important to consider the self-concept not only as multidimensional but also as hierarchically organized. From our own perspective, these advances suggest that it will be useful to go beyond the measurement of global self-esteem in unemployed samples to the measurement of separate facets of the self-concept such as a person's positive attitude to self, perceived competence, perceived power, and perceived activity.

The emphasis on different selves is also apparent in self-discrepancy theory, the second current development in the psychology of the self-concept that I wish to describe. There have been discussions in the past of the effects of discrepancies between different aspects of the self such as the actual self and ideal self or the actual self and the ought self, sometimes linked to psychodynamic theory (e.g., Piers & Singer, 1971; Schafer, 1967) or to other areas of psychology or sociology (e.g., Mead, 1934; Rogers, 1961; Wylie, 1979).

Higgins (1987) has recently developed a systematic framework for classifying these discrepancies. He assumes that there are three basic domains of the self; the actual self, the ideal self, and the ought self. The actual self refers to the attributes that someone (yourself or another) believes you actually possess. The ideal self refers to attributes that someone (yourself or another) would like you, ideally, to possess. The ought self refers to attibutes that someone (yourself or another) believes you should or ought to possess. These three domains of the self can be considered from two different perspectives. The first perspective is one's own personal standpoint and the other is the perspective of some significant other person (e.g., mother, father, friend, spouse). The three different domains can be considered in relation to these two different standpoints or perspectives to yield six basic types of self-state representations: actual/own, actual/other, ideal/own, ideal/other, ought/own, and ought/other.

Higgins (1987) asserts that the first two self-state representations (especially the first) constitute what is usually referred to as the self-concept. The final four self-state representations function as self-directive standards or self-guides (see also Higgins, Strauman, & Klein, 1986). People differ in the self-guides that they are attempting to meet, some self-guides being more personally relevant than others. Thus, some individuals may be especially motivated to meet an ideal/own self-guide; others may be more concerned with meeting a self-state representation that concerns what some significant other believes they should be like (i.e., an ought/other self-guide).

According to Higgins (1987), "Self-discrepancy theory postulates that we are motivated to reach a condition where our self-concept matches our personally relevant self-guides" (p. 321). He cites previous discussions that involve the notion that standards are motivating and that self-regulation involves the reduction of discrepancies (e.g., Carver & Scheier, 1981; Duval & Wicklund, 1972; Miller et al., 1960). However, he asserts that "self-discrepancy theory differs from these other theories in proposing that different types of chronic discrepancies between the self-concept and different self-guides, as well as between different self-guides, are associated with different motivational predispositions" (p. 322).

He singles out four types of discrepancy for further attention: actual/own with ideal/own, actual/own with ideal/other, actual/own with ought/own, and actual/own with ought/other. These different discrepancies are assumed to be associated with different emotions. Thus, when there is a discrepancy between the actual/own self-concept and the ideal/own self-guide the person is predicted to be vulnerable to dejection-related emotions such as disappointment and dissatisfaction. A discrepancy between the actual/own self-concept and the ideal/other self-guide is also assumed to be associated with dejection-related emotions but, in this case, the emotions are shame and embarrassment about not meeting the standards of others. When the discrepancy is between the actual/own self-concept and the ought/other self-guide, the person is predicted to be vulnerable to agitation-related emotions, especially fear and feeling threatened. A discrepancy between the actual/own self-concept and the ought/own self-guide is also assumed to be associated with agitation-related emotions, but in this case the emotions are guilt, self-contempt, and uneasiness.

This form of analysis therefore enables one to distinguish the conditions that give rise to different emotions such as disappointment, shame, fear, and guilt. Higgins (1987) relates his analysis to other discussions of these emotions, considers the question of the availability and accessibility of self-discrepancies, presents some empirical evidence in support of his position, and compares his approach with other evidence and theories that concern self-beliefs and affect.

How might this analysis be applied to the study of the psychological impact of unemployment? It may clarify the conditions that determine different emotional states in unemployed people, depending on discrepancies between their actual self-concepts and their salient self-guides. Thus, some unemployed people may feel dejected and disappointed because there is a disjunction that involves the actual self and what they would ideally like to be. Others may experience shame and embarrassment because there is a large discrepancy between how they currently see themselves and what they perceive to be the wishes of others. Some may be vulnerable to a range of emotions or have limited vulnerability depending upon the magnitude and salience of the self-discrepancies. Note that Higgins (1987) believes that particular individuals can possess none of the discrepancies, all of them, or any combination of them. Hence, there can be a wide range of individual differences depending upon the availability and accessibility of self-discrepancies. Curiously, there is little discussion of anger as an emotion or of other emotions such as envy that one might expect the unemployed to experience. Nor does the theory deal with positive emotions such as feeling happy, satisfied, calm, and secure, except in relation to the absence of particular forms of discrepancy (Higgins, 1987, p. 336). The theory does not provide links to action; the major focus so far has been on the emotional consequences of self-discrepancies and the conditions under which self-guides and self-discrepancies might relate to motivated action have not been developed. Hence, there are many gaps still to be filled.

Nevertheless, it is apparent that self-discrepancy theory, as well as the other recent approaches to the self-concept that I have discussed take us further than earlier forms of analysis. These new developments could be usefully applied to the study of the psychological impact of unemployment, going beyond the more descriptive accounts that typify much of the discussion of unemployment and the self-concept.

Stress and Coping Models

For most people, loss of a job may be viewed as a stressful event. There is now a vast literature on how people cope with stress and negative life events (e.g., Brown & Harris, 1978; Dohrenwend & Dohrenwend, 1974; Fisher & Reason, 1988; Goldberger & Breznitz, 1982; Holmes & Rahe, 1967; Kobasa, Maddi, & Courington, 1981; Kobasa, Maddi, & Kahn, 1982; Lazarus & Folkman, 1984; Pearlin & Schooler, 1978; Thoits, 1983; Turner, 1983) and the concepts and models that have been developed in this general area can be applied to how people deal with the stress of unemployment. It should be pointed out, however, that the concepts of stress and coping are themselves controversial and that those who work in this area do not always agree on how to define them. For example, stress can be located within the person or the focus can be on stressful events in the environment. An influential current perspective on stress and coping comes from the work of Lazarus and his colleagues and I draw on their discussion in what follows. Lazarus and Folkman (1984) adopt a relational definition of stress that takes both person and environment into account: "Psychological stress is a particular relationship between the person and the environment that is appraised by the person as taxing or exceeding his or her resources and endangering his or her well-being" (p. 19). Note that this definition specifies two central processes, cognitive appraisal and coping, that are assumed to mediate the person-environment relationship. We will briefly refer to each.

Cognitive appraisal refers to how an individual evaluates or construes a particular transaction or set of transactions between the person and the environment with respect to relevance for well-being. The distinction is made between *primary appraisal*, identified by the question "Am I in trouble or being benefited, now or in the future, and in what way?" and *secondary appraisal*, identified by the question "What if anything can be done about it?" Primary appraisal can be of three kinds: (1) irrelevant, (2) benign-positive, and (3) stressful. An encounter with the environment that has no implication for a person's well-being falls into the irrelevant category. If the person construes the outcome of the encounter as positive or likely to be positive, preserving or enhancing well-being, then the appraisal is benign-positive. When the encounter involves harm/loss, threat, and challenge, then it is appraised as stressful. In harm/loss some negative event has already occurred, such as injury or illness or loss of a loved one. In threat, there is the potential for harm/loss. In challenge the cognitive appraisal focuses upon the potential for gain or growth arising from the encounter.

It should be evident that cognitive appraisals following loss of a job could involve one or more of the three types of appraisal just mentioned. The unemployed person has suffered an important loss in income and other benefits since he or she no longer has a job; the event may also be construed as threatening because there is the potential for future harm/loss (e.g., steady erosion of one's savings, increasing restriction on social activities); the event may also be seen as a challenge if the unemployed person focuses on new opportunities that might occur and that ought to be explored. According to Lazarus and Folkman (1984), a threat appraisal is characterized by negative emotions such as fear, anxiety, and anger. In contrast, a challenge appraisal is characterized by positive emotions such as eagerness, excitement, and exhilaration. These various positive and negative emotions would be expected to occur following loss of a job, depending on the dominant kind of appraisal made by the person. Thus, some may feel depressed, fearful, and angry about the loss and its implication for the future; other unemployed individuals may react with some degree of interest and anticipation as they look to the future.

Secondary appraisal refers to how a person evaluates what might and can be done in a stressful encounter with the environment, that is, to how one might cope with the stressful event. The degree of stress and the quality of the emotional reaction are shaped by the interaction of primary and secondary appraisals. In the case of an unemployed person, this interaction would involve the person's appraisal of how severe the effects of the job loss are now and will be in the future and how well-equipped the person is to deal with or cope with the job loss (e.g., by finding another job). A person may also make reappraisals of the situation that are based on new information from the environment and from the individual's own reactions to the stressful event. Some of these reappraisals can be defensive in nature, influenced by a person's needs rather than by environmental pressures. People may also differ in their vulnerability to stress, depending upon their important commitments and the resources they have for warding off threats to those commitments.

Lazarus and Folkman (1984) discuss cognitive appraisal processes in detail, observing that appraisals are influenced by both person factors and situation factors. Among the person variables that influence appraisals are an individual's commitments (or dominant motives, goals, and values) and beliefs (e.g., beliefs about personal control and existential beliefs). Among the situation variables that influence appraisals are the novelty, predictability, uncertainty, temporal characteristics, ambiguity, and timing of stressful events. There is not space to discuss these variables in detail but they can obviously be related to the experience of unemployment. For example, loss of a job would be more stressful when a person is highly committed to employment and believes that there is little that one can personally do to change the event. The appraisal would also be more stressful when the person construes the situation as involving a high degree of unpredictability and uncertainty and when the person believes that it may take considerable time to get another job.

Lazarus and Folkman (1984) define coping as: ". . . constantly changing cognitive and behavioral efforts to manage specific external and/or internal demands that are appraised as taxing or exceeding the resources of the person" (p. 141). Coping is therefore conceived of as a changing process that differs from automatized adaptive behavior and that is not necessarily equated with adaptational success or with mastery. They consider two main forms of coping: (1) emotion-focused coping, where coping is directed toward regulating the emotional response to the problem, and (2) problem-solving coping where coping is directed toward managing or altering the problem that is causing the distress. Lazarus and Folkman discuss various examples of emotion-focused and problem-focused coping and they also consider the availability or otherwise of coping resources that help to buffer the effects of stress. These coping resources include health and energy, positive beliefs, commitments that sustain coping, problem-solving skills, social skills, social support, and material resources. Coping can also be affected by constraints that restrict the use of resources. These constraints include personal constraints, environmental constraints, and level of threat.

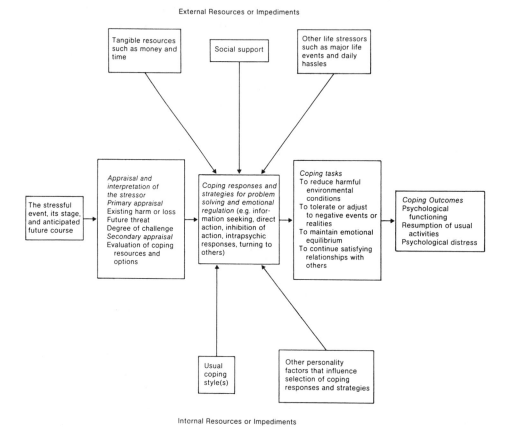

Figure 4.1. The coping process. (From Taylor, S.E. (1986), *Health Psychology.* Copyright 1986 by Random House. Reprinted with permission.)

These distinctions can also be applied to the analysis of unemployment effects. For example, one could examine various types of emotion-focused and problem-focused coping among unemployed people (e.g., defensive strategies, selective attention, positive comparisons, reappraisals, active problem-solving), the effects of resources such as social support and welfare payments, and the degree to which unemployed people are constrained in the degree to which they can use available resources. Warr's (1987a) review of unemployment research indicates that many of these variables have been studied.

Many of the variables discussed by Lazarus and Folkman (1984) and by other researchers concerned with stress and coping have been included in a summary diagram by Taylor (1986) that relates to the coping process. This summary is presented in Figure 4.1. It will be observed that cognitive appraisals, internal and external resources and constraints, and forms of coping are included as variables in Figure 4.1. The figure helps to flesh out the wide range of variables that could be considered in investigations of the psychological impact of unemployment within the general framework of the psychology of stress and coping.

There is plenty of scope for setting up studies of unemployment effects that use this framework. Some of the North American research includes variables that are important in the analysis of coping (e.g., Buss & Redburn, 1983; Cobb & Kasl, 1977; House, 1981; Kasl & Cobb, 1982). For example, Kasl and Cobb (1982) discuss their longitudinal study of the effects of plant closure and job loss as an illustration of the complexity that one finds when investigating stress effects in a field setting. They investigated the effects on male workers of a plant closure in both a large metropolitan area and a rural community over a period of time, collecting information some four to seven weeks before the plant closed and at different intervals thereafter, until about two years after the plant closed. They obtained information on a range of variables using both subjective and objective measures. For example, questionnaire and interview measures of such variables as self-blame, job satisfaction, health, work-role deprivation, perceived social support, and personality variables were included as well as psychophysiological measures based on blood and urine specimens, blood pressure, and pulse rate plus other objective and sociodemographic measures. A control sample of male workers who were continuously employed men in comparable jobs was also included in the design. These controls were studied over the same period of time as those whose jobs were terminated and the same assessment procedures were used.

The findings from this study are too complex to summarize in any detail. Most of the dependent variables were sensitive to the change in employment status that occurred when the plant workers moved from employment to unemployment but there was a tendency for the men who continued to be unemployed to return to baseline levels on the variables some four to eight months after the plant closure. Kasl and Cobb (1982) note that:

> This pattern suggests that the men did not maintain a state of arousal, distress, and sense of work role deprivation as long as the unemployment lasted; rather, they showed evidence of adaptation, so that following an initial period of unemployment those remaining unemployed could not be distinguished from those finding a new job. (p. 450)

Some of the effects were moderated by the social setting (urban or rural). For example, in the urban setting, men in poorer health tended to report more job-loss stress; in the rural setting, men with less perceived social support tended to report more job-loss stress. And levels of depression, anxiety-tension, and low self-esteem increased when testing occurred soon after job loss for the unemployed men in the urban setting when compared with the unemployed men in the rural setting.

Kasl and Cobb (1982) discuss the strengths and limitations of their longitudinal study in regard to how far one can make causal inferences and they

caution against cross-sectional analyses that compare employed and unemployed individuals—"these are inherently ambiguous observations in need
of clarification with respect to causality" (p. 461). They also emphasize the
importance of using both objective and subjective measures of dependent
variables. An idiographic, subjectivistic approach to stress that relies on perceived and self-reported stimulus conditions and perceived and self-reported
responses or outcomes may trap the researcher in an intrapsychic network of
associations. The various subjective measures ". . . may be but different
invitations to the subject to describe the nature and amount of his distress"
(p. 463). There is a twofold challenge:

> . . . to develop relatively objective measurement procedures for subjective
> constructs and to develop complex data analysis strategies so that objective
> and relatively superficial indicators can reveal some of the subjective and
> idiosyncratic import that they may have for particular individuals. (p. 463)

There are other North American investigations that have also been concerned with the effects of unemployment on health and that have studied
variables that relate to stress and coping. We have already noted the use of
aggregate time series designs to study the relationship between economic
downturns, health service utilization, and reports about health (e.g., Brenner, 1973, 1983; Catalano, Dooley, & Jackson, 1981, 1985; Dooley & Catalano, 1984a, 1984b; Dooley et al., 1988) and panel studies that select samples
and examine health variables over time using longitudinal data collection
(e.g., Cobb & Kasl, 1977; Kasl & Cobb, 1982). Other recent panel studies
include those by Dew, Bromet, and Schulberg (1987), Elder and Caspi
(1988), Parnes and King (1977), Pearlin, Lieberman, Menaghan, and Mullan
(1981), Grayson (1985), Liem and Liem (1988), and Linn, Sandifer, and Stein
(1985). Some of the more recent European research is described in Schwefel,
Svensson, and Zöllner (1987) and in the recent collection of articles in the
Journal of Social Issues (Dooley & Catalano, 1988). Both sources describe
panel studies conducted in Europe (e.g., Brenner & Starrin, 1988; Iverson &
Sabroe, 1987, 1988; John, 1987). We do not have space to describe the results
of these investigations.

Kessler, House, and Turner (1987) discuss some of the methodological
issues associated with the use of aggregate time series and panel study designs
and they describe a recent study of their own that was cross-sectional in nature and involved currently unemployed, previously unemployed, and stably
employed respondents obtained by sampling households in high unemployment census tracts in southeastern Michigan in 1984. In other articles they
present the results of statistical analyses that indicate the effects of both
modifying and mediating variables on the health-related variables that they
studied for their three samples (Kessler, Turner, & House, 1987, 1988). They
used various strategies to assess the impact of selection bias in their study (see
also Kessler, 1987). They found that unemployment had health-damaging
effects in the population that they sampled that were severe enough to be

considered clinically significant. They also found that coping, social support, and a positive self-concept were significant modifers of the health-damaging effects of unemployment. These resources attenuated the effects of un-employment on ill health, social support and the self-concept having the strongest and most consistent effects. Analyses concerned with locating mediating variables showed that there were two clear mechanisms through which unemployment causes ill health. The first was financial strain; in its absence the effects of current unemployment were halved. The second mechanism concerned the presence or absence of other stressful events. The negative effects of unemployment were compounded by the presence of other stressful life events. Hence, unemployed people who were also vulnerable to other negative life events were especially at risk. Kessler, Turner, and House (1987) note that there may be other intervening mechanisms that may either compound or buffer the negative effects of unemployment on health-related variables (e.g., employment commitment, marital harmony).

In the United Kingdom both Fineman (1983) and Payne and Hartley (1987) have used models that include stress and coping variables (see also Cullen, Ronayne, Cullen, Ryan, & Wynne, 1987). Fineman's (1983) model is pre-sented in Figure 4.2 and is clearly indebted to the earlier analyses of Howard and Scott (1965) and Lazarus (1966). Fineman (1983) applied the model in his study of white collar unemployment. Payne and Hartley (1987) describe a model that was adapted from the demands, supports, and constraints model developed by Payne (1979). This model proposes that ". . . the stressfulness of the environment is a function of the relative balance between the problems facing the unemployed and the degree of support and/or constraint under which these problems are faced" (p. 33). The model is presented in Figure 4.3 and it can be seen that there are four sets of variables: perceptions of the environment, affective states, personal attributes, and conditioning variables such as social class, financial position, and health. Double-headed arrows are used to indicate that effects can flow both ways. For example, perceptions of the environment (e.g., supports, demands, constraints, opportunities) can in-fluence current affect; current affect (e.g., anxiety and depression) can in-fluence perceptions of the environment. Single-headed arrows denote one-way effects. For example, financial worries can influence the felt threat of continuing unemployment. Payne and Hartley (1987) applied their model to a study of the affective experience of unemployed men and found that the severity of problems experienced by their unemployed sample predicted level of psychological symptoms even when conditioning variables and personal attributes were controlled.

The preceding review concerned with stress and coping models is a selec-tive one, designed to give the main flavor of this approach rather than to present an exhaustive account. The latter task would occupy a lot more space because the literature on stress, coping, life events, social support, vulnerabil-ity, resources, constraints, and other such variables has become very large in recent years. Clearly, however, this general approach is very relevant to how

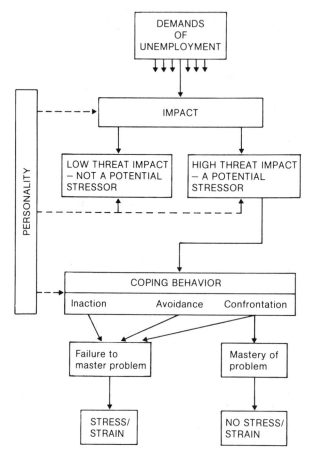

Figure 4.2. A framework of the stress process in unemployment. (From Fineman, S. (1983), *White Collar Unemployment: Impact and Stress.* Copyright 1983 by Wiley. Reprinted with permission.)

people cope with the stress of unemployment. It is likely that we will see many more applications of this approach in unemployment research in the future.

Expectancy-Value Theory

It is also possible to develop hypotheses about aspects of the unemployment experience by using theoretical approaches that come from the psychology of motivation. Motivational theories should enable one to predict such features of an unemployed person's behavior as the amount of effort a person puts into looking for a job, how long a person persists in the job search before turning

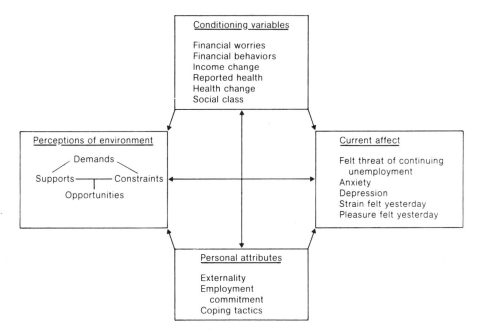

Figure 4.3. A stress model of the psychological experience of unemployment. (From Payne, R., & Hartley, J. (1987), "A Test of a Model for Explaining the Affective Experience of Unemployed Men," in *Journal of Occupational Psychology, 40*, pp. 31–47. Copyright 1987 by the British Psychological Society. Reprinted with permission.)

to other activities, and the nature of the choices that a person makes between alternative activities.

My interest in the psychology of motivation relates specifically to a class of models that goes by the name of expectancy-value (or expectancy-valence) theory. Researchers who use this general class of models attempt to relate a person's actions to the perceived attractiveness or aversiveness of expected outcomes. What a person does is seen to bear some relation to the expectations that the person holds and to the subjective value of the outcomes that might occur following the action. The expectations encompass both beliefs about whether a particular action can be performed to some required standard that defines a successful outcome and beliefs about the various positive and negative consequences that might occur as a result of the action. Whether or not a person has a tendency to act in a particular direction will depend on that person's expectation about whether he or she can perform the action to the required standard, thereby achieving a successful outcome, on a further set of expectations about the possible consequences of the outcome, and on the valence (or subjective value) associated with the action outcome. Those actions will be preferred that can be coordinated to the dominant motivational tendencies (or action tendencies) that relate to a combination of these expectations and valences. Usually, the combination is assumed to be a multiplicative one.

The expectancy-value approach has had a wide application in psychology and goes by a variety of names. Some 30 years ago I noted that there were a number of expectancy-value models in existence and that they had emerged from diverse areas of psychology (Feather, 1959a)—level of aspiration (Lewin, Dembo, Festinger, & Sears, 1944), the analysis of a rat's bar-pressing performance (Tolman, 1955), the theory of decision making (Edwards, 1954), social learning and clinical psychology (Rotter, 1954), risk-taking behavior and achievement motivation (Atkinson, 1957), and from my own research into committed and wishful choices between alternative goal objects (Feather, 1959b). Those models took a different point of view from the drive theories that were then very much in vogue (Hull, 1943; Spence, 1956). They emphasized the cognitive structuring of reality by an active organism and the purposive quality of its behavior within a means-end framework.

In each of these early models the behavior that occurred in a given situation was related to a resultant that maximized the combination of expectations and subjective values (or valences). The organism was assumed to select that course of action associated with the maximum subjectively expected utility, resultant weighted valence, resultant motivation, behavior potential, choice potential, performance vector, or whatever the maximized combination was called.

I brought the picture up to date in 1982 in my edited book, *Expectations and Actions* (Feather, 1982c). New developments and critiques of expectancy-value models were described in relation to seven different contexts: achievement motivation, attribution theory, information feedback, social learning theory, values and attitudes, organizational psychology, and decision making. There have been further developments since 1982, especially from attribution theory (Weiner, 1986) and from the study of volition (Heckhausen, 1986; Kuhl, 1985, 1987). We will describe attribution theory in a subsequent section. Renewed interest in the nature of volition has emerged from West German research where both Kuhl (1985, 1987) and Heckhausen (1986) have reminded us of early contributions by Ach (1910) on intention and commitment. These authors distinguish between motivation and volition. Kuhl (1985, 1987) asserts that volition involves a degree of commitment to a planned course of action that is also protected and maintained once initiated by processes of action control. Kuhl relates volition and action control to an information-processing model that involves memory systems and motivational maintenance systems. The distinction between motivation and volition that he captures in this model is evident in the following extract (Kuhl, 1987):

> People do not always act according to their current hierarchy of motivational tendencies. Somebody who has just decided to stop smoking might feel a stronger urge to smoke than to chew gum, but he or she may end up enacting the initially weaker motivational tendency (i.e., chewing gum) as a result of a

superordinate control process which gradually moves the relative strengths of the two competing action tendencies in favor of the intentional commitment. (pp. 280–281)

Expectancy-value approaches that assume that actions are guided by some combination of expectancies and subjective values also have to allow for the fact that the routine use of convenient heuristics may circumvent more rational forms of judgment that involve conscious reflection (e.g., Kahneman, Slovic, & Tversky, 1982; Nisbett & Ross, 1980). Thus, people do not always reflect on alternative courses of action, estimating the probabilities of occurrence and weighing the different subjective values of outcomes and consequences. They may make their judgments on the basis of quite simple rules and they may also be dominated by situational constraints, social norms, group pressures, task requirements, and other imposed conditions. These various contributions imply that expectancy-value models have boundary conditions (see also Feather, 1982b, pp. 397–400; 1988a) and that they need to be supplemented by other principles. Nevertheless, the expectancy-value framework has been a very useful and influential approach in motivational psychology and continues to be a major focus of research.

Expectancy-value theorists have been concerned not only with relating behavior to action tendencies that are based upon a combination of expectations and subjective values. They also have developed ideas about the nature and determinants of expectations and subjective values (or valences). I have already noted that different kinds of expectations have been distinguished in the literature (e.g., outcome expectations, efficacy expectations), a point that I will return to subsequently when describing self-efficacy theory. Various determinants of a person's expectation of success at a task have been specified such as the person's own past performance at the same or similar tasks and information about the nature of the task and the performance of others. Thus, expectations of success would be higher if a person had a consistent pattern of success at the task or knew that most people were able to succeed, and they would be lower otherwise (see Feather, 1982a; Weiner, 1980, 1986, for fuller discussions).

The valences or subjective values of events and outcomes have had rather less attention. I have conceptualized valences in terms of anticipated positive of negative effects (i.e., anticipated satisfaction or dissatisfaction; Feather, 1986b, 1988a, 1988b, in press). It is obvious, however, that we need much more conceptual analysis of how links with the affective system are made, whether on the basis of past learning or built-in mechanisms. The wider analysis of valences is a neglected area in psychology that deserves far more attention than it has so far received. I have assumed that the valences of events and outcomes are influenced by general personality dispositions (needs and values) but they are not the only influences (Feather, 1982a, 1982b). There are also other variables that have effects (e.g., the objective characteristics of possible outcomes, the difficulty of the task, the amount of personal control that one can exert, moods and other states of the person). Although it is possible to list various factors that influence the subjective attractiveness and aversiveness of objects and events, we are still a long way from having a comprehensive theory about the processes that determine valences or demand characteristics in particular situations.

How can these ideas be applied in unemployment research? I have analysed job-seeking behavior in relation to the expectancy-value framework (Feather & O'Brien, 1987). One can assume that the action tendency relating to job-seeking will depend on the strength of a person's expectation that he or she will find employment following attempts to do so and on the perceived attractiveness of having a job. The expectation would be weaker following many unsuccessful attempts to obtain employment than after few unsuccessful attempts. The attractiveness or positive valence of having employment would be influenced by a person's needs and values and by other factors such as the nature of the specific job that is applied for. This analysis is described in more detail in Chapter 8 of this book. I have also analyzed depressive responses to unemployment in relation to action tendencies, expectations, and valences (Feather & Barber, 1983; Feather & Davenport, 1981). This analysis is presented in Chapter 6.

My use of the expectancy-value framework in the context of unemployment research has been relatively "broad-brush," making use of the sorts of measures that one can obtain in applied settings. I have not been concerned with recent extensions of the approach or with the other reformulations, modifications, and alternative approaches noted earlier. I have been more interested in discovering just how far one can take the traditional analysis of behavior in terms of expectations and subjective values or valences, in the full realization that this form of analysis can only give a partial account of findings but, I hope, not a misleading one.

Attribution Theory

One can also approach the analysis of unemployment effects by using ideas from attribution theory. It is now over 30 years since Heider (1958) published his seminal work on the psychology of interpersonal relations in which he presented a wide range of influential ideas that included phenomenological accounts of perceived causality and the naive or common-sense analysis of action. This publication was followed some 10 years later by influential analyses of causal attributions by Jones and Davis (1965) and by Kelley (1967) that were based to a large extent on Heider's writings and that helped to give further focus to the field. The literature is now voluminous and it is clear that attribution theory has had an impact on many areas in contemporary psychology (Harvey & Weary, 1984, 1985; Jaspars, Fincham, & Hewstone, 1983; Kelley & Michela, 1980; Shaver, 1985; Weiner, 1986). As so often happens in psychology, the field has become somewhat fragmented and specialized as it has been more intensively investigated, though there are recent attempts to integrate attribution concepts into theories that deal with general domains. (e.g., Weiner, 1986).

Attribution theory is basically concerned with how people explain outcomes, what determines their attributions, and how their attributions influence what they believe might happen in the future, how they feel, and what they do. These various aspects can be examined in depth. There is an extensive research literature on antecedents of causal attributions, how attributions can be measured, the various errors and biases that occur when people make causal attributions either as actors or as observers, how causal attributions might be classified in terms of a more parsimonious framework of dimensions, the functions of attributions, and the consequences of causal attributions in regard to expectancy change, affect or emotion, and behavior. There have also been theoretical discussions that take up such issues as the distinction between cause and reason; self-blame and the attribution of responsibility; legal, philosophical, and psychological approaches to the analysis of causality; the interdependence of cognition and affect; and the limits and shortcomings of social judgment.

How might some of these ideas be applied to the analysis of unemployment effects? I have been particularly interested in how people explain unemployment, what determines their causal attributions, whether their causal attributions differ depending on whether they are employed or unemployed, and whether different kinds of attributions are linked to different reported feelings and other components of a person's total belief system, such as a person's dominant values. For example, one would expect to find increasing attribution to external causes as unemployment rates rise. If a lot of people are without jobs then it becomes less plausible to blame unemployment on internal causes such as a person's lack of ability or effort and more plausible to blame factors in the environment such as socioeconomic conditions and poor government. How people attribute causality for unemployment would also relate to whether or not they are unemployed or have had a history of unemployment. Following the Jones and Nisbett (1972) analysis of actor-observer differences in causal attributions, one might expect to find that unemployed people (actors) would be more likely to attribute their unemployment to situational causes than would those who are not unemployed (observers). The latter may be more likely to blame the unemployed for their unemployment, appealing less to situational causes and more to personal causes. The causal attributions for unemployment would also relate to general attitude/value orientations such as the degree to which a person has conservative values or believes in the Protestant work ethic (Feather, 1984b, 1985a: Furnham, 1982b) or believes that the world is a just place where people get what they deserve (Lerner, 1980).

In addition, however, one might expect to find different reported feelings about being unemployed that depend in part upon the causal attributions that an unemployed person makes. Weiner, Russell, and Lerman (1978, 1979) found that there were outcome-dependent affects (happiness following a positive outcome, frustration or dissatisfaction following a negative outcome) that depended on attainment or nonattainment of a goal and not on the cause of those outcomes. There were also specific affects that were linked to particular kinds of causal attributions. Thus, feelings of self-esteem and pride were associated with successful outcomes that could be ascribed to the self (e.g., to personality, effort, ability) rather than to external causes (e.g., luck, ease of the task). Weiner (1986) discusses other affects that are linked to the attributional dimensions of locus, stability, and controllability and documents the evidence that supports these linkages. For example, feelings of anger are elicited when failure (or nonattainment of a goal) is ascribed to the controllable actions of others, whereas feelings of pity are elicited when another person's failure is ascribed to uncontrollable causes. In the context of unemployment, this type of analysis implies that most unemployed people will feel frustrated or dissatisfied because they have not been able to attain the goal of finding a job, that those who are unemployed will be pitied if their unemployment is perceived to be largely outside of their control, and that the unemployed themselves will feel angry if they perceive that their unemployment is caused by outside forces that involve other people who control their access to jobs.

Weiner's analysis of emotional reactions obviously assumes that how we think will influence how we feel. This is a cognitive theory of emotion that is clearly compatible with other theories that assert that emotions are guided by how people construe or appraise situations (e.g., Arnold, 1960; Lazarus, 1966; Lazarus & Folkman, 1984). Weiner's (1986) attributional analysis is also applied to the analysis of expectancy change where a lot of evidence is martialled to support the principle that "changes in expectancy of success following an outcome are influenced by the perceived stability of the cause of the event" (p. 114). As a particular example, expectancies of success would be less likely to decrease following failure if the failure can be attributed to unstable causes (e.g., bad luck). Failure to get a job following a job interview might not result in a lower expectation of success for future job interviews if the unemployed person believed that the failure was due to the fact that he or she was inappropriately dressed—a cause that can easily be changed in the future. Expectations about getting a job would also be less likely to fall following an unsuccessful attempt if the unemployed person believed that the employment situation was volatile and that the availability of jobs could vary from time to time.

Weiner's complete model is presented in Figure 4.4. As applied to the unemployment context, the model implies that a person who loses a job will feel sad and frustrated, assuming that loss of a job is construed as a negative outcome. The person will undertake a causal search to determine why the outcome occurred, especially if the job was an important part of that person's life or if loss of the job was unexpected. The cause that is chosen will be related to causal antecedents. For example, a person may attribute loss of the job to some personal deficiency because he or she has a consistent record

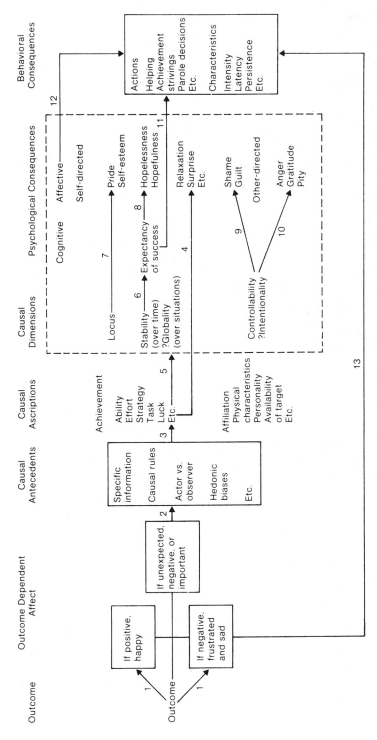

Figure 4.4. An attributional model of motivation and emotion. (From Weiner, B. (1986), *An Attributional Theory of Motivation and Emotion*. Copyright 1986 by Springer-Verlag. Reprinted with permission.)

of losing jobs in the past while others have managed to retain their jobs. Another person may relate the job loss to poor economic conditions because many other people have also lost their jobs despite the fact that they are competent workers.

The attributions that are made also have consequences depending on their location within a dimensional space that is structured in relation to the dimensions of locus (internal, external), stability (stable, unstable), and controllability (controllable, uncontrollable). These attributional consequences involve both expectation change and affective reactions. For example, attribution of the job loss to stable causes may determine reduced expectancies of finding a job in the future whereas attribution to unstable causes may produce only minor changes in expectancies; an attributed cause of unemployment that is seen to be under the control of others (e.g., government inaction to relieve unemployment) may elicit anger; a cause that is seen by the person as involving an uncontrollable aspect of the self may elicit shame; a cause that is seen by the person as involving a controllable aspect of self may elicit guilt.

We should note that the affective consequences could be complex depending upon the causal attributions made and their dimensional location. A person, for example, could experience dissatisfaction, diminished self-esteem, and feelings of hopelessness and shame following job loss if the cause of unemployment was ascribed to internal, stable, uncontrollable factors and if the expectancy of finding another job in the future was very low. This pattern of affect would be different if the job loss was ascribed to external, unstable, controllable factors, in which case the person might experience dissatisfaction but no loss of self-esteem and might remain angry but hopeful about finding another job.

Finally, Weiner assumes that expectancy and affect together determine action. An unemployed person whose expectation of finding a job is low and who feels ashamed of being unemployed and perhaps also depressed, may be less likely to look for a job than one who is more hopeful and whose self-esteem is higher. Weiner (1986) presents empirical support for his model, especially in regard to the achievement context, but indicates that the theoretical network has general application beyond the domain of achievement strivings.

Some of the research from my program has been concerned with the causal attributions that people make for unemployment and with the consequences of these attributions. This research was not based upon Weiner's model, though the results can be interpreted within that framework. I have described Weiner's model because it provides a rich source of ideas for the analysis of motivation and emotion in everyday life, encompassing both stressful and nonstressful outcomes. Future studies of unemployment effects could draw from this model, especially if they are to be concerned with the mediating affects of causal attributions. An appeal to the role of causal attributions also forms part of recent developments in learned helplessness theory, a topic that we turn to in the next section.

Helplessness Theory

The earlier statement of helplessness theory by Seligman (1975) related learned helplessness to an expectation that outcomes were independent of responses. In the reformulation of the theory by Abramson, Seligman, and Teasdale (1978), the expectation of uncontrollability of outcomes remained central to the theory but it was supplemented by attributional variables that enabled one to make predictions about depression. It is the association between learned helplessness and depression that is the main concern of this discussion.

According to Abramson et al. (1978):

1. Depression consists of four classes of deficits: motivational, cognitive, self-esteem, and affective.
2. When highly desired outcomes are believed improbable or highly aversive outcomes are believed probable and the individual expects that no response in his repertoire will change their likelihood (helplessness) depression results.
3. The generality of the depressive deficits will depend on the globality of the attribution for helplessness, the chronicity of the depression deficits will depend on the stability of the attribution for helplessness, and whether self-esteem is lowered will depend on the internality of the attribution for helplessness.
4. The intensity of the deficits depends on the strength, or certainty, of the expectation of uncontrollability and, in the case of the affective and self-esteem deficits, on the importance of the outcome. (p. 68)

This form of analysis resembles Weiner's (1986) attributional theory of motivation and emotion in that it relates affect and behavior to expectations and causal attributions. In this case, however, the expectations concern whether or not outcomes are seen as uncontrollable and the attributions are related to dimensions of locus, stability, and globality. The locus dimension is used to distinguish personal helplessness from universal helplessness. Personal helplessness occurs when the person expects that the outcome is not contingent on any response in his or her repertoire but also believes that relevant others may have the response in their repertoires. For example, a student who has studied very hard may attribute failure at a mathematics exam to lack of ability at mathematics while at the same time continuing to believe that others can pass mathematics exams. Universal helplessnes occurs when the person expects that the outcome is not contingent on any response in any person's repertoire (self or other). For example, a father may believe that there is nothing that he or anyone else can do to cure his child's leukemia. Self-esteem deficits are assumed to occur in cases of personal helplessness but not when helplessness is universal. The degree to which causes are seen as stable and global is assumed to influence the chronicity and generality of helplessness via the expectation of uncontrollability. When an expectation is based upon stable and global causes, helplessness extends over time and may generalize across a range of situations.

Recently, in a further elaboration of the model, Peterson and Seligman (1984) have assumed that the causal attributions that an individual makes in a particular situation may be influenced by the individual's explanatory style (see also Feather & Tiggemann, 1984). Some people, for example, may be more prone to make internal, stable, and global causal attributions for negative outcomes than are others. Because of their explanatory style, they would be more at risk for developing depressive symptoms when they miss out on highly desirable outcomes or see them as unlikely or suffer highly aversive outcomes or see them as likely.

What implications does this approach have in relation to the psychological impact of unemployment? Abramson et al. (1978) specifically refer to the unemployment context when they discuss self-esteem deficits. They compare two individuals who are depressed

> because they expect that regardless of how hard they try they will remain unemployed. The depression of the person who believes that his own incompetence is causing his failure to find work will feel low self-regard and worthlessness. The person who believes that nationwide economic crisis is causing his failure to find work will not think less of himself. Both depressions, however, will show passivity, negative cognitive set, and sadness, the other three deficits, since both individuals expect that the probability of the desired outcome is very low and that it is not contingent on any responses in their repertoire. (p. 66)

Their discussion suggests (as does Weiner's) that a person's reactions to being unemployed will depend in part upon how the unemployment is explained. Affective and behavioral responses will be influenced by whether or not the cause of unemployment is seen as internal or external, stable or unstable, global or specific, and whether outcomes are seen as contingent upon responses or independent of responses (controllable or uncontrollable). In the learned helplessness analysis, however, what remains central is a person's expectation that outcomes are uncontrollable or independent of response. It could be argued that this expectation of uncontrollability develops in unemployed people over time as they unsuccessfully try to find a job. Nothing they do seems to change the situation. Despite their efforts they still remain unemployed. On the basis of this learning, these unemployed people may shift to a condition of helplessness, believing that obtaining employment is largely independent of what they can do.

There are some apparent differences between Weiner's (1986) formulation and the revised learned helplessness model, although both approaches have some aspects in common (e.g., the postulated attribution-expectancy-behavior sequence). Discussion of these differences is beyond the scope of this presentation (see Weiner, 1986, pp. 219–222). Weiner (1986) is cautious in extending his analysis to depression. Earlier he observed that what seems to be important in depression is a low expectation of goal attainment based on stable causes. According to Weiner (1980), depression may then by seen to involve hopelessness (the low expectation) and negative affects "which may be generated by internal or external ascriptions, or by the negative outcome of an event" (p. 404). This discussion implies that one needs to distinguish between a person's expectation of goal attainment and a person's expectation of uncontrollability and between the conditions of hopelessness and helplessness. It may be the case that hopelessness (low expectation of goal attainment) rather than helplessness (response-outcome independence) is the more appropriate concept to stress in the analysis of depression (or, at least, for some forms of depression). Weiner's (1986) more recent position is that, given the complex nature of clinical depression and its determinants, it might be "more useful to move away from clinical depression and consider what might be called discouragement, demoralization, or despondency from an attributional perspective" (pp. 221–222). Research from my own program has investigated nonclinical depression (or feelings of sadness and disappointment) among unemployed people as well as depressive symptoms in the more clinical sense. These studies, which also involve attributional variables, will be described subsequently.

Self-Efficacy Theory

It is also possible to relate research on the psychological impact of unemployment to theoretical ideas that come from Bandura's social cognitive theory in which the concept of self-efficacy has an important role (Bandura, 1977, 1982, 1986, 1988). Social cognitive theory emphasizes such factors as past learning in social contexts, the effects of role models, the individual's ability to self-regulate and monitor behavior in relation to internal standards and social influence, the capacity for individuals to discriminate between situations and to generalize past learning, the effects of cognitive expectancies in the initiation and maintenance of action sequences, and the role of self-generated affective consequences (Bandura, 1986). It can be seen, therefore, that the approach makes contact with some of the other forms of analysis already discussed in this chaper—for example, with self-theory, stress and coping models, expectancy-value theory, attribution theory, and helplessness theory—but it does so within its own wide-ranging framework of ideas.

According to Bandura (1988), the "capacity to exercise self-influence by personal challenge and evaluative reaction to one's own attainments provides a major cognitive mechanism of motivation and self-directedness" (p. 41). People react to discrepancies between the goals they set and the feedback they obtain about their performance attainments. These discrepancies involve internal standards and knowledge about performance and they provide an important basis for self-evaluative reactions. Fulfilment of valued goals or standards gives rise to self-satisfactions; dissatisfactions arise from failure to achieve these desired goals or standards.

A person might react to self-dissatisfaction arising from performance that falls short of standards by enhanced effort, that is, negative discrepancies and their affective consequences can be motivating. In other cases, however, a large negative discrepancy can discourage further effort. A person's judgment of self-efficacy is important in determining which of these reactions occurs. Bandura (1988) indicates that "it is partly on the basis of the self-beliefs of efficacy that people choose what challenges to undertake, how much effort to expend in the endeavor, how long to persevere in the face of difficulties. . . ." (p. 42). These self-beliefs also affect the extent to which people are vulnerable to stress and despondency when they confront difficulties and suffer failure. Those "who harbor self-doubts about their capabilities are easily dissuaded by failure. Those who are assured of their capabilities intensify their efforts when they fail to achieve what they seek and they persist until they succeed" (Bandura, 1988, p. 42).

Bandura (1977) distinguishes efficacy expectations from outcome expectations. Thus, "an outcome expectancy is defined as a person's estimate that a given behavior will lead to certain outcomes. An efficacy expectation is the conviction that one can successfully execute the behavior required to produce the outcomes." (p. 193). Elsewhere perceived self-efficacy is defined as "people's judgments of their capabilities to organize and execute courses of action to attain designated types of performances" (Bandura, 1986, p. 391). The distinction between efficacy and outcome expectations recognizes that the person can perceive the likely consequences of actions without being able to execute these actions successfully. An unemployed person, for example, may believe that getting a job will lead to a lot of positive rewards but may also believe that he or she does not have the skills necessary to get a job. Similar distinctions between different types of expectation have been made by Heckhausen (1977)—see also Feather (1982b, p. 407). Bandura's discussion of outcome expectations and efficacy expectations obviously relates to the variable called expectancy of success (or expectancy of goal attainment) in expectancy-value models and in Weiner's (1986) attributional analysis. A person's expectancy of success refers to the expectation that a defined outcome will occur if a particular action is performed (Atkinson, 1982, pp. 17–21). Clearly, beliefs about self-efficacy will influence a person's expectancy of success. These expectancies are embedded in a whole structured set of beliefs that concern what may lead to what—for example, beliefs about the implications of actions as far as outcomes are concerned and about the implications of outcomes as far as further consequences are concerned.

There is now an extensive body of research into the effects of differences in self-efficacy, with applications to many different areas—for example, the treatment of phobias, recovery from heart attacks, academic performance, self-regulatory behavior (see Bandura, 1986). The dynamic interplay between self-evaluation, perceived self-efficacy, and self-set standards has been investigated in a series of studies in which discrepancy levels are varied systematically and the effects of self-reactive influences and self-efficacy on effort expenditure are examined (e.g., Bandura & Cervone, 1983, 1986). Findings from these studies show how the different factors discussed by Bandura act in concert. For example, a person with high self-efficacy for goal attainment whose level of performance falls short of a goal or standard may produce heightened effort; if there is a low sense of self-efficacy combined with low dissatisfaction about a substandard performance level, then the person may produce much less effort. Self-efficacy is itself influenced by performance relative to standards. Bandura (1988) notes that when people fail to meet a challenging goal:

> some become less sure of their efficacy, others lose faith in their capabilities, but many remain unshaken in the belief that they can obtain a standard. . . . Surpassing a taxing standard through sustained strenuous effort does not necessarily strengthen self-beliefs of efficacy. . . . Although, for most people, high accomplishment strengthens their self-beliefs, a sizable number who drive themselves to hard-won success are left with self-doubts that they can duplicate the feat. (p. 48)

Personal goal-setting is also influenced by perceived self-efficacy, higher goals being set by people who perceive themselves to be more capable.

Bandura (1986, 1988) considers various properties of goals, the question of commitment to goals, the hierarchical nature of goal systems, and relations between goal discrepancies and mood. He relates his discussion of the impact of goal systems to other analyses of goal-directed behavior (e.g., Locke, Motowildo, & Bobko, 1986; Locke, Shaw, Saari, & Latham, 1981).

Bandura's discussion of the dynamic interplay between goal-setting, feedback, performance, affective reactions to discrepancies, and perceived self-efficacy could be applied to the analysis of behavior following loss of a job, enabling one to account for such behaviors as persistent job seeking and withdrawing from job seeking after a number of failures. For example, one would expect that a person with high perceived self-efficacy relating to the responses that are necessary to obtain employment would persevere longer when looking for a job than one whose perceived self-efficacy is low, though repeated failure to obtain employment may ultimately erode beliefs in one's capability to organize and execute the actions that are necessary to get a job. Feelings of dissatisfaction would be more intense for unemployed people who set very high goals as far as their desired employment is concerned and who consistently fail to get the kind of job they desire, when compared with those who are willing to settle for jobs that may not be in the ideal range.

Bandura's discussion of the joint effects of efficacy beliefs and outcome beliefs can also be related to possible alternative reactions to unemployment. Figure 4.5 summarizes different possible effects that different patterns of outcome and efficacy beliefs are likely to produce, according to Bandura (1982). If a person has a high sense of personal efficacy and believes that the environment will reward performance attainments, then positive, assured actions are likely to follow (see upper right-hand quadrant in Figure 4.5). High self-efficacy coupled with beliefs that the environment is unresponsive and that actions are not likely to lead to rewarding outcomes may result in social activism and attempts to change the environment (upper left-hand quadrant).

OUTCOME JUDGMENT

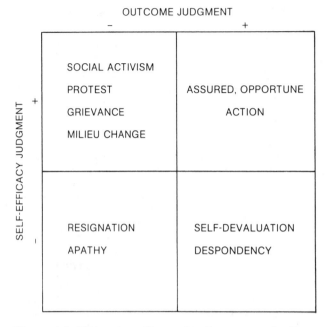

Figure 4.5. Interactive effects of self-percepts of efficacy and response outcome expectations on behavior and affective reactions. (From Bandura, A. (1982), "Self-Efficacy Mechanism in Human Agency," in *American Psychologist, 37*, pp. 122–147. Copyright 1982 by the American Psychological Association. Reprinted with permission.)

When self-efficacy is low, however, and the environment is perceived as unresponsive, resignation and apathy may result (lower left-hand quadrant). Finally, when self-efficacy is low and the environment is seen to reward responses, self-devaluation and despondency may follow (lower right-hand quadrant).

This analysis implies that psychological reactions to unemployment will vary depending upon the particular combination of outcome and efficacy beliefs. For example, the analysis suggests that unemployed individuals who believe that they have the necessary skills and abilities to enable them to get a job and who also believe that getting a job will be followed by positive consequences will actively continue to seek employment. However, if these individuals have little confidence in their capabilities and believe that their job-seeking attempts are futile, then they will become resigned and apathetic (if they believe that the environment is unrewarding) or suffer low self-esteem and despondency (if they believe that the environment does reward appropriate behaviors). As Bandura (1982) indicates:

> When people have a low sense of personal efficacy and no amount of effort by themselves or comparative others produces results, they become apathetic

and resigned to a dreary life. The pattern in which people see themselves as ineffectual but see similar others enjoying the benefits of successful effort is apt to give rise to self-disparagement and depression. Evident successes of others make it hard to avoid self-criticism. (p. 141)

We should note that this analysis should be considered within the context of Bandura's wider framework, which relates the maintenance and regulation of behavior not only to efficacy and outcome expectations but also to personal standards, goals and goal systems, feedback, and discrepancy-generated affect. As noted previously, for example, dissatisfaction and mounting despondency can also follow from a failure to match performance with high personal standards.

Life-Span Developmental Psychology

A final source of ideas that is relevant to unemploymemt research may be found in the study of development across the life span. Unemployment affects people of all ages—the young person who has recently left school, the middle-aged person, the older person close to retirement.

Warr (1987a) compares the impact of unemployment on middle-aged men and teenagers in terms of his vitamin model. He notes that the evidence consistently points to the particularly negative effects that unemployment has on the affective well-being of middle-aged men, especially if they have families to support. Financial demands are likely to be high for middle-aged men because they may have children to support and mortgages to repay (Estes & Wilensky, 1978). Their loss of income following job loss may also be dramatic, especially if they were on high salaries or received extra payments. They also lose their valued role as a provider for the family and as an employed person contributing to the labor force. Their unemployment generates ambiguity and uncertainty about the future that affects their lives more generally. They are also at a stage of the life cycle that is often accompanied by questions about one's life, achievements, and future.

The situation of unemployment is different for the teenager who has recently left school. Warr (1987a) notes that as a group they are less affected by unemployment than are middle-aged people. Some may not have had jobs; others may have lost a job for which the income was relatively low. Hence, financial loss, when it occurs, is less. Moreover, many teenagers still receive support from their families and their financial requirements are generally less than for older groups because they have less responsibilities. A lot of teenagers continue to live with their parents and thus have physical security. They may retain their interpersonal contacts because they still have networks of friends from school with whom they mix and who participate with them in established patterns of leisure activities. Despite these factors that may ameliorate the negative effects of unemployment, teenagers still suffer from not having a job for a number of reasons. As Warr (1987a) points out, "gaining a job is of special significance for adolescents, marking the end of childhood dependence and representing entry into the adult world" (p. 228). The teenager's independence and autonomy is therefore likely to be retarded by unemployment and the development of competence is also inhibited because the school-leaver who fails to find a job is denied the opportunity of learning new skills in the workplace. Hence the teenager is denied an adult role, at least as this role is construed by most societies, and the failure to make this transition from adolescence to adulthood via employment (and what employment brings) has consequences for establishing a person's identity, autonomy, and competence.

This comparison between the psychological effects of unemployment on middle-aged men and teenagers highlights the different roles and responsibilities that are associated with different parts of the life cycle. It also draws attention to "markers," such as getting a job, that are signals of the transition from adolescence to adulthood. Psychologists working in the area of life-span developmental psychology discuss these sorts of variables, often in relation to stages. For example, Erikson, (1950, 1959, 1968, 1980, 1982), in his well-known theory of ego development across the life span, describes eight different stages from infancy to old age that relate to major conflicts between opposing trends (e.g., trust versus mistrust, industry versus inferiority, intimacy versus isolation). Resolution of the conflict at each stage is assumed to strengthen the self. Each step is assumed to grow out of the previous one and the personality incorporates in some form the strengths and weaknesses of the manner in which the conflicts have been resolved throughout earlier stages.

At adolescence, for example, there is a search for fidelity and the basic conflict is between identity and identity confusion. Resolution of this conflict is assumed to lead to the establishment of a new sense of identity that integrates the past, present, and future and that also provides some stability in a changing world together with a feeling of self-regulation and direction. Successful passage through adolescence involves resolution of most problems of identity confusion and one sees the progressive development of increasingly mature interpersonal relationships in which the self enters into shared intimacy with others. This development involves questioning how the crises of preceding developmental stages were resolved and the formation of a new ego-identity that enables the person to fit into the wider social world. Although occupational identity is assumed to be an important concern of adolescence, it is not the only one. Adolescents are also concerned with their gender identity and their ideals and basic values (see Feather, 1980). The task of forming an identity is heavily influenced by culture. Finally, individuals differ in the way they cope with the adolescent experience and there are asynchronies and regressions in development that cut across the themes that I have outlined. I have discussed other theoretical views on adolescence elsewhere (Feather, 1980).

Erikson sees the major task of middle adulthood as resolving the conflict between generativity and the forces of self absorption and stagnation. Generativity is expressed in a concern with establishing the next generation and it can be expressed in the bearing and rearing of children, or by other contributions to society that involve care, guidance, productivity, or creativity. Thus, it can be manifested at the occupational level as well as at the family level. Where generativity is not achieved, a sense of stagnation may develop and the person may become overinvolved with self.

There are other theoretical accounts of stages of development throughout the life cycle to which I could refer (e.g., Havighurst, 1973; Levinson, Darrow, Klein, Levinson, & McKee, 1978) that also involve the assumption that the different "seasons" of a person's life are characterized by different concerns, roles, responsibilities, and conflicts. Thomae and Lehr (1986) indicate that "the idea of ordering the human life cycle into stages or universal crises or concerns has influenced the work of many life span developmental psychologists" (p. 432). However, just as there is reason to be skeptical of well-defined stages in the way people react to unemployment (Chapter 3), so one might question the idea that people move through stages in their lives that are defined by crises or conflicts (Thomae & Lehr, 1986). There are differences in the life situations of individuals and in individuals' reactions to these situations that are not easy to capture in terms of general stage theories. These theories tend to be set within the framework of psychodynamic ideas and they are illustrated by findings from limited samples. As Thomae and Lehr (1986) point out:

> If psychologists expose themselves to the life histories of average people stressed and torn by the great interventions in their lives by history or by loss of friends and other significant others, by conflicts between parents and children, between husbands and wives, between employer and employee, and by illness, failure, and frustrations, they will find it less easy to construct an orderly sequence for these events. (p. 442)

In the context of unemployment effects, it may be more useful to look for differences between different groups in relation not only to their age but also in terms of their gender and other personal and background characteristics. That is not to say that age location along the life span is not an important variable. There are clear differences in the concerns that people have and in the roles and responsibilities that they assume as they grow older. These have to be taken into account in any explanation of unemployment effects.

Life-span developmental psychology is also important in the present context because it draws attention to different kinds of effects that can occur across the life span and to the methodologies that can be used to unravel these effects. Change and development occur in a wider social and cultural milieu and are influenced by secular trends and events and by the influence of history and tradition. The individual has to adjust not only to changing internal conditions, but also to external influences such as economic crises, wars, periods of affluence, and changes in social and political institutions that may have lasting effects on developmental outcomes over time. These kinds of influences have received a great deal of emphasis from those who work in the fields of political socialization, generational analysis, and life-span developmental psychology. For example, Bengtson and Starr (1975), in a discussion of youth, generations, and social change, argue that:

> The analysis of contemporary youth is enhanced from a perspective that allows consideration of time-related processes of maturation (individual development or aging) and period change (cultural development); of the lineage (socialization) relationship that bonds the generations together; of the structural elements of age strata; and of generations as historically conscious aggregates. Four factors can be seen as influencing differences or similarities across contemporaneous age groups: aging (maturation) effects, lineage (socialization) effects, period (historical) effects, or generation unit (ideological) effects. (p. 236)

In a similar manner, Jennings and Niemi (1975) distinguish between life-cycle effects (the kinds of change that are endemic to the life course), generational effects (differences in the shared community of experiences that different age cohorts undergo), and period or *zeitgeist* effects (those influences that reflect important trends and events during a period of history and that have roughly common impact on most segments of society). Similarly Baltes, Reese, and Lipsitt (1980) distinguish between age-normative influences that affect almost every person in a particular culture at about the same point in the life span, history-normative influences that are the result of circumstances existing at a particular historical moment and that affect all people who are alive at the time, and nonnormative influences that are more restricted in scope and do not affect all members of a society or all members of a cohort. Examples of age-normative effects are walking, talking, puberty, marriage, parenthood, and retirement. Examples of history-normative effects are the effects of new inventions such as the computer or the effects of medical improvements, economic crises, and wars. Examples of nonnormative influences are sudden illness or disease or a motor accident or winning the lottery. All of these influences have effects on the course of a person's development. These different influences interact in complex ways to produce age-related changes in development (Perlmutter & Hall, 1985).

These relatively new theoretical perspectives on change and development have been paralleled by the emergence of more sophisticated procedures for analyzing the relative effects of different influences. These procedures involve a combination of longitudinal and cross-sectional designs in which data are collected for different segments of society in a sequential way, starting at different points in history and following up different age cohorts over long periods of time. Obviously these procedures are time-consuming, complex, and costly but they are necessary if we are to advance our understanding of the basis for stability and change in behavior across the life course in relation to individuals and groups (Baltes, Reese, & Lipsitt, 1980; Baltes, Reese & Nesselrode, 1977; Elder, 1980; Schaie, 1983).

What are the implications for research into the psychological impact of unemployment? These forms of analysis alert us to the need to consider different kinds of influences that can affect how individuals react to unemployment. These reactions can be related to the age-normative influences that are present at a particular age and to historical and nonnormative influences. As noted earlier, one would expect different reactions to unemployment when unemployed teenagers are compared with unemployed middle-aged men, mainly on the basis of age-normative factors (Chapter 9). But history-normative influences may also play a part, as when those born during the Great Depression are compared with those born in the more affluent 1960s, or when changes in legislation about social welfare affect financial provisions for unemployed people, or when a worsening economic crisis sharply reduces the number of jobs available. Finally, nonnormative influences also have effects on how individuals cope with unemployment, as when a sudden, debilitating illness leads to loss of a job. Carefully designed studies enable the researcher to go part of the way toward disentangling some of these influences. In a later chapter (Chapter 8), for example, I will describe a longitudinal study in which an attempt was made to control for history-normative effects.

Concluding Comments

In the last two chapters I have reviewed some theoretical approaches that are relevant to the analysis of the psychological effects of unemployment, moving from theories that specifically relate to the context of work, employment, and unemployment to theories that are more general in their scope. I had two main aims in mind. The first was to prepare the reader for the studies to be described in subsequent chapters of this book that draw upon some to the theoretical ideas that have been presented. The second aim was to indicate that there are various approaches that can be applied to the study of unemployment effects, some of which deserve more attention in this context than they have had in the past. Thus, the second aim was heuristic, based on the belief that we can go further than we have done so far in applying psychological theories to applied problems such as the analysis of the psychological effects of unemployment.

The theories that I reviewed vary considerably in their emphasis. Most of those described in the present chapter have an individualistic focus and are largely cognitive in their orientation, though that does not mean that they ignore feelings or affect. Indeed, affect plays a central role in these theories, whether it be in terms of self-esteem, anticipated positive or negative affect, feelings that relate to outcomes and to causal attributions, the affect that comes with states of hopelessness and helplessness, or feelings of dissatisfaction that occur when goals are not attained. The main approaches described in the preceding chapter have a more environmental focus, though they also involve assumptions about individual needs. Jahoda (1985) is explicit in emphasizing the importance of institutional arrangements that constrain or enable the degree to which individuals can satisfy their needs—"the fit or misfit between socially imposed experiences and human needs" (p. 18). She believes that in the unemployment area, theory building is not the overarching aim. Instead, theories are used as background tools for planning research and interpreting results.

It will be noted that there is no general theory that can be applied to all aspects of the unemployment experience. Instead there are theories that are more relevant to our understanding of affective reactions and psychological well-being, theories that can be applied to the analysis of behavior following job loss such as job-seeking behavior, and theories that take account of age-related variables. No doubt there are other theoretical approaches that could also be usefully applied in future research in this area including those from other disciplines (e.g., sociology), but those that I have reviewed in the last two chapters provide a fair sampling of relevant approaches from psychology.

Finally, I have not attempted to present a critical analysis of each approach because that would have taken me too far afield. It is sufficient at this stage to indicate that there are psychological approaches that can be used to frame research into the psychological impact of unemployment and that take us beyond descriptive statements about the unemployment experience toward a deeper understanding.

Chapter 5

Scales and Measures

The preceding chapters provide us with a framework or context in which we can locate our own studies of the psychological impact of unemployment. The remaining chapters of this book will focus upon these investigations which began in the late 1970s and have continued throughout the 1980s. Most of these studies were concerned with the psychological impact of youth unemployment although, in recent years, the consequences of unemployment for older age groups have also been examined. As will become evident, I have addressed a wide range of questions in this research program using procedures that have become more sophisticated as the program developed.

The main findings from these studies will be presented in the chapters that follow. In the present chapter I will describe some of the scales and measures that were used in the research. Having this material together in one place permits an economy of description and a ready source of access for the reader who wishes to check on points of detail. The scales and measures to be described relate to the self-concept, value and attitudes, affective reactions and psychological well-being, expectations and valences, internal-external locus of control, causal attributions, time structure, and an assortment of other variables. As noted in the previous chapters, these variables have been of interest to researchers concerned with the effects of both employment and unemployment.

Self-Concept Measures

Two types of self-concept measures have been used: (1) a measure of global self-esteem and (2) a more differentiated measure of aspects of the self-concept based upon semantic differential ratings of self. I will describe each in turn.

Table 5.1. Items used in global measure of self-esteem.

Item
1. I feel that I'm a person of worth, at least on an equal plane with others.
2. I feel that I have a number of good qualities.
3. I am able to do things as well as most other people.
4. I feel I do not have much to be proud of.
5. I take a positive attitude toward myself.
6. I think that I am no good at all.
7. I am a useful person to have around.
8. I feel that I can't do anything right.
9. When I do a job, I do it well.
10. I feel that my life is not very useful.

Global Self-Esteem

A measure of global self-esteem based upon the Rosenberg Self-Esteem Scale (RSE; Rosenberg, 1965) has been used in a number of investigations (Feather, 1982e; Feather & Barber, 1983; Feather & Bond, 1983; Rowley & Feather, 1987). The scale is presented in Table 5.1. It contains 10 items of which six are worded positively and four are worded negatively. Respondents check one of five answers for each statement to indicate how true they believe the statement is for self (Almost always true, Often true, Sometimes true, Not often true, Never true). Responses to each item are scored from 1 to 5 in the direction of increasing self-esteem. Total self-esteem scores can therefore vary from 10 to 50. Internal reliabilities for this scale are typically high. For example, Feather and Barber (1983) report a coefficient alpha (Cronbach, 1951) of 0.83 for a sample of 116 unemployed respondents.

The RSE has been used extensively in research (e.g., Bachman, O'Malley, & Johnston, 1978). Recently, Demo (1985) used confirmatory factor analysis to show that the RSE provides a valid measure of experienced self-esteem. In some studies scores based on the positive items in the scale have been separated from those based on the negative items on the assumption that individuals uncouple positive and negative self-esteem, especially under conditions of adversity (Warr & Jackson, 1983).

Differentiated Measures

Consistent with recent developments in self theory that examine various aspects of the self (Chapter 4), we have also used measures of different components of the self-concept in some of our investigations (Feather, 1983a; Feather & O'Brien, 1986a, 1986b). Subjects were asked to rate self using 25 bipolar adjective scales presented in semantic differential format (e.g., successful-unsuccessful, friendly-unfriendly, happy-sad, weak-strong). For each scale subjects checked a category on a seven-point scale to describe "how you see yourself." Responses were intercorrelated and then factor-analyzed, using the principal factor solution with iterated communalities followed by varimax rotation for factors with eigenvalues greater than one (the PA/2 solution in Nie, Hull, Jenkins, Steinbrenner, & Bent, 1975). This procedure has enabled the construction of subscales that measure separate aspects of the self-concept, as defined by the meaningful factors that emerged from the factor analysis. For example, the following six scales were constructed by Feather and O'Brien (1986a, 1986b) on the basis of this procedure. The adjective in italics for each item indicates the direction in which the item was scored for each item, scores from 1 to 7 being assigned. The internal reliabilities are those for employed and unemployed groups who were tested in 1981 as part of a longitudinal study of school-leavers (Feather & O'Brien, 1986a, 1986b).

Competence. This scale involved the following nine bipolar adjective scales: *successful*-unsuccessful, worthless-*valuable*, dull-*bright*, pessimistic-*hopeful*, *useful*-useless, apathetic-*purposeful*, *competent*-incompetent, unconfident-*confident*, and *satisfied*-dissatisfied. Total competence scores could range from 9 to 63. Internal reliabilities were 0.86 and 0.87 for employed and unemployed groups tested in 1981.

Positive Attitude. This scale involved the following three bipolar adjective scales: *good*-bad, *pleasant*-unpleasant, and *friendly*-unfriendly. Total positive attitude scores could range from 3 to 21. Internal reliabilities were 0.70 and 0.62 for the employed and unemployed groups tested in 1981.

Depressive Affect. The scale involved the following four bipolar adjective scales: happy-*sad*, elated-*depressed, tense*-relaxed, and satisfied-*dissatisfied.* Total depressive affect scores could range from 4 to 28. Internal reliabilities were 0.75 and 0.80 for the employed and unemployed groups tested in 1981.

Potency. This scale involved the following four bipolar adjective scales: *tough*-tender, weak-*strong, rugged*-delicate, and *hard*-soft. Total potency scores could range from 4 to 28. Internal reliabilities were 0.73 and 0.67 for the employed and unemployed groups tested in 1981.

Activity. This scale involved the following three bipolar adjective scales: lazy-*busy*, passive-*active*, and *fast*-slow. Total activity scores could range from 3 to 21. Internal reliabilities were 0.64 and 0.60 for the employed and unemployed groups tested in 1981.

Anger. This scale involved the following two bipolar adjective scales: *angry*-calm and quiet-*restless*. Total anger scores could range from 2 to 14. Internal reliabilities were 0.34 and 0.57 for the employed and unemployed groups tested in 1981.

A similar factor structure was obtained in a study with Adelaide schoolchildren (Feather, 1983a), except that the set of factors obtained with this sample was somewhat less differentiated.

Value Measures

In the course of the research program a number of value measures have been used. These range from measures of differentiated work values to more general measures of human values.

Work Values

Three scales were used to assess desired work values in the longitudinal study conducted by Feather and O'Brien (1986a, 1986b). These scales were designed to measure desired skill utilization, desired variety, and desired influence in a person's ideal job and they were developed in previous studies (O'Brien, 1980; O'Brien & Dowling, 1980; O'Brien, Dowling, & Kabanoff, 1978). Respondents were asked to indicate how much opportunity for skill use, variety, or influence they would like to have in their ideal job and these three categories of work value were further specified by the items included in each scale.

The desired *skill utilization* scale involves four items concerned with opportunities for learning new jobs, working in the way you think best, using abilities, and using education and experience. The categories of response are: Not at all, A little, Some, A great deal, and A very great deal. Answers are coded 1 to 5 for each item and total skill-utilization scores can therefore vary from 4 to 20. Internal reliabilities were 0.67 and 0.69 for the employed and unemployed groups tested in 1981.

The desired *variety* scale involves four items concerned with change or variety in jobs, change in location, variation of work pace, and frequency of interaction with different people. The categories of response are the same as those used in the skill-utilization scale and they are coded in the same way. Total variety scores can therefore range from 4 to 20. Internal reliabilities were 0.65 and 0.61 for the employed and unemployed groups tested in 1981.

The desired *influence* scale involves five items concerned with deciding about the design of the workplace, speed of work, new skills learned, organization of work, and choice of coworkers. The response categories are: No influence, A little influence, Some influence, A great deal of influence, and A very great deal of influence. Answers are again coded from 1 to 5 for each item and total influence scores can therefore range from 5 to 25. Internal reliabilities were 0.74 and 0.81 for the employed and unemployed groups tested in 1981.

Corresponding scales were also used in the longitudinal study to measure skill utilization, variety, and influence *actually* experienced by employed workers in their jobs (O'Brien & Feather, 1989).

Protestant Ethic Values

I have included a measure of so-called Protestant ethic values in a number of the studies from our research program (Feather, 1982e, 1984b; Feather &

O'Brien, 1986a, 1986b). Weber's (1904–1905/1976) classic analysis of the origins of the modern capitalistic spirit emphasized that Protestant asceticism "looked upon the pursuit of wealth as an end in itself as highly reprehensible; but the attainment of it as a fruit of labor in a calling was a sign of God's blessing" (1976, p. 172). The moral outlook stressed the virtues of hard work, self-discipline, the denial of pleasure for its own sake, and individual activism as a person attempted to fulfill his or her duty in a calling or vocation.

The Protestant ethic (PE) scale developed by Mirels and Garrett (1971) was based on Weber's analysis and it was used in our studies. This scale consists of 19 items, 16 of which are worded, and thus scored, positively and three have reverse scoring. The scale emphasizes the virtues of industriousness, asceticism, and individualism (e.g., "Any man who is able and willing to work hard has a good chance of succeeding"; "Most people spend too much time in ·unprofitable amusements"; "The self-made man is likely to be more ethical than the man born to wealth.") The usual response format for each item is a scale ranging from "I disagree very much" (−3) to "I agree very much" (+3), excluding 0. This format was used in our earlier studies (Feather, 1982e, 1984b). In those studies we converted responses to a 1 to 7 scale measuring the extent of belief in the work ethic by adding a constant of 4 to each item. Total PE scores in these studies could therefore range from 19 to 133. In the longitudinal study involving school-leavers (Feather & O'Brien, 1986a, 1986b) we used a 1 to 6 rating scale and total PE scores could therefore range from 19 to 114. Internal reliabilities for the scale are at a respectable level. For example, in the longitudinal study internal reliabilities of 0.75 and 0.74 were obtained for the employed and unemployed groups tested in 1981.

Employment Value

Three items have been used to measure employment value (Feather, 1983a, 1986a; Feather & Davenport, 1981; Feather & O'Brien, 1986a, 1986b). They are as follows (the end labels are in parentheses): "Should a job mean more to a person than just money?" (Not at all/Yes, definitely); "Does most of the satisfaction in a person's life come from his/her work?" (Definitely not/Yes, definitely); "How much should people be interested in their work?" (No need to be interested/People should be very interested). In most of our studies, each item involved a 1 to 7 scale and responses were scored 1 to 7 in the direction of increasing value attached to work or employment. In these cases total employment value scores could range from 3 to 21. Internal reliabilities obtained from the longitudinal study of school-leavers (Feather & O'Brien, 1986a, 1986b) were 0.46 for the employed group and 0.59 for the unemployed group.

The scale is designated a measure of employment value on the basis of the results of a factor analysis (Feather & O'Brien, 1987), which showed that the scale had a loading of 0.41 on a factor that we called the internal work ethic. The Mirels and Garrett (1971) PE scale had a loading of 0.61 on the same factor.

Table 5.2. Items in employment commitment scale (Rowley & Feather, 1987).

Item
1. Even if I won a great deal of money in the lottery, I would want to continue working somewhere.
2. Having a job is very important to me.
3. I hate being on the dole.
4. I get bored without a job.
5. The most important things that have happened to me have involved my job.
6. If the unemployment benefit was really high, I would still prefer to work.
7. I really must get a job or I'll lose my self-respect.
8. Being unemployed is about the worst thing that ever happened to me.

Employment Commitment

Rowley and Feather (1987) used an eight-item measure of employment commitment in their study of the impact of unemployment in relation to age and length of unemployment. This scale was similar to the one used by Warr and Jackson (1984) but with minor modifications to suit the Australian context. The eight items are presented in Table 5.2. Subjects used a scale with five response categories from "Disagree a lot" (scored 1) to "Agree a lot" (scored 5) to answer each item. The internal reliability for the scale was 0.85.

Rokeach Value Survey

The Rokeach Value Survey (RVS; Rokeach, 1973) was included in one investigation of beliefs about unemployment with high school students (Feather, 1985a). The RVS contains one set of terminal and one set of instrumental values. I used Form D of the RVS in which the values are printed on removable gummed labels. The values in Form D are presented in alphabetical order and each value is accompanied by a short definition. The set of 18 terminal values concerns general goals or end states of existence (e.g., freedom, happiness, salvation, wisdom). The other set of 18 instrumental values concerns modes of conduct or ways of behaving (e.g., being broad-minded, honest, loving, responsible). In the usual procedure, subjects are asked to rank the 18 terminal values and then the 18 instrumental values in "their order of importance to *you*, as guiding principles in *your* life," using the standard instructions (Rokeach, 1973, pp. 357–361). Subjects arrive at their final rank orders by rearranging the gummed labels within each value set so that the final rank orders indicate "how you really feel."

As in other studies in the Flinders value program (Feather, 1975, pp. 23–24), the ranks from 1 (most important) to 18 (least important) were transformed to z scores corresponding to a division into 18 equal areas under the normal curve (Cohen & Cohen, 1975, p. 265). This transformation was made on the assumption that it is easier for subjects to distinguish between the relative importance of values at the extremes of the scale than among those that they rank in the middle. These transformed ranks constitute the measures of value importance and they can range from 1.91 (most important) to −1.91 (least important).

Affect and Psychological Well-Being

Various measures of affective reactions and psychological well-being have been included in the research program. These have involved both scales and single items. For example, scales to measure stress symptoms and life satisfaction were used in the longitudinal study of school-leavers (Feather & O'Brien, 1986a, 1986b) as well as single-item measures of disappointment, helplessness, guilt, anger, and depressed feelings about being unemployed.

Stress Symptoms Scale

In the longitudinal study we used a scale developed by O'Brien in previous research into work, health, and leisure (O'Brien, 1981; O'Brien et al., 1978). The stress symptoms score was based upon responses to 20 items that covered a wide variety of stress symptoms (e.g., indigestion, sleeplessness, loss of appetite). For each item subjects used a four-point scale to rate how often they experienced the health problem. The scale was labeled "many times" at one end and "never" at the other end and responses were coded from 1 to 4. Total stress symptoms could therefore range from 20 to 80 with *lower* scores denoting higher stress. Internal reliabilities were 0.87 and 0.90 for the employed and unemployed groups tested in 1981.

Life Satisfaction Scale

A scale developed by Quinn and Shepard (1974) was used in the longitudinal investigation of school-leavers and it was also employed in previous research into work, health, and leisure (O'Brien, 1981; O'Brien et al., 1978). In this scale 10 items are presented in semantic differential format to provide a general measure of satisfaction with life. Subjects describe how they feel by rating their present life on the following seven-point bipolar adjective scales (the adjective in italics for each item indicates the direction in which the item is scored, scores from 1 to 7 being assigned): boring–*interesting*, *enjoyable*–miserable, *easy*–hard, useless–*worthwhile*, *friendly*–lonely, *full*–empty, discouraging–*hopeful*, tied down–*free*, disappointing–*rewarding*, *brings out the best in me*–doesn't give me much of a chance. Total life satisfaction scores could therefore range from 10 to 70. Internal reliabilities were 0.85 and 0.86 for the employed and unemployed groups tested in 1981.

General Health Questionnaire

The General Health Questionnaire (GHQ) was developed by Goldberg (1972, 1978) as a measure of psychological distress. The 12-item version of the

GHQ was recommended by Banks et al., (1980) for use as an indicator of mental health in occupational studies. Indeed, the GHQ has figured prominently in the Sheffield studies concerned with the psychological effects of unemployment (Warr, 1987a). We have also used it in one or another of its versions (Bond & Feather, 1988; Rowley & Feather, 1987). For example, Rowley and Feather (1987) used the 12-item version in their study of the impact of unemployment in relation to age and length of unemployment. In this version subjects answered questions about how they have been feeling over the past few weeks in comparison to how they usually felt (e.g., "Have you been able to concentrate on whatever you're doing?"; "Have you lost much sleep over worry?" "Have you felt constantly under strain?"; "Have you been feeling unhappy and depressed?"). Subjects responded to each item on a four-point Likert scale with verbal labels (e.g., Better than usual, Same as usual, Less than usual, Much less than usual) keyed to scores from 0 to 3, with higher scores indicating higher levels of psychological distress. Scores could therefore range from 0 to 36. The internal reliability for the scale was 0.89.

Beck Depression Inventory

We have used the Beck Depression Inventory (BDI), either in its long or short version, in some of the studies from our research program (Bond & Feather, 1988; Feather, 1982e; Feather & Barber, 1983; Feather & Bond, 1983). The long form of the BDI (Beck, 1967) consists of 21 items that cover a range of symptoms associated with depression (e.g., sadness, pessimism, social withdrawal, somatic preoccupation). Each item involves four alternatives that span increasing degrees of intensity for the depressive symptom that is involved. These alternatives are coded from 0 to 3. Subjects are asked to pick out the alternative that "best describes the way you feel today, that is, right now." In the long version of the test, total BDI scores can range from 0 to 63; in the shorter 13-item version (Beck & Beck, 1972) total BDI scores can range from 0 to 39. Internal reliabilities for these scales tend to be high. For example, Feather and Barber (1983) reported an internal reliability of 0.83 for the short form of the BDI administered to their unemployed sample; Feather and Bond (1983) reported internal reliabilities of 0.82 and 0.85 for their samples of employed and unemployed graduates, respectively, also for the short form to the BDI.

Hopelessness Scale

I have also used the Hopelessness Scale developed by Beck, Weissman, Lester, and Trexler (1974) as a measure of general pessimism or hopelessness in a study conducted with Adelaide schoolchildren (Feather 1983a). Bond and Feather (1988) have also used the measure in their study of various correlates of structure and purpose in the use of time. This scale consists of 20 items in true-false format, some of which are reverse scored (e.g., "I look forward to the future with hope and enthusiasm," "I don't expect to get what I really want," "Things just won't work out the way I want them to"), with a possible range of scores from 0 to 20. Bond and Feather (1988) report an internal reliability of 0.77 for the scale.

Single-Item Measures

In addition to the scales described in the previous sections, I have also included single-item measures of affect in most of the studies from our research program. For example, items concerning feelings of disappointment and helplessness about unemployment have been used in a number of our studies (e.g., Feather, 1983a, 1986a; Feather & Barber, 1983; Feather & Davenport, 1981). The unemployment disappointment variable was called *depressive affect* in the report of the Feather and Davenport (1981) study. Measures of anger, guilt, and depression about being unemployed have also been included. All of these single-item measures formed part of the questionnaire used in the longitudinal study of school-leavers (Feather & O'Brien, 1986a, 1986b, 1987). The relevant items presented to unemployed respondents in that study were as follows (end-labels for each scale are in parentheses):

Unemployment Disappointment. Subjects used a seven-point scale to answer the following question: "When you think about being unemployed, or the possibility of being unemployed, how does it make you feel?" (Really glad/ Really depressed).

Unemployment Guilt. Subjects used a seven-point scale to answer the following question: "How guilty do you feel about your unemployment?" (Not at all guilty/Very guilty).

Unemployment Anger. Subjects used a seven-point scale to answer the following question: "How angry do you feel about your unemployment?" (Not at all angry/Very angry).

Unemployment Helplessness. Subjects used a seven-point scale to answer the following question: "How helpless do you feel about your unemployment?" (Completely in control/Very helpless).

Unemployment Depression. Subjects used a seven-point scale to answer the following question: "How depressed do you feel about your unemployment?" (Not at all depressed/Very depressed).

Causal Attributions

Various measures of how respondents explain unemployment have been included in our research program. These measures span explanations of youth unemployment in general as well as causal attributions for a person's own

Table 5.3. Explanations for youth unemployment used by Feather and O'Brien (1986a, 1986b).

Items
1. Lack of good education among unemployed youth.
2. Failure of the schools to provide proper counseling and guidance about employment.
3. Lack of work experience among unemployed youth.
4. Lack of effort by unemployed youth in trying to get jobs.
5. Lack of specific work skills among unemployed youth.
6. Temporary bad luck.
7. Prejudice and discrimination against unemployed youth.
8. Not being able to handle job interviews very well.
9. Unemployed youth being too choosy about the sorts of jobs they are prepared to take.
10. Employers objecting to poor appearance (e.g., hair, clothing, neatness) among unemployed youth.
11. Lack of genuine interest among unemployed youth in getting jobs.
12. The economic situation in Australia.
13. Failure of the government to help create jobs for unemployed youth.
14. Getting the dole offers an attractive alternative to working.
15. The unions are affecting employment for young people by causing too many strikes, keeping wages too high, or some other reason.
16. There is too much competition for jobs.
17. Most jobs are too dull or uninteresting to apply for.
18. Failure of private industry to provide jobs for unemployed youth.
19. Too many married women in the workforce taking jobs young people could hold.
20. Technological change; machines replacing people.
21. Decline in manufacturing industries in Australia.

unemployment. Hence we have been concerned with general beliefs about the causes of unemployment as well as beliefs that focus upon a person's own unemployed condition. In some cases items have been combined into scales; in other cases single-item measures have been employed.

Explanations of Youth Unemployment

Some of our studies have presented subjects with lists of possible explanations for youth unemployment. Table 5.3 presents 21 such explanations that were presented to all subjects in the longitudinal study of school-leavers (Feather & O'Brien, 1986a, 1986b). Subjects rated each explanation on a five-point scale ranging from "Not important at all" (scored 1) to "Very important" (scored 5). The ratings for the 21 items were then intercorrelated using the data obtained in 1981 and the matrix of product moment correlations was factor-analyzed using the principal factor solution with iterated communalities followed by varimax rotation for factors with eigenvalues greater than one (the PA/2 solution in Nie et al., 1975). We were able to identify four interpretable factors and we derived four scales on the basis of this analysis.

One scale we called *economic recession* and it involved six items: (a) the economic situation in Australia; (b) failure of government to help create jobs for unemployed youth; (c) there is too much competition for jobs; (d) failure of private industry to provide jobs for unemployed youth; (e) technological change, machines replacing people; and (f) decline in manufacturing industries in Australia. Total scores could range from 6 to 30. Internal reliabilities were 0.68 and 0.64 for the employed and unemployed groups tested in 1981.

The second scale we called *lack of motivation*. It involved four items: (a) lack of effort by unemployed youth in trying to get jobs; (b) unemployed youth being too choosy about the sorts of jobs they are prepared to take; (c) lack of genuine interest among unemployed youth in getting jobs; and (d) getting the dole offers an attractive alternative to working. Total scores could range from 4 to 20. Internal reliabilities were 0.63 and 0.65 for the employed and unemployed groups tested in 1981.

The third scale we called *competence deficiency*. It involved four items: (a) lack of a good education among unemployed youth; (b) failure of schools to provide proper counseling and guidance about employment; (c) lack of work experience among unemployed youth; and (d) lack of specific work skills among unemployed youth. Total scores could range from 4 to 20. Internal reliabilities were 0.67 and 0.73 for the employed and unemployed groups tested in 1981.

The fourth scale we called *appearance/interview inadequacy*. This scale involved two items: (a) not being able to handle interviews very well and (b) employers objecting to poor appearance (e.g., hair, clothing, neatness) among unemployed youth. Total scores could range from 2 to 10. Internal reliabilities were 0.40 and 0.73 for the employed and unemployed groups tested in 1981.

Similar sets of items have been used in earlier studies (Feather, 1983a, 1985a; Feather & Barber, 1983; Feather & Davenport, 1981). For example, Feather and Davenport (1981) asked unemployed subjects to rate 28 reasons for youth unemployment on a five-point scale in regard to how important each reason was "as a direct cause of your being unemployed." They constructed two scales on the basis of a factor analysis. These scales were called *external difficulty* and *competence deficiency* and they were similar to the economic recession and competence deficiency variables already described. The studies reported by Feather (1983a, 1985a) used similar procedures except that ratings of the importance of the different causes were made for youth unemployment in general rather than for one's own unemployment.

Finally, Feather and Barber (1983) used eight items as the basis for constructing indexes of internal and external causes of unemployment in their study of depressive reactions and unemployment. In each case unemployed subjects rated each possible cause of unemployment according to how true they though it was in relation to their own unemployment. They used rating scales numbered from 1 to 7 with "Not true at all" at the low end of the scale and "Very true" at the high end.

Four items stated possible internal causes of unemployment as follows: (a) "I seem to lack the ability and confidence to get a job"; (b) "I'm the sort of person who doesn't believe in having to exert myself too hard to achieve things"; (c) "I find that my mood at the time influences whether or not I get the job I'm looking for"; and (d) "Although I try hard sometimes, I simply have not made the effort recently." Responses to these four items were summed to provide a measure of *internal attribution*, which could range from 4 to 28. The internal reliability for the scale was 0.47.

Four items stated possible external causes for unemployment: (a) "Jobs are difficult to find because of economic conditions that are beyond the control of governments and employers and also beyond the control of those seeking employment"; (b) "Jobs are very difficult to find and this is due to the deliberate policies of the government and/or employers. These policies are also unlikely to change in the near future"; (c) "I have simply been unlucky so far, but my luck could change"; and (d) "Some of the employers I contacted would not give me a job because they seemed to take a personal dislike to me, but this may not be true of all employers." Responses to these four items were summed to provide a measure of *external attribution* that could also range from 4 to 28. The internal reliability for the scale was 0.22.

These procedures for assessing beliefs about the importance of different reasons for unemployment evolved from earlier research into how people explain poverty (Feagin, 1972; Feather, 1974). Similar procedures have been used in Britain by Furnham (1982a, 1982b, 1982c). Feagin (1972) classified reasons for poverty as individualistic, societal, or fatalistic. This classification captures the basic distinction between internal and external causes but it does not do justice to the more differentiated set of factors that we have found in the factor-analytic studies of reasons for unemployment that we have conducted.

Attributional Style

Research on depression and causal attribution suggests that there may be reliable individual differences in the attributional style that people adopt to explain good and bad events. Seligman and his colleagues, for example, argue that depression-prone individuals may tend to attribute bad outcomes to internal, stable, and global factors, and good outcomes to external, unstable, and specific factors (Abramson et al., 1978). More recent contributions refer to explanatory style rather than to attributional style (Peterson & Seligman, 1984) but the idea that particular styles of explanation can be a risk factor in depression is still basic.

I developed a balanced measure of attributional style based on descriptions of a similar measure, the Attributional Style Questionnaire (ASQ) used by Seligman, Abramson, Semmel, and von Baeyer (1979; see also Peterson et al., 1982). My measure, called the Balanced Attributional Style Question-

Table 5.4. Hypothetical events used in balanced attributional style questionnaire.

Outcome	Type of situation	Events
Good	Achievement	(4) You start a small business and it's a success. (7) You apply for a job that you want badly and you get it. (9) You do very well in a sporting contest. (13) You score well in a final examination at school, college, or university.
Good	Affiliation	(2) You go to a party at which most people are friendly towards you. (10) You go out on a date and it all goes well. (12) Someone you know invites you to a party. (16) A group that you like accepts you as a member.
Bad	Achievement	(1) You have been looking for a job unsuccessfully for some time. (6) You score poorly in a final examination at school, college, or university. (11) You start a small business and it's a failure. (15) You do very poorly in a sporting contest.
Bad	Affiliation	(3) You go out on a date and it all goes badly. (5) Someone you know fails to invite you to a party. (8) A group that you like rejects you as a member. (14) You go to party at which hardly anyone speaks to you.

Note: Numbers in parentheses refer to the order of events in the actual questionnaire.
Source: From Feather, N.T., & Tiggemann, M. (1984), "A Balanced Measure of Attributional Style," in *Australian Journal of Psychology*, *36*, pp. 267–283. With permission of the authors and by courtesy of the Australian Psychological Society.

naire (BASQ), was included in an early study that involved employed and unemployed groups (Feather, 1982e). Information about the test characteristics of the BASQ has been provided by Feather and Tiggemann (1984) and results linking BASQ measures to other variables such as self-esteem, depression, and Protestant ethic values have been reported in other articles (Feather, 1983b, 1983c, 1987b).

The BASQ consists of 16 items that present brief descriptions of hypothetical situations (see Table 5.4). Four of these items describe achievement situations with positive outcomes, four describe achievement situations with negative outcomes, four describe affiliation situations with positive outcomes, and four describe affiliation situations with negative outcomes. The general instructions ask subjects to vividly imagine themselves in the situations that follow and to think what might have caused each event ("the *major* cause if this event happened to *you*"). They write this cause down for each situation and then use rating scales numbered from 1 to 7 to answer three questions about the cause and one question about the situation before going on to the next situation. The instructions for the BASQ ask respondents to treat each situation independently. Respondents are also told that they can use any part of the rating scale when answering a question. Finally, they are again requested to answer the questions "as they apply to how *you* feel."

The questions answered by respondents for each item are concerned with the internality, stability, and globality of the major cause they write down and with the importance of the situation. These questions are as follows (the end-labels are in parentheses):

Internality. Is the cause (of the event) due to something about you or something about other people or circumstances? (Totally due to other people or circumstances = 1; Totally due to me = 7).

Stability. In the future (when the event occurs), will this cause again be present? (Will never again be present = 1; Will always be present = 7).

Globality. Is the cause something that just influences the event, or does it also influence other areas of your life? (Influences just this particular situation = 1; Influences all situations in my life = 7).

Importance. How important would this situation be if it happened to you? (Not at all important = 1; Extremely important = 7).

Various combinations of items can be used to provide subscales for the attributional dimensions of internality, stability, and globality, and for the importance of situations. In the study comparing employed and unemployed groups (Feather, 1982e), I collapsed across the achievement-affiliation distinction so as to obtain separate internality, stability, globality, and importance scores for the eight good events and the eight bad events. The scores obtained for each of the eight subscales involving eight items each could range from 8 to 56.

The internality, stability, and globality subscales can also be combined to form two measures of composite attributional style, one for good events and one for bad events, based on 24 ratings each. The scores obtained for each of the two composite scales can range from 24 to 168. Note, however, that there has been some criticism of the use of composite measures of this kind (Perloff & Persons, 1988).

Responses to the importance items can also be examined (e.g., Feather, 1982e, 1987b). I assumed that responses to these items would reflect differences in levels of general motivation or interest. Low levels of importance across the various situations sampled in the BASQ can then be assumed to denote lack of interest or apathy. This variable is relevant to unemployment research because studies of the effects of unemployment conducted in the 1930s provided evidence for increased levels of resignation and apathy among the unemployed (Chapter 2). Importance scores for the good and bad events sampled in the BASQ can be used to investigate whether differences in regard to apathy can be observed in regard to current employment and unemployment.

One can also code the major causes that subjects write down for the eight good and eight bad events. I have used the threefold classification described by Janoff-Bulman (1979) and by Peterson, Schwartz, and Seligman (1981) in which causes are categorized as characterological, behavioral, or external (Feather, 1982e, 1983b, 1983c). A cause is coded as characterological when it refers to some stable, relatively unmodifiable characteristic that a person is said to possess (e.g., business ability, shyness, sporting talent), as behavioral when the cause refers to some action or intention of the person that influences the event (e.g., lack of effort, preparation, a desire to succeed), and as external when the cause refers to situations or external circumstances that produce the event (e.g., other people, luck, the economic situation). I have also added a mixed category, which is used when the cause implies a mixture of attributions (e.g., similar interests, compatibility between person and groups).

Single-Item Measures

Single-item measures that relate to causal attributions have also been used in our research program. Feather and Davenport (1981) included the following item in their study of young unemployed people: "How much do you think that your unemployment is your own fault?" (Not my fault at all/All my own fault) and referred to this item as *internal attribution*. Feather (1983a, 1986a) used a similar item with schoolchildren: "How much do you think the unemployed generally are to blame for being unemployed?" (Not their fault at all/All their own fault).

Feather and O'Brien (1987) used a simple version of the attributional style procedure by asking unemployed subjects in their longitudinal study of school-leavers to write down "What you believe to be the major cause of *your* unemployment." Subjects then used seven-point scales to answer the following five questions concerned with the internality, stability, globality, personal uncontrollability, and external uncontrollability of the cause they wrote down (end-labels are in parentheses):

Internality. The question was: "Is the cause of your unemployment something about you or something about other people or circumstances?" (Totally due to other people or circumstances/Totally due to me).

Stability. The question was: "In the future, if your unemployment continues, will this cause still be present?" (Will never again be present/Will always be present).

Globality. The question was: "Is the cause something that influences your unemployment only, or does it also influence other areas of your life?" (Influences just this particular situation/Influences all situations in my life).

Personal Uncontrollability. The question was: "Can you do anything to change the cause of your unemployment?" (I can easily change the cause of my unemployment/Totally beyond my power to change the cause of my unemployment).

External Uncontrollability. The question was: "Can any other person or group change the cause of your unemployment?" (Others can easily change the cause of my unemployment/Totally beyond any other person's or group's power to change the cause of my unemployment).

Measures of perceived uncontrollability or helplessness have also been included in other studies in the program (Feather, 1983a, 1986a; Feather & Barber, 1983). Feather and Barber (1983) asked their unemployed subjects: "Can the cause of your unemployment be changed by anyone, whether by you or by anyone else?" (Can easily be changed/Totally beyond anyone's power to change it). Feather (1983a) asked schoolchildren a similar question relating to unemployment generally. In another study (Feather, 1986a) schoolchildren were asked two questions: (1) "How helpless do you feel about whether or not you will get a job when you start to look for one" (Not helpless at all/Very helpless) and (2) "Do you think you have much control over whether or not you will get a job when you start to look for one?" (A lot of control/Not much control at all).

External Locus of Control

We included a scale designed to measure individual differences in external control of reinforcements in the longitudinal study of school-leavers (Feather & O'Brien, 1986a, 1986b, 1987). Nine items were selected from the Rotter (1966) Internal-External Control Scale based upon a factor analysis of student data conducted by O'Brien & Kabanoff (1981). These were items 3, 7, 11, 15, 16, 17, 18, 20, and 22 from the original scale. Each item had two alternatives, one internal and the other external. Responses to the items were coded in the direction of external control to give a possible score range from 0 to 9. This scale provides a general measure of the extent to which subjects see personal outcomes and reinforcements as due to external agents such as social forces, luck, and fate as opposed to internal factors such as effort, personal action, and abilities. The internal reliabilities were 0.44 and 0.48 for the employed and unemployed groups tested in 1981.

Expectation and Valence Measures

Expectation Measures

As noted previously, we have used the framework of expectancy-value (valence) theory to model job-seeking behavior and other aspects of the unemployment experience (Feather & Davenport, 1981; Feather & O'Brien,

1987). The expectation measures have related to a person's confidence about finding a job at various points (e.g., just prior to leaving school or in the present). Thus, Feather and Davenport (1981) asked their unemployed subjects to answer three questions (end-labels are in parentheses): (1) "How confident are you of getting a job in the near future?" (Not at all confident/ Very confident); (2) "What would you say your chances were of getting a job, compared with other people of your age who are unemployed?" (Much less/ Much more); and (3) "How confident were you of getting a job when you first left school?" (Not at all confident/Very confident). Feather and Barber (1983) used the following two questions with their unemployed sample: (1) "Think back to the time immediately before you left school. How confident do you think you were then about finding a job?" (Not at all confident/Very confident); (2) "Now think over your current situation. How confident are you now about finding a job?" (Not at all confident/Very confident). They used these items to measure initial and present expectations of success. Similar items were included in questionnaires that were administered to children still at school (Feather, 1983a, 1986a), except that questions were rephrased to relate to the different population that was tested (e.g., "How confident are you about finding a job when you start to look for one?"; "How difficult do you think it will be for you to get a job when you complete your education?"; and "How long do you think it will take for you to get a job when you start to look for one?" In all of these studies subjects provided ratings either on 1 to 5 or 1 to 7 scales to indicate their answers.

The items that were included in the longitudinal study of school-leavers were based upon those used in the earlier studies (Feather & O'Brien, 1986a, 1986b, 1987). Each item involved a seven-point scale with "Not very confident" and "Very confident" as the end labels. Three items were used: (1) "Think back to the time immediately before you left school. How confident were you then about finding a job?"; (2) "Now think over your current situation. How confident are you about finding the job you really want in the near future?"; and (3) "How confident are you about finding any kind a job at all in the near future?" We called these variables *initial job confidence, desired job confidence,* and *any job confidence.* A factor analysis indicated that two of these variables (desired job confidence, any job confidence) clustered together with three other variables (unemployment helplessness, stability of cause, and personal uncontrollability—see Feather and O'Brien (1987). After reverse coding, scores on the latter three items were combined with scores on the two confidence items to define a variable called *control-optimism,* linking confidence about finding a job with feelings of control and self-efficacy. Total control optimism scores could range from 5 to 35. The internal reliability was 0.68 for unemployed subjects tested in 1982.

A similar factor was also found in a factor analysis that involved data from schoolchildren (Feather, 1986a). In this case, however, the five variables that defined the factor involved low confidence and high perceived uncontrollability or helplessness and the factor was called *helplessness-pessimism.*

Hence this factor was a reflected version of the factor found in the longitudinal study.

Valence Measures

In earlier studies I referred to the three-item measure of employment value (see earlier section) as a measure of employment valence or employment importance (e.g., Feather, 1983a, 1986a; Feather & Bond, 1983; Feather & Davenport, 1981). The results of the factor analysis of data from unemployed respondents in the longitudinal study of school-leavers (Feather & O'Brien, 1987) showed, however, that the three-item measure of employment value clustered with other value measures to define a factor called *internal work ethic* and that this factor was separate from another factor that we called *job valence*. The job valence variable was defined by three items: job need, unemployment disappointment, and unemployment depression. The latter two items have already been described in the section on affective measures. The job need item was as follows: "How much do you feel that *you* need a job?" (Don't really need one/Desperate to have a job). Subjects used a seven-point rating scale to answer the item.

The measure of job valence therefore combines reported need for a job with affective reactions of disappointment and depression about not finding employment. This definition of the concept is consistent with Lewin's original use of the term (Lewin, 1938, pp. 106–107) in which valences were related to psychological needs and tension systems and to the perceived nature of the object or activity to which the valence applied. It is also consistent with discussions of valence in the recent literature that link the concept with the affective system (e.g., Feather, 1986b, 1987a, 1988a, in press). For example, I have argued that valences are closely tied to the affective system and that anticipated affect is a key indicator of the strength of positive and negative valences (Feather, 1986b). The distinction between values and valences recognizes that the former variables are more stable and dispositional in nature, whereas the latter are more closely tied to the immediate situation and current concerns.

Time Structure

As I noted in Chapter 3, Jahoda (1981, 1982) considers that paid employment has a number of latent functions in addition to enabling a person to earn a salary (a manifest function). One of the broad categories of experience that employment is assumed to provide is the imposition of a time structure on the waking day so that the use of time is organized and time markers are available for events (e.g., lunch breaks) that occur consistently on a daily basis.

Feather and Bond (1983) developed a measure of time structure, conceived as the extent to which individuals see their use of time to be structured and purposeful. They used the Time Structure Questionnaire (TSQ) in a study that compared employed and unemployed university graduates in regard to a range of measures. The original version of the scale was published in the Feather and Bond (1983) article as well as information about subscales (called engagement, direction, structure, and routine) that were based upon the results of a factor analysis.

The TSQ has since been revised and extended and the most recent version, which involves 26 items, is presented in Table 5.5. Items are answered by using a 1 to 7 scale with "Yes, always" and "No, never" as the endpoints, except for Item 16 where the endpoints are "Would have no idea" and "Yes, definitely"; Item 20, "No structure at all" and "Very structured"; Item 21, "Change very frequently" and "My important interests are always the same"; and Item 22, "No purpose at all" and "A great deal of purpose."

Information about test characteristics and about variables that correlate with the TSQ is presented in Bond and Feather (1988). A factor analysis of the TSQ identified five interpretable factors. These factors (and the items that had the highest loadings for each factor) were as follows: (1) *Sense of Purpose* (Items 4, 8,18, 19 and 25); (2) *Structured Routine* (Items 3, 9, 15, 16, and 20); (3) *Present Orientation* (Items 5, 24, and 26); (4) *Effective Organization* (Items 1, 11, 12, and 13); and (5) *Persistence* (Items 7, 14, and 23). Bond and Feather (1988) report internal reliabilities of 0.88, 0.92, and 0.91 for the TSQ for three different samples of subjects. Rowley and Feather (1987) report an internal reliability of 0.65 for a five-item measure of time structure based on the TSQ.

Action Measures

We have been interested in variables that relate to actions or behaviors in some of our studies. For example, Feather and O'Brien (1987) and Rowley and Feather (1987) examined job-seeking behavior, Feather and Bond (1984) investigated potential social action, and a recent study (Feather, 1989a) included measures of behavior change following job loss.

Job-Seeking Behavior

A single-item measure of job-seeking behavior has been used in some of the studies from our research program (e.g., Feather, 1982e; Feather & O'Brien, 1987). Subjects were asked: "How frequently do you look for a job?" They checked a six-point scale labeled "Not looking for a job," "When I feel like it," "Monthly," "Weekly," "Every couple of days," and "Daily." Responses were coded 1 to 6, with higher numbers keyed to more frequent job-seeking activity.

Rowley and Feather (1987) used a measure of job-search activity that listed six specific methods of job search (checking CES self-service notice boards;

Table 5.5. Items in the time structure questionnaire.

---

1. Do you ever have trouble organizing the things you have to do? (No)
2. Do you ever find that time just seems to slip away? (No)
3. Do you have a daily routine which you follow? (Yes)
4. Do you often feel that your life is aimless, with no definite purpose? (No)
5. Many of us tend to daydream about the future. Do you find this happening to you? (No)
6. And what about the past? Do you find yourself dwelling on the past? (No)
7. Once you've started an activity do you persist at it until you've completed it? (Yes)
8. Do you ever feel that the things you have to do during the day just don't seem to matter? (No)
9. Do you plan your activities from day to day? (Yes)
10. Do you tend to leave things until the last minute? (No)
11. Do you find that during the day you are often not sure what to do next? (No)
12. Do you take a long time to "get going"? (No)
13. Do you tend to change rather aimlessly from one activity to another during the day? (No)
14. Do you give up easily once you've started something? (No)
15. Do you plan your activities so that they fall into a particular pattern during the day? (Yes)
16. Could you tell how many useful hours you put in last week? (Yes)
17. Do you think you do enough with your time? (Yes)
18. Do you get bored with your day-to-day activities? (No)
19. Looking at a typical day in your life, do you think that most things you do have some purpose? (Yes)
20. Do your main activities during the day fit together in a structured way? (Yes)
21. Do the important interests/activities in your life tend to change frequently? (No)
22. Do your main interests/activities fulfill some purpose in your life? (Yes)
23. Do you have any difficulty in finishing activities once you've started them? (No)
24. Do you spend time thinking about opportunities that you have missed? (No)
25. Do you ever feel that the way you fill your time has little use or value? (No)
26. Do you spend time thinking about what your future might be like? (No)

Note: The key for scoring each item is given in parentheses. For example, ratings in the direction of the *no* pole were scored as indicating more time structure for Items 1, 2, 4, and so forth, and ratings in the direction of the *yes* pole were coded as indicating more time structure for Items 3, 7, 9, and so forth.

Source: From Bond, M.J., & Feather, N.T. (1988), "Some Correlates of Structure and Purpose in the Use of Time," in *Journal of Personality and Social Psychology*, *55*, pp. 321–329. Copyright 1988 by the American Psychological Association. Reprinted with permission.

checking newspaper "Vacancies" section; visiting or phoning employers; placing a personal advertisement in a newspaper; writing to employers; asking friends or relatives) as well as a seventh category, "Other." Subjects were asked to state the number of times they had used each method in the previous two weeks. Their responses to the seven categories were summed to provide an overall score called *job-search frequency*. Rowley and Feather (1987) also summed the number of different methods that each subject identified using, regardless of the number of times each was used. This second measure was called *job-search methods* (see also Feather, 1989a).

Feather and Davenport (1981) included in their study two measures of effort expended by unemployed subjects in trying to find a job, in addition to ratings by subjects of how much they wanted or needed a job. These measures applied to the situation when subjects first left school and to their current situation. The two measures of effort were (end-labels are in parentheses): (1) "How hard would you say you tried to get a job immediately after leaving school?" (Didn't try at all/Tried as hard as I could); (2) "How hard would you say you are trying now to get a job?" (Not trying hard at all/Trying as hard as I can). Subjects provided responses on a five-point rating scale.

A much more general measure of self-rated activity was obtained in the longitudinal study of school-leavers (Feather & O'Brien, 1986a, 1986b) based upon semantic differential ratings of self. This three-item measure of activity was described earlier in this chapter.

Potential Social Action

In their study of employed and unemployed university graduates Feather and Bond (1983, 1984) included an item concerned with potential social action based on procedures developed in an earlier study by Feather and Newton (1982). Respondents were presented with a request in the style of a pamphlet labeled *"Would You Help?"* A preliminary statement indicated that:

> Many groups within the community are speaking out against unemployment and are also helping unemployed people in their own way. Let us assume that one such group is the *Campaign to Assist Unemployed Youth.* This group has no political affiliations at all but is simply concerned with finding ways in which unemployed youth can be assisted.

Respondents were then asked to suppose that their present commitments left them with about 10 hours each week available for other activities. On this basis they were asked to check any of the following 11 ways in which they would be willing to assist the campaign, checking as many statements as they wanted to: (a) sign a petition to be sent to the proper authorities; (b) sign a petition to be published in the local newspapers; (c) write your own letter to the local newspapers; (d) join the group (no financial contribution required); (e) contribute some money; (f) attend meetings to become informed and help make plans; (g) stuff and address envelopes (containing pamphlets); (h) telephone people to ask their support; (i) hand out pamphlets on street corners; (j) participate in peaceful rallies and marches; (k) help organize peaceful rallies and marches. They could also check a category indicating that they did not want to help the campaign at all. The number of volunteer actions checked (0 to 11) was the first measure of willingness to assist the organization.

The second measure was obtained by asking respondents to check how many hours per week (0 to 10) they would be prepared to contribute to the campaign, assuming they had 10 hours of uncommitted time available each week.

Behavior Change

Warr (1984b) and Warr and Payne (1983) have conducted studies of reported behavior change after job loss. Unemployed respondents were asked to indicate whether they currently do more or less of each of the activities on a list of activities compared to what they were doing at the same time of year when they were employed. The activities covered domestic work (e.g., prepare meals for yourself), domestic pastimes (e.g., watch television), other pastimes (e.g., just look around shops without buying anything), book reading (e.g., visit the public library in order to borrow books), recreation (e.g., take part in sports), entertainment through money (e.g., go to a pub or a club for a drink), and social contacts (e.g., spend time with friends). The response categories were: More than when I was employed; Same as when I was employed; Less than when I was employed; and I never do that.

I have used the same procedure in a recent study of unemployed people who were contacted via an organization concerned with helping unemployed individuals of mature age (Feather, 1989a).

Financial Stress and Strain

Various measures of financial stress and strain have been used in the Sheffield studies (e.g., Jackson & Warr, 1984; Warr, Banks, & Ullah, 1985; Warr & Jackson, 1985). We have used similar measures in our recent research. Thus, Rowley and Feather (1987) included a measure of financial strain in their investigation of unemployment in different age groups. Subjects were asked, "Thinking back over the past month, how often have you had serious financial worries?" Subjects circled a number on a five-point scale (Never = 0, Hardly ever = 1, Frequently = 2, Nearly all the time = 3, All the time = 4).

The same question was included in a recent study in the Flinders program that involved mature age, unemployed subjects (Feather, 1989a). In addition, subjects were asked the seven questions listed in Table 5.6 that covered various areas that might be affected by financial stress. They responded to each question by using a seven-point scale labeled "Definitely not" (scored 1) at the low end and "Yes, definitely" (scored 7) at the high end. After reverse coding, the ratings for the seven items were summed to obtain a measure of global financial stress.

Studies conducted in North America have also included measures designed to assess financial strain. For example, Kessler et al., 1987) used the six-item scale developed by Pearlin et al. (1981) to measure this variable and found

Table 5.6. Items used in financial stress scale (Feather, 1989a).

Item
1. Are you able to afford a home suitable for yourself/your family?
2. Are you able to afford furniture or household equipment that needs to be replaced?
3. Are you able to afford the kind of car you need?
4. Do you have enough money for the kind of food you/your family should have?
5. Do you have enough money for the kind of medical care you/your family should have?
6. Do you have enough money for the kind of clothing you/your family should have?
7. Do you have enough money for the leisure activities you/your family want(s)?

that unemployment results in increased financial strain which, in turn, results in negative health effects.

Unemployment History

We have included measures of a person's unemployment history in our studies. The items relate to length of unemployment and number of job applications. For example, duration of unemployment was assessed in the longitudinal study of school-leavers (Feather and O'Brien, 1986a, 1986b, 1987) by asking subjects, "Approximately how long (in weeks) have you been looking for work?" Number of job applications was assessed by asking subjects, "Approximately how many jobs have you applied for since you became unemployed? (include both full-time and part-time jobs)."

It is recognized that these measures are prone to errors in recall and that they may be subject to distortion. It is possible to develop more differentiated measures of a person's employment and unemployment history that take account of differences between people in the extent to which they move into and out of employment, how many jobs they have had in the past, and how long they remain in jobs on the average. Such measures should be introduced in future studies.

Social Support

Some recent studies of the psychological impact of unemployment have examined the extent to which social support may mitigate the negative consequences of unemployment (e.g., Kessler et al., 1987, 1988). We included two items designed to measure support in our longitudinal study of school-leavers (Feather & O'Brien, 1986a, 1986b, 1987). The first item asked, "How well do you think your parents understand you—your feelings, your likes, your dislikes, and any problems that you have?" Subjects checked a five-point scale labeled "Not well at all" at the low end and "Very well" at the high end and responses were coded from 1 to 5. The second item asked, "When you have any kind of personal problem, how often do your parents give you their support and guidance?" Subjects checked a five-point scale labeled "Never" at the low end and "Always" at the high end and responses were coded 1 to 5. Responses to the two items were highly correlated for unemployed subjects tested in 1982 ($r = 0.72$). Hence, the responses were added for each respondent to obtain a total support score, which had a possible range from 2 to 10. The internal reliability was 0.83.

It should be noted that this measure of support related specifically to parental support (an appropriate focus, given the population of young people who were sampled) and that the measure was not designed to sample the different forms that support can take (e.g., material, informational, and emotional support), as is now frequently the case in studies of social support (e.g., Cohen & Syme, 1985; Cutrona, 1986; Sarason & Sarason, 1985).

The recent literature provides a number of examples of different approaches that could be used to assess social support in studies specifically directed to examining how reactions to unemployment may be moderated by the amount of social support that is available within family and community networks. The appropriateness of these measures has to be evaluated in relation to the particular population being sampled. For example, I incorporated some of the more complex procedures into a recent study in an attempt to take account of various kinds of support obtained from different people and agencies but I found that the mature age, unemployed subjects who were tested had difficulty with the questions, perhaps because I asked for too much information (Feather, 1989a). It should be possible, however, to design simpler measures of support that can be widely used with unemployed people and that distinguish between different kinds of support and different sources of support.

Conclusion

In this chapter I have reviewed the basic scales and measures that have been included in our research program. It is obvious that we have used a variety of different methods, selected from many different areas. Their use in more than one study has provided the opportunity for the empirical and conceptual replication of findings, and it has allowed a degree of convergent validation in regard to the procedures that have been employed.

Chapter 6

Youth Unemployment: Single-Group Studies

The next two chapters provide reviews of our cross-sectional studies concerned with the psychological impact of unemployment as perceived by young people. My description of these studies will proceed from those that involved single groups to those that were designed to provide comparisons between groups. The single-group studies were based on three main kinds of subject population: young unemployed people who were seeking jobs, students in the last years of high school, and university students. They will be described in this chapter. The comparison-group studies compared data obtained from unemployed respondents with data obtained from respondents of similar age who had jobs. They will be described in the next chapter.

Research with Unemployed Groups

Two studies will be described, the first by Feather and Davenport (1981), the second by Feather and Barber (1983). In the Feather and Davenport (1981) study we tested a sample of 212 unemployed young people (150 males, 60 females, 2 of unspecified gender) from metropolitan Adelaide, South Australia. These subjects were contacted through helping agencies concerned with unemployment. Subjects answered a questionnaire under anonymous conditions. The questionnaire was administered in small group settings during July and August 1978. The mean age of the sample was 19.76 years, 96% were unmarried, and 60% said that they lived at home with their parents. The mean reported length of unemployment for the sample was 30.59 weeks (median = 19.69 weeks).

The questionnaire included three questions designed to measure both present expectations of success about getting a job and initial expectations of success when subjects first left school; the three-item measure of employment value described previously; two items designed to measure present and initial effort expended in trying to find a job; two items concerned with how much subjects wanted or needed a job both currently and initially when they first left school; 28 possible reasons for unemployment, which subjects rated in regard to how important they were in relation to their own unemployment; a measure of internal attribution for unemployment designed to assess how much subjects thought their unemployment was their own fault; a measure of unemployment disappointment assessing how depressed subjects felt about being unemployed; and a set of background and demographic items. Most questions involved the use of five-point rating scales.

As noted previously (Chapter 5), two scales were constructed on the basis of a factor analysis of the intercorrelations of the importance ratings for the 28 reasons for youth unemployment. The first of the derived scales was called *external difficulty* because the four items making up the scale all referred to some external condition that was causing unemployment ("The government isn't doing enough to help create jobs", "Private industry is deliberately reducing the number of jobs available"; "The unions are affecting unemployment by causing too many strikes, keeping wages too high, or some other reason"; and "The economic situation in Australia"). The second scale was called *competence deficiency* because the four items making up the scale all referred to some personal defect in skill, ability, or experience as a cause of present unemployment ("I haven't got enough education"; "I haven't got enough experience"; "I haven't got the specific skills that many employers require"; "There's too much competition for the kind of job I want").

The major focus of this study was on depressive affect or unemployment disappointment. Using ideas from expectancy-value theory, we predicted that unemployment disappointment would be positively related to a person's initial expectation of success, that is, that subjects would report feeling more disappointed when high initial expectations of getting a job were disconfirmed. We also predicted that unemployment disappointment would be higher when employment was valued more, when subjects reported that they were trying hard to find a job, and when they indicated high levels of need for a job when compared with lower levels on the employment value, effort, and need variables.

These predictions were generally confirmed by the results. Table 6.1 presents the mean ratings for the major variables in relation to four categories of affect and the results of a 2×4 analysis of variance with gender (male, female) as the first factor and affect (glad, neutral, depressed, very depressed) as the second facor. The four categories of affect corresponded to ratings of one and two (glad), three (neutral), four (depressed), and five (very depressed) on the five-point rating scale for unemployment disappointment. The respective percentages of subjects in each category were 14.2% (glad), 32.2% (neutral), 27.5% (depressed), and 26.1% (very depressed).

It can be observed that subjects in the higher categories of unemployment disappointment reported significantly higher levels of initial confidence, employment value, present effort, initial need, and present need. In each case, mean scores on the variable increased with a shift from the "glad" category to

Table 6.1. Mean ratings of major variables in relation to four categories of affect.

Variable	Range	Affect category				Main effect of depressive affect, $F(3,201)$
		Glad ($n = 30$)	Neutral ($n = 68$)	Depressed ($n = 58$)	Very depressed ($n = 55$)	
Expectation of success						
Initial confidence	1–5	3.07	4.01	4.26	4.30	7.38***
Present chances	1–5	2.53	3.15	2.93	2.85	3.02*
Present confidence	1–5	3.03	3.18	3.14	3.09	0.03
Employment value	3–15	9.77	11.03	11.19	11.76	3.47*
Motivation to work						
Initial effort	1–5	3.47	3.93	4.02	4.31	2.32
Present effort	1–5	2.47	3.21	3.24	3.62	5.06**
Initial need	1–5	3.27	4.09	4.42	4.46	7.17***
Present need	1–5	2.20	3.32	4.07	4.15	25.17***
Causal attribution						
Internal attribution	1–5	3.40	2.51	2.19	2.22	7.05***
Competence deficiency	4–20	13.67	12.40	14.17	13.00	2.44
External difficulty	4–20	12.27	13.53	14.60	14.45	2.80*

Note: There were minor variations in ns due to missing data in some analyses (1–3 cases).
*$p < 0.05$; **$p < 0.01$; ***$p < 0.001$.
Source: From Feather, N.T., & Davenport, P.R. (1981), "Unemployment and Depressive Affect: A Motivational and Attributional Analysis," in Journal of Personality and Social Psychology, 41, pp. 422–436. Copyright 1981 by the American Psychological Association. Reprinted with permission.

the "very depressed" category. Thus, the subjects with higher levels of unemployment disappointment were those who indicated that they were initially more confident of getting a job and more in need of a job after leaving school, who viewed employment as something to be valued, and who reported high levels of present effort and present need.

Table 6.1 also shows that subjects in the higher categories of reported unemployment disappointment were more likely to blame their unemployment on external difficulties and less likely to blame themselves for being unemployed when compared with subjects in the lower categories of reported unemployment disappointment.

These results were supported by a correlational analysis that also showed that internal attribution was negatively related to both initial confidence and the two measures of need, and that external difficulty was positively related to both initial confidence and the two measures of need. The relevant correlations are presented in Table 6.2. Thus, subjects who reported that initially they were relatively confident of getting a job and who reported high levels of need for a job were more likely to attribute their unemployment to external difficulties and less likely to blame themselves, when compared with subjects whose initial expectations of employment and levels of need were lower. A further analysis also showed that ratings of confidence, effort, and need tended to be lower for the present situation in which subjects found themselves when compared with the situation on first leaving school. These differences are consistent with the assumption that repeated failure to get a job will lead to decreasing expectations of success and to changes in motivational variables.

The reader is referred to the original article for details of other significant findings. Feather and Davenport (1981) viewed their results as consistent with the implications of an expectancy-value analysis, which assumes that the positive motivation or tendency to seek employment is related to the multiplicative combination of expectation of success and the perceived net attractiveness (or valence) of employment itself. They also noted that their results did not appear to be compatible with a learned helplessness view that implies that individuals who report high levels of depressive affect will be more passive and less motivated. Instead, their findings showed that higher levels of unemployment disappointment were associated with higher levels of frustrated motivation.

Feather and Davenport (1981) were careful to qualify their results. They observed that their data were based on verbal reports, some of a retrospective nature, and that the conclusions would be strengthened if behavioral data could be obtained. They also recognized that their sample involved young unemployed people who were in contact with helping agencies and that it did not include those who had withdrawn from the job search. They suggested that a longitudinal study was needed so that changes in expectations, levels of motivation, affect, and attributions could be observed over a long time span for the same group of subjects. One would then be in a stronger position to

Table 6.2. Product-moment intercorrelations between major variables together with means and standard deviations.

Variable	2	3	4	5	6	7	8	9	10	11	12	13	M	SD
1. Initial confidence	0.16*	0.09	0.07	0.13	0.15*	0.53***	0.19**	-0.29***	-0.04	0.21**	0.06	0.29***	4.00	1.30
2. Present chances		0.28***	0.23**	0.01	0.03	0.07	0.19**	-0.07	-0.09	0.05	0.01	0.07	2.92	0.94
3. Present confidence			0.22**	-0.08	0.14*	0.05	0.19**	0.00	-0.10	-0.03	0.14*	0.01	3.13	1.20
4. Employment value				0.13	0.12	0.12	0.18*	-0.01	0.03	0.11	0.15*	0.23**	11.10	2.69
5. Initial effort					0.23**	0.30***	0.15*	-0.09	0.08	0.01	0.10	0.19**	3.99	1.35
6. Present effort						0.13	0.30***	-0.13	-0.11	0.06	0.06	0.25***	3.22	1.35
7. Initial need							0.31***	-0.29***	0.09	0.14*	0.08	0.29***	4.16	1.27
8. Present need								-0.32***	0.06	0.16*	0.05	0.50***	3.57	1.28
9. Internal attribution									0.03	-0.17*	-0.02	-0.29***	2.49	1.32
10. Competence deficiency										0.12	0.09	-0.00	13.24	3.83
11. External difficulty											-0.03	0.20**	13.84	4.08
12. Sex												0.09	1.29	0.45
13. Depressive affect													3.61	1.11

Note: The *n*s range from 209 to 212 due to missing data. Two-tailed tests of significance were used.
*p < 0.05; **p < 0.01; ***p < 0.001.
Source: From Feather, N.T., & Davenport, P.R. (1981), "Unemployment and Depressive Affect: A Motivational and Attributional Analysis," in *Journal of Personality and Social Psychology, 41*, pp. 422–436. Copyright 1981 by the American Psychological Association. Reprinted with permission.

make statements about causal antecedents. They observed that the measure of depressive affect or unemployment disappointment was a situation-specific measure and that it could not be taken as equivalent to measures concerned with chronic forms of depression that generalize across situations (e.g., the Beck Depression Inventory; Beck, 1967).

They also considered the effects of prolonged unemployment, arguing that their motivational analysis did not deny that long-term unemployment may be associated with a complex set of cognitive, motivational, and affective reactions or with high level of chronic depression among some people. Thus, there may be some people who become depressed after prolonged unemployment because they are predisposed by earlier experiences to develop depressive disorders (Beck, Rush, Shaw, & Emery, 1979). Also, because prolonged unemployment can have devastating effects on many aspects of a person's life, one would expect depressive reactions to relate to the whole range of negative consequences and not only to frustrated work motivation. Prolonged unemployment may also result in qualitative changes in causal attributions so that attributions to internal, global, stable, and uncontrollable factors become more frequent, despite the evidence that many of the causes of unemployment are external and socioeconomic. Doubts about self-efficacy may also occur along with higher levels of pessimism about the likelihood of getting a job. Chronic forms of depression may occur as a result of some of these effects. Within this total picture, however, the findings of the Feather and Davenport (1981) study do suggest that a contributing factor leading to the depressive affect or disappointment that follows unsuccessful attempts to obtain employment is the frustration of the motivation to work.

Their findings were followed up by Feather and Barber (1983) in their study of depressive reactions and unemployment. Feather and Barber (1983) distinguished between two patterns of unemployment effects. The first they called the frustrated work motivation pattern; the second they called the self-denigration pattern. They identified the findings of the Feather and Davenport (1981) study with the frustrated work motivation pattern, conceptualized within the framework of expectancy-value theory. Unemployment disappointment was more intense among unemployed individuals who valued employment, had high expectations of finding a job, and reported high levels of need and effort in relation to obtaining employment. As noted previously, Feather and Davenport (1981) also found that higher levels of depressive affect or unemployment disappointment were accompanied by an increasing tendency to blame present difficulties on relatively stable, external factors rather than on internal factors. Thus, the situation-specific affect reported by subjects was linked to the external, frustrating situation rather than to deficiencies that they perceived themselves to possess.

Feather and Barber (1983) noted that the affect associated with frustration may be complex in nature, involving not only depression and disappointment but also resentment and hostility, especially when the frustrated positive motivation is linked to external causes. Weiner's (1986) recent statement of his attributional theory of emotion and motivation relates anger to beliefs that the causes of a negative outcome are external and controllable. Assuming that the single-item measure of unemployment disappointment used by Feather and Davenport (1981) could have measured anger as well as disappointment about not finding a job, their results can be seen as consistent with Weiner's (1986) analysis. Scores on their measure of unemployment disappointment were positively related to the importance subjects assigned to reasons for unemployment that involved external difficulties that were controllable in nature (e.g., "The government isn't doing enough to create jobs").

As I observed in previous discussion, Feather and Davenport (1981) recognized that it would be a mistake to equate unemployment disappointment with depressive symptomatology. Disappointment may involve a mixture of emotions (e.g., sadness, anger, guilt). It is often transient and situation-bound, occuring in its own right, as when a person feels sad and disappointed about failing to achieve a goal or after suffering some other aversive consequence. The distinction between transient disappointment or sadness and more general forms of depression is well recognized in the literature (e.g., Beck, 1967; Depue & Monroe, 1978; Jacobson, 1971).

The second pattern of unemployment effects described by Feather and Barber (1983) concerns the development of depression and negative attitudes toward the self. Thus, more severe, enduring, and generalized forms of depression may tend to develop when aversive events continue despite a person's efforts to prevent them and where, over time, a person's expectations of achieving desired goals or avoiding negative consequences signal a state of hopelessness. Under these conditions one might also find increasing evidence of self-blame and self-esteem deficits. Cognitive and attributional analyses of depression involving concepts of helplessness, hopelessness, attributional styles, negative cognitive sets, and faulty information processing are consistent with these ideas (e.g., Abramson et al., 1978; Beck, 1967, 1976; Peterson & Seligman, 1984; Weiner, 1986—see also Chapter 4).

A movement from transient, situation-specific affective states to more general depression may occur in some people following prolonged and repeated periods of unemployment. These more significant forms of depression may be accompanied by diminished self-esteem; perceptions that unemployment will continue irrespective of one's actions (helplessness); very low expectations of finding a job (hopelessness); and a tendency for the depressed person to attribute bad outcomes to internal, stable, and global causes although, in the case of unemployment, some external attribution to socioeconomic causes may become woven into the depressive symptomatology (Feather & Davenport, 1981). In addition, the unemployed person whose depression is more general and severe may display greater evidence of motivational deficits that involve lack of effort and apathy when compared with the unemployed person whose depression is less severe and generalized.

Feather and Barber (1983) drew upon their distinction between the frustrated motivation pattern and the self-denigration pattern of unemployment effects to predict that different patterns of correlations may be associated with situation-specific depressive reactions to unemployment and the more chronic and generalized depressive symptomatology that may accompany prolonged unemployment. They predicted that:

1. Situation-specific depressive affect about unemployment will be associated with high expectations of getting a job, the importance of having employment, and external attributions about the causes of unemployment.
2. More general depressive symptomatology will be associated with low expectations of getting a job and low self-esteem, internal attributions about the causes of unemployment, and perceived uncontrollability or helplessness about changing the causes of unemployment.
3. Depressive symptoms of a more general kind, internal attributions and perceived uncontrollability will be associated with an unsuccessful employment history that extends over time.

They tested these three predictions with a sample of 116 unemployed subjects (64 males, 52 females) currently without any full-time or part-time employment, who were contacted through helping agencies in metropolitan Adelaide, South Australia, over a three-week period in June 1980. Most of their subjects were under 25 years of age (mean = 20.06 years) and they had been looking for paid employment for a mean of 57.51 weeks (median = 36.50 weeks).

The subjects completed a questionnaire either individually or in small group settings under anonymous conditions. The questionnaire included two items designed to measure present and initial expectations of finding a job (i.e., currently and just before subjects left school); the same measure of unemployment disappointment as was used in the Feather and Davenport (1981) study—"When you think about being unemployed, how does it make you feel?" (Very glad/Very depressed); four items designed to measure internal attributions for each subject's current unemployment and four items to measure external attributions (see Chapter 5); an item designed to measure perceived uncontrollability—"Can the cause of your unemployment be changed by anyone, whether by you or by anyone else?" (Can easily be changed/Totally beyond anyone's power to change it); and an item designed to assess employment value—"How important to you is the fact that you are unemployed?" (Not at all important/Extremely important). Subjects answered all of these items by using seven-point rating scales. They also completed the measure of global self-esteem based on the Rosenberg (1965) Self-Esteem Scale and the short form of the Beck Depression Inventory (BDI; Beck & Beck, 1972). The questionnaire also contained items concerned with unemployment history (weeks out of work, number of job applications), as well as standard demographic and backgound items.

The main results of this study are presented in Table 6.3. Analyses of differences between means showed that present confidence about finding a job was

Table 6.3. Means and standard deviations of major variables and correlations with depressive affect, BDI depression, number of weeks out of work, and number of unsuccessful job applications.

Variable	Range	M	SD	r With			
				Depressive affect	BDI depression	Weeks out of work	Number of unsuccessful job applications
Expectation of success							
Initial confidence	1–7	4.73	1.95	−0.12	−0.17	−0.08	0.08
Present confidence	1–7	3.12	1.92	−0.07	−0.08	−0.03	0.04
Employment importance	1–7	5.68	1.84	0.44***	0.19	−0.02	0.17
Perceived uncontrollability	1–7	3.37	1.79	−0.12	0.31***	0.23*	−0.01
Attribution measures							
Internal causes	4–28	13.02	5.13	0.05	0.28**	0.32***	0.20*
External causes	4–28	17.53	4.46	0.19*	0.03	0.12	−0.07
Self-esteem score	10–50	39.23	6.38	−0.13	−0.46***	−0.12	−0.11
Depressive affect	1–7	5.26	1.57	—	0.13	−0.05	−0.01
BDI depression	0–39	6.06	5.65	0.13	—	0.11	0.26*

Note: BDI = Beck Depression Inventory, $N = 116$. There were some variations from this N due to a small number of missing cases for some variables. Ns for correlations involving weeks out of work ranged from 95 to 110 due to some missing cases. Ns for the correlations involving number of unsuccessful job applications ranged from 91 to 99 due to some missing cases. Two-tailed tests are reported for the correlations. For weeks out of work, $M = 57.51$, $SD = 67.86$; for number of unsuccessful job applications, $M = 62.39$, $SD = 98.72$. Weeks out of work and number of unsuccessful job applications were positively correlated, $r(93) = 0.40$, $p < 0.001$.

*$p < 0.05$; **$p < 0.01$; ***$p < 0.001$.

Source: From Feather, N.T., & Barber, J.G. (1983). "Depressive Reactions and Unemployment," in *Journal of Abnormal Psychology*, 92, pp. 185–195. Copyright 1983 by American Psychological Association. Reprinted with permission.

significantly lower than initial confidence immediately before leaving school, as recalled retrospectively. As in the Feather and Davenport (1981) study, subjects tended to attribute their unemployment more to external causes than to internal causes.

The statistically significant correlations in Table 6.3 support the first two predictions. Ratings of unemployment disappointment or depressive affect were positively related to employment value and subjects' endorsement of external causes. The BDI depression scores were positively related to subjects ratings of the perceived uncontrollability of the cause of their unemployment and to their endorsement of internal causes. These BDI scores were negatively related to self-esteem scores, that is, those higher in depressive symptoms were lower in self-esteem. Note, however, that unlike the results of the Feather and Davenport (1981) study, unemployment disappointment was not related to expectations of finding a job. Thus, the positive relation between these variables found in the earlier study was not replicated. Note also that the situation-specific measure of unemployment disappointment and the global measure of depressive symptoms were unrelated. One could not use scores on the specific measure to predict more clinically significant forms of depression.

The results also provided some support for the third prediction. Subjects who had a longer history of unemployment and those who reported having made more unsuccessful job applications were more likely to see the causes of their unemployment as internally based. More frequent unsuccessful applications for jobs were associated with higher BDI depression scores. Ratings of the perceived uncontrollability of the cause of unemployment tended to be higher among those subjects who had been employed for longer periods. But there was no evidence that self-esteem scores and ratings of confidence about finding unemployment were lower among those subjects who had been out of work longer or who had made more unsuccessful attempts to obtain employment. As would be expected, there was a statistically significant positive correlation ($r = 0.40$, $p < 0.001$) between the two measures pertaining to unemployment history (weeks out of work, number of unsuccessful job application).

The findings from the Feather and Barber (1983) study support the view that unemployment disappointment or the situation-specific depressive affect that accompanies failure to find a job and depression conceived as a set of symptoms that might follow prolonged and repeated periods of unemployment have somewhat different correlates. One set of relations seems to reflect frustrated work motivation. The negative affective reactions that are involved correspond to those that may follow any unsuccessful attempt to achieve a positively valued goal when expectations are within the realms of possibility and goal attainment is blocked by external forces. The other set of relations brings with it depressive symptoms that have a more general focus and involves self-blame, diminished self-esteem, and beliefs that it might be difficult to alter the negative condition.

The results are also consistent with the view that depression more generally conceived, internal attributions for unemployment, and beliefs that it may be beyond anyone's power to change the causes of unemployment may be a consequence of increasing length of unemployment and more frequent failures in job applications. These results, however, were not entirely consistent from measure to measure and it is clear that they need to be supported by findings from longitudinal studies that take account of life circumstances, coping responses, and the details of unemployment history. It is at least possible that some people lack self-esteem and are highly depressed to begin with, even before they try to enter the labor market. It is also likely that the depressive symptomatology that may accompany unemployment involves not only internal attributions but ascriptions to external causes as well (see Feather & Davenport, 1981).

Feather and Barber (1983) also conducted a hierarchical multiple regression analysis in order to determine the relative contribution of the major variables to unemployment disappointment and BDI depression (see Table 6.4). As one would expect, the results of this analysis were consistent with those from the analysis of the simple correlations (Table 6.3). Two points are of particular interest. First, the attribution variables added very little to the variance in each analysis. This result implies that one should not give sovereign status to attributional variables as precursors of affective reactions to unemployment. It is important to assess a range of other variables as well, especially those that relate to the personal and social costs of not having a job and the different ways in which people learn to cope with negative outcomes. Second, with all of the variables in the equation it was possible to account for 31% and 40% of the variance in unemployment disappointment and BDI depression, respectively, Hence, a lot of the variance in these two measures was still unexplained.

The two studies that I have discussed in this section are somewhat unique in that each drew upon psychological theories concerned with motivation and emotion (expectancy-value theory, attribution theory, helplessness theory). Thus, they marked an advance over descriptive accounts concerned with the psychological impact of unemployment. Feather and Davenport (1981) and Feather and Barber (1983) were aware that their studies would have been improved had they been able to obtain wider samples of unemployed people, had they been able to use scales with known psychometric properties for all of the variables that they measured, and had they been able to study the effects of unemployment on their young subjects over time. But the design of research in naturalistic settings has to allow for the practicalities of what is possible. Within these constraints, the two studies described in this section provided useful findings about the psychological impact of unemployment. They also demonstrated that it is possible to link hypotheses about unemployment effects to wider perspectives grounded in psychological theory.

Table 6.4. Multiple correlations and proportions of variance explained from hierarchical multiple-regression analyses.

		DEPENDENT VARIABLES						
		Depressive Affect			BDI Depression			
Step	Independent variable	R	R^2	R^2 change	R	R^2	R^2 change	
1	Weeks unemployed + unsuccessful job applications	0.046	0.002	0.002	0.256	0.066	0.066*	
2	Age + sex	0.118	0.014	0.012	0.335	0.112	0.047	
3	Internal causes	0.135	0.018	0.004	0.424	0.180	0.067**	
4	External causes	0.245	0.060	0.042*	0.424	0.180	0.000	
5	Perceived uncontrollability	0.289	0.083	0.023	0.519	0.270	0.090**	
6	Employment importance	0.499	0.249	0.166***	0.557	0.310	0.040*	
7	Initial confidence + present confidence	0.525	0.276	0.027	0.578	0.334	0.024	
8	Self-esteem	0.553	0.306	0.030	0.631	0.398	0.064**	

*$p < 0.05$; **$p < 0.01$; ***$p < 0.001$.
Source: From Feather, N.T., & Barber, J.G. (1983). "Depressive Reactions and Unemployment," in Journal of Abnormal Psychology, 92, pp. 185–195. Copyright 1983 by the American Psychological Association. Reprinted with permission.

Research with Student Groups

Secondary School Students

The three studies to be described in this section involved samples of students who were either attending secondary schools or at university. The first two studies in this section take us away from young unemployed samples to schoolchildren in their last years of high school. I initiated these studies in order to obtain information about how children who are still at school interpret the causes of unemployment, how they view their own prospects of finding a job, and how they believe they would react if they were unemployed. It is important to discover the beliefs that schoolchildren hold about unemployment before they leave school, not the least because their subsequent attempts to find work may be influenced by these beliefs. Research might also provide insights into variables that may be related to these beliefs—variables that might include socioeconomic status and gender, socialization experiences, and other more general beliefs, attitudes, and values held by the individual. Investigation of this wider set of variables may itself provide useful evidence that is relevant to theoretical principles that come from particular areas of psychology.

The first study that I will describe was designed to test a number of general predictions. I expected that children's beliefs about the causes of unemployment would emphasize both internal and external causes. There is a wide range of comment and discussion about the causes of present-day unemployment that comes from various information sources. These commentaries and debates vary in the degree to which they are well-informed and they span both individual and socioeconomic explanations of the unemployed condition. Previous studies have shown that people refer to both internal and external factors when they explain poverty (Feather, 1974, 1975; Furnham, 1982c) and one would expect them to do the same when explaining unemployment. Indeed, the design of both the Feather and Davenport (1981) and Feather and Barber (1983) studies allowed for different kinds of internal and external attributions of unemployment. Research in Britain has done the same (e.g., Furnham 1982a, 1982b, 1988).

There is an important theoretical point to be made, however, when one considers the explanations for unemployment that schoolchildren see as important and those that are endorsed by the unemployed themselves. Given the fact that children still at school do not have first-hand experience of the employment situation, their judgments about the causes of unemployment are from the point of view of observers rather than actors. They might therefore be more likely to regard internal dispositional and motivational factors such as lack of ability and insufficient effort to find a job as important causes of unemployment than would unemployed individuals. The unemployed would be more likely to refer to the importance of external, situational causes in what is probably a more differentiated and informed view of their unem-

ployed condition. This expected difference is consistent with discussions by
Jones and Nisbett (1972) and Nisbett and Ross (1980) of actor-observer differences in causal attribution (see also Watson, 1982). The evidence also
shows that attributions for negative events tend to be more external than
attributions for positive events (Feather, 1983b, 1986a, 1987b). One would
expect this general bias to influence attributions for the negative event of
unemployment when compared with the positive event of employment,
though real-life experiences would temper the general bias.

It can also be argued that children's beliefs about employment and unemployment will vary according to the type of school they attend. I was interested
in the comparison between children attending government-funded or state
schools and children attending independent schools where parents pay fees.
Children attending the more expensive independent schools are more likely to
have parents who score higher on a variety of socioeconomic indicators (e.g.,
income, education, occupation). These parents would communicate beliefs,
attitudes, and values to their children that differ in some respects from those
held by parents with fewer resources and different "class" backgrounds.
These differences are not easy to specify and there is undoubtedly a great
deal of overlap between different segments of the population in the distribution of beliefs, attitudes, and values. One can speculate, however, that
the value systems of those more affluent parents who are committed to the
elite independent schools will reflect more concern with achievement, competence, and self-direction, and that these parents will tend to have beliefs
and attitudes that are relatively conservative in the political-economic
sense (Feather, 1972, 1975; Kohn, 1977; Rokeach, 1973). The more affluent
parents also have more opportunity to send their children to the schools that
reinforce the sorts of value and belief systems that they themselves hold
(Feather, 1975). The different kinds of school provide different inputs, though
the dimensions of variation in school ethos are not always easy to specify and
the extent of variation within each type of school (state or independent) is
probably considerable. Finally, the realities of the job market may be such
that children from independent schools more readily obtain employment
when they complete their education. This knowledge presumably influences
student expectations about their future job prospects.

All of the considerations suggest that work-related beliefs will vary depending upon the school attended. I predicted that children from the more elite
independent schools would be more confident about getting a job and that
their beliefs about the causes of unemployment would be more likely to
reflect values and political-economic views that are of a more conservative
kind, with an emphasis on the virtues of hard work and individual competence. These differences between children attending independent and state
schools would be accentuated in cases where students from the state schools
are drawn from predominantly working-class areas with political social, and
economic beliefs toward the left of the political spectrum.

One might also expect to find gender differences in how secondary school students view their future prospects that also relate to different socialization experiences and to the realities of the labor market. For example, some evidence suggests that female subjects are less confident about succeeding at achievement tasks when compared with male subjects (e.g., Feather, 1969; Lenney, 1977). This difference has not been consistently found, however, and its occurrence probably depends on a number of interacting determinants. However, when this possible difference is linked to the fact that female school-leavers may suffer some disadvantage in finding jobs when compared with male school-leavers, it suggests that female school-leavers who are still at school will be less confident about finding a job when compared with their male peers and that they will perceive the job market as more difficult to enter.

This first study with schoolchildren was also designed to investigate relations between variables similar to those that were included in the two studies described in the previous section, to study relations between reported beliefs and expectations and more general personality variables, and to obtain information about some of the correlates of a student's decision to leave school early or later.

There were 650 subjects (383 males, 266 females, one who did not specify gender) who were involved in the study. The sample was drawn from year 9 and year 10 classes from two state schools and three independent schools in metropolitan Adelaide. The mean age of the sample was 14.34 years and most subjects were 14 or 15 years of age. Further details about the sample are provided in the original report (Feather, 1983a).

Subjects completed a questionnaire under anonymous conditions, administered by their teachers at the five schools in October 1980 in regular class hours. Subjects answered most of the questions that concerned work and unemployment by using seven-point rating scales. The following items fall into that class (some of them were described in Chapter 5). There were two questions relating to confidence about finding a job and difficulty in finding a job for which ratings were summed to provide a measure of job expectation. Two questions concerned the value of employment (satisfaction derived from work, interest in work). Ratings were summed to give a measure of employment value. Two questions concerned how much subjects needed or wanted a job. Ratings were summed to provide a measure of job need. The single-item measure of unemployment disappointment used by Feather and Davenport (1981) and by Feather and Barber (1983) was also included in the questionnaire. Two questions concerned predictions about future unemployment. One related to unemployment rate ("What percentage of people in your class do you think will be unemployed four months after completing their education?"). Subjects circled a percentage from a scale from 0 to 100 presented in five unit gradations. The second related to unemployment length ("For how many years do you think that high rates of unemployment among young people will continue?"). Subjects answered by ticking a scale that went from 1 year to 10 years in one-year units, and from 10 years to 20 years in two-year units, with "more than 20 years" as the last point on the scale.

In addition to these items subjects rated a set of 19 reasons for youth unemployment as not important (1), somewhat important (2), or very important (3). These reasons sampled a wide range and they included individualistic or internal reasons (e.g., "Lack of effort by unemployed youth in trying to get jobs"), societal or external reasons (e.g., "Failure of the government to help create jobs for unemployed youth"), and fatalistic reasons (e.g., "Temporary bad luck"). These reasons were similar to those used in earlier research on poverty by Feagin (1972) and Feather (1974) and some had a more specific source in the Feather and Davenport (1981) and Feather and Barber (1983) studies. A factor analysis of the intercorrelations of the importance ratings for the 19 reasons led to the development of five scales that defined particular kinds of reasons: lack of motivation, economic situation, lack of skill, lack of education, and interview/appearance inadequacy.

Subjects also answered two further questions concerning the causes of unemployment. One assessed internal attribution: "How much do you think the unemployed generally are to blame for being unemployed?" (Not their fault at all/All their own fault). The second assessed perceived uncontrollability: "Can the causes of unemployment be changed by you or by anyone else?" (Can easily be changed/Totally beyond anyone's power to change it).

The following scales were also completed by subjects: (1) the nine-item measure of external locus of control (Chapter 5) that was based on a factor analysis of responses to the Rotter (1966) measure of external control (O'Brien and Kabanoff, 1981); the Hopelessness Scale developed by Beck et al. (1974); and (3) a set of 25 bipolar adjective scales for each of which subjects were asked to circle a number from 1 to 7 that best describes "how you see yourself." A factor analysis of the intercorrelations between these self-ratings enabled the development of the following four scales that were assumed to measure self-esteem, potency or power, tension, and depression (the adjective in italics indicates the direction in which the item was scored for each variable). The self-esteem scale was based on 12 items (*successful*-unsuccessful, worthless-*valuable*, dull-*bright*, *pleasant*-unpleasant, pessimistic-*hopeful*, *useful*-useless, apathetic-*purposeful*, *friendly*-unfriendly, *interested*-bored, *competent*-incompetent, unconfident-*confident*, and *satisfied*-dissatisfied); the potency scale on 3 items (*tough*-tender, *rugged*-delicate, and *hard*-soft); the tension scale on two items (*angry*-calm, and *tense*-relaxed); and the depression scale on two items (happy-*sad* and elated-*depressed*).

Other questions answered by subjects were designed to obtain information about family background and school performance. For example, subjects indicated in what year they planned to leave school (year 9, year 10, year 11, year 12, don't know) and how their marks compared with those of other students in their year (well above average, above average, average, below average, well below average). The latter variable was scored from 1 to 5 in the direction of increasing quality of performance and will be referred to as the school performance variable.

What were the main findings from this study? The mean importance ratings for the set of reasons for youth unemployment considered for the entire sample showed that subjects were biased toward internal explanations that blamed the unemployed for their present condition (Feather, 1983a). Thus, the reasons rated as most important related to internal or personal causes such as lack of effort, lack of genuine interest, lack of education, and poor appearance, although failure of the government to create jobs (an external cause) was also seen to be relatively important. The least important reasons were judged to be too many married women in the workforce holding down jobs, most jobs too dull and uninteresting to apply for, and temporary bad luck. These results are in contrast to those obtained by Feather and Barber (1983), where external reasons were rated as more important than internal reasons by the unemployed themselves. They also contrast with results obtained by Feather and Davenport (1981)—see Feather (1983a) for details—and suggest that the schoolchildren sampled in the present study ("observers") were more inclined to blame the unemployed for their present condition than the unemployed were themselves ("actors"). I noted before that attribution theorists have argued for an actor-observer bias in the way individuals assign causality for behaviors and outcomes, with observers more likely to cite dispositional factors (e.g., traits, abilities, attitudes), whereas actors may lean more toward a situational interpretation of events (Nisbett & Ross, 1980).

The main findings relating to group differences are presented in Table 6.5, which also includes the results of 2×2 analyses of variance with gender (male, female) as the first factor in each analysis and type of school (state, independent) as the second factor. Table 6.5 shows that students from the state schools had lower mean internal attribution scores, that is, they were less likely to blame the unemployed for their unemployed condition when compared with the independent school students. Further analyses showed that students from the state schools were more likely to endorse the following reasons for unemployment as important when compared with students from the independent schools: poor appearance, the economic situation in Australia, government failure to create jobs, failure of private industry to provide jobs, and too many married women in the workforce. Students from the state schools also had higher scores on the attribution scales concerned with the economic situation and interview/appearance inadequacy. Thus, students from the two types of school perceived the causes of youth unemployment in different ways.

The independent school children also had higher expectations about finding a job, valued employment more, predicted that unemployment would go on longer, reported higher school performance, saw themselves as more de-

Table 6.5. Mean ratings for attribution items, for work/unemployment items, and for general measures.

MEAN RATINGS

Variable	Range	Males		Females		All subjects	F for sex	F for school	F for interaction
		State (N = 121)	Independent (N = 262)	State (N = 115)	Independent (N = 151)				
Attribution measures									
Internal attribution	1–7	3.72	4.10	3.65	3.91	3.91	2.06	10.67***	0.38
Perceived uncon-trollability	1–7	3.98	3.96	3.70	4.09	3.95	0.08	2.27	3.71
Work/unemployment items									
Job expectation	2–14	8.72	9.37	8.18	8.79	8.90	9.43**	11.32***	0.01
Employment value	2–14	10.36	10.75	9.73	10.25	10.38	11.15***	6.99**	0.14
Job need	2–14	12.06	12.22	11.63	11.45	11.91	19.62***	0.00	1.35
Unemployment disappointment	1–7	5.37	5.87	5.87	5.62	5.72	0.16	2.79	13.08***
Unemployment rate	0–100	45.41	38.70	39.41	43.58	41.19	0.15	1.06	7.88**
Unemployment length	1–20	10.86	12.43	9.31	13.17	11.75	0.06	19.95***	3.86*
General measures									
External control	0–9	4.10	4.05	4.30	4.45	4.20	5.59*	0.08	0.45
Hopelessness	0–20	4.72	4.55	5.04	4.56	4.67	0.19	1.03	0.26
Self-esteem	12–84	64.08	63.34	63.38	64.34	63.72	0.20	0.00	0.95
Potency	3–21	13.90	13.79	10.66	11.01	12.59	146.26***	0.16	0.80
Tension	2–14	6.62	6.89	6.49	6.76	6.74	0.44	1.86	0.00
Depression	2–14	5.49	5.87	5.56	5.94	5.76	0.15	3.96*	0.00
School performance	1–5	3.26	3.49	3.18	3.60	3.42	0.51	28.22***	2.40
Anticipated year of leaving school	9–12	11.14	11.79	11.35	11.86	11.64	4.10*	110.66***	1.60

Note: N = 650. There were variations from this N due to missing data on some variables.
*p < 0.05; **p < 0.01; ***p < 0.001.
Source: From Feather, N.T. (1983a), "Causal Attributions and Beliefs About Work and Unemployment Among Adolescents in State and Independent Secondary Schools," in *Australian Journal of Psychology, 35,* pp. 211–232. With permission of the author and by courtesy of the Australian Psychological Society.

pressed, and anticipated staying at school longer when compared with the state school students. All of the differences that I have mentioned were statistically significant and they are generally consistent with predictions.

The results in Table 6.5 also show that there were gender differences on some of the variables. Male subjects had significantly higher expectations of finding a job, higher employment value scores, higher job need scores, and higher potency scores when compared with female subjects. The female subjects were higher in external control and they anticipated staying at school longer. Analyses of the importance ratings for the individual items concerned with reasons for unemployment showed that female subjects rated the following reasons for youth unemployment as more important than did male subjects: prejudice and discrimination, failure to handle interviews, and disruptive actions of the unions. These mean differences were also statistically significant and the gender differences as a whole are generally consistent with predictions.

I will conclude by presenting some of the correlations that occurred between selected variables. Table 6.6 presents the partial correlations of job expectation, unemployment disappointment, depression, and anticipated year of leaving school with other variables involved in the study, controlling for gender of subject and type of school. I will not attempt to summarize all of these results (see Feather, 1983a). It is clear, however, that this analysis adds to our understanding of the variables that are associated with expectations, situation-specific disappointment about unemployment, self-rated feelings of depression, and students' reports of when they anticipate leaving school. For example, job expectations were positively related to a set of variables that included internal attribution, positive self-esteem and higher levels of school performance, and negatively related to feelings of hopelessness, tension, and depression; unemployment disappointment was positively related to higher levels of employment value and job need, as was the case in the Feather and Davenport (1981) study but, surprisingly, also positively related to a tendency to blame the unemployed for their unemployment; the nonspecific measure of depression was related to a set of variables that together imply a negative view of self, pessimism, external control, powerlessness, tension, low expectations, and lower levels of school performance. Students' reported intentions to continue at school and hence to leave school later were associated with their overall assessment of their competence as reflected in school marks, self-esteem, and internal control.

The results in Table 6.6 show in particular that those young people who anticipated feeling disappointed about not getting a job were those who were more likely to report that they valued work or employment and that they needed a job. These relations were present before the search for employment began and they indicate that some of the linkages that have been demonstrated in previous studies with the unemployed (Feather & Barber, 1983; Feather & Davenport, 1981) also occur among students who are still at school as they predict the negative affective consequences of frustrated work motivation.

Table 6.6. Partial correlations relating job expectation, unemployment disappointment, depression, and anticipated year of leaving school to other variables for all subjects holding sex of subject and type of school constant.

Variable	Unemployment disappointment	Job expectation	Depression	Anticipated year of leaving school
Attribution measures				
Lack of motivation	0.07	0.09*	−0.06	−0.01
Economic situation	−0.02	−0.02	−0.03	−0.04
Lack of skill	0.02	−0.04	0.00	0.02
Lack of education	0.00	0.02	0.02	0.00
Interview/appearance inadequacy	0.07	−0.03	0.00	−0.12**
Internal attribution	0.13***	0.15***	−0.06	−0.02
Perceived uncontrollability	0.04	−0.01	0.05	0.03
Work, unemployment items				
Job expectation	0.01	—	−0.22***	−0.01
Employment value	0.23***	0.10*	−0.08*	0.03
Job need	0.39***	0.08	−0.17***	0.02
Unemployment disappointment	—	0.01	−0.05	0.05
Unemployment rate	−0.07	−0.11**	0.05	0.08
Unemployment length	0.03	−0.03	0.02	−0.05
General measures				
External control	−0.10*	−0.10*	0.22***	−0.13**
Hopelessness	−0.06	−0.41***	0.33***	−0.06
Self-esteem	0.16***	0.31***	−0.52***	0.13**
Potency	−0.11**	0.08	−0.11**	−0.13***
Tension	−0.09*	−0.12**	0.33***	−0.06
Depression	−0.05	−0.22***	—	−0.04
School performance	0.06	0.20***	−0.19***	0.35***
Anticipated year of leaving school	0.05	−0.01	−0.04	—

Note: $N = 650$ but there were variations from this N due to missing data on some variables. Two tailed tests of significance were used.
*$p < 0.05$; **$p < 0.01$; ***$p < 0.001$.

Source: From Feather, N.T. (1983a), "Causal Attributions and Beliefs About Work and Unemployment Among Adolescents in State and Independent Secondary Schools," in *Australian Journal of Psychology, 35,* pp. 211–232. With permission of the author and by courtesy of the Australian Psychological Society.

Finally, I return to the findings about causal attributions or explanations for youth unemployment. I have already noted that the results were consistent with research on actor-observer differences in causal attributions and with the literature on attribution errors (Jones & Nisbett, 1972; Nisbett & Ross, 1980; Watson, 1982). They also demonstrate the value of going beyond laboratory studies to real-life settings because the more detailed analyses revealed differences relating to type of school attended and gender that extend our understanding of the factors that influence the way individuals explain events and outcomes.

Our results imply that the explanations that people give for events such as poverty and unemployment can be understood not only as products of cognitive processing but as social products as well. They reflect the background of a person's social experience in different settings as channeled through family, school, groups, the media, and other sources of influence. These various socializing agents shape a person's construction of social reality and the nature of their impact varies from person to person depending upon where a person is located in the social structure. The views about social reality that emerge involve integrated systems of beliefs, attitudes, and values that have some consistency about them and that are important in social judgment, social interaction, and self-definition. At a general level these constructions provide a person with a framework for making sense out of the mass of information that is a continuing and inevitable part of daily existence, and they guide both thought and action. Their reality is a psychological reality that may involve both accurate and inaccurate inferences from the social world as it exists. Many of these ideas have been discussed before (Feather, 1971, 1975) and, in different versions, by other authors.

The second study that I will describe in this section also involved secondary school students. It extended the analysis of explanations for youth unemployment to a wider set of reasons and examined relations between scores on derived attribution subscales and measures of social class, voting preference, and personal value priorities (Feather, 1985a). I also conducted multivariate analyses in order to discover sets of variables that predicted employment value and helplessness and pessimism about unemployment (Feather, 1986a).

There were 334 subjects (167 males, 164 females, three who did not specify gender) who participated in the study. They were drawn from year 11 classes in five state high schools in metropolitan Adelaide. The schools were selected from different catchment areas so as to ensure that the sample as a whole would span a wide range of socioeconomic status. Most students were 16 years of age and they were tested in August–September 1983.

Subjects completed a questionnaire that contained the relevant measures. Their teachers administered the questionnaire during regular class sessions and it was answered under anonymous conditions. The questionnaire consisted of three main sections. The first section contained a set of 27 possible explanations for youth unemployment. Subjects rated each of these explanations for their importance using a five-point scale. A factor analysis of the intercorrelations between these ratings enabled the construction of six derived attribution scales that overlapped with some of the scales obtained in previous studies (Feather, 1983a; Feather & Davenport, 1981). The scales (with examples of reasons with high factor loadings) were as follows: lack of motivation ("Lack of effort by unemployed youth in trying to get jobs"), recession and social change ("The economic situation in Australia"), competence deficiency ("Lack of good education among unemployed youth"), defective job creation ("Failure of the government to help create jobs for unemployed youth"), personal handicap ("Sickness and physical handicap among unemployed people"), and specific discrimination ("Prejudice and discrimination against unemployed youth").

The second section of the questionnaire contained Form D of the Rokeach Value Survey (Rokeach, 1973) for which subjects were instructed to rank 18 terminal values in order of importance for self and then to do the same for 18 instrumental values (see Chapter 5).

The last section of the questionnaire contained background and demographic questions, as well as specific items concerned with employment and unemployment. Some of these items were identical to those used in the study that I have just discussed (Feather, 1983a). These were measures of unemployment disappointment, interest in work, satisfaction from having a job, need for a job, want for a job, confidence about finding a job, difficulty in finding a job, internal attribution, school performance, and anticipated year of leaving school. In addition, there were items concerned with unemployment time ("How long do you think it will take for you to get a job when you start to look for one?"), helplessness ("How helpless do you feel about whether or not you will get a job when you start to look for one?"), perceived uncontrollability ("Do you think you have much control over whether or not you will get a job when you start to look for one?"), as well as questions that concerned whether subjects had received guidance at school about jobs and whether they had any work experience at all (e.g., occasional work, regular part-time work, visits to industries or firms). Subjects answered most of the items that concerned employment or unemployment by using seven-point rating scales with end-labels that were equivalent to those that were used in previous studies (see Feather, 1985a, 1986a, for details).

Although these students were below the voting age, I also included a measure of hypothetical voting preference ("If you had the vote, which political party do you think you would vote for?"). Their responses were coded in the direction of preference for the more conservative political party. A measure of social class was obtained that was based on the occupational status and level of education of each subject's father or guardian.

The results relating to the attribution measures are presented in Table 6.7. It can be seen that these secondary school students saw explanations that referred to external socioeconomic conditions (recession/social change, defective job creation) and explanations that concerned lack of skill (competence deficiency) as relatively important reasons for youth unemployment. As

Table 6.7. Mean scores for scales and product-moment correlations.

Variable	Range	Midpoint	M	SD	Correlations			
					Internal attribution	Sex of subject	Social class	Conservative voting preference
Derived scales								
Lack of motivation	5–25	15	16.72	4.21	0.26***	-0.06	-0.04	0.04
Recession/social change	5–25	15	19.71	3.45	-0.16**	-0.04	-0.08	0.02
Competence deficiency	5–25	15	18.10	3.56	0.00	-0.02	-0.06	-0.08
Defective job creation	2–10	6	7.11	1.89	-0.09	-0.04	-0.29***	-0.23***
Personal handicap	2–10	6	5.75	2.04	0.02	-0.02	-0.15*	-0.11
Specific discrimination	2–10	6	7.12	2.01	0.05	-0.01	-0.03	-0.05
Other variables								
Internal attribution	1–7	4	3.69	1.42	—	-0.01	0.14*	0.16*
Sex of subject	—	—	—	—	-0.01	—	-0.02	0.05
Social class	—	—	—	—	0.14*	-0.02	—	0.26***

Note: $N = 334$. There were minor variations from this N because of missing cases on some items. Sex was coded as follows: male = 1, female = 2. Voting preference was coded Labor (left wing) = 1, Liberal (right wing) = 2. All tests of significance are two-tailed.
$*p < 0.05$; $**p < 0.01$; $***p < 0.001$.
Source: From Feather, N.T. (1985a), "Attitudes, Values, and Attributions: Explanations of Unemployment," in Journal of Personality and Social Psychology, 48, pp. 876–889. Copyright 1985 by the American Psychological Association. Reprinted with permission.

was the case in the previous study (Feather, 1983a), explanations that referred to lack of motivation were also seen as relatively important.

The correlations in Table 6.7 show that explanations concerned with defective job creation (by either the government or private industry) tended to be rated as less important by subjects whose voting preference was more conservative in orientation (i.e., they favored the more-to-the-right Liberal party rather than the more-to-the-left Labor party), and as less important by subjects whose social class indexes were higher. Conservative voting preference was positively related to social class and internal attribution (i.e., to blaming youth unemployment on the unemployed themselves). The internal attribution measure was positively related to the lack-of-motivation scale and negatively related to the recession/social-change scale, reflecting the internal and external characteristics of the explanations that made up these respective scales. Subjects with higher social class indexes were more likely to have higher internal attribution scores. Thus, like those subjects with a conservative voting preference, they were more likely to blame unemployment on the unemployed themselves.

The detailed results concerning relations between the value priorities assessed by the Rokeach Value Survey (Rokeach, 1973) and the various measures listed in Table 6.7 are presented in the original report (Feather, 1985a). The correlations were low but they demonstrated meaningful patterns. For example, general social values (a world at peace, equality) tended to be higher in relative importance for those subjects who blamed youth unemployment on external, socioeconomic factors (recession/social change, defective job creation). These two values were assigned lower priority in their value systems by those subjects who were higher in internal attribution and social class. Values that reflected individualistic concerns (capable, courageous, intellectual) were assigned higher priority by those subjects who were more inclined to blame unemployment on lack of skill (competence deficiency).

I interpreted these findings as demonstrating that subjects' explanations of events are a function of their attitudes and values, pointing to the need to consider causal attributions and other types of explanation in relation to the motivational and affective concerns of individuals. The explanations that people provide for events are not neutral beliefs that are the end-products of unbiased, rational information processing. They are linked to other beliefs, attitudes, and values within the total belief system in ways that give meaning and consistency to the events that occur. Thus the explanations that individuals construct have functional significance in terms of a complex set of determinants involving cognition, motivation, and affect. As I noted when discussing the results of the previous study, they are also related to socializing influences that are linked to where a person is located in the social structure. Thus, both internal dynamics and external forces affect the explanations that individuals offer for events and outcomes.

When a factor analysis was conducted of the intercorrelations between the items concerned with employment and unemployment, two patterns of rela-

Table 6.8. Means, standard deviations, and factor loadings after varimax rotation.

				Factor loadings	
Variable	N	M	SD	Factor I	Factor II
Work interest	331	6.01	1.04	0.50	−0.19
Job satisfaction	331	3.88	1.60	0.40	−0.05
Job need	330	5.58	1.20	0.70	0.05
Job want	333	6.26	1.13	0.83	0.00
Unemployment disappointment	333	5.68	1.29	0.65	0.02
Job confidence	333	4.91	1.35	0.01	−0.69
Job difficulty	333	3.64	1.50	0.00	−0.65
Unemployment time	317	11.98	7.75	−0.21	0.53
Helplessness	333	3.41	1.49	0.18	0.54
Uncontrollability	331	3.70	1.62	−0.15	0.47

Note: All variables except unemployment time were assessed by using 1–7 rating scales (midpoint = 4). Higher scores on the job confidence and job difficulty scales indicated that subjects were more confident about getting a job and believed that a job would be easier to get.
Source: From Feather, N.T. (1986a), "Employment Importance and Helplessness About Potential Unemployment Among Students in Secondary Schools," in *Australian Journal of Psychology*, *38*, pp. 33–44. With permission of the author and by courtesy of the Australian Psychological Society.

tions were obtained that were similar to those that have already been discussed in relation to the other studies already described in this chapter. The factor loadings are presented in Table 6.8. Measures of employment value, need for a job, and feeling depressed or disappointed about hypothetical future unemployment clustered together to define a factor that was called *employment importance*. The other pattern of relations revealed by the factor analysis linked measures of helplessness and uncontrollability with low confidence about job prospects, high perceived difficulty, and more pessimism about how long it would take to find a job. This pattern defined the *helplessness-pessimism* factor and it resembled the self-denigration pattern described by Feather and Barber (1983). Had measures of general depressive symptoms and self-esteem been included, one would have expected helplessness-pessimism to be associated with more evidence of depressive symptoms and lower self-esteem.

Further analyses were conducted to discover the correlates of the helplessness-pessimism and employment importance factors. The relevant correlations are reported in Table 6.9. The results of a path analysis testing a possible causal model for helplessness-pessimism are presented in Figure 6.1. The correlations show that higher scores on the helplessness-pessimism factor were significantly associated with less job guidance, less tendency to blame unemployment on the unemployed (lower internal attribution), lower school performance, and lower social class. Higher scores on the employment importance factor were significantly associated with more job guidance and

Table 6.9. Means, standard deviations, and intercorrelations involving factor scores and other variables.

Variable	Variable										N	M	SD
	1	2	3	4	5	6	7	8	9	10			
1. Helplessness-pessimism		−0.01	−0.20***	−0.26***	−0.19***	−0.01	0.08	−0.03	−0.18**	0.08	309	−0.02	0.85
2. Employment importance			0.16**	0.00	−0.09	−0.09	0.17**	0.05	−0.10	0.07	309	0.02	0.89
3. Job guidance				0.11*	−0.03	−0.02	0.10	0.02	0.07	0.10	333	2.91	0.82
4. Internal attribution					0.01	−0.01	0.03	−0.02	0.14*	−0.01	332	3.69	1.42
5. School performance						0.31***	0.07	−0.17**	0.15*	−0.08	333	3.40	0.78
6. Year leave school							0.01	−0.08	0.02	0.04	275	1.73	0.44
7. Father employed								0.03	0.24***	0.01	286	0.89	0.32
8. Work experience									−0.04	0.00	332	0.90	0.30
9. Social class										−0.02	270	0.03	0.87
10. Sex of subject											331	1.50	0.50

Note: Ns for anticipated year of leaving school, father's employment status, and social class were lower because subjects who checked "Don't know" and "Not applicable" categories were excluded. Helplessness-pessimism and employment importance were factor scores. Sex of subject was coded male = 1, female = 2. Coding of other variables is described in the text.
*$p < 0.05$; **$p < 0.01$; ***$p < 0.001$.

Source: From Feather, N.T. (1986a), "Employment Importance and Helplessness About Potential Unemployment Among Students in Secondary School," in *Australian Journal of Psychology, 38,* pp. 33–44. With permission of the author and by courtesy of the Australian Psychological Society.

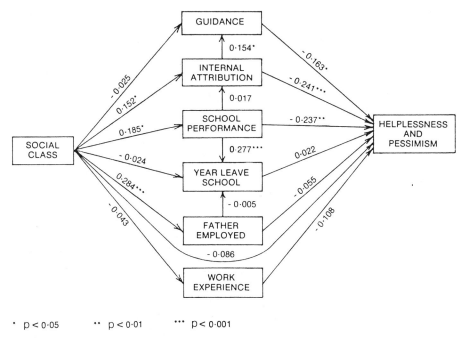

* p < 0·05   ** p < 0·01   *** p < 0·001

Figure 6.1. Path diagram linking social class and other variables to helplessness-pessimism. The numbers on the lines are standardized beta coefficients. $*p < 0.05$; $**p < 0.01$; $***p < 0.001$. (From Feather, N.T. (1986a), "Employment Importance and Helplessness About Potential Unemployment Among Students in Secondary Schools," in *Australian Journal of Psychology, 38*, pp. 33–44. With permission of the author and by courtesy of the Australian Psychological Society.)

subjects having fathers or guardians who were employed. Higher internal attribution for unemployment, higher school performance, and having a father or guardian in employment, were all significantly associated with higher social class. Staying at school longer and less work experience were both associated with higher school performance. More job guidance was positively related to internal attribution for unemployment. There were no significant gender differences for any of the variables listed in Table 6.9. Again, some of these correlations were consistent with the patterns found previously (Feather, 1983a).

Note, however, that there were also some differences between the results of this study and those obtained in the Feather and Davenport (1981) and Feather and Barber (1983) studies, which investigated young unemployed subjects rather than students still at school. Further analysis of the variable called unemployment disappointment showed that it was not linked to attribution to external causes as was found by Feather and Davenport (1981) and by Feather and Barber (1983)—see Tables 6.2 and 6.3. The correlation between unemployment disappointment and internal attribution was not negative, as one might expect it to be given the previous results, but it was close to zero. Moreover, in the previous study with schoolchildren there was a positive correlation between unemployment disappointment and internal attribution (see Table 6.6). Furthermore, as I indicated when describing the results of the Feather and Barber (1983) study, those unemployed subjects who had higher scores (i.e., more depressive symptoms) on the short form of the Beck Depression Inventory (Beck & Beck, 1972) were more likely to appeal to internal causes when accounting for their unemployment and to see the situation as uncontrollable. In the present study with schoolchildren, helplessness-pessimism about finding a job was more likely to be associated with external attributions.

Why did these differences occur? They probably reflect both sample effects and the effects of differences in the measures used. Schoolchildren and young unemployed people make judgments about unemployment from very different perspectives. The unemployed can call upon their own direct experience whereas schoolchildren are making outsider guesses about hypothetical future events in the context of the school situation. Moreover, the attribution measures used with the unemployed samples related to their own personal experience; the attribution measure used with the schoolchildren, both in this study and in the previous one, was not in terms of their own experience but referred to the general explanation of an important social event. It is likely that students who blamed the external situation held beliefs that people are largely controlled by external circumstances as far as employment prospects are concerned. These beliefs became part of the structure of helplessness-pessimism about employment possibilities. Consistent with this interpretation is the finding from the previous study with schoolchildren that depressed mood (as measured by semantic differential scales) was positively correlated with a short version of Rotter's (1966) external locus of control scale (see Table 6.6.). Depression, pessimism, external control, powerlessness, low grades, and low self-esteem clustered together for this group.

The findings from these studies with student samples are consistent with the view that children at school generalize from their past and present experience when they are asked to make judgments about a hypothetical future event. Thus, children win or lose at sport, obtain high or low grades at school, are ignored or encouraged by their parents, and so on. These kinds of events shape views of self and have predictable effects on expectations, motivation, and affect. Children can appeal to this background of knowledge when predicting their reactions to positive and negative events in the future. The legacy of present and past experience thereby provides a basis for predicting future reactions.

Possible future events as construed by the person can also have effects on the present. Thus, children can be assumed to assess their job prospects and to work through the implications of not obtaining employment, drawing upon their own backgrounds and personal experience in their attempts to come to terms with future possibilities. The process is probably similar in some respects to anticipatory socialization, a term used by Rosenberg (1957) to describe the process whereby aspects of a student's chosen occupation come to be incorporated into his or her chosen self-image even before the student enters the occupational practice. In a similar way, one might expect to find that an individual's current views of self and his or her behavior will be influenced by expectations about the prospects of future employment and unemployment and that the process of coming to terms with future job prospects will begin before the individual even attempts to enter the workforce. Future expectations will thus have an effect on a person's current attitudes, values, and behavior. These processes that involve the effects of the past, present, and anticipated future deserve more detailed investigation as they affect individual reactions to possible life events such as unemployment.

Finally, one can consider the possibility of using the two independent factors (employment importance and helplessness-pessimism) in research concerned with other reactions to unemployment. In discussing the results of the second study with schoolchildren (Feather, 1986a), I indicated the possibility of classifying individuals simultaneously on both factors and investigating behaviors that might be associated with the separate classifications. For example, one would expect that individuals with high scores on the employment importance factor and low scores on the helplessness-pessimism factor would engage in more active job search when compared with individuals with low scores on the employment importance factor and high scores on the helplessness-pessimism factor. These kinds of predictions could be developed in terms of the expectancy-value framework (Feather, 1982c; Chapter 4) because helplessness-pessimism defines a variable that involves both outcome and efficacy expectations and employment importance defines a variable that encompasses the valence (perceived attractiveness and aversiveness) of the employment outcome. As we will see in Chapter 8, this suggestion has been realized in the analysis of data obtained from our longitudinal study (Feather and O'Brien, 1986a, 1986b, 1987), using a more differentiated measure of job valence and variable called control-optimism, which can be seen as the reverse of the helplessness-pessimism variable (Chapter 5).

University Students

The third study to be described in this section involved university students rather than secondary school students. There were 265 introductory psychology students (95 males, 170 females) at Flinders University who participated in the study. The ages of most students ranged from 17 to 22 (mean = 21.93, *SD* = 6.94). Subjects were tested in March 1983 and they completed a questionnaire that was administered in small group settings during the first week of their course. Names were not required on the questionnaire.

The questionnaire contained the 27 possible explanations for youth unemployment that had been used in the study with secondary school students just described (Feather, 1986a). As in that study, subjects rated each reason for importance, using a five-point scale ranging from *not important at all* (1) to *very important* (5). A factor analysis of the intercorrelations between the ratings for the different reasons enabled the construction of seven derived attribution scales. These scales (with examples of reasons with high factor loadings) were as follows: lack of motivation ("Lack of genuine interest among unemployed youth in getting jobs"), competence deficiency ("Lack of work experience among unemployed youth"), defective government ("Failure of the government to help create jobs for unemployed youth"), personal handicap ("Lack of intelligence or ability among the unemployed"), social change ("Technological change; machines replacing people"), economic recession ("Worldwide recession and inflation"), and specific competition ("An influx of immigrants has taken up all available jobs"). These factors resemble those that were found in the other studies that I have described (Feather, 1983a, 1986a; Feather & Davenport, 1981).

Subjects also completed the Conservatism Scale (C Scale) devised by Wilson and Patterson (1968) and discussed by Wilson (1973). The C Scale consists of 50 items. Each item relates to some familiar or controversial issue or concept (e.g., the death penalty, evolution theory, chastity, church authority, strict rules, legalized abortion, and so forth). Subjects were asked, "Which of the following do you favor or believe in?" and they answered each item by circling "yes," "?," or "no." Items were coded in the conservative direction and a total conservatism score based on the 50 items was obtained.

Subjects were also asked "Which political party do you prefer or usually vote for?" and a measure of conservative voting preference was constructed on the basis of their answers. This measure contrasted the more-to-the-right Liberal party voters with the more-to-the-left Labor party voters. The same comparison was made in the study with the secondary school students except that the voting preference measure was realistically based for the university students rather than hypothetical.

Finally, subjects provided information about the usual demographic and background variables. A measure of social class was constructed that was based on the occupational status and level of education of each subject's father or guardian (Feather, 1986a).

It was predicted that there would be differences between individuals in the degree of importance they attached to the explanations for youth unemployment that related to their level of conservatism assessed generally via questionnaire (the C Scale) and specifically via conservative voting preference (right wing versus left wing). Given the fact that conservative individuals are more likely to endorse Protestant ethic values that relate to the virtues of hard work, self-discipline, the denial of pleasure for its own sake, and individual activism (Feather, 1984b), one would also expect them to assign more importance to reasons for unemployment that concerned lack of effort, lack of interest, hedonistic self-indulgence, and perhaps also lack of ability and skill. Those individuals who are less conservative in their attitudes may be more willing to endorse explanations for unemployment that refer to external conditions such as the economic situation, the policies of the government, and the failure of private industry to provide jobs. Their lower conservatism would be manifested in a greater inclination to blame established authority for current high rates of unemployment, especially if authority is seen as conservative in its attitudes toward social issues.

The results are presented in Table 6.10. There it can be seen that explanations that referred to external socioeconomic conditions (defective government, social change, economic recession) were seen as more important reasons for youth unemployment than were explanations that blamed unemployment on individual factors (lack of motivation, personal handicap). The means for the former explanations were all above the midpoint of the respective scale and those for the latter explanations were below the midpoint. Note, however, that competence deficiency or lack of skill was also seen as a relatively important reason for unemployment. These results are similar to those that were obtained in the corresponding study with secondary school students (Table 6.7), except that the university students in the present study did not see lack of motivation as an important reason for youth unemployment, whereas this was a relatively important reason for those still at secondary school (Feather, 1983a, 1986a).

The correlations in Table 6.10 show that the results were in the expected direction. Conservative subjects were more likely to blame unemployment on lack of motivation, personal handicap, social change, and specific competition (positive correlations) and less conservative subjects were more inclined to blame defective government and economic recession (negative correlations). Conservative voting preference was positively associated with level of conservatism and subjects who were higher in social class tended to favor the more conservative political party. All of these correlations were statistically significant.

Like the results for the secondary school students described previously, these findings again showed that subjects' explanations of events were a function of their attitudes and values, in this case the extent to which they favored a conservative position. The results were consistent for both the general and specific measures of conservatism and they strengthen our earlier conclusion that the explanations that people provide reflect their basic cognitive and affective orientations.

Concluding Comments

All of the studies described in this chapter involved single groups and all were correlational in nature. These studies were set within the context of psychological theories concerned generally with motivation, cognition, and affect and with the effects of socialization. The results do not provide precise tests of these theories but they can be interpreted in relation to these theories.

Table 6.10. Mean scores for scales and product-moment correlations.

Variable	Range	Midpoint	M	SD	Correlations			
					Sex of subject	Social class	Conservatism	Conservative voting preference
Derived scales								
Lack of motivation	5–25	15	13.87	4.48	0.03	0.10	0.35***	0.23***
Defective government	7–35	21	23.79	5.18	0.13*	0.06	0.08	0.04
Competence deficiency	4–20	12	15.37	2.87	0.08	−0.14*	−0.19**	−0.42***
Personal handicap	3–15	9	7.46	2.69	0.09	0.08	0.27***	0.14*
Social change	4–20	12	13.88	3.09	−0.02	−0.05	0.26***	0.20**
Economic recession	3–15	9	13.02	1.99	0.07	−0.07	−0.23***	−0.10
Specific competition	2–10	6	4.80	2.13	−0.06	−0.04	0.29***	0.16*
Other variables								
Sex of subject	—	—	—	—	—	−0.05	0.03	−0.10
Social class	—	—	—	—	−0.05	—	0.02	0.27***
Conservatism	0–100	50	35.93	11.63	0.03	0.02	—	0.37***

Note: $N = 265$. There were minor variations from this N because of missing cases on some items. Sex was coded as follows: male = 1, female = 2. Voting preference was coded Labor (left-wing) = 1, Liberal (right-wing) = 2. All tests of significance are two-tailed.
*$p < 0.05$; **$p < 0.01$; ***$p < 0.001$.
Source: From Feather, N.T. (1985a), "Attitudes, Values, and Attributions: Explanations of Unemployment," in Journal of Personality and Social Psychology, 48, pp. 876–889. Copyright 1985 by the American Psychological Association. Reprinted with permission.

What are some of the main conclusions? First, there was evidence that variables that concern employment value, need for a job, and negative affective reactions about not finding a job (e.g., disappointment, depressive affect) are linked together. The two studies with young unemployed individuals showed that the negative affective reactions were also associated with a tendency for the unemployed to blame their unemployment on outside forces, that is, to employ external rather than internal attributions. Feather and Barber (1983) called this pattern of relations the frustrated motivation pattern and recognized that the negative affect associated with not having a job could involve anger as well as disappointment. However, the negative affect–external attribution linkage was not found in the two studies that involved secondary school students. Its occurrence probably depends upon a person having direct experience with unemployment.

Second, there was also evidence that variables that relate to low confidence about finding a job, feelings of helplessness, powerlessness, low self-esteem, and depression are linked together. Feather and Barber (1983) referred to this pattern as the self-denigration pattern of relations and they found that depressive symptoms were associated with a tendency for the unemployed to blame themselves for their unemployment. However, the depression–internal attribution linkage was not found in the two studies that involved secondary school students. As for the previous case, its occurrence probably depends upon a person having direct experience with unemployment, especially over a long time period.

Third, how individuals assigned importance to different kinds of reasons for youth unemployment depended upon their attitudes and values and on past and present socialization influences coming from family, school, peer group, and so forth. The studies with secondary school students and with university students demonstrated these kinds of effects. Findings from these studies reinforce the view that an individual's beliefs about unemployment relate both to the internal dynamics of the person's cognitive-affective system and to the cumulative effects of past and present experience within the social environment.

Fourth, results that concerned relations between measures of confidence about getting a job and disappointment about not finding one were inconsistent from study to study. In one study (Feather & Davenport, 1981), the correlation between measures of initial confidence and depressive affect was positive, supporting the prediction that negative affect following failure is likely to be higher when initial expectations of success are high than when they are low (see also Feather, 1963, 1969). But in the other studies described in this chapter no reliable relations between these variables were found. Feather and Barber (1983) concluded that although there are undoubtedly cases where shame and disappointment about failure are more intense when one's hopes are initially high, there would also be cases where this relation may not be observed. For example, failure when an expectation is low may in some cases be compatible with low self-esteem and depressive symptomatology. And failure when an expectation is high may be cushioned if a person's self-esteem remains unchallenged and continues to be preserved. Positive relations between initial confidence and shame and disappointment about failure are probably more likely to be found when the failure can be attributed to internal causes such as low ability or insufficient effort, that is, where it signals some personal inadequacy. But linkages between expectations and depressive affect may be attenuated under conditions where attributions tend to be to external circumstances, as when present-day unemployment is attributed to an adverse economic climate. What may be central is how the failure reflects upon a person's view of self (see also Feather, 1988b).

Fifth, the results of our studies highlight the importance of considering a person's direct experience when interpreting differences and correlations. This became clear when the findings for employed samples and student samples were compared. In the present context, differences in results led us to speculate about actor-observer effects and about the role that direct experience with unemployment has in determining subjects' beliefs about the causes of youth unemployment.

We will return to some of these issues in later chapters, especially within the context of our longitudinal study (Feather & O'Brien, 1986a, 1986b, 1987), where it was possible to obtain further evidence about some of the linkages that have been discussed.

Chapter 7

Youth Unemployment: Comparison-Group Studies

The previous chapter reviewed the results of studies in which single groups were the focus of interest. This chapter reviews studies from our research program in which information was collected from both employed and unemployed groups and where the findings from the two groups were then compared. Like the single-group studies, these comparison studies were cross-sectional in nature in the sense that the information was obtained from the different groups at about the same time and there was no attempt to follow up the groups longitudinally over an extended time period. Two studies will be described. The first involved samples of young employed and unemployed subjects from the population at large, the second involved a more selective sample of young people who had recently graduated from Flinders University.

Employed Versus Unemployed Groups: General Population

The study to be described in this section was one of the earliest to be conducted in our research program (Feather, 1982e). It was designed to explore a number of variables that have featured in the literature on causal attribution, learned helplessness, perceived controllability, self-esteem, and values. These variables were depressive symptoms, self-esteem, Protestant ethic values, attributional style, and apathy or general lack of interest.

What were the main predictions in this early study? First, I expected to find that unemployed subjects would be lower in self-esteem and more depressed when compared with those who have jobs. Both the 1930s' literature and the recent literature on unemployment effects describe adverse consequences of unemployment that may involve negative changes in a person's self-concept and negative affective reactions (e.g., Eisenberg & Lazarsfeld, 1938; Feather, 1985c; Fryer & Payne, 1986; Kelvin & Jarrett, 1985; Warr, 1987a, 1987b).

This literature is too large to summarize here but some of the arguments for differences between employed and unemployed groups will be presented.

It is reasonable to argue that depressive symptoms and self-esteem loss can be outcomes of the negative experiences associated with the unsuccessful search for employment. These negative experiences relate to the various costs of failing to obtain a job. They include not only the loss of material benefits but wider costs as well that are associated with being in a jobless environment (Kelvin & Jarrett, 1985; Warr, 1987a, 1987b). One would expect these negative experiences to determine some cognitive and affective changes relating to a person's view of self, especially if the unemployment occurs over a long period and under conditions where there are few positive factors like social support to buffer the negative effects. It is also possible that selection factors may operate to produce group differences such that individuals who have low self-esteem and who suffer from depression are less likely to find jobs. Those who get jobs may tend to be higher in self-esteem and lower in depressive symptoms, presenting a happier and more confident self to interviewers who select from among job applicants. One can also argue that employment in contemporary society is an important ingredient in defining a person's sense of identity and worth (Erikson, 1968; Gurney, 1980a, 1980b; Super & Hall, 1978) and that good-quality work environments provide features that are conducive to positive physical and mental health (Jahoda, 1982; Warr, 1987a, 1987b). These various lines of argument all imply the predicted group differences in depressive symptoms and self-esteem.

Second, I expected to find differences between the employed and unemployed groups in regard to Protestant ethic (PE) values, that is, for values that emphasize the virtues of effort, hard work, individualism, the denial of pleasures, and so forth. Different lines of argument can again be developed. If one wanted to blame the victim one might assume that those people without jobs were those who were not trying hard enough to get employment and that those with jobs were more committed to hard work and individual enterprise. On that basis, one would predict that the unemployed would have less commitment to PE values when compared with the employed. But that kind of argument would oversimplify the complex social, political, and economic forces that underlie present-day structural unemployment and do less than justice to the many highly motivated people who are seeking work. One can also argue, however, that prolonged experience with unemployment may lead to attitude and value shifts in the direction of establishing a new self-concept in which the virtues of having paid employment are no longer seen as important as they were. That is, the unemployed person adjusts cognitively and affectively to the experience of unemployment. Adjustments that deemphasize a commitment to paid employment and PE values may be more likely to occur when unemployment rates are high and where unemployment can readily be attributed to external causes such as the socioeconomic situation. In addition, some kinds of employment where hard work and effort are essential for success may have the effect of reinforcing PE values. These arguments imply that one would expect to find less evidence of PE values among an unemployed sample when compared with an employed sample.

We are on less solid ground in predicting differences between employed and unemployed groups in regard to attributional style. This is partly because the concept of attributional style is dispositional in nature. Thus, Peterson and Seligman (1984) view attributional style (or explanatory style, to use their preferred term) as a trait, "analogous to liberalism in politics or vanity in interpersonal relations" (p. 371). However, they do not regard it as invariant. Like liberalism and vanity, it has a certain amount of plasticity. They propose that a person's characteristic way of explaining good and bad events and outcomes should be treated as both a dependent variable that can be modified by life events and an independent variable that can influence or modify future events, as when a depressive explanatory style influences the development of depressive symptoms following a negative life event.

The first possibility mentioned by Peterson and Seligman (1984) is of more concern here. Does the experience of employment or unemployment affect a person's attributional style? If so, in what ways? One could argue that attributional styles may move toward the external pole among the unemployed, given the fact that unemployed subjects tend to give more emphasis to external causes in their explanations of unemployment (Chapter 6). In contrast, attributional styles may shift toward the internal pole among those employed individuals who work in jobs that demand competence and effort. As a counterargument, however, one could also propose that those unemployed who suffer a loss in self-esteem and become highly depressed as a result of their unemployment may shift toward explaining negative events in their lives in terms of internal, stable, and global causes—the depressive attributional style described by Peterson and Seligman (1984). In the end, what happens would depend on how stable attributional styles are and on other factors that might shift a person's characteristic ways of explaining events and outcomes, such as the importance of the event or outcome that is experienced. I predicted in the study being described that young unemployed people may show evidence of an attributional style in which both good events and bad events are more likely to be attributed to external causes. I also suggested that this external orientation may become linked to beliefs that life is somewhat capricious and that the causes of good and bad events may vary from occasion to occasion. That is, one might expect to find that the unemployed will also tend to perceive the causes of good and bad events as relatively less stable and more specific when compared with the judgments of the employed group. But I made these predictions recognizing that one could argue for other possible differences that are also plausible.

Finally, I predicted that subjects in the unemployed group would display more apathy and resignation than subjects in the employed group. The Eisenberg and Lazarsfeld (1938) review of the unemployment research in the 1930s indicated that being without a job may lead to diminished motivation and a state of apathy and resignation (see Chapter 3). Prolonged unemployment, despite repeated attempts to find a job, would ultimately determine reduced expectancies and a reduction in the motivation to seek employment (Feather & Davenport, 1981). It may also lead to a reevaluation of personal goals so that some goals that were seen as initially important by the individual are subsequently not only assessed as unattainable but perhaps also as less important.

The concept of apathy implies low levels of motivation and lack of interest across a range of situations. Thus, people with high levels of apathy would be expected to judge outcomes and events that may occur, or have in fact happened to them, as relatively less important when compared with people who are less apathetic. This conceptualization was the basis for the measure of apathy used in the present study.

Two groups of subjects (employed, unemployed) were tested during September/October 1979. The employed sample comprised 78 subjects (39 males, 39 females) and the unemployed sample 69 subjects (32 males, 37 females), none of whom were students but who all lived in metropolitan Adelaide. Subjects in the employed sample were slightly older than those in the unemployed sample (means of 21.44 years and 19.94 years, respectively). The unemployed sample had been unemployed for a mean of 31.32 weeks (median = 18 weeks). Both samples came from families in which the fathers had attained similar average levels of education.

Subjects in the two samples completed a questionnaire either individually or in small group settings. Names were not required on the questionnaire. There were five parts of the questionnaire and these comprised the Balanced Attributional Style Questionnaire (BASQ; Feather & Tiggemann, 1984), a modified version of the Rosenberg (1965) measure of global self-esteem (Bachman et al., 1978), the Mirels and Garrett (1971) Protestant Ethic (PE) Scale, the 21-item version of the Beck Depression Inventory (BDI; Beck, 1967), and a final section that included background and demographic items and questions that concerned unemployment history and job-search activity. These scales have been described in Chapter 5.

The BASQ was scored so as to provide separate internality, stability, globality, and importance scores for the eight good events and for the eight bad events as described in Chapter 5 (see also Feather & Tiggemann, 1984). This method involved summing across the achievement and affiliation situations for either good or bad outcomes (Table 5.4). The causes that subjects wrote down for each event were also coded on the basis of the classification used by Janoff-Bulman (1979) and by Peterson et al. (1981) in which causes are categorized as characterological, behavioral, or external. The self-esteem scale was scored both in terms of the total score and for scores based on the six positive items and the four negative items considered separately. Each subset of items was scored so that a high score indicated a favorable assessment of self-worth. This more differentiated scoring procedure was used because Warr and Jackson (1983) found that negative self-esteem items discriminated between employed and unemployed young people whereas positive self-esteem items did not. They suggested that people may distinguish between positive and negative aspects of self. The negative status that comes with being unemployed may sensitize unemployed subjects to negative aspects of themselves. The BDI and the PE Scale were scored in the usual manner (Chapter 5). The apathy score was based on the importance ratings for the eight good events and the eight bad events in the BASQ, considered separately. Low importance scores across situations were assumed to denote a general lack of interest or apathy.

The main results for this study are presented in Table 7.1. The reader is referred to the original article for further details (Feather, 1982e). Table 7.1 shows that, as predicted, the unemployed subjects had higher depression scores on the BDI. They also had lower self-esteem scores when compared with the employed subjects. This difference also occurred when the self-esteem scores were based on the positive items and negative items considered separately. So in this study, both sets of self-esteem items discriminated between the employed and unemployed groups. The PE scores for male subjects were much lower on the average for the unemployed group when compared with the employed group but there was little difference between the mean PE scores for the unemployed female subjects when compared with the employed female subjects.

The unemployed male subjects provided lower importance ratings for good events and bad events on the average when compared with the employed male subjects (i.e., they showed more evidence of lack of interest or apathy over the range of good and bad events). The results for the female subjects were less clear-cut. Thus, the prediction that unemployment would be associated with lower levels of general interest (or more apathy) received its best support from the results of the male subjects.

The results for the internality, stability, and globality scores derived from responses to the BASQ indicated very few differences that achieved conventional levels of statistical significance. There was no firm evidence that the experience of employment or unemployment influenced attributional style, assessed by the way individuals rated the perceived causes of a range of good or bad events for internality, stability, and globality. I have also conducted correlational analyses that demonstrate statistically reliable correlations between internality, stability, and globality scores for a wider sample and scores on the BDI, the self-esteem scale, and the PE scale (Feather, 1983c, 1987b; Feather & Tiggemann, 1984). But consideration of these results would take us too far afield.

Some further results are worthy of note. Those unemployed subjects who reported being out of work longer tended to have lower self-esteem ($r = -0.39, p < 0.001$). The behaviorally oriented measure of "How frequently do you look for a job?" (see Chapter 5) was positively related to self-esteem scores ($r = 0.26, p < 0.05$), to PE scores ($r = 0.26, p < 0.05$), to importance scores for good events ($r = 0.27, p < 0.05$), and to importance scores for bad events ($r = 0.24, p < 0.05$). This behavioral measure, however was negatively

Table 7.1. Mean ratings from attribution questionnaire and mean scores for BDI, self-esteem, and Protestant ethic for employed and unemployed samples.

| | | GROUP (EMPLOYED/UNEMPLOYED) | | | | F Values For | | |
| | | Males | | Females | | | | |
Variable	Outcome	Employed (N = 39)	Unemployed (N = 32)	Employed (N = 39)	Unemployed (N = 37)	Group effect	Sex effect	Group × sex effect
BDI depression	—	5.21	11.84	6.36	10.73	21.04***	0.01	0.91
Self-esteem								
Total	—	40.92	37.16	38.54	35.76	9.05**	3.17	0.21
Positive items	—	24.28	22.13	22.74	21.14	7.81***	3.67	0.17
Negative items	—	16.64	15.03	15.79	14.62	7.39***	1.60	0.18
Protestant ethic	—	82.72	72.41	82.62	84.65	2.27	4.76*	5.44*
Internality	Good events	41.15	37.06	38.90	39.72	1.85	0.00	4.60*
	Bad events	35.92	35.41	33.00	36.31	1.45	0.90	2.54
Stability	Good events	43.74	40.09	41.79	40.59	5.79*	0.66	1.53
	Bad events	33.18	33.78	32.21	34.06	1.33	0.13	0.34
Globality	Good events	40.10	36.66	38.26	37.78	2.34	0.14	1.40
	Bad events	31.05	30.31	26.87	30.81	1.67	2.43	3.32
Importance	Good events	45.36	38.41	46.74	44.49	14.14***	8.93**	3.82
	Bad events	39.54	35.13	39.47	40.14	1.97	3.22	3.87*

Note: There were minor variations from the *N*s listed due to a small number of missing cases. Attribution and importance ratings could range from 8 to 56.
*p < 0.05; **p < 0.01; ***p < 0.001.
Source: From Feather, N.T. (1982e), "Unemployment and Its Psychological Correlates: A Study of Depressive Symptoms, Self-esteem, Protestant Ethic Values, Attributional Style, and Apathy," in *Australian Journal of Psychology*, 34, pp. 309–323. With permission of the author and by courtesy of the Australian Psychological Society.

related to BDI depression ($r = -0.24$, $p < 0.05$), and to weeks out of work ($r = -0.27$, $p < 0.05$). These results indicate that both lower self-esteem and less effort to find a job were associated with increasing length of unemployment. They also show that the active pursuit of employment tended to be more frequent among those with higher self-esteem, stronger PE values, and higher levels of concern about positive and negative events (lower apathy). But frequency of job search was lower among those unemployed subjects who reported more depressive symptoms. These findings may imply a sort of reciprocal determinism (Bandura, 1986) in which the state of continued unemployment has effects on the person, and the person, so modified by his or her experiences, begins to behave in ways that alter the probability of finding a job.

Finally, the results indicated some gender differences that at the very least caution one against generalizing across the two sexes when stating conclusions about unemployment effects. Some of the findings were more clear-cut when the employed and unemployed male groups were compared than when the comparison involved the two female samples. Perhaps the male subjects who were sampled saw employment as a more central concern in their lives, as an essential part of the male role and a basic aspect of masculine identity. The female subjects may not have seen getting a job as such an important aspect of their life plans or as so crucial to their self-definition. They may have been more prepared for and more open to other possibilities such as working in the home or getting married and starting a family. An analysis showed that PE scores, which might be assumed to reflect in part a person's commitment to employment, were positively correlated with self-esteem for all male subjects when the employed and unemployed groups were combined ($r = 0.24$, $p < 0.05$) but negatively correlated for all female subjects ($r = -0.18$, ns). The difference in these two correlations was statistically significant ($p < 0.05$). These results support the view that the male subjects may have partly defined their self-esteem in terms of values relating to work and individual effort.

Both Warr (1987a, 1987b) and Warr and Parry (1982) have discussed the effects of unemployment on women—see also Warr et al. (1988). Warr notes that it is important to distinguish between jobless women who have a strong desire for paid work (the unemployed) and others who have no such desire (the nonemployed). In a review of 38 previous investigations, Warr and Parry (1982) found no significant difference for married women in affective well-being between those with or without paid employment, and more recent evidence appears to be consistent with that conclusion (Warr, 1987a). For unmarried women, however, there was a difference; paid employment was found to be significantly beneficial. Warr (1987a) suggests that married women without a job are more likely to be "nonemployed" than those who are single, divorced, or separated and that there are basic differences between the environments of married and unmarried women who are employed, unemployed, or nonemployed, depending also on whether or not they have children to nurture and support. Warr (1987a) discusses these differences in terms of the nine environmental features described in his vitamin model, on the assumption that these environmental differences would be associated with differences in psychological well-being.

Employed Versus Unemployed Groups: University Graduates

The second study involved a much more selective sample of young people, namely, recent graduates from Flinders University, Adelaide, who were either in paid employment or unemployed. Like the previous study this study was also concerned with differences in self-esteem and depressive symptoms between employed and unemployed groups. Its main aim, however, was to investigate differences between employed and unemployed people in their reports about how they use and structure their time. To what extent do they see their time as filled with useful activity? Does their use of time demonstrate purpose? Do they plan their daily activities or do they allow time to slip away? Do they follow a daily routine?

One of the findings from the study of the unemployed in the Austrian village of Marienthal (Jahoda et al., 1933) was that the unemployed suffered a disintegration in their sense of time. Indeed, in her subsequent discussion of the manifest and latent functions of paid employment, Jahoda (1979, 1981, 1982) included the imposition of a time structure as an important latent consequence of having a job. This consequence, along with the other latent consequences that were assumed to follow paid employment (shared experiences and contacts with people, collective goals and purposes, the assignment of status and identity, and required regular activity), were seen as beneficial for psychological well-being. Jahoda proposed that if a person is deprived of these categories of experience, then the psychological consequences may be negative (see Chapter 3 for a fuller discussion).

Feather and Bond (1983) investigated these ideas in the study under discussion. We predicted that the unemployed subjects would report less structure and purpose in their use of time when compared with the employed subjects. In addition, however, we were interested in variables that might correlate with individual differences in reported time use. We expected that difficulties in the use of time would covary with diminished self-esteem and a higher frequency of depressive symptoms. Hepworth (1980) found that unemployed men who could not fill their time meaningfully reported poorer mental health on the GHQ (Goldberg, 1972). One would expect that this kind of relation would generalize beyond unemployed samples and that a reported lack of structure and purpose in a person's life would be associated with low self-esteem and heightened depression among the employed as well as among the unemployed.

Following the findings from the study described in the previous section (Feather, 1982e), we also predicted that our unemployed subjects would have lower self-esteem and higher levels of depressive symptoms when compared with those in paid employment.

Finally, it was also predicted that among the unemployed those who see involvement in a job as important would have lower self-esteem, more depressive symptoms, and would report less structure and purpose in their use of time than those for whom employment is less valued. The more employment is seen to be as attractive and fulfilling in a personal sense, the more one would expect to find negative consequences when a person is deprived of employment. On the other hand, one would expect that among the employed those who see involvement in employment as important would have higher self-esteem, lower depressive symptoms, and would show more structure and purpose in their use of time when compared with those for whom employment is less valued. The employment status of the former people is compatible with their view that having a job is important and one would expect the consequences of their employment to be more positive for them. This line of argument implies opposite relations between a measure of employment value on the one hand and measures of self-esteem, depressive symptoms, and time structure on the other when employed and unemployed samples are compared.

At the time of the study there was already some evidence that was consistent with this last prediction. Stafford, Jackson, and Banks (1980), using the measure of employment commitment developed by Warr, Cook, and Wall (1979) and the GHQ measure of mental health (Goldberg, 1972), found that high employment commitment was associated with good mental health for the employed, whereas for the unemployed high employment commitment was associated with poor mental health. Warr (1987a) has recently updated these findings by referring to our studies with unemployed samples in which measures of employment value (Feather & Davenport, 1981) or employment importance (Feather & Barber, 1983) were included and to other studies of affective states and psychological well-being among the unemployed that were conducted by the Sheffield group or came from elsewhere (e.g., Jackson, Stafford, Banks, & Warr, 1983; Jackson & Warr, 1984; Shamir, 1986a; Ullah et al., 1985; Warr & Jackson, 1985: Warr et al., 1985).

There were 43 subjects (13 males, 30 females) who were unemployed in our sample and 255 subjects (156 males, 99 females) who had full-time paid employment. The mean age of the unemployed sample was 26.45 years and the mean age of the employed sample was 26.46 years. The mean reported length of unemployment for the unemployed sample was 29.70 weeks (median = 26.50) and the mean reported length of employment in the present job for the employed sample was 19.60 months (median = 9.29 months). All of the subjects were graduates from Flinders University who had completed their degrees in 1979 and 1980. Other details of the sampling can be found in Feather and Bond (1983).

Subjects completed a questionnaire that was mailed to them. It included the early 17-item version of the Time Structure Questionnaire (TSQ). The most recent version (Bond & Feather, 1988) was described in Chapter 5. The items covered such aspects of time use as organization, purpose, routine, planfulness, inertia, daydreaming, and so forth. Some of these items were suggested by Jahoda's (1979) discussion of how unemployment affects a person's sense of time. Subjects used a 1 to 7 rating scale to answer each item so that possible scores could range from 17 to 119. Higher scores indicated more structure and purpose in a subject's use of time.

In addition to this total score, four additional scores were obtained. These scores were based upon scales determined by the results of a factor analysis. Four factors emerged from this analysis and items with high loadings on these factors were selected to form the derived scales. The first scale involved four items that referred to engagement, purpose, meaning, and interest in daily life. We called it the *Engagement Scale*. The second scale involved three items that referred to lack of direction, aimless activity, and difficulty in initiating activity. We called it the *Direction Scale*. The third scale involved three items that referred to inertia and lack of structure or organization in the use of time. We called it the *Structure Scale*. The fourth scale involved two items that referred to routine and planning. We called it the *Routine Scale*. The specific items making up each of these scales are described in the original report (Feather & Bond, 1983).

Subjects also used 1 to 7 rating scales to answer the three-item measure of employment value first used by Feather and Davenport (1981) and described in Chapter 5. It will be recalled that these items concerned whether having a job meant more to the person that just money, whether most of the satisfaction in a person's life comes from his/her work, and how much should people be interested in their work. The modified version of the Rosenberg (1965) Self-Esteem Scale was used to measure global self-esteem and, following Warr and Jackson (1983), scores were again partitioned in terms of responses to the six positive items and the four negative items. The 13-item short form of the Beck Depression Inventory (BDI, Beck & Beck, 1972) was used to measure depressive symptoms. More detailed information about these scales is presented in the original report (Feather & Bond, 1983) and in Chapter 5.

The mean scores for the employed and unemployed groups on these variables are reported in Table 7.2 along with some results of a 2×2 analysis of variance applied to each measure, with gender (male, female) as the first factor and employment status (employed, unemployed), as the second factor. Table 7.2 shows that, as predicted, the unemployed sample had significantly higher depression scores and lower scores on most of the measures of time use. They also had lower self-esteem scores on the negative items of the self-esteem scale when compared with the employed sample. The mean levels of depression were in the minimal range for the employed subjects and in the mild range for the unemployed subjects, using the Beck and Beck (1972) classification. Note, however, that differences between the employed and unemployed groups were not statistically significant in regard to structure, total self-esteem, self-esteem based on the positive items, and employment value.

There were three statistically significant main effects of gender that indicated male/female differences irrespective of employment status. The female

Table 7.2. Mean scores and standard deviations for employed and unemployed samples and results of analysis of variance.

| Variable | Range | Employed (n = 255) | | Unemployed (n = 43) | | F values for main effect of group |
		Mean	SD	Mean	SD	
Use of time						
Total score	7–119	79.30	14.85	74.49	16.56	4.17*
Engagement	4–28	20.31	4.67	17.74	5.19	9.60**
Direction	3–21	15.55	3.65	13.98	4.53	7.46**
Structure	3–21	11.81	3.71	12.84	4.05	2.00
Routine	2–14	9.62	2.44	8.72	2.78	7.59**
Self-esteem						
Total	10–50	41.93	5.13	40.43	8.10	1.32
Positive items	6–30	25.04	3.17	24.86	5.07	0.02
Negative items	4–20	16.91	2.56	15.57	3.45	5.18*
BDI depression	0–39	2.57	3.35	5.44	5.55	16.05***
Employment value	3–21	16.33	2.20	16.16	3.29	1.75

Note: There were minor variations from the *n*s listed due to occasional missing cases.
$*p < 0.05; **p < 0.01; ***p < 0.001$.
Source: From Feather, N.T., & Bond, M.J. (1983), "Time Structure and Purposeful Activity Among Employed and Unemployed University Graduates," in *Journal of Occupational Psychology*, *56*, pp. 241–254. Copyright 1983 by the British Psychological Society. Reprinted with permission.

subjects tended to have higher scores on the routine scale (means of 9.84 versus 9.23), lower total self-esteem scores (means of 40.87 versus 42.37) and higher employment value scores (means of 16.90 versus 15.86) when compared with the male subjects. The lower self-esteem scores for the female subjects involved the negative items (means of 16.06 versus 17.22) but not the positive items (means of 24.81 versus 25.17).

The correlations between variables are presented in Table 7.3. They generally supported the predictions. More structured and purposeful use of time as indexed by the total TSQ score and by scores on the derived scales was positively related to self-esteem and negatively related to the BDI depression scores for both the employed and unemployed samples (with the exception of the routine scores). The correlations involving the separate measures of self-esteem were very similar to those obtained by using the total self-esteem scores except that for both groups the scores based on the negative items were more strongly linked to engagement (positively) and to BDI depression (negatively) than the scores based on the positive items. As in the study described in the previous section (Feather, 1982e), self-esteem and BDI depression scores were negatively correlated.

Table 7.3. Correlations between use of time measures and other major variables for employed and unemployed samples.

Variable	EMPLOYED GROUP					UNEMPLOYED GROUP				
	Self-Esteem			BDI depression	Employment value	Self-Esteem			BDI depression	Employment value
	Total	Positive items	Negative items			Total	Positive items	Negative items		
Use of time										
Total score	0.46***	0.40***	0.42***	−0.41***	0.23***	0.48**	0.43**	0.51***	−0.46**	−0.50***
Engagement	0.47***	0.35***	0.52***	−0.45***	0.14*	0.38*	0.30	0.46**	−0.51***	−0.40**
Direction	0.32***	0.32***	0.25***	−0.29***	0.25***	0.42**	0.41**	0.38*	−0.41**	−0.44**
Structure	0.32***	0.30***	0.27***	−0.28***	0.19*	0.46**	0.45***	0.42**	−0.30	−0.33*
Routine	0.10	0.13*	0.04	−0.01	0.15*	0.02	−0.03	0.02	0.03	−0.14
Self-esteem										
Total	—	0.92***	0.87***	−0.54***	0.07	—	0.97***	0.93***	−0.69***	−0.31*
Positive items		—	0.61***	−0.39***	0.09		—	0.80***	−0.61***	−0.24
Negative items			—	−0.61***	0.02			—	−0.73***	−0.36*
BDI depression				—	−0.01				—	0.27

Note: $n = 255$ for employed group and $n = 43$ for unemployed group, except for minor variations. Tests of significance of correlations are two-tailed.
*$p < 0.05$; **$p < 0.01$; ***$p < 0.001$.
Source: From Feather, N.T., & Bond, M.J. (1983), "Time Structure and Purposeful Activity Among Employed and Unemployed University Graduates," in *Journal of Occupational Psychology, 56,* pp. 241–254. Copyright 1983 by the British Psychological Society. Reprinted with permission.

Of particular interest is the fact that the correlations between the use of time scores and employment value were in opposite directions for the employed and unemployed samples. As predicted, correlations between employment value and the use of time scores were negative for the unemployed group. Thus, those unemployed subjects who saw employment as important were more likely to report difficulties in their use of time when compared with unemployed subjects who valued employment less. In contrast, among the employed sample, higher employment value scores were positively correlated with total scores on the TSQ and with more purposeful engagement, more directed activity, more structure, and more routine in the use of time. Thus, for the employed group, subjects with higher employment value scores were more likely to report that their use of time was structured and purposeful.

Note also that those unemployed respondents with higher employment value scores were more likely to report lower self-esteem and a higher frequency of depressive symptoms when compared with those unemployed respondents who had lower employment value scores (rs of -0.31 and 0.27, respectively). The corresponding correlations were close to zero in the employed sample.

These results clearly demonstrate that how people use their time is an important variable in the study of employment and unemployment. As predicted, the unemployed subjects showed less engagement, less direction, and less routine in their use of time and their overall score was also lower. In a general sense, their use of time indicated less organization and less purpose. This result is not altogether surprising given the fact that employment imposes its own goals, structures, and routines on those who are employed, whereas the unemployed do not have these job-related requirements. Hence the unemployed have to fall back on their own resources and make the best they can of an uncertain world that does not include the regimen of paid employment. These employed/unemployed differences in the use of time are consistent with those found in the 1930s (Eisenberg & Lazarsfeld, 1938), and they indicate that these earlier findings have some generality across time.

Our results also show, however, that the use of time measures were related to other variables in addition to employment and unemployment. For both the employed and unemployed groups, these measures correlated with individual differences in self-esteem, BDI depression, and employment value. The results are consistent with Hepworth's (1980) finding that ability to organize one's time is a good predictor of mental health. They extend this earlier finding to new variables and indicate that the relations found are general ones that apply to both employed and unemployed samples.

As was the case in the study by Stafford et al. (1980), employment value emerged as an important moderator of the correlations but, in this case, mainly for the time-related variables where the correlations between these variables and the measure of employment value were in the opposite direction for the employed sample (positive correlations) and the unemployed sample (negative correlations). This strong reversal in the direction of correlations did not occur, however, for the correlations between employment value and the measures of self-esteem and depressive symptoms when the two samples were compared. It was only in the unemployed sample that these correlations were statistically significant, with higher employment value linked to lower self-esteem and more depressive symptoms. Not being able to achieve the valued goal of paid employment was therefore associated with negative emotional consequences and diminished self-esteem. I noted in Chapter 6 that Feather and Davenport (1981) found a positive relation between employment value and unemployment disappointment for a young unemployed sample. I also reported that Feather and Barber (1983) found that the addition of a cruder measure of employment importance significantly incremented the variance accounted for in both a situation-specific measure of depressive affect or unemployment disappointment (that probably also tapped hostility and anger) and in the BDI measure of depressive symptoms (Table 6.4) for their young unemployed sample. So there is other evidence from our studies that is consistent with the correlations between employment value, self-esteem, and depressive symptoms reported in Table 7.3 for the unemployed sample in the study under discussion.

These results, like all of the other findings from our research program that I have presented so far, came from a cross-sectional study. Cause-effect relations in the present context are most appropriately tested in longitudinal studies that investigate the effects of changes in employment status over time as people move into and out of employment. In the present study, for example, it is possible that those individuals who were low in self-esteem and high in depressive symptoms were less likely to get jobs to begin with and that their unemployment was also a consequence of a general lack of purpose and time structure in their lives. Alternatively, the relative deficiencies in the temporal variables displayed by the unemployed sample might be linked to the higher frequency of depressive symptoms reported by this sample, that is, the employed/unemployed differences in time structure and purpose might be further reflections of the differences in reported depression. One could also argue that disintegration in a person's management of time might be a precursor of both depression and loss of self-esteem, or that employment and unemployment might have direct effects on the temporal measures as Jahoda's (1979, 1981, 1982) analysis suggests, given the radically different nature of the task situations (see also Warr, 1987a). I could go on listing alternative models. The point is clear, however, that controlled, longitudinal studies are necessary to assist in sorting out cause-effect relations. These studies should include behavioral measures of how people use their time (e.g., time budgets) as well as subjective reports.

It will be observed that in contrast to the results of the study discussed in the previous section (Feather, 1982e), total self-esteem scores were not significantly lower for the unemployed subjects when compared with employed subjects. This failure to replicate the previous finding may be due to differences in the populations that were sampled in the two studies. Young graduates have undergone unique sets of educational experiences that may help to immunize them against some of the initial shock of not getting a job and perhaps subsequently as well. Prior to seeking employment, the successful graduate has presumably developed some skills in structuring time and developing a sense of purpose and autonomy. Given their past record of achievement, the unemployed young graduates in the Feather and Bond (1983) study may have been able to maintain relatively high levels of self-esteem even in the face of unemployment.

The present results are consistent with those obtained by Shamir (1986b) in a recent Israeli study involving adults with university degrees who had several years of work experience. Shamir (1986b) found from both cross-sectional analyses and longitudinal analyses of data that global self-esteem, assessed by the Rosenberg (1965) Self-Esteem Scale, was not related to employment status (employed versus unemployed) nor affected by changes in employment status. However, the psychological well-being of respondents in Shamir's (1986b) study was lower for unemployed subjects and was sensitive to changes in employment status. Other research has also shown that unemployment has a negative psychological impact on highly educated and professional groups (e.g., Fineman, 1983; Kaufman, 1982; Leventhman, 1981), although Schaufeli (1988b) has recently drawn attention to some inconsistencies in the results of studies with white-collar professionals. Shamir (1986b) also found that global self-esteem had a significant moderator effect on relations between employment status and three indicators of psychological well-being (morale, depressive affect, and anxiety), with the high-self-esteem individuals showing more resistance to the negative impact of unemployment on psychological well-being when compared with the low-self-esteem individuals. Shamir (1986b) argues that his results are consistent with the view that self-esteem is a relatively stable personality characteristic, less likely to be modified by social circumstances than other variables. Kessler et al. (1988) also found that high self-esteem acted as a resource, reducing the damage that unemployment inflicts.

Other researchers have reported findings that indicate no reliable differences in the self-esteem of well-educated professionals who are either employed or unemployed (see Schaufeli, 1988b; Shamir, 1986b for reviews). For example, Hartley (1980) found no difference in the self-esteem of managers who were employed compared to those who were unemployed. Using data from a national panel survey, Cohn (1978) also found no evidence from a longitudinal analysis for a decrease in "satisfaction with self" as a result of job loss among highly educated white-collar workers. A significant decrement in self-satisfaction with job loss occurred, however, among blue-collar workers and less educated white-collar workers. Cohn (1978) also found that dissatisfaction with self was accentuated when there was a lack of an external cause to which unemployment could be attributed. Specifically, dissatisfaction with self was significantly greater for those unemployed who lived in areas where the local unemployment rate was low when compared with those living in areas where the unemployment rate was high. Cohn (1978) comments that ". . . it appears that when an environmental indicator of external cause for employment status change is available to the individual, the experience of status change does not have as great effect on self-attitude as when such an indicator is absent" (p. 90). This argument is consistent with Kelvin and Jarrett's (1985) discussion of the effects of unemployment on the self-concept (Chapter 4) and with my earlier discussion of attributional changes and their possible effects on the development of depressive symptoms (Feather, 1982e; Feather & Barber, 1983; Feather & Davenport, 1981). Also consistent with this discussion is the finding by Jackson and Warr (1987) that unemployed men in areas of England and Wales, where unemployment was chronically high, had significantly better psychological health when compared with those in areas of moderate or lower unemployment. Note, however, that Dooley et at. (1988), in their Los Angeles study, found that the aggregate unemployment rate had an adverse effect on their subjects when psychological symptoms were investigated.

It seems clear that the effects of unemployment on self-esteem depend upon the nature of the population being studied, with less evidence of decrements in self-esteem following job loss among more educated, white-collar individuals. Note, however, that in the present study lower self-esteem was found when self-esteem scores based on the negative items were uncoupled from self-esteem scores based on the positive items (Table 7.2). Shamir (1986b), however, on the basis of a factor analysis of the items in the global measure of self-esteem used in his study (Rosenberg, 1965), found no justification for dividing global self-esteem into positive and negative components. The factor analysis supported a one-factor solution. However, some earlier factor analyses of the Rosenberg Self-Esteem Scale with less selected groups have provided two-factor solutions that suggested a separation of the positive and negative items (Dobson, Goudy, Keith, & Powers, 1979). I have found the same kind of division in a recent factor analysis of the self-esteem scale (Rosenberg, 1965) that I described in Chapter 5 (see Table 5.1). Factor analyses using data from two separate samples (high school students, university students) indicated separate rotated factors for the positive and negative items. Note, however, that in the previous study (Feather, 1982e), I found that both kinds of self-esteem score were lower for unemployed individuals when compared with employed individuals, not just the scores based on the negative items (Table 7.1). The evidence suggests, however, that we should continue to partition global self-esteem into separate components based on the positive and negative items. Although scores on the two sets of items are positively correlated (Table 7.3), there may be qualitative differences in the self-esteem that is based on endorsement of the positive items and the self-esteem that is based on rejection of the negative items. As Warr and Jackson (1983) suggest, the latter measure of self-esteem may be more affected by adverse conditions such as unemployment or other negative life events.

Finally, the results showed that there were significant gender differences on some of the variables. The female respondents were significantly lower in self-esteem (especially when self-esteem was based on the negative items) and they had significantly higher scores on the routine variable when compared with the male respondents. A similar gender difference in self-esteem was found in the earlier study that involved a nonstudent sample (Feather, 1982e) and in a study involving a sample of first-year psychology students (Feather, 1985b), but only the latter difference was statistically significant. Shamir (1986b) also found that the self-esteem of the men in his sample was higher than that of the women. In a longitudinal study, Gurney (1980a) found evidence suggesting that self-esteem increased among female school-leavers who obtained jobs but not among male school-leavers who found jobs. Wylie (1979), in a comprehensive review of the literature, concluded that there is no firm evidence to support the view that women generally have lower self-esteem than men. We need more research to discover the precise conditions under which gender differences in self-esteem occur. I will return to the question of gender differences in self-esteem in the next chapter in relation to a more differentiated measure of self-esteem.

A significant gender difference also occurred in regard to the measure of employment value, with female respondents having significantly higher scores when compared with male respondents. In the previous study (Feather, 1982e), I found than the unemployed female respondents had lower apathy scores that the unemployed male respondents, higher scores on the measure of Protestant ethic values (Mirels & Garrett, 1971), and they reported higher levels of job-seeking activity. In the Feather and Barber (1983) study, unemployed female subjects reported higher ratings of importance than did unemployed male subjects. A greater concern about the value of work or employment among female respondents has therefore been found in other studies in our research program. However, this finding may not generalize to other populations. Warr, Jackson, and Banks (1982) found in a study of teenagers with limited qualifications that unemployed women in one of the cohorts tested showed less employment commitment and higher psychological well-being with longer unemployment. A high proportion of the unemployed women who were not seeking work had withdrawn from the labor market for family reasons (e.g., to have a baby). In one of the single-group studies described in the last chapter, I found that female students still at secondary school had significantly higher employment value scores when compared with male students (Feather, 1983a) but no statistically significant gender differences were found on a measure of employment importance used with high school students in a later study also described in Chapter 6 (Feather, 1986a).

With some of the findings that I have been discussing in this section we confront a perplexing problem that appears in a lot of the unemployment literature, namely, inconsistent results from study to study on some of the major variables. I will return to this problem at the end of this book. In some cases the inconsistencies can be attributed to differences in the samples that were tested; in other cases to differences in the measures that were used. Differences in the actual nature of the employment and unemployment experience, variables relating to unemployment history, cultural attitudes toward the unemployed, the way a society copes with unemployment, and other kinds of variables such as support and financial strain are also important. Studies also vary in the level of sophistication of the analyses that researchers use to deal with the data and control for important variables. Research would profit by more conceptual input to guide investigations, enabling one to move toward a better understanding of the impact of employment and unemployment on health and behavior.

Further Research on Time Structure

We have conducted further research since the Feather and Bond (1983) study, using a revised version of the Time Structure Questionnaire (TSQ), mainly with student samples. In a recent study (Bond & Feather, 1988) we found that TSQ total scores were positively correlated with a sense of purpose in life, self-esteem, reported health, present standing and optimism about the future, Type A behavior, and more efficient study habits, and were negatively correlated with depression, psychological distress, anxiety, neuroticism, physical symptoms, hopelessness, and anomie. Perceived use of time also varied with role demands, such as whether a person was single or married, employed or unemployed, or a part-time or full-time student. We also investigated relations between factor scores derived from a factor analysis of the TSQ items and the variables just mentioned. The five factors that were identified were called Sense of purpose, Structured routine, Present orientation, Effective organization, and Persistence. Details of the correlational analysis involving these factors are presented in the original report (Bond & Feather, 1988).

   We argued in the context of these findings that there is a need for further research that investigates interrelations between the perceived use of time, role demands, and personality variables. These studies might focus on changes in life circumstances that are forced upon people (e.g., unemployment, chronic illness) and those that are a normal part of most people's experience as they grow older (e.g., marriage, having children, retirement). Our results highlight the importance of a person's sense of purpose and structure in daily life. At a theoretical level, sense of purpose can be linked to theories that relate actions to goal structures. Examples of such theories are those that specify variables that are assumed to influence goal-directed action tendencies (e.g., expectancy-value theories; Feather, 1982c, 1986b, 1988a, 1988b, in press) and the volitional control of action (e.g., Kuhl, 1987; Kuhl & Beckmann, 1985). Some of these motivational approaches also take time perspective and future orientation into account, as in the work of De Volder and Lens (1982), Gjesme (1981), Lens (1986), Nuttin (1985), Van Calster,

Lens, and Nuttin (1987), and Raynor and Entin (1982). In addition to these theories, there are other related approaches from cognitive psychology that emphasize that actions are determined by goals, plans, and feedback (e.g., Anderson, 1985; Frese & Sabini, 1985; Miller et al., 1960). From a different perspective, Bandura (1986) has also emphasized the effects of goals, feedback, and other variables in his social-cognitive analysis of thought and action (see also Locke et al., 1981; Locke et al., 1986).

Although a sense of purpose is a subjective variable, it should be possible to relate a person's sense of purpose to theoretical variables such as a strong action tendency or a dominant intention or to the presence of goals and plans that are in the process of being executed. One's purposes help to shape the direction of thought and action. Studies have shown that students who saw goals in the distant future as more attractive and who assigned more instrumental value to studying hard in order to reach these distant goals, demonstrated more study persistence (De Volder & Lens, 1982); that students who perceived that their school results were instrumental for success in the future and who had a more positive affective attitude toward the future showed stronger study motivation and higher academic performance (Van Calster et al., 1987); that workers who were laid off for a seven-week period but who had a sense of purpose for the future coped better in their use of time than those who were made redundant (Fryer & McKenna, 1987); and that students in the Bond and Feather (1988) study who had more of a sense of purpose in their use of time showed better adjustment across a range of measures than those who had less of a sense of purpose. All of these findings suggest that sense of purpose is an important variable that deserves further investigation. In particular, more analysis is needed of how this variable might be integrated into theories concerned with motivation, action, and adjustment.

We also require a similar conceptual analysis of the factor that Bond and Feather (1988) called structured routine because this factor has been neglected by psychologists, except in its more extreme manifestations (e.g., obsessive-compulsive neuroses). The imposition of an orderly structure on daily activities, however, also has its healthy consequences and is an essential aspect of planning. Having a routine, however, is not the same as having a plan although the two are related. A routine has a stability about it that extends over time and pertains to a particular set of activities within a defined situation. A plan can change from time to time depending on the circumstances. It may be important to distinguish between a routine that is imposed on a person by virtue of external conditions (e.g., performing a task according to certain prescribed steps) and a routine that is self-generated rather than imposed from the outside. These different sources of routine may have different implications for psychological well-being and for attitudes toward the task.

It is also of interest to note that recent research on action styles has provided evidence for factors concerned with goal orientation and planfulness (Frese, Stewart, & Hannover, 1987). These factors resemble the purpose and routine factors described by Bond and Feather (1988) but they are not identical to them. It is clear, however, that there is now converging evidence from a number of different areas indicating that purpose and structure are important variables in the analysis of action and psychological well-being, and that these variables are worthy of more attention in the future. Our studies on the use of time therefore have wider significance.

Other research on time use in relation to unemployment has been conducted by Bostyn and Wight (1987), Kilpatrick and Trew (1985), Miles (1983), Rowley and Feather (1987), Warr et al. (1985), Warr (1984b), and Warr & Payne (1983). Some of these studies have examined reported behavior changes that occur after job loss by using self-reports (e.g., Warr, 1984b; Warr & Payne, 1983); others have classified time use on the basis of evidence obtained from time diaries (e.g., Kilpatrick & Trew, 1985). In the Kilpatrick and Trew (1985) study with a sample of unemployed men in Northern Ireland, it was found that it was possible to cluster subjects into four main groups in relation to the time they spent at various activities. Those unemployed men who spent a lot of time on active leisure and work-related activities fell into the Active cluster; those who spent more of their time with others than did members of any other cluster fell into the Social cluster; the men in the Domestic cluster spent a lot of their time on domestic chores; and those in the Passive cluster spent a large amount of time on passive leisure and child-care activities compared with the other groups. The men in the latter two clusters were more home-centered than those in the former two clusters. Kilpatrick and Trew (1985) found that psychological well-being, assessed by the 12-item version of the GHQ (Goldberg, 1978), became progressively poorer as one moved from the active to the social to the domestic to the passive cluster. They also reported other differences between the four groups in regard to background characteristics and unemployment history.

Fryer and McKenna (1987) compared two groups of men, both of whom came from engineering companies in an industrial town in a high unemployment area in the north of England. One group consisted of middle-aged men who were made redundant; the other group involved middle-aged men who were laid off for a period of seven weeks with the knowledge that they would be reemployed. Fryer and McKenna (1987) conducted detailed interviews of the men in the fifth week after the end of employment and they collected information on perceived health using the GHQ (Goldberg, 1972) and the Nottingham Health Profile (Hunt, McEwen, & McKenna, 1985). They found that the redundant men suffered greater difficulties in their use of time when compared with the temporarily laid-off men and they exhibited higher levels of psychological distress. Fryer and McKenna (1987) observed that the most obvious difference between the laid-off and redundant groups was ". . . the temporary and circumscribed nature of the former and the uncontrolled and potentially limitless nature of the latter. It was uncertainty about the future . . . that distinguished the two situations for the participants" (p. 71). They also noted that the redundant men suffered a greater drop in weekly disposable income than the laid-off men and they suggested that this relative difference was probably also instrumental in producing their greater distress. There was a lot of individual variation in how time was used and in the ways in which the experience of lack of employment was negative. On a theoretical level, Fryer and McKenna (1987) argued that their results posed a problem for Jahoda's (1982) explanatory claim that deprivation of the five latent or unintentional consequences of employment would have negative effects because, as a group, the laid-off men did not manifest as negative a response to being without a job as the redundant men. This difference occurred despite the fact that both were deprived of the latent functions of employment mentioned by Jahoda (1982). Fryer and McKenna (1987) claimed that Jahoda's account omitted orientation toward the future and the role of planning.

In a similar vein and consistent with my discussion of our studies on time structure (Bond & Feather, 1988; Feather & Bond, 1983), I would argue that the redundant participants had less sense of purpose and structure when compared with the laid-off participants. The goal structures of the latter participants would not be much affected because of the temporary nature of their unemployment but, for those made redundant, the change in situation would have profound effects on the meaning and direction of their lives.

Warr (1987a) views the results of the Fryer and McKenna (1987) study as demonstrating the positive effects on mental health of having environmental clarity, one of the environmental features listed in his vitamin model. The temporarily laid-off men had less deterioration in this feature. The two groups also differed in valued social position, another of the environmental features, with the unemployed group suffering a greater deterioration in regard to that feature. Warr (1987a) discusses the consequences of unemployment for a person's sense and use of time in terms of a reduction in externally generated goals, a further environmental feature in his vitamin model. Thus, "fewer demands are made, objectives are reduced, and purposeful activity is less encouraged by the environment. Routines and cycles of behaviour are less often set in motion, and opportunities for 'traction' and 'flow'. . . may be limited" (p. 213). He goes on to observe that "an absence of demands can produce an excess of time and remove the need to choose between activities or to allocate fixed amounts of time to individual tasks. . ." (p. 213). A general reduction in those demands that are linked to particular points (such as mealtimes or the start of a working day) may lead to a loss of temporal differentiation. "Time-markers which break up the day or week and indicate one's position in it are no longer as frequent or as urgent" (p. 213). Hence, the unemployed person may have a prolonged sense of waiting and a feeling that each day lacks structure. In terms of the vitamin model, it would be expected that these changes in purpose and structure linked to a reduction in externally generated goals and organized routines would be accompanied by reduced psychological well-being as evidenced by feelings of boredom, negative affective states, and so forth.

In conclusion, it seems that the evidence for the proposition that unemployment is accompanied by objective and subjective changes in the use of time is consistent. These changes can be related to reductions in the environmental features described by Warr (1987a) and, more generally, to decreases in the extent to which daily activities have structure and purpose and are organized in relation to long-term goals and plans. The evidence also indicates that a lack of structure and purpose in the use of time is linked to negative consequences over a wide range of variables.

Potential Social Action

In the questionnaire used in the Feather and Bond (1983) study, we included two measures of potential social action that were described in Chapter 5. These measures concerned how many volunteer actions and how many volunteer hours our respondents would be willing to contribute to assist a hypothetical social organization called the Campaign to Assist Unemployed Youth. Our main interest was in discovering whether social protest is a function of the discrepancy between expectations and outcomes.

We predicted that potential social action about current levels of unemployment in Australian society would be more likely to occur when present employment status (including unemployment) is highly discrepant in a negative sense with initial job expectations than when the discrepancy between expected job levels and current job status is less. Thus, we expected that potential social action would be more evident among the unemployed than among the part-time employed or those in full-time paid employment. The job expectations of the unemployed would be completely disconfirmed by their lack of employment in comparison with partly employed and fully employed people who at least have jobs. Moreover, it was expected that potential social action would be more evident among those unemployed people whose job expectations were initially high and among those partly and full employed people whose current employment level was negatively discrepant with their initial expectations.

These predictions may be related in a general way to psychological theories that deal with the effects of frustration, inequity, relative deprivation, and the affective consequences of expectation/outcome discrepancies. Each of these approaches suggests that a negative discrepancy between a desired expected state and a current state may be associated with negative affects such as disappointment, resentment, and anger and may be followed by actions that relate to the discrepancy. These various approaches differ in the variables that they emphasize, though there is some overlap between them—see Cook, Crosby, and Hennigan (1977), Crosby (1976, 1982), Crosby and Gonzales-Intal (1984), and Walker and Pettigrew (1984) for a discussion of relative deprivation theory in relation to the other approaches.

We also investigated the role of other variables in relation to potential social action. For example, some results summarized by Rosenthal and Rosnow

(1975) suggest a sex difference in volunteering, with females more likely to volunteer than males (though the results are somewhat mixed). Furthermore, Lipset (1972) reported that student activists in universities in the 1960s were more often found in the social sciences, the humanities, and the more purely theoretical fields of science (in that order), than in the more vocational, professional, and experimental fields. We were able to examine the relationship of potential social action to both of these variables (sex of subject, type of graduate) and, in addition, to investigate in an exploratory way some other variables that might be associated with a person's expressed intention to assist a hypothetical social movement concerning unemployment.

The sampling procedure has already been described in relation to the study of time structure discussed in a previous section of this chapter. In the present analysis we also included a sample of 48 respondents who reported that they were in part-time or casual employment in addition to the 255 respondents who reported that they were in full-time paid employment and the 43 respondents who reported that they were currently unemployed and seeking employment (see Feather & Bond, 1984, for details).

Employed respondents used 1–7 scales labeled from "Very high" (7) to "Very low" (1) to rate six characteristics of a job in terms of level hoped for ("The highest level you could *have reasonably hoped for* in a first job after graduation, relative to others in your field"), level expected ("The level you really *expected* to achieve in a first job after graduation, relative to others in your field"), level tolerated ("The lowest level you would have *tolerated* in a first job after graduation, relative to others in the same field"), first job ("What your *first* job after completing your first degree or diploma was actually like, relative to others in the same field"), and current job (What your *current* job is like, relative to others in the same field"). Unemployed respondents used the same rating scales to rate the six job characteristics in terms of level hoped for, level expected, level tolerated, and first job (if applicable), but not current job because they were unemployed. This procedure was derived from a study of education and employment (Jones, 1981). Note that some of these ratings involved retrospective judgments (e.g., level hoped for, level expected) that could be subject to some distortion in the light of subsequent events and personal wishes.

The six characteristics of a job that were rated were salary, advancement, security, responsibility, skills, and people, and each of these characteristics was accompanied by short examples to specify its meaning further (e.g., examples given for security were guaranteed work and position and superannuation; examples given for skills were opportunity to use learned skills and to develop new skills).

To simplify the subsequent analysis the ratings were summed for each respondent across the six job characteristics to obtain total scores for each set of ratings. These total scores could therefore range from 6 to 42. These new variables will be called total level hoped for, total level expected, total level tolerated, total first job level, and total current job level. This procedure was justified by the uniformly statistically significant positive correlations that were obtained between the ratings across each set of ratings for the six job characteristics and by interitem reliabilities for each scale that exceeded 0.75 (Cronbach, 1951).

The major analysis to test the hypothesis about expectation/outcome discrepancies used the total level expected and total current job level variables. The measures of potential social action (i.e., number of volunteer actions, number of volunteer hours) were based on the procedure developed by Feather and Newton (1982); they were described in Chapter 5. The actions and hours volunteered by respondents related to a hypothetical social organization called the Campaign to Assist Unemployed Youth.

What were the main results? Table 7.4 presents the mean scores concerned with job characteristics and potential social action in support of the campaign. One-way analyses of variance showed that the unemployed group volunteered significantly more hours to assist the campaign than did the other two groups but differences between the three groups in the number of volunteer actions were not statistically significant. The three groups had similar hoped-for and tolerated levels summed across the six job characteristics. The employed group, however, reported significantly higher expected levels when compared with the other two groups and the unemployed group reported significantly lower levels relating to the first job held. In general, these results are consistent with prediction at the level of group differences. The unemployed group, whose current employment status was most discrepant with initial job expectations, tended to volunteer more actions and more hours, especially in comparison with the employed group.

Analyses also showed that for the relatively large group of employed graduates, female respondents volunteered more activities and hours to the campaign when compared with male respondents. Graduates from the humanities, social sciences, and education schools of the university tended to volunteer more activities and hours when compared with graduates from the science/medical schools (see Feather & Bond, 1984, for details). These results were as predicted.

Hierarchical multiple regression analyses were also conducted for each of the action measures for the full-time employed group (Table 7.5). These analyses showed that for both volunteer actions and volunteer hours the addition of sex of respondent, type of graduate, and the interaction term (current level × level expected) to the regression equation led to increments in the variance accounted for in the dependent variable. The number of activities volunteered to the campaign tended to be higher among graduates who were female and came from the humanities/social sciences/education schools of the university. Note, however, that the addition of all variables to the equation accounted for only a relatively small percentage of the variance (15% for volunteer actions, 21% for volunteer hours).

The nature of the significant interaction effect (current level × level expected) is presented in Figure 7.1 for both volunteer actions and volunteer

Table 7.4. Mean scores on job characteristics, and action measures for employed, partly employed, and unemployed samples.

Variable	Range	Group			F
		Full-time employed ($N = 255$)	Partly employed ($N = 48$)	Unemployed ($N = 43$)	
Job characteristics					
Total level hoped for	6–42	32.88	31.67	32.56	1.10
Total level expected	6–42	28.22	25.79	26.67	4.09*
Total level tolerated	6–42	20.75	18.24	19.50	2.91
First job level	6–42	26.35	20.98	15.29	26.09**
Current job level	6–42	29.79	24.27	—	—
Action measures					
Number of volunteer actions	0–11	3.57	4.35	4.07	1.87
Number of volunteer hours	0–10	1.96	2.28	2.88	3.67*

Note: There were variations from the Ns listed due to some missing cases. The two measures of social action were positively correlated, $r(329) = 0.72$, $p < 0.001$.
*$p < 0.05$; **$p < 0.001$.
Source: From Feather, N.T., & Bond, M.J. (1984). "Potential Social Action as a Function of Expectation-Outcome Discrepancies Among Employed and Unemployed University Graduates," in Australian Journal of Psychology, 36, pp. 205–217. With permission of the authors and by courtesy of the Australian Psychological Society.

Table 7.5. Results of hierarchical multiple regression analysis for the full-time employed group with action measures as dependent variables.

		DEPENDENT VARIABLE							
		Number of Volunteer Actions				Number of Volunteer Hours			
Step	Independent variable	R	R^2	R^2 change	Simple r	R	R^2	R^2 change	Simple r
1.	Sex of respondent	0.139	0.019	0.019*	0.14*	0.155	0.024	0.024*	0.16*
2.	Age of respondent	0.183	0.034	0.014	0.11	0.173	0.030	0.006	0.06
3.	Father's education level	0.250	0.063	0.029*	-0.18**	0.200	0.040	0.010	-0.11
4.	Type of graduate	0.302	0.091	0.028*	-0.23***	0.268	0.072	0.032**	-0.22***
5.	Relative grades at university	0.312	0.097	0.006	0.09	0.271	0.073	0.002	0.06
6.	Use of career guidance	0.318	0.101	0.004	0.13*	0.280	0.078	0.005	0.14*
7.	Months since leaving university	0.321	0.103	0.002	-0.03	0.285	0.081	0.003	-0.04
8.	Employment value	0.323	0.105	0.001	0.06	0.307	0.094	0.013	0.14*
9.	Need for a job	0.349	0.122	0.017*	-0.12	0.327	0.107	0.012	-0.09
10.	Difficulty of obtaining a job	0.354	0.126	0.004	0.10	0.333	0.111	0.004	0.10
11.	Total current job level	0.360	0.130	0.004	-0.04	0.393	0.155	0.044**	-0.18**
12.	Total job level expected	0.360	0.130	0.000	-0.01	0.395	0.156	0.001	0.03
13.	Current level × Level expected	0.392	0.154	0.024*	-0.05	0.459	0.210	0.055**	-0.14*

Note: Sex of respondent was coded 1 = male, 2 = female; father's education level was coded 1 to 4 in the direction of higher levels of education; type of graduate was coded 1 = social sciences/humanities/education graduate, 2 = sciences/medicine graduate. Tests of significance are two-tailed for the simple rs.
*$p < 0.05$; **$p < 0.01$; ***$p < 0.001$.

Source: From Feather, N.T., & Bond, M.J. (1984), "Potential Social Action as a Function of Expectation-Outcome Discrepancies Among Employed and Unemployed University Graduates," in *Australian Journal of Psychology, 36*, pp. 205–217. With permission of the authors and by courtesy of the Australian Psychological Society.

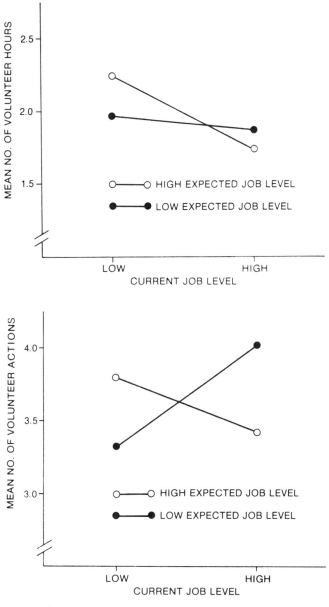

Figure 7.1. Mean number of actions and mean number of hours volunteered to Campaign in relation to high and low current job levels and high and low expected job levels for the employed sample. (From Feather, N.T., & Bond, M.J. (1984), "Potential Social Action as a Function of Expectation-Outcome Discrepancies Among Employed and Unemployed University Graduates," in *Australian Journal of Psychology*, *36*, pp. 205–217. With permission of the authors and by courtesy of the Australian Psychological Society.)

hours. In Figure 7.1 respondents were classified as high or low in total expected job characteristics and as high or low in total current job levels according to whether they were above or below the median of the respective distribution (*Mdn.* = 27.72 for the distribution of total expected job levels; *Mdn.* = 30.68 for the distribution of total current job levels). Figure 7.1 shows that willingness to assist the campaign either by volunteering actions or hours was more likely to occur when low current job levels were associated with relatively high initial expectations (i.e., a negative discrepancy). This result is in line with prediction. It is interesting to note that at least in the case of volunteer actions, willingness to assist was also more likely to occur when high current job levels were associated with relatively low initial expectations (i.e., a positive discrepancy). This latter effect was not predicted and needs to be replicated. If these two types of effect hold up in future research then it could be argued that both positive and negative discrepancies between expected and current levels of employment may elicit a sense of injustice and concern among the full-time employed, which may be reflected in some expressed intention to act on behalf of the disadvantaged.

Analyses that were similar to those just described were also conducted for the partly employed and unemployed groups but they were hampered by the small sample sizes. There was no evidence that measures of willingness to assist the campaign were positively related to initial expectations about job levels for the unemployed group as had been predicted (see Feather & Bond, 1984).

What implications do these results have for theoretical approaches such as relative deprivation theory that emphasize the effects of disconfirmed expectations? In a review of relative deprivation studies, Muller (1980) concluded that "strong claims about frustration or relative deprivation being the 'root' psychological cause of protest and violence must be rejected" (p. 84). Muller (1980), however, on the basis of the evidence, is willing to grant that "one kind of frustration—that arising from perceived discrepancy between one's just desserts and one's actual attainment—may bear a modest relationship to individual propensity for participating in political protest and violence" (p. 84)—see also Gurr (1970).

It is clear that predictions that relate protest behavior to relative deprivation are not always confirmed and that there is a need for more detailed theoretical analyses that take account of a range of preconditions and mediating variables both at the psychological and sociological levels of inquiry. Crosby's (1976, 1982) contributions are a step in this direction. She has been mainly interested in egoistical deprivation and the conditions that make one feel deprived. Her most recent formulation stresses that wanting and deserving are two essential preconditions of felt deprivation, which she equates with resentment or a sense of grievance (Crosby, 1982). Moreover, she maintains that "the perception that others are better off than oneself, the thought that one is less well off than expected, and the belief that conditions will not improve probably all amplify feelings of grievance" (p. 153).

Walker and Mann (1987) found evidence that measures of egoistical relative deprivation predicted the number of stress symptoms that were reported by unemployed people better than measures of fraternalistic relative deprivation. In contrast, fraternalistic relative deprivation predicted protest orientation better than egoistical relative deprivation measures. Egoistical relative deprivation refers to the outcomes of intraindividual or interindividual comparisons; fraternalistic relative deprivation involves comparisons between an individual's membership group and some other reference group. Clearly the egoistic-fraternalistic distinction will be an important one in future research. Our study may be seen as involving measures relating to egoistical relative deprivation rather than to fraternalistic relative deprivation.

The results of the multiple regression analysis applied to data from the employed graduates (Table 7.5) may be compared with those from recent studies of job satisfaction that found that congruency between desired and perceived job characteristics accounted for less than 3% of the variance in satisfaction scores whereas job attributes accounted for up to 40% of the variance (O'Brien & Dowling, 1980; O'Brien & Humphrys, 1982). Note that the discrepancy investigated in the present study concerned expected/actual differences rather than ideal/actual differences. Nevertheless, the differences between groups reported in Table 7.4 could be interpreted as reflecting the effects of current job levels rather than discrepancies. The results in Table 7.5 showed that the addition of the interaction term significantly incremented the variance in both action measures. But at least in the case of volunteer hours, the addition of current job level to the regression equation also led to a significant increment in the variance accounted for. Finally, in a recent investigation of relative deprivation ideas, Taylor (1982) found that:

> The gap between expectations and actual outcomes did not relate to satisfaction as the past/present relative deprivation theories predict. . . . Instead of supporting the relative deprivation predictions, these data suggest the simpler conclusion that the trend of recent experience is a reasonably strong predictor of satisfaction: people are satisfied if their economic situation is improving, dissatisfied if their situation has declined. (p. 31)

Though Taylor's "trend of recent experience" implies widening or narrowing of gaps between expectations and current status, the evidence just summarized indicates that it is important to distinguish between the separate contributions of expected status and current status, and their interaction in any study that investigates the effects of disconfirmed expectations. It is likely that some reactions to unemployment and underemployment may relate more to the current conditions of a person's life than to negative gaps between expectations and outcomes. For example, in the present study the same multiple regression analysis described earlier was applied to other data obtained from the full-time employed group involving depression scores from the short form of the Beck Depression Inventory (Beck & Beck, 1972), self-esteem scores from the 10-item adaptation of the Rosenberg (1965) scale

(Bachman et al., 1978), and to scores from the specially designed questionnaire (TSQ) concerned with the structured and purposive use of time (Feather & Bond, 1983). In each case, the addition of total current job level significantly incremented the variance accounted for in the respective dependent variable but the addition of the expectation measure and the interaction term did not. Lower depression, higher self-esteem, and more structured and purposive use of time were all significantly associated with higher current job levels. The respective correlations of each variable with total current job levels were $r = -0.30$, $p < 0.001$ for depression; $r = 0.28$, $p < 0.001$ for self-esteem; and $r = 0.34$, $p < 0.001$ for the use of time.

An obvious implication of these findings is that future investigations should pay more attention to qualitative differences in job levels among employed people and to the effects of these differences on a range of cognitive, affective, and behavioral variables. A primary focus on expectation/outcome discrepancies could divert attention from effects that are more closely associated with the actual and/or perceived conditions of a person's employment situation than with the size and direction of perceived gaps. While some variables (e.g., a sense of grievance and possible social protest) may depend in part upon job-related expectation/outcome discrepancies, other variables (e.g., depression, self-esteem, the perceived use of time) may be more closely tied to the positive and negative features of actual job levels and to the wider effects that current job conditions (e.g., low salary, lack of security) have on individual lives (see Chapter 8).

Finally, some further qualifications are in order. It is important to remember that the present study of potential social action involved a hypothetical situation (assisting a fictional campaign), the expectation measure was retrospective in nature and perhaps therefore subject to some distortion, the sampling was from a relatively selected population (university graduates), and the investigation was concerned with the analysis of behavioral intentions at the individual psychological level rather than with more structured forms of collective action. Future research is needed to investigate social and political action as it occurs among the unemployed and underemployed in real-life settings, using representative samples and allowing for a wide range of variables at the individual, social-psychological, and sociological levels of inquiry. The evidence so far seems to show that the unemployed do not become mobilized as a political force but instead show low levels of political involvement (Marsh, Fraser, & Jobling, 1985). They may, however, express verbal attitudes in favor of political action, lawbreaking and violent change (e.g., Breakwell, 1986; Clark, 1985; Gaskell & Smith, 1985), though these attitudes may not be translated into action (Jackson, 1985). Banks and Ullah (1987) found that the young unemployed people in their sample were more disaffected with the political system and more likely to support the British Labour party than those young people who were employed. Both groups showed a low level of interest and involvement in politics. Banks and Ullah (1988) suggest that research should now move beyond party political questions to broader issues concerned with the attitudes of the unemployed to trade unions, law and order, government, citizenship, sexual politics, and so forth.

Chapter 8

Youth Unemployment: Longitudinal Studies

A recurrent theme in my discussion of the single-group studies and comparison-group studies described in the two preceding chapters has been recognition of the need to conduct longitudinal investigations of the effects of employment and unemployment. Without these kinds of studies results are ambiguous. It is always possible in cross-sectional studies to present alternative interpretations of the results. For example, if one finds that depressive symptoms are associated with unemployment in a correlational study one can either argue that this is because individuals who are depressed to begin with find it difficult to obtain jobs or because being unemployed leads to depressive symptoms. Warr (1987a) observes that the former type of interpretation is more likely to apply for cross-sectional studies when unemployment rates are very low. When there is an easy labor market it seems more reasonable to assume that those who fail to get jobs are likely to be those with personal attributes that impede them from becoming employed. When unemployment rates are high, however, and a lot of people miss out on obtaining employment, the interpretation in terms of prior characteristics becomes less plausible and it seems more reasonable to assume that differences are produced by the employment or unemployment experience (Spruit, Bastiaansen, Verkley, Van Niewenhuijzen, & Stolk, 1985; White, 1983).

Tracking events over time in a longitudinal investigation helps to reduce the ambiguity although, even then, it is not easy to arrive at conclusions about causes because of the large number of variables that may influence outcomes and the difficulty of controlling them and specifying how they might interact.

In this chapter I will describe a longitudinal study of the effects of employment and unemployment that involved samples of young people who had recently left school (Feather & O'Brien, 1986a, 1986b, 1987).

Longitudinal Study of School-Leavers

A number of studies appeared in the 1980s that tracked young people over time as they moved into and out of employment. Studies from the Sheffield group involved at least two different samples of young people. One set of studies used samples of less-qualified, 16-year-old school-leavers from a large northern city in England (Banks & Jackson, 1982; Jackson et al., 1983; Stafford, Jackson, & Banks, 1980). Another set of studies used samples of unemployed, poorly qualified West Indian and white 17-year-olds who were drawn from 11 urban areas in England (Banks & Ullah, 1985, 1988; Ullah et al., 1985; Warr et al., 1985). Two major Australian studies have been conducted in metropolitan Adelaide, South Australia. One set of studies used samples of school-leavers in each of their last three years of high school, drawn from 12 randomly selected high schools and subsequently followed up over a number of years (Tiggemann & Winefield, 1984; Winefield & Tiggemann, 1985; Winefield, Tiggemann, & Goldney, 1988). We conducted the other set of studies, also involving school-leavers from Adelaide high schools (Feather & O'Brien, 1986a, 1986b, 1987; O'Brien & Feather, 1989). Other Australian studies of school-leavers using a longitudinal design have been conducted by Gurney (1980a, 1980b, 1981), Patton and Noller (1984), and the Australian Council for Educational Research. I have reviewed the Australian research on unemployment up to 1985 (Feather, 1985c). A recent general review that examines Australian research on young people in work and education has been prepared by Blakers (1987).

It is important to note differences in the populations studied in these various investigations. The Sheffield studies were concerned with less-qualified young people; the studies conducted in metropolitan Adelaide spread the net more widely and were not restricted to school-leavers who were less qualified but to all school-leavers. These kinds of differences as well as cultural differences and differences in the measures that were used help to account for some of the variation in results.

It would be simplistic to expect the same pattern of results to emerge from studies of young school-leavers when compared with those obtained from studies using adult populations. As I noted in Chapter 4, adults have different roles and responsibilities when compared with young people who have just left school and one would expect the effects of unemployment to be more drastic for them, especially if they have families to support, debts to pay off, and limited financial resources. The young unemployed person is typically in a more favorable situation where he or she can fall back on parents for support while still retaining social links with friends from school. The young person may have no history of employment at all. He or she is concerned with finding a full-time job for the first time and not with regaining employment. The sudden change in status from being a student to having paid employment may have important psychological effects that could overshadow the effects of a delay in obtaining a first job.

There have been a number of longitudinal studies of adult samples moving into and out of employment. Some of these have come from the United Kingdom (e.g., Jackson & Warr, 1984; Payne, Warr, & Hartley, 1984; Stokes & Cochrane, 1984; Warr & Jackson, 1984, 1985, 1987); some from North America (e.g., Cobb & Kasl, 1977; Cohn, 1978; Dooley et al., 1988; Elder & Caspi, 1988; Liem & Liem, 1988; Linn et al., 1985; and some from other countries (e.g., Brenner & Starrin, 1988; Iverson & Sabroe, 1987; Schaufeli, 1988b; Shamir, 1986b). Recent reviews of longitudinal studies have been provided by O'Brien (1986), Schaufeli (1988b), and Warr (1987a) and the general conclusion is that unemployment has adverse effects on psychological health in adults, especially for less qualified men who have limited financial resources to draw upon. Reemployment improves their psychological health. Because the conditions of the lives of unemployed adults differ so much from those of unemployed young people who are seeking to enter the labor market, the findings from these adult studies will not be a focus of the present chapter. The main aim is to describe the longitudinal study of school-leavers that we conducted (Feather & O'Brien, 1986a, 1986b, 1987) and to relate the findings from this research to the results of other longitudinal studies with young people.

The variables that we examined in this longitudinal study spanned a wide range and included measures concerned with self-evaluation, values, affective reactions, job expectations, need for employment, employment value, external locus of control, and explanations for unemployment, most of which were described in Chapter 5. The list involved variables that have long been of interest to investigators in this field (e.g., self-esteem, depression) and some that have only recently become a focus of attention (e.g., Protestant ethic values, causal attributions).

The research began in 1980 and extended over a two-year period. Use of a longitudinal design enabled us to make stronger inferences about possible cause-effect relations. We were able to observe the degree to which findings were replicated from year to year and to study patterns of change over the time periods that were sampled.

The study was also designed so as to control in a quasi-experimental way for the possible effects of testing procedures and societal influences on the variables of interest. To accomplish this control, we used a design suggested by the literature on quasi-experimentation (e.g., Cook & Campbell, 1979) and by previous research in political socialization, generational differences, and life-span developmental psychology (e.g., Feather, 1980; Jennings & Niemi, 1975; Schaie, 1983; Chapter 4).

Testing effects occur when repeated assessment of the same sample using the same measures has unintended consequences due to possible practice and reactivity effects (Cook & Campbell, 1979). Subjects may react in different ways on subsequent occasions because they become familiar with the items and remember some of the previous responses (a practice effect) or because the previous exposure to the items causes them to react differently for reasons other than familiarity (a reactivity effect).

Societal or historical effects occur because each age cohort lives through a shared set of environmental circumstances that differ from those experienced by a different age cohort (cohort effects) or because there are environmental changes or conditions that would be expected to affect all members of a population, regardless of cohort membership (period effects). For example, in the present context, historical or societal effects of the latter type might occur following the enactment of new legislation concerning social welfare provisions for the unemployed or because of a worsening economic crisis that sharply reduces the number of jobs available. Such changes in the external conditions might alter a person's view of unemployment and its effects quite apart from any effects of the unemployment experience itself.

I described these different kinds of effects in Chapter 4 when discussing contributions from life-span developmental psychology. It is possible to disentangle those effects by using appropriate quasi-experimental designs. It is important to do so in order to gauge the extent to which any reliable differences that are obtained can be attributed to the employment or unemployment experience per se rather than to the effects of repeated testing or to unknown historical/societal factors. We made no specific predictions about testing effects and historical/societal effects in our study but we did attempt to control for them.

We had a number of hypotheses in mind that guided our choice of variables. First, we expected that unemployment, particularly if prolonged, would have some negative effects on young individuals (e.g., diminished self-worth, decreased confidence, increasing negative affect) and that employment would have some positive effects (e.g., enhanced self-worth, increased satisfaction with life). I have noted some of these effects in previous chapters and other researchers have also drawn attention to them in studies of school-leavers (e.g., Banks & Jackson, 1982; Banks & Ullah, 1988; Gurney, 1980a; Jackson et al., 1983; Patton & Noller, 1984; Tiggemann & Winefield, 1984; Ullah et al., 1985; Warr et al., 1985; Winefield & Tiggemann, 1985) though, as I indicated previously, findings vary across studies because of differences in the populations that were sampled, the measures that were used, the time periods that were studied, or because of other unknown factors. The longitudinal design of our study enabled us to discover whether any differences that were obtained between groups were outcomes of the unemployed/employed experience or whether they were present before our respondents left school and attempted to enter the labor market.

Second, we expected that explanations of unemployment would be affected by a person's actual experience in the job market and the extent to which the job search was successful or unsuccessful. Specifically, we predicted that unemployed individuals would be more likely to blame youth unemployment on external socioeconomic factors (at least initially), whereas those who obtained employment would be more likely to explain youth unemployment in terms of internal factors such as lack of ability and lack of effort. Findings from cross-sectional studies show that the unemployed tend to blame their condition on external factors while the employed are relatively more inclined to appeal to internal factors when accounting for unemployment (e.g., Feather & Barber, 1983; Feather & Davenport, 1981; Furnham, 1982a, 1982b; Chapter 6). But a longitudinal design is again necessary to enable the investigation of possible causal links.

Third, we expected to find differences between male and female respondents on some of the variables we measured. For example, Warr et al. (1985) claim that women tend to obtain lower scores than men on measures of psychological health and that the sorts of activities that individuals engage in during unemployment probably vary according to gender. Their results supported their claim (see also Donovan & Oddy, 1982). It is now commonplace to draw attention to possible gender differences in reactions to employment and unemployment that reflect different gender roles and differences in life situations (e.g., Feather, 1982e, 1983a, 1985c, 1987a; Gurney, 1980a; Tiggemann & Winefield, 1984; Warr, 1987a; Warr & Parry, 1982; Warr et al., 1988; Winefield & Tiggemann, 1985). Consistent with these discussions, we expected to find that female respondents in our study would report more stress symptoms and would rate themselves as higher on external locus of control and lower on perceived power when compared with male respondents.

Details of the samples and procedures used in the study are presented in the original reports (Feather & O'Brien, 1986a, 1986b, 1987). Samples of male and female subjects were drawn from year 10, year 11, and year 12 classes in 15 state high schools in metropolitan Adelaide. These are the last three years of high school in South Australia with the age of most students ranging from 15 to 18. Three main samples were obtained: (1) group A—2976 students who were first tested in 1980 in 10 high schools when they were students and subsequently tested in 1981 and 1982 when they were either unemployed, employed (full-time or part-time), or still at school or in further education (e.g., tertiary studies); (2) group B—480 subjects who were selected in 1980 from two high schools but tested only in 1981 and 1982; and (3) group C—545 subjects who were selected from the 1980 school enrollments from three high schools but tested only in 1982. These latter two samples also contained unemployed, employed, and student respondents. Together, the three samples allowed us to assess and control for testing effects.

In order to assess the impact of societal or "history" effects (e.g., change in government policies, economic fluctuations, changes in the unemployment rate) that might influence changes in the dependent variables across time, a fourth sample of 930 students from year 10, 11, and 12 classes in three state high schools in metropolitan Adelaide was selected and tested in 1982 (group D).

The first test session for group A was conducted in the schools in 1980 with the assistance of the teachers who were briefed beforehand. Respondents in group D (the "societal" control group) also completed the questionnaires at school in 1982. The test session occupied about 45 minutes and respondents were asked to provide their names and addresses so that they could be approached for subsequent testing where necessary. Names and addresses were also selected for groups B and C to enable subsequent testing. Questionnaires were mailed to groups A and B in 1981 and to groups A, B, and C in 1982. Testing occurred during September/October of each year, so there was an interval of approximately one year between successive tests. Reply-paid envelopes, follow-up letters, and phone calls were used in an attempt to increase the response rate. Using the size of the initial school sample as the base, there were 74% in group A who returned questionnaires at their first retest in 1981 and 66% at the second retest in 1982. Group B consisted of those 80% who returned questionnaires mailed to them in 1981; 92% of these respondents returned questionnaires at their first retest in 1982. Group C consisted of those 58% who returned questionnaires mailed to them in 1982.

The questionnaire varied in its format depending upon whether it was administered in the schools or mailed out subsequently (see Feather & O'Brien, 1986a, 1986b, 1987, for details). The mailed questionnaires had a general section to be completed by all respondents and other sections to be completed (where appropriate) by those who were full-time unemployed, full-time employed, part-time employed, or either still at school or in further education (e.g., tertiary studies). The results that I will report relate only to those who were full-time unemployed or full-time employed.

The major variables have been described in detail in Chapter 5. Those that were the basis of employed versus unemployed comparisons over time were as follows:

1. Six differentiated measures of the self-concept derived from a factor analysis. Scores were based upon subjects' ratings of self on bipolar adjective scales presented in semantic differential format. The six scales were called Competence, Positive attitude, Depressive affect, Potency, Activity, and Anger.
2. A number of value measures. These were the three scales designed to measure desired skill-utilization, desired variety, and desired influence in a person's ideal job (e.g., O'Brien & Dowling, 1980); the 19-item measure of Protestant ethic (PE) values (Mirels & Garrett, 1971); and the three-item measure of employment value (Feather & Bond, 1983; Feather & Davenport, 1981).
3. The nine-item locus of control scale (O'Brien & Kabanoff, 1981).
4. A number of measures of affective reactions. These were the Stress Symptoms Scale (O'Brien et al., 1978); the 10-item Life Satisfaction Scale (O'Brien et al., 1978; Quinn & Shepard, 1974); and the single-item measure of unemployment disappointment.
5. The single-item measures of job expectancy and job need.
6. Four differentiated measures of causal attributions for youth unemployment derived from a factor analysis. Scores were based on how subjects rated various possible explanations of youth unemployment for impor-

tance. The four scales were called Economic recession, Lack of motivation, Competence deficiency, and Appearance/interview inadequacy.

7. Background and demographic items (e.g., gender, age, religion, ethnic background, education, and occupation of mother, father, or guardians).

8. Teachers' ratings of academic potential (available for a high proportion of the students who were sampled in 1980). Students were rated as either in the top 33%, the middle 33%, or the bottom 33% as far as academic potential was concerned.

Analyses of the data involving the appropriate control-group comparisons showed that testing effects and societal or history effects were minimal (see Feather & O'Brien, 1986b; O'Brien & Feather, 1989). The longitudinal analyses of the data used $2 \times 2 \times 2$ analyses of variance for a repeated measures design with gender (male, female) as the first factor, employment status (employed, unemployed) as the second factor, and time (e.g., 1980 versus 1981) as the third factor. Time was treated as the within-subject variable. Thus, in each analysis the comparison across time involved a comparison of scores for respondents who were at school with the scores of these same respondents when they subsequently became full-time employed or full-time unemployed.

In order to attribute an effect on a variable to employment or unemployment one needs to demonstrate patterns of change in the variable across time that differ depending on whether subjects subsequently became employed or unemployed. The crucial term in the analysis is the employment status × time interaction term because it takes account of these relative changes. A significant employment status × time interaction effect might or might not be accompanied by a statistically significant main effect of employment status. A significant main effect of employment status that is not accompanied by a significant time × employment status interaction effect would suggest that differences between employed and unemployed groups were present while respondents were still at school, that they were again evident when respondents subsequently became employed or unemployed, and that any changes that occurred across time were similar for both groups.

Three basic analyses were conducted that varied in the time comparisons that were made (1980 versus 1981, 1980 versus 1982, 1981 versus 1982) and in the subjects who were involved in these comparisons. There is not space to present the results from all of these analyses. Instead, in Table 8.1 I present a sample of the results in which the mean scores for the different variables for respondents who were employed or unemployed in 1982 were compared with the mean scores for these same subjects when they were still at school in 1981.

It can be seen that there were several significant main effects of employment status. When compared with those respondents who became employed, those who became unemployed reported lower competence, more depressive affect, and less activity in their self-ratings. Those who became unemployed tended to have lower Protestant ethic scores and to see employment as less

Table 8.1. Results of longitudinal analyses for respondents from groups A and B who were employed or unemployed in 1982.

Variable	Possible score range	Theoretical midpoint	At School (1981)		Employed/Unemployed in 1982		d.f.s and F Values			
			Employed in 1982 Mean	Unemployed in 1982 Mean	Employed in 1982 Mean	Unemployed in 1982 Mean	d.f.	Time (T)	Employment status (E)	T × E
Self-concept measures										
Competence	9–63	36	45.36	43.62	46.98	42.42	1,588	11.15***	19.72***	13.66***
Positive attitude	3–21	12	16.68	16.60	16.88	16.56	1,606	2.35	1.92	0.91
Depressive affect	4–28	16	12.95	13.77	12.56	14.55	1,601	0.59	13.09***	7.48**
Potency	4–28	16	17.36	17.33	17.33	16.86	1,605	0.89	0.44	1.68
Activity	3–21	12	15.36	14.73	15.62	14.17	1,601	0.52	16.30***	8.87**
Anger	2–14	8	7.31	7.20	7.24	7.80	1,603	0.70	1.44	8.19**
Value measures										
Skill utilization	4–20	12	15.88	15.69	16.08	15.84	1,602	3.74	0.85	0.02
Variety	4–20	12	13.10	13.05	13.39	13.29	1,600	7.61**	0.28	0.04
Influence	5–25	15	16.22	16.62	16.44	16.28	1,591	2.97	0.61	0.41
Protestant ethic	19–114	66.5	74.34	72.48	74.26	71.30	1,551	0.62	5.24*	1.11
Employment value	3–21	12	15.87	14.95	15.73	14.97	1,598	0.72	14.49***	0.15
Affective measures										
Stress symptoms	20–80	50	60.76	55.78	61.18	56.29	1,529	1.48	17.09***	0.02
Life satisfaction	10–70	40	48.38	46.90	50.59	45.48	1,583	12.45***	15.70***	15.29***
Unemployment disappointment	1–7	4	5.51	5.32	5.62	5.38	1,602	2.70	6.91**	0.09
Job need	1–7	4	5.90	5.52	5.85	5.63	1,601	0.06	9.37**	1.19
External control	0–9	4.5	5.02	5.39	5.25	5.89	1,562	14.97***	9.78**	1.96
Unemployment attributions										
Economic recession	6–30	18	23.16	23.02	23.06	23.78	1,584	0.28	0.31	4.84*
Lack of motivation	4–20	12	13.61	13.70	14.11	12.92	1,578	2.44	3.79	12.88***
Competence deficiency	4–20	12	14.61	15.10	14.63	15.12	1,579	0.02	2.91	0.09
Appearance/interview inadequacy	2–10	6	7.68	7.69	7.74	7.98	1,596	2.00	0.58	0.95

Note: Due to missing cases on variables, *n*s for employed subjects ranged from 426 to 479; *n*s for unemployed subjects ranged from 107 to 132. Lower scores on the stress symptoms scale denote higher stress.
*p < 0.05; **p < 0.01; ***p < 0.001.
Source: From Feather, N.T., & O'Brien, G.E. (1986b). "A Longitudinal Study of the Effects of Employment and Unemployment on School-Leavers," in *Journal of Occupational Psychology, 59,* pp. 121–144. Copyright 1986 by the British Psychological Society. Reprinted with permission.

attractive (i.e., their employment value scores were significantly lower). They reported more stress symptoms and their life satisfaction scores were lower. They also expressed less disappointment about being unemployed, less need for a job, and their external control scores tended to be higher. All of these differences emerged from the analysis as significant main effects. They were present both when respondents were at school and when they subsequently became employed or unemployed. Most of the main effects of employment status just noted were also statistically significant in the other two longitudinal analyses (1980 versus 1981; 1980 versus 1982) but there were some exceptions (see Feather & O'Brien, 1986b, for details). In the other two analyses there was also a significant difference in self-rated positive attitude, with the unemployed respondents rating themselves lower on this variable.

The main effects of time of testing tended to be inconsistent from analysis to analysis except for external control scores, which showed a consistent increase across time in all three analyses.

As already noted, statistically significant employment status × time interaction effects are required if one is to attribute changes in variables across time to the experience of employment or unemployment. Table 8.1 shows that there were seven such effects. The most consistent effects (i.e., those that occurred in at least two of the three longitudinal analyses) were for the following variables: competence, depressive affect, activity, life satisfaction, economic recession, and lack of motivation. There was no consistent pattern of change for the first three variables for respondents who subsequently became employed across the three longitudinal analyses. Depending on the analysis, mean scores were similar, showed a slight increase, or decreased marginally across time (see Feather & O'Brien, 1986b). In contrast, there were consistent effects for those respondents who subsequently became unemployed. Competence, activity, and life satisfaction scores decreased but depressive affect scores increased for members of this group as their status changed from students at school to unemployed members of the workforce. These results demonstrate that the unemployment experience had some negative effects, consistent with the first hypothesis.

The statistically significant interaction effects for the two attribution variables (economic recession, lack of motivation) reflected the following changes: those who became employed showed a slight decrease in the tendency to blame youth unemployment on factors relating to economic recession but scores on the economic recession variable increased across time for those respondents who became unemployed. In marked contrast, employment appeared to lead to an increased tendency for respondents to blame unemployment on lack of motivation, whereas unemployment led to a reduced tendency for respondents to endorse lack of motivation as an explanation for youth unemployment. These results were consistent with our second hypothesis.

A further analysis that involved variables (e.g., job expectancy, teachers' ratings of academic potential) that were assessed for all subjects only when they were still at school showed that those students who were subsequently unemployed had lower self-rated confidence of finding a job (job expectancy) when they were at school and lower teachers' ratings of academic potential when compared with those students who obtained employment (Feather & O'Brien, 1986b). The analysis also showed that the unemployment rate was higher for those who left school earlier, that is, after completing year 10, when compared with those who stayed at school longer (years 11 and 12). It was also higher for female respondents when compared with male respondents.

What are we to make of these findings? First, they tell us that there were group differences to begin with on a fairly wide range of variables. These differences occurred before our subjects attempted to enter the workforce and they were maintained subsequently. Thus, they were present across the time intervals that were sampled, that is, before respondents left school and after they became employed or unemployed. Most of them emerged as main effects of employment status from the analyses and they encompassed such differences as lower self-rated competence, lower positive attitude toward self, lower self-rated activity, higher self-rated depression, lower life satisfaction, higher stress symptoms, lower PE values, lower employment value, and lower need for a job for those who became unemployed when compared with those who found jobs. Differences also emerged on selected variables assessed only at school (e.g., lower job expectancies and lower teachers' ratings of academic potential for those who subsequently become unemployed). The set of variables that I have described can be thought of as risk factors or predisposing factors for subsequent unemployment. Young people still at school could be differentiated in regard to these variables, enabling one to separate those who were more at risk as far as finding a job was concerned from those who were less at risk.

There were some differences, however, that became more pronounced over time, apparently as a result of the unemployment experience. Unemployed respondents tended to rate themselves as even less competent, less active, and less satisfied with life and even more depressed after they left school and became unemployed. They were also more likely to blame youth unemployment on causes relating to the economic recession and less likely to attribute youth unemployment to lack of motivation after they had experienced unemployment themselves. As noted, the corresponding changes on these variables for employed respondents were much less systematic and, with the exception of the attribution measures, it was difficult to detect a consistent pattern of change across time that might relate to the experience of becoming employed. These various differences emerged from the analyses as statistically significant employment status × time interactions and they provide important evidence for the impact of employment status on the variables that were investigated.

The results that I have reported are robust not only in the statistical sense but also because they were replicated in at least two of the three comparisons allowed for by the three-phase longitudinal design that we used. The design also provided the opportunity for evaluating both the possible effects of repeated testing of respondents and the possible influence of societal/historical factors and other influences that might affect responses over the 1980–1982 interval, independently of the effects of employment-unemployment experiences. In general, however, there was little evidence for either procedural effects or general societal effects and this conclusion is strengthened by the fact that replicated effects were obtained over the time periods that were investigated.

How do our results relate to other recent findings in the literature? The negative effects of unemployment that we found are consistent with the results of cross-sectional and longitudinal studies summarized by Warr (1987a) and with Jahoda's (1982, 1988) contention that unemployment has adverse effects on most people. They are also consistent with Australian findings reported by Patton and Noller (1984) who found, in a longitudinal study of school-leavers, that an unemployed group increased their scores on depression and external locus of control and decreased their self-esteem scores, whereas an employed group showed no significant changes. Note, however, that Patton and Noller (1984) found no differences between their groups on these variables when their respondents were still at school, whereas we did find evidence of differences on some of our variables (see also Tiggemann & Winefield, 1984; Winefield & Tiggemann, 1985). Cochrane (1983) found initial differences in depression between employed and unemployed applicants for the Australian Regular Army, with higher depression for those who were unemployed. Unemployed recruits who underwent an 11-week training program in the army had sharply reduced depression scores at the post-test but no significant change occurred for the previously employed recruits who underwent the same training program. However, there were no differences between the groups in self-esteem either at pre- or post-test. Other studies from the Australian literature on the psychological impact of unemployment have documented adverse effects on psychological well-being (see Feather, 1985c), but most of these investigations have been cross-sectional in nature rather than longitudinal.

How can we explain the negative effects of unemployment that were evident in the replicated results of the present investigation? We can appeal to the various theories described in earlier chapters in this book. I will not attempt to apply these forms of analysis, however, mainly because this longitudinal study was not designed to test competing theories but rather to provide reliable information about the effects of employment and unemployment for a wide range of variables over a two-year time span.

However, some specific points can be made in relation to the main changes that were found. The diminished self-rated activity reported by the unemployed respondents can be interpreted as indicating that the unemployed situation provided reduced structure and purpose in the use of time when compared with the school situation (Feather & Bond, 1983; Jahoda, 1982;

Kilpatrick & Trew, 1985). The changes in self-rated competence and depressive affect that were obtained for those school-leavers who became unemployed can be seen as the cognitive and affective consequences of negative experiences in the job market, as their expectations were reduced by failure and important goals were not realized (Feather & Barber, 1983; Feather & Davenport, 1981). There may well have been social comparison effects on the self-concept as our unemployed subjects saw some of their peers getting jobs while they themselves were unsuccessful.

The changes in attributions that occurred can be related to respondents' direct experience with the job market. Thus, the realities of a difficult labor market as experienced by the unemployed and their knowledge that they want a job and have tried to obtain one would lead them to discount lack of motivation as an explanation for youth unemployment and to shift their attributions towards the external pole. The success experienced by the employed respondents in their search for a job would be expected to lead to a contrasting pattern of attributions with more emphasis on motivation and effort and less emphasis on the external, socioeconomic situation.

Finally, the diminished life satisfaction reported by the unemployed respondents can be related to the fact that they were denied the financial rewards, higher standards of living, and other positive environmental features that can come with paid employment and were excluded from an important role that is assumed to be a normal part of one's experience in a setting that offers the possibility of satisfying some basic human needs (Jahoda, 1982; Warr, 1987a).

Note that the various theoretical ideas that we have referred to are not mutually exclusive but overlap. Moreover, it is important to recognize that there are individual differences in the way people react to unemployment. Some unemployed individuals cope better than others and some may even find sources of satisfaction in the alternative life-styles that they adopt (Fryer & Payne, 1986).

Our findings provided little consistent evidence that the experience of employment enhanced psychological well-being. This is in contrast to the results of recent Australian studies by Gurney (1980) and Tiggemann and Winefield (1984). The latter authors concluded that their results were "consistent with a notion of paid work leading to growth rather than of unemployment leading to debilitation" (p. 41). These studies and the present one differ, however, in a number of respects. We were able to provide replicated findings over three time periods (T_1 to T_2, T_1 to T_3, and T_2 to T_3) and we used a different set of measures, some of which were more differentiated than those used previously (e.g., the subvarieties of self-concept measures, values, affective measures, attributions, etc.). Nevertheless, it is surprising that we found little consistent evidence for the positive effects of the employment experience itself when compared with the previous school experience. We can speculate that in some respects both school and employment serve similar functions (e.g., by providing a structure and purpose to daily life, shared experiences and contacts with other people, activity, opportunities for skill-utilization and achievement, and so forth), though obviously there are also basic differences in the psychological significance of the two settings. The contrasting experiences of school and unemployment may be greater for most young people and therefore more likely to determine differences.

The findings concerning attributions for unemployment are consistent with the results of the studies that I described in earlier chapters that showed that the unemployed are likely to see external factors (e.g., the economic situation, the policies of the government and employers) as important causes of their unemployed condition (e.g., Feather & Barber, 1983; Feather & Davenport, 1981), whereas the employed are more likely than the unemployed to blame unemployment on individualistic factors such as lack of effort (e.g., Furnham, 1982a). The results of this longitudinal study showed, however, that these differences were minimal while respondents were still at school (Table 8.1) but emerged as effects of the experience of employment and unemployment when respondents were tested subsequently. Note, however, that Schaufeli (1988a), using the Causal Dimensions Scale (Russell, 1982), found that a sample of Dutch professional graduates did not change their causal attributions when they actually became employed or unemployed six months after their final exam. There was evidence of a self-serving bias in causal attributions in his sample (Feather, 1983b). Differences between the results of his study and ours probably relate to the differences in the samples and measures that were used and to cultural differences in the way unemployment is managed (Schaufeli, 1988a).

Our results also suggest that those who obtained jobs saw themselves as somewhat more active and motivated as far as commitment to employment was concerned. The various analyses showed that the subsequently employed respondents scored higher both at school and on the post-tests on self-rated activity, job need, employment value, unemployment disappointment, and Protestant ethic (PE) values. These various findings indicate that there were some motivational and attitude differences between those who obtained jobs and those who became unemployed, though in all of the analyses the measures of employment value, unemployment disappointment, and job need were high when compared with the midpoints of the respective scales, indicating relatively strong commitment to enter or remain in the workforce (see Table 8.1).

Finally, we turn to the question of gender differences. Table 8.2 presents a sample of these results. The consistent gender differences that we obtained were as follows: male respondents tended to score higher on self-rated potency and desired skill-utilization and influence in one's job; female respondents tended to score higher on self-rated positive attitude, stress symptoms, unemployment disappointment, and external control. They were also more likely than male respondents to blame youth unemployment on socioeconomic conditions (economic recession). Male respondents had higher self-rated confidence about finding a job (i.e., higher job expectancies) when they were at school but teachers' ratings of their academic potential tended to be lower when compared with the ratings obtained by female students.

Table 8.2. Mean scores from cross-sectional analyses for employed and unemployed male and female respondents in 1981.

MEAN SCORES IN 1981

Variable	Males		Females		d.f.	F values		
	Employed	Unemployed	Employed	Unemployed		Sex (S)	Employment status (E)	S × E
Self-Concept Measures								
Competence	47.36	44.00	47.20	42.97	1,644	0.25	22.89***	0.29
Positive attitude	16.63	15.65	17.38	17.42	1,659	22.53***	2.64	4.07*
Depressive affect	12.05	13.12	11.66	12.97	1,657	1.06	7.81**	0.08
Potency	18.43	18.62	14.55	15.26	1,657	177.23***	1.78	0.51
Activity	15.59	14.14	15.96	13.99	1,657	1.17	30.02***	0.66
Anger	7.09	7.43	7.08	7.49	1,657	0.00	2.53	0.02
Value Measures								
Skill utilization	15.95	16.35	15.53	15.22	1,653	8.24**	0.00	2.01
Variety	12.82	12.67	12.93	12.97	1,654	0.47	0.03	0.13
Influence	16.30	17.16	15.74	15.71	1,650	6.87**	1.03	1.54
Protestant ethic	75.24	70.31	74.17	73.13	1,613	0.14	5.84*	2.82
Employment value	15.56	15.10	15.56	16.03	1,650	0.52	0.04	2.43
Affective Measures								
Stress symptoms	63.10	60.96	57.59	54.72	1,609	47.73***	6.04*	0.12
Life satisfaction	50.41	48.76	52.86	47.75	1,637	6.22*	14.95***	3.30
Unemployment disappointment	5.29	5.02	5.79	5.51	1,655	25.83***	5.05*	0.00
Job need	5.80	5.35	5.89	5.64	1,650	1.64	7.44**	0.63
External control	5.10	4.98	5.35	5.07	1,630	2.51	1.42	0.20
Unemployment Attributions								
Economic recession	22.31	23.72	23.33	23.72	1,637	7.21**	4.62*	1.68
Lack of motivation	14.41	11.79	14.43	12.93	1,643	0.77	36.79***	2.87
Competence deficiency	14.40	14.32	15.13	15.77	1,650	11.69***	1.03	1.23
Appearance/interview inadequacy	7.78	7.18	8.04	7.81	1,651	5.94*	5.21*	1.15

Note: Due to missing cases on variables, ns for the employed group ranged from 510 to 552 and for the unemployed group from 119 to 128. Lower scores on the stress symptoms scale denote higher stress.

*$p < 0.05$; **$p < 0.01$; ***$p < 0.001$.

Source: From Feather, N.T., & O'Brien, G.E. (1986b). "A Longitudinal Study of the Effects of Employment and Unemployment on School-Leavers," in Journal of Occupational Psychology, 59, pp. 121–144. Copyright 1986 by the British Psychological Society. Reprinted with permission.

The gender differences in potency, external control, and stress symptoms were consistent with our third hypothesis. They agree with previous results. For example, I found that female students were higher in external control in the study with secondary school students from state and independent schools (Feather, 1983a; Chapter 6; see also O'Brien & Kabanoff, 1981). The female respondents in the present study saw themselves as less in control of their lives and less powerful and they were less confident about finding employment, despite the more positive ratings for academic potential that they received from their teachers. Warr et al. (1985) reported that women typically obtain lower scores than men on measures of psychological health. The fact that the female respondents reported experiencing stress symptoms more frequently is consistent with the findings that Warr et al. report. The higher scores for male respondents on desired influence in the workplace probably reflect male gender-role characteristics in that men in general tend to describe themselves as more assertive and independent than do women (Antill, Bussey, & Cunningham, 1985; Spence & Helmreich, 1978). These differences become incorporated into individual value systems and self-concepts and one would expect them to influence preferences and behavior in particular situations such as the workplace (Feather, 1984a, 1987a; Feather & Said, 1983; Warr & Parry, 1982).

Transitions Between Employment and Unemployment

The findings that were described in the previous section compared the scores on a range of variables for respondents when they were still at school with the scores of the same respondents one year later when they were either in full-time paid employment or unemployed. The data analysis showed that the experience of unemployment influenced changes on some variables, especially those that pertained to self-rated competence, activity, depressive affect, and satisfaction with life, where changes were in the direction of reduced psychological well-being and diminished self-regard. Explanations of youth unemployment were also affected by the employment/unemployment experience. For some variables, however, differences between those who found jobs and those who failed to gain employment were not affected by the subsequent experience of employment or unemployment. The results therefore provided evidence for the psychological impact of unemployment in regard to changes on some variables. At the same time, however, they caution us against treating school-leavers as a homogeneous population while they are still at school, given the stable differences that were found between the employed and unemployed groups both at school and on the subsequent post-tests.

The data set obtained from our longitudinal study is a very rich one and it provides a basis for investigating many different kinds of questions. We have also analyzed the data with a view to finding whether or not different patterns of employment and unemployment have different effects on individuals

(Feather & O'Brien, 1986a). Do the effects of unemployment differ for those who become unemployed after holding a job when compared with those who were also unemployed on a previous occasion? Conversely, do the effects of employment differ for those who become employed after a period of unemployment when compared with those who were also employed on a previous occasion? Are differences between employed and unemployed individuals most apparent when individuals with a pattern of consistent unemployment are compared with individuals with a pattern of consistent employment than when comparisons involve different degrees of employment and unemployment?

What kinds of effects might be predicted? Jackson et al. (1983) and Warr and Jackson (1985) have recently reported evidence that is relevant to the question of the effects of changes in employment status on psychological well-being. Jackson et al. (1983) conducted a longitudinal analysis of data from two separate cohorts of lower qualified 16-year-olds who had left school in a large northern city in England and who were interviewed on two or three subsequent occasions. They found that a shift from unemployment to employment over two testing occasions was accompanied by a reduction in psychological distress as measured by the General Health Questionnaire (GHQ; Goldberg, 1972), while a shift from employment to unemployment was accompanied by an increase in psychological distress. They also found that distress scores for those who were either employed or unemployed on two testing occasions were very similar on each pair of occasions but the distress scores were much higher for those who were unemployed than for those who were employed.

Evidence concerning the effects of changes in employment status also comes from a recent study by Warr and Jackson (1985). They reinterviewed a large sample of men in Britain nine months after a first interview in which they obtained measures of psychological health and commitment to the labor market. Warr and Jackson (1985) found some evidence of deterioration in psychological health as measured by the GHQ but only for a subsample that had been unemployed for less than three months at the time of the first interview and who remained continuously unemployed. These results suggested that unemployment has its major effect on psychological health in the first few months after job loss. All measures of health showed large improvements for those regaining paid work by the time of the second interview.

On the basis of the findings from these two studies and other investigations of job loss (e.g., Cobb & Kasl, 1977; Cohn, 1978), we expected that movement from employment to unemployment among our school-leavers would be accompanied by negative effects of various kinds (e.g., more stress, reduced life satisfaction) and that the reverse transition from unemployment to employment would lead to changes in the positive direction (e.g., less stress, increased life satisfaction). We also expected that there would be more evidence of positive advantage among school-leavers who were employed on both testing occasions when compared with those who were unemployed on both testing occasions.

Table 8.3 presents the mean change scores from 1981 to 1982 for four subgroups (employed-employed, employed-unemployed, unemployed-employed, unemployed-unemployed) defined according to their employment status in 1981 and 1982. The means of the scores on each variable from which the change scores were derived are presented in the original report (Feather & O'Brien, 1986a).

The change scores were analyzed by using a $2 \times 2 \times 2$ analysis of variance with gender of subject (male, female) as the first factor in the analysis, employment status in 1981 (employed, unemployed) as the second factor, and whether or not a respondent had changed status from 1981 to 1982 (same, different) as the third factor. A similar type of analysis was used by Jackson et al. (1983). We expected that change to a different employment status from 1981 to 1982 would be positive for measures related to psychological well-being (e.g., fewer stress symptoms, more life satisfaction) when the change was from unemployment to employment, and negative (e.g., more stress symptoms, less life satisfaction) when the change was from employment to unemployment. Hence the primary focus was on the interaction term from each analysis of variance relating to the initial status $\times$ change interaction.

As Table 8.3 shows, very few of these interactions were statistically significant. Those that were significant at conventional levels concerned causal attributions for youth unemployment. A change from employment to unemployment was accompanied by an increased attribution of youth unemployment to socioeconomic causes and decreased attributions to lack of motivation and appearance/interview inadequacy. A change from unemployment to employment was accompanied by the reverse pattern. Respondents in this subgroup were less likely to attribute youth unemployment to socioeconomic causes and more likely to blame it on lack of motivation and appearance/interview inadequacy.

Protestant ethic scores, life satisfaction scores, and unemployment disappointment scores tended to decrease with a shift from employment to unemployment and to increase with a shift from unemployment to employment. In these cases, however, significant levels for the interaction term ($p < 0.10$) only approached conventional levels of statistical significance.

These effects are weaker than those that I reported in the previous section where the transition was from school to paid employment or from school to unemployment. They were also weaker when compared with the adverse effects of unemployment on psychological well-being found by Jackson et al. (1983). Why did these differences occur? In regard to the former difference, I can only speculate that the different forms of analysis involved samples of young people who differed in regard to important variables. Those who left school and could not find a job may have scored lower on some of the key indicators of self-concept and affective well-being when compared with those who were at least able to find paid employment, and these differences may have persisted despite subsequent events. Alternatively, it may be the case that, for whatever reason, some transitions are more dramatic in their effects than others as far as young people are concerned. Shifts from employment to

Table 8.3. Results of ANOVA of change scores.

| Variable | MEAN CHANGE SCORES FOR SUBGROUPS | | | | d.f. | F Values |
| | Employed in 1981 | | Unemployed in 1981 | | | Initial status × status change interaction |
	Same status in 1982 (E–E)	Different status in 1982 (E–U)	Same status in 1982 (U–U)	Different status in 1982 (U–E)		
Self-Concept Measures						
Competence	0.36	−0.74	2.42	0.67	1,485	0.04
Positive attitude	−0.00	0.08	−0.35	−0.02	1,500	0.10
Depressive affect	0.43	0.54	0.74	0.66	1,494	0.02
Potency	0.26	0.13	0.08	−0.12	1,498	0.01
Activity	−0.22	−1.17	0.55	0.71	1,499	1.59
Anger	0.21	0.92	0.13	0.12	1,499	0.92
Value Measures						
Skill utilization	0.03	0.50	0.08	0.05	1,496	0.43
Variety	0.21	1.13	0.03	−0.02	1,494	0.95
Influence	0.40	1.25	−0.08	0.15	1,486	0.27
Protestant ethic	0.48	−2.90	2.41	4.62	1,446	3.30*
Employment value	0.05	−0.79	0.52	−0.53	1,483	0.01
Affective Measures						
Stress symptoms	−0.83	1.52	−0.92	−0.51	1,432	0.44
Life satisfaction	−0.58	−2.24	−2.25	1.14	1,473	3.06*
Unemployment disappointment	0.07	−0.46	0.20	0.41	1,491	3.45*
Job need	0.11	0.08	0.24	0.15	1,487	0.07
External control	−0.01	0.57	0.23	−0.03	1,460	1.76

Unemployment Attributions						
Economic recession	0.23	1.25	0.67	−1.05	1,468	5.12**
Lack of motivation	0.29	−2.23	0.21	1.63	1,479	16.28***
Competence deficiency	−0.07	−0.71	0.56	0.46	1,483	0.31
Appearance/interview inadequacy	−0.14	−0.54	0.02	0.82	1,485	4.04**

Note: A negative change on the stress symptoms scale denotes increased stress.

$*p < 0.10; **p < 0.05; ***p < 0.001.$

Source: From Feather, N.T., & O'Brien, G.E. (1986a), "A Longitudinal Analysis of the Effects of Different Patterns of Employment and Unemployment on School-Leavers," in *British Journal of Psychology, 77,* pp. 459–479. Copyright 1986 by the British Psychological Society. Reprinted with permission.

unemployment may not be as dramatic as some other transitions because young people are still in the process of formulating the direction that they want their lives to take and movement between jobs may be seen as a normal part of this process.

The fact that our results were not as strong as those obtained by Jackson et al. (1983) may also relate to sample differences, given the fact that they studied less-qualified young people whereas we sampled from a population with a wider range of ability. The difference in results may also be a function of the measures used. For example, Jackson et al. (1983) used the 12-item version of the GHQ as their measure of psychological well-being. This measure was devised for assessing through self-report the probability of minor psychiatric disorders. It samples a variety of possible reactions that a person might recently have experienced (e.g., lack of concentration, lack of sleep, unhappiness, decision problems, loss of confidence, strain, feelings of worthlessness, diminished confidence, difficulties in coping). Hence it is related to a person's immediate life situation. The variable in our study that was probably closest conceptually to the GHQ was present life satisfaction (e.g., whether one's life is boring or interesting, useless or worthwhile, full or empty, disappointing or rewarding, friendly or lonely). We found that our respondents reported diminished life satisfaction with a shift to unemployment when the shift was from school (Table 8.1) and from employment (Table 8.2). So this measure was sensitive to the unemployment experience just as Jackson et al. (1983) found the GHQ to be. Both measures are keyed to the way individuals feel about their current life situation.

Other measures from our study may have been less sensitive to change across the one-year time interval that was used. For example, the value measures may have related to relatively stable features of the person (e.g., Protestant ethic values) or to relatively stable ideals (e.g., desired levels of skill use, influence and variety in one's ideal job), and they may have been less amenable to change than affective states that are more closely related to the immediate conditions of a person's life (Feather, 1989b). Warr (1984c) suggests that types of psychological well-being may be classified into less constant features and more constant features and simultaneously into positive, negative, and global types of well-being. Among the measures we used, present life satisfaction would qualify as a less constant global aspect of well-being while our self-concept and value measures would tend to fall into the more constant class. Warr and his colleagues appear to have given more emphasis to the less constant features of psychological well-being in their research program. The GHQ, for example, is a measure of less constant negative well-being and ratings of strain and pleasure (Warr & Payne, 1982) also relate to less stable aspects of experience. Warr (1984c) reports that while unemployed people have lower psychological well-being in respect of the less constant features, the pattern of results is much more variable in respect of the more constant features of well-being such as self-esteem. According to Warr (1984c), findings to date suggest that unemployment affects negative self-esteem (e.g.

Feather & Bond, 1983; Warr & Jackson, 1983) but not positive or global self-esteem (e.g. Feather & Bond, 1983; Hartley, 1980; Warr & Jackson, 1983), although he qualifies the latter conclusion by indicating that studies of the unemployed over much longer time periods need to be conducted (see also my discussion in Chapter 7).

Changes in the more stable aspects of self will probably depend upon the particular experiences that a person undergoes and the way these experiences are interpreted. A person's self-perception of competence may be preserved, for example, despite repeated failure to get a job, if that person continues to blame the external economic situation for his or her unemployed condition. The person could maintain a low expectation of finding employment yet still have a sense of competence because unemployment is attributed to the external situation. The attribution findings from the present study are of particular interest in this regard. Shifts from employment to unemployment or vice versa led to predictable changes in the degree to which current youth unemployment was attributed to the economic recession, lack of motivation, and appearance/interview inadequacies. The changes that occurred were such as to preserve or enhance a positive view of self because those moving to employment became more internal in their attributions for youth unemployment and those moving to unemployment became more external. If, however, a person were to remain unemployed over a long period of time, despite repeated efforts to obtain employment, and if that person saw that most others who were similar in many respects to self were finally able to get a job, then that person's own causal attributions for being unemployed may shift from external to internal and self may be seen as deficient in competence and ability. Under these conditions one would expect to find self-esteem deficits, associated depressive symptoms, and feelings of hopelessness and helplessness (Feather & Barber, 1983). A negative view of self might also develop when the unemployed come to believe that others despise and deprecate them for their failure to find a job (Breakwell, Collie, Harrison, & Propper, 1984). Note that we did find evidence in the present study that the shift from school to unemployment was associated with decrements in three of the differentiated aspects of the self-concept, namely, self-rated competence, self-rated depressive affect, and self-rated activity.

Moderating Effects

Analyses were also conducted to determine whether employment commitment had moderating effects on any of the variables that were assessed in our longitudinal study when employed and unemployed samples were compared. I noted some of the evidence for such moderating effects in Chapter 7 in regard to our previous studies (Feather & Barber, 1983; Feather & Bond, 1983; Feather & Davenport, 1981). Thus, Feather and Davenport (1981) found that ratings of depressive feelings about unemployment were positively correlated with a measure of employment value (or how attractive and important work or employment was seen to be by respondents in their unemployed sample). Feather and Barber (1983) found that the addition of a measure of employment importance to the regression equation significantly incremented the variance in measures of unemployment disappointment and depressive symptoms for a young unemployed group. Feather and Bond (1983) subsequently found a positive correlation in a sample of young employed graduates between the same measure of employment value and the extent to which these employed respondents saw their use of time as structured and purposeful. In contrast, the correlation between employment value and the use of time measure was negative for a sample of young unemployed graduates. The more these young unemployed people saw employment as important for themselves, the less likely were they to see their use of time in a positive light. Those with higher employment value scores in the unemployed group were also more likely to report lower self-esteem and a higher frequency of depressive symptoms but the correlations between employment value and these two variables (self-esteem and depressive symptoms) were nonsignificant for the employed sample. Warr (1987a) has summarized some of the recent evidence that supports the conclusion that employment commitment has a moderating effect on psychological well-being for unemployed groups.

The Jackson et al. (1983) study provides an example of the moderating effects of employment commitment for samples of young people. Jackson et al. (1983) found that the changes in distress levels that they observed were moderated by employment commitment (or the degree to which a person wants to be engaged in paid employment). Larger increases in psychological distress as assessed by the GHQ occurred for high-commitment people who became unemployed and larger decreases were found for high-commitment people who become employed when the employment commitment scale described by Warr et al. (1979) was used. Cross-sectional findings from their study also provided consistent evidence across occasions and cohorts for the moderating effects of employment commitment. For employed groups, those who were higher in employment commitment tended to report lower levels of psychological distress but for unemployed groups higher employment commitment scores were positively associated with levels of psychological distress (see also Stafford et al., 1980). Warr & Jackson (1985) also found that increases in psychological ill-health as measured by the GHQ were positively related to employment commitment scores for their sample of continuously unemployed men. However, employment commitment had no impact on changes following reemployment, in contrast to the results of the Jackson et al. (1983) study. Hence, there is some inconsistency in these results, at least in regard to the moderating effects of employment commitment when there is a change from unemployment to employment.

We continued this line of research by examining the possible moderating effects of need for a job, employment value, and Protestant ethic values on measures of psychological well-being for both employed and unemployed groups. Although these measures differ in their item content and probably in some of their underlying dimensions, each may be assumed to tap aspects of employment commitment or the degree to which a person wants to be engaged in paid employment. In line with the Jackson et al. (1983) findings, we expected all three variables to have similar moderating effects with high levels on the variables being positively associated with psychological well-being for the employed sample and negatively associated with psychological well-being for the unemployed sample. Also in line with the Jackson et al. (1983) findings, we expected that higher levels on each variable would amplify increases in psychological well-being when employment status changed from unemployed to employed and would also amplify decreases in psychological well-being when employment status changed from employed to unemployed.

The relevant correlations are presented in Table 8.4 separately for employed and unemployed respondents in 1981. The results are surprising. In contrast to the Jackson et al. (1983) findings, there was no consistent evidence that any of the measures that were assumed to reflect employment importance moderated psychological well-being across the employed and unemployed groups so as to produce relations that differed in their sign. For example, life satisfaction scores were not positively correlated with job need, Protestant ethic values, and employment value for the employed group and negatively correlated with these variables for the unemployed group. Instead, the correlations were positive and statistically significant for both groups. Similar patterns of significant positive correlations consistently occurred for competence, positive attitude, activity, desired skill utilization in one's job, unemployment disappointment, and lack of motivation, while significant negative correlations were evident for depressive affect and external control. Thus, irrespective of group, there was a tendency for respondents with higher scores on job need, Protestant ethic values, or employment value to rate themselves as higher on competence, positive attitude towards self, activity, desired skill utilization in one's job, life satisfaction, and unemployment disappointment, and to rate themselves as lower on external control and depressive affect when compared with respondents whose scores on job need, Protestant ethic values, or employment value were lower. The former respondents were also more likely to blame unemployment on lack of motivation when compared with respondents with lower levels of job need, Protestant ethic values, and employment value.

Note also that the intercorrelations between job need, Protestant ethic values, and employment value were all positive and statistically significant, supporting the assumption that the three measures could be taken as reflecting in part the importance of obtaining employment for the individual, a variable corresponding to what Jackson et al. (1983) call employment commitment.

Analyses of the change scores for each of the four subgroups (i.e., employed-employed, employed-unemployed, unemployed-employed, and unemployed-unemployed) failed to detect any consistent evidence that the

Table 8.4. Partial correlations holding sex of subject constant for employed and unemployed male and female respondents in 1981.

	PARTIAL CORRELATIONS					
	Job Need		Protestant Ethic Values		Employment Value	
	Employed	Unemployed	Employed	Unemployed	Employed	Unemployed
Self-Concept Measures						
Competence	0.15***	0.11	0.19***	0.24**	0.15***	0.30***
Positive attitude	0.14***	0.20*	0.11*	0.05	0.13**	0.22*
Depressive affect	-0.12**	-0.18*	-0.07	-0.26**	-0.05	-0.28**
Potency	0.02	0.05	0.08	0.16	-0.04	0.09
Activity	0.16***	0.24**	0.18***	0.14	0.13**	0.15
Anger	-0.11*	-0.08	-0.04	0.02	-0.20***	-0.13
Value Measures						
Skill utilization	0.05	0.10	0.12**	0.14	0.22***	0.19*
Variety	0.03	-0.08	0.04	-0.12	0.03	0.12
Influence	0.02	-0.04	-0.09*	0.06	0.00	-0.00
Protestant ethic	0.26***	0.30***	—	—	0.27***	0.48***
Employment value	0.22***	0.33***	0.27***	0.48***	—	—
Affective Measures						
Stress symptoms	-0.00	0.07	0.07	-0.20*	0.05	-0.02
Life satisfaction	0.11*	0.11	0.13**	0.29**	0.11*	0.26**
Unemployment disappointment	0.36***	0.36***	0.24***	0.15	0.24***	0.19*
Job need	—	—	0.26***	0.30***	0.22***	0.33***
External control	-0.04	-0.09	-0.23***	-0.09	-0.15***	-0.17

Unemployment Attributions						
Economic recession	0.06	0.01	−0.13**	0.06	0.03	0.10
Lack of motivation	0.17***	0.24**	0.29***	0.34***	0.08	0.18
Competence deficiency	0.09*	0.05	0.07	0.13	0.12**	0.09
Appearance/interview inadequacy	0.19***	0.07	0.07	0.13	0.12**	−0.01

Note: Due to missing cases on variables, *n*s for the employed group ranged from 510 to 552 and for the unemployed group from 119 to 128. Lower scores on the stress symptoms scale denote higher stress. All tests of significance are two-tailed.

$*p < 0.05$; $**p < 0.01$; $***p < 0.001$.

Source: From Feather, N.T., & O'Brien, G.E. (1986a), "A Longitudinal Analysis of the Effects of Different Patterns of Employment and Unemployment on School-Leavers," in *British Journal of Psychology*, 77, pp. 459–479. Copyright 1986 by the British Psychological Society. Reprinted with permission.

variables that were assumed to reflect employment importance or commit-ment moderated changes in psychological well-being from employment to unemployment or vice-versa (see Feather & O'Brien, 1986a, for details).

This failure to replicate the Jackson et al. (1983) findings on the moderating effects of employment commitment is probably attributable in part to the different measures that we used in our study. The scales used by Jackson et al. (1983) to measure employment commitment and psychological well-being contain some items for which responses are almost logically entailed depend-ing on whether a person is employed or unemployed. For example, agreeing with the item "Work will make me feel that I'm doing something with my life" or with the item "I get bored with no work to do" (both from the em-ployment commitment scale) implies that an unemployed person would be less likely to endorse, respectively, the item "felt that you're playing a useful part in things" or the item "been able to enjoy your normal day-to-day activi-ties" (both from the GHQ). Similarly, an employed person who agreed with the item "If I was out of work I wouldn't feel right" (from the employment commitment scale) would be more likely to endorse the item "been feeling reasonably happy all things considered" (from the GHQ). In all of these cases there are consistency pressures relating to item content that would move the respondent in the direction of the pattern of relations that Jackson et al. (1983) obtained, quite apart from the theoretical expectation that attainment of important goals like getting a job should have positive consequences and nonattainment of important goals should have negative consequences.

The measures we used to reflect employment commitment were clearly different from the measures used to assess psychological well-being and the obtained correlations were similar for both employed and unemployed sam-ples. No moderating effects were found that resembled the Jackson et al. (1983) findings, though such effects have emerged when other variables have been investigated (e.g. time structure, Feather & Bond, 1983). We do not discount the possibility that variables such as employment commitment have moderating effects on reactions to employment and unemployment but pat-terns of correlations can be expected to vary depending upon the measures of commitment that are used and the dependent variables that are being assessed. Note also that the results from the Sheffield group in regard to the moderating effects of employment commitment are not entirely consistent, as I indicated when describing the results of the Jackson et al. (1983) and Warr & Jackson (1985) studies (see also Fryer, 1988; Fryer & Payne, 1986, p. 258; Payne & Hartley, 1984).

The preceding discussion implies that we need to analyze conceptually what is meant by employment commitment. In Chapter 6, I described the results of a single-group study with high school students that showed that a variable called employment importance, defined by variables involving job need, job want, work interest, job satisfaction, and unemployment disappointment, could clearly be distinguished in a factor analysis from helplessness-pessimism about finding a job. The results presented in Table 8.4 imply that employment importance is linked to the self-concept, underlying values, causal attributions, and the affective system. These results therefore inform us further about some of the correlates of employment importance and, at a theoretical level, they enhance our understanding of the network of variables that relate to the motivational concept of valence as applied to the employment outcome.

At a conceptual level, I prefer to conceive of the attractiveness of paid employment in terms of the concept of valence. In Chapter 5, I described a measure of employment valence that was derived via factor analysis and that was based on three variables (job need, unemployment disappointment, and unemployment depression). Clearly, therefore, this measure of valence assumes linkages to the motivational and affective system (see also Lewin, 1936, 1938). This measure has been used in a study of job-seeking behavior that was developed within the framework of expectancy-value (valence) theory (Feather & O'Brien, 1987).

Job-Seeking Behavior

Our study of job-seeking behavior was developed within the general framework of expectancy-value (valence) theory. It will be recalled that this motivational approach relates a person's actions to the expectations that the person holds and to the subjective value of the outcomes that might occur following the action. This kind of analysis has a long history in psychology (Feather, 1959a) and continues to be a dominant approach in the psychology of motivation (see Chapter 4). It was discussed by various authors in my 1982 book, *Expectations and Actions* and new developments and critiques were presented in that context (Feather, 1982c).

As used by expectancy-value theorists, the concept of expectation typically refers to a person's expectations about the implications of actions when behavior is instrumental to ends or outcomes. One should note, however, that theorists have distinguished between different kinds of expectations (e.g., Bandura, 1977, 1982, 1986; Feather, 1982a, pp. 63–65; Heckhausen, 1977, 1986). In our study of job-seeking behavior (Feather & O'Brien, 1987), we treated expectations as action-outcome expectancies (Heckhausen, 1977) that relate to the likelihood of finding a job given attempts to do so. We assumed that these expectations may also become fused with beliefs about control over outcomes. Thus, low expectations of finding a job, reflected in feelings of hopelessness and pessimism, may also be linked with feelings of helplessness about one's potential for changing outcomes, and high expectations, reflected in feelings of hopefulness and optimism, may also be linked to beliefs that one has some control over outcomes and can change them for the better. This assumption was supported by the results of the factor analysis described in Chapter 5 (pp. 99–100) which provided the basis for constructing the measure of control-optimism that we used. This measure comprised the following five variables: unemployment helplessness (reverse coded), desired job confidence, any job confidence, stability (reverse coded), and personal uncontrollability (reverse coded). Thus those subjects with higher scores on the control-optimism variable were less likely to report feeling helpless, more likely to report that they were confident about finding a job, and less likely to see the cause of their unemployment as stable and unchangeable.

Our measure of the subjective value or valence of finding a job was also constructed on the basis of the factor analytic findings described in Chapter 5 (p. 100). This measure comprised the following three variables: job need, unemployment disappointment, and unemployment depression. It will be observed that this kind of measure links valences conceptually to the motivational and affective system. This definition is consistent with Lewin's (1938, pp. 106–107) usage of the term. He introduced the concept of valence to refer to the perceived attractiveness or aversiveness of regions of the psychological environment and assumed that valences could be related to psychological needs and tension systems and to the perceived nature of the object or activity to which the valence applied. Further theoretical developments linked the valence of an outcome to perceived instrumentality as far as "flow-on" consequences were concerned (e.g. Mitchell, 1982; Vroom, 1964), to general human values that can function like needs to induce valences on means and ends (Feather, 1979, 1982b, 1988a, 1988b, in press; Feather & Newton, 1982), and to affective reactions of pleasure and disappointment when goals are attained or not attained, respectively (Feather, 1982a, pp. 70–71; 1982b). Indeed, I have argued that valences are closely tied to the affective system (Feather, 1986b) and that anticipated affect is an important indicator of the strength of positive and negative valences.

How was the expectancy-value (valence) approach applied to job-seeking behavior among the unemployed respondents sampled in our longitudinal study? We developed the following major predictions:

1. Frequency of job-seeking behavior will be positively related to an unemployed person's expectation of finding employment.
2. Frequency of job-seeking behavior will be positively related to the extent to which an unemployed person sees employment as attractive or positively valent.
3. Measures of expectation and valence in combination will provide better prediction of job-seeking behavior than either measure alone.

These three hypotheses are consistent with an expectancy-value analysis of motivated behavior. Some evidence supporting the first two predictions can be found in the results of the Feather and Davenport (1981) study. Table 6.2 shows that the measures of initial effort and present effort spent in trying to get a job, both of which can be taken as measures of job-seeking activity, were positively related to the measures of initial need and present need, respectively, and to the measure of unemployment disappointment. Initial effort and present effort were also positively linked to initial confidence and present confidence, respectively, though the correlations were very low. As noted previously, measures of need and disappointment were components of the derived measure of job valence used in the study presently under discussion.

We were also able to test the following subsidiary hypotheses that concerned variables assumed to determine expectations and valences:

1. An unemployed person's expectation of finding employment will be negatively related to the number of previous unsuccessful attempts to find a job. Research on expectations has consistently shown that they are responsive to success and failure experiences, especially when success or failure occurs on a regular basis (Feather, 1982c). In the present context this implies that repeated failure to find employment should be accompanied by reduced expectations (Feather & Barber, 1983 Feather & Davenport, 1981).

2. An unemployed person's expectation of finding employment will be negatively related to length of unemployment; that is, a prolonged period of unemployment will be associated with lower expectations. This hypothsis is linked to the previous one because it is reasonable to assume that people who have been unemployed longer have had more unsuccessful experiences in applying for jobs than those who have had shorter periods of unemployment.

3. An unemployed person's expectation of finding employment will be positively related to the degree of social support that person receives. The availability of support and understanding from others (e.g., parents) helps to reduce feelings of hopelessness and helplessness so that a person maintains some optimism and control despite failing to find a job. Various authors have pointed to the importance of social support in relation to coping (e.g. Brown & Harris, 1978; Cobb, 1976; Dooley et al., 1988; Kessler, et al., 1988; Lazarus & Folkman, 1984; Pearlin et al., 1981; Schaefer, Coyne, & Lazarus, 1982; Ullah et al., 1985). There is also a growing literature concerned with the measurement of social support (e.g. Cohen & Syme, 1985; Cutrona, 1986; Sarason & Sarason, 1985; Ullah et al., 1985). One way in which social support might operate is by maintaining or enhancing a person's optimism that positive solutions to problems can be found and that he or she has some control over the course of events.

4. The perceived attractiveness of employment will be a positive function of the strength of an unemployed person's work ethic or Protestant ethic (PE) values; that is, employment will have stronger positive valence for individuals with strong PE values than for those people for whom these values are weaker (Feather & Davenport, 1981, p. 434). As noted previously (Feather, 1982d, 1986b, 1987a), general values may be assumed to be a class of variables that influence specific valences. Just as food is more attractive when a person is hungry or a successful outcome in a skill situation is more attractive for a person with a strong achievement motive (Feather, 1982a), so getting a job should have higher positive valence for a person with strong PE values.

We also investigated gender differences in the variables that were measured. As noted previously, studies indicate that there may be some differences in the way unemployment affects men and women, though these differences depend upon a range of variables that relate to nonoccupational roles such as whether or not the person is single or married and has children (Warr & Parry, 1982). Thus, Warr (1984a) reports that studies conducted by the Sheffield research group show that unemployment has the same pattern of negative effects on psychological well-being in male and female teenagers (typically unmarried and without children), although the females generally report lower psychological well-being. In the study described here we were able to investigate whether there were gender differences in job-seeking behavior and in other variables such as expectations and degree of social support received. Some studies suggest that women may be less confident than men and have lower expectancies of success, especially in achievement situations (e.g. Lenney, 1977). Given the emphasis on assertiveness and independence in the male sex role (Feather, 1980, 1987a), one might also expect young men to be less likely to seek and receive social support than young women (Vaux, 1985). It was possible to investigate these predictions in the study under discussion.

These hypotheses were tested in the longitudinal study against the data obtained from 320 respondents (140 males, 179 females, 1 who did not specify gender) who were unemployed in 1982 and a smaller sample of 131 respondents (52 males, 77 females, 2 who did not specify gender) who were unemployed in 1981. All of these subjects reported that they were full-time unemployed.

The major variables that were included in the analysis were control-optimism, job valence, social support from parents, duration of unemployment (number of weeks spent looking for a job), the number of job applications made by each respondent since becoming unemployed, the Mirels and Garrett (1971) measure of Protestant ethic values, and frequency of job-seeking behavior defined by each respondent's answer to the question "How frequently do you look for a job?" Respondents answered this question by checking one of six categories that ranged from "Not looking for a job at all" (1) to "Daily" (6). These variables have been described in detail in Chapter 5.

The detailed results are presented in the original report (Feather & O'Brien, 1987). Table 8.5 presents the correlations between variables for both the 1981 and 1982 samples. Figure 8.1 presents the results of a path analysis that explored the structure of relations for the 1982 sample. Some of the main findings based on the correlations reported in Table 8.5 and elsewhere were as follows: (1) job-seeking behavior was positively related to job valence but unrelated to control-optimism; (2) job-seeking behavior was positively related both to length of time unemployed and the number of unsuccessful job applications; (3) job valence was positively related to the work ethic; (4) control optimism was negatively related to the length of time unemployed (both samples) and negatively related to the number of unsuccessful

Table 8.5. Correlations between variables for 1981 and 1982 unemployed respondents.

Variable	Control-optimism	Job valence	Support	Duration unemployed	Job applications	Sex of respondent	Work ethic	Job seeking
Control-optimism	—	-0.26***	0.12*	-0.26***	-0.20***	-0.04	0.06	-0.07
Job valence	-0.04	—	0.07	0.11*	0.16**	-0.00	0.19***	0.40***
Support	0.14	0.20*	—	-0.08	-0.01	0.16**	0.12*	0.04
Duration unemployed	-0.19*	0.14	-0.09	—	0.45***	0.01	0.03	0.15**
Job applications	-0.13	0.08	-0.13	0.28**	—	0.06	-0.06	0.28***
Sex of respondent	-0.01	0.23**	0.21*	0.10	0.08	—	-0.05	-0.02
Work ethic	0.27**	0.31***	0.17	-0.13	-0.10	0.12	—	0.11*
Job seeking	-0.17	0.30***	-0.11	0.18*	0.26**	0.04	-0.06	—

Note: Tests of significance are two-tailed. Sex of respondent was coded 1 = male, 2 = female. Correlations for the 1982 sample are above the diagonal; correlations for the 1981 sample are below the diagonal.
$*p < 0.05$; $**p < 0.01$; $***p < 0.001$.
Source: From Feather, N.T., & O'Brien, G.E. (1987), "Looking for Employment: An Expectancy-Valence Analysis of Job-Seeking Behaviour Among Young People," in *Journal of Occupational Psychology*, 78, pp. 251–272. Copyright 1987 by the British Psychological Society. Reprinted with permission.

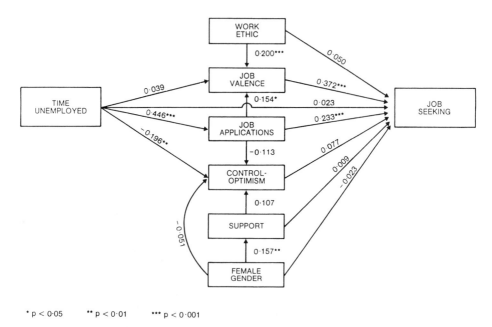

* p < 0·05   ** p < 0·01   *** p < 0·001

Figure 8.1. Path diagram linking job-seeking behavior with other variables. The numbers on the lines are standardized beta coefficients. (From Feather, N.T., & O'Brien, G.E. (1987), "Looking for Employment: An Expectancy-Valence Analysis of Job-Seeking Behaviour Among Young People," in *Journal of Occupational Psychology*, 78, pp. 251–272. Copyright 1987 by the British Psychological Society. Reprinted with permission.)

job applications (1982 sample only); (5) control-optimism was positively related to support received from parents (1982 sample only); (6) number of unsuccessful job applications was positively related to length of time unemployed; (7) support from parents was higher for female subjects when compared with male subjects; (8) job-seeking behavior was positively related to a general measure of negative affect associated with unemployment. Some of these relations between variables were reduced in magnitude by the path analysis (see Figure 8.1).

The results of a hierarchical multiple regression analysis for both samples are presented in Table 8.6. In these two analyses we considered a wider range of variables in relation to job-seeking behavior. In particular, we added measures of social class and teachers' ratings of academic potential as described previously. The measure of social class was based upon the levels of education that respondents reported both parents had completed at school or subsequently and on the status of the occupation of the father (Brotherton, Kotler, & Hammond, 1979). Teachers' ratings were obtained when respondents were at school; they involved teachers assigning students to either the top 33%, the

Table 8.6 Multiple correlations and proportions of variance explained from hierarchical multiple regression analysis.

Step	Independent variable	Job Seeking: 1982 Sample			Job Seeking: 1981 Sample		
		R	R^2	R^2 change	R	R^2	R^2 change
1	Social class + academic potential + age + sex	0.089	0.008	0.008	0.085	0.007	0.007
2	Support	0.101	0.010	0.002	0.136	0.019	0.011
3	Work ethic	0.143	0.020	0.010	0.143	0.020	0.002
4	Duration unemployed + job applications	0.330	0.109	0.088***	0.292	0.086	0.065*
5	Control-optimism	0.330	0.109	0.000	0.315	0.099	0.014
6	Job valence	0.471	0.222	0.113***	0.440	0.194	0.094**
7	Control-optimism × job valence	0.477	0.228	0.006	0.445	0.198	0.004

*$p < 0.05$; **$p < 0.01$; ***$p < 0.001$.
Source: From Feather, N.T., & O'Brien, G.E. (1987), "Looking for Employment: An Expectancy-Valence Analysis of Job-Seeking Behaviour Among Young People," in Journal of Occupational Psychology, 78, pp. 251–272. Copyright 1987 by the British Psychological Society. Reprinted with permission.

middle 33%, or the bottom 33% as far as academic potential was concerned. An interaction term involving the product of control-optimism and job valence was also added to the regression equation.

These results in Table 8.6 are consistent from sample to sample and they reinforce those that emerged from the previous analyses. Only two variables significantly added to the variance accounted for in job-seeking behavior; a history of job seeking as indicated by the combination of length of unemployment with number of unsuccessful job applications and job valence. More detailed inspection of the results for the job history variables indicated that it was job applications that accounted for the increase rather than duration of unemployment. Note that the interaction term did not add significantly to the variance accounted for in the dependent variable. Thus, there was no support for the hypothesis that job-seeking behavior would be better predicted from a combination of measures of expectation and valence (additive or multiplicative) than from either measure alone. With all variables in the equation we were able to account for around 20% of the variance in job-seeking behavior.

Finally, an analysis of data for those respondents who reported they were unemployed in both 1981 and 1982 found no statistically significant correlations linking the 1981 variables in Table 8.4 with job-seeking behavior in 1982. Nor was job-seeking behavior in either 1981 or 1982 reliably predicted by variables assessed while respondents were still at school in 1981. Many of the variables assessed at school overlapped with those assessed subsequently for the unemployed samples (competence, positive attitude, depressive affect, potency, activity, anger, desired work values, work ethic, external control, job need, stress symptoms, and life satisfaction). These negative results indicate the difficulty of predicting job-seeking behavior one or two years in advance of the actual situation of unemployment.

These results are only partially consistent with an expectancy-value (valence) analysis because the measure of valence predicted job-seeking behavior but the measure of control-optimism did not. This is a surprising result because, as noted previously, measures of confidence about finding a job, need for a job, and disappointment or depressive affect about being unemployed predicted effort expended in finding a job in the Feather & Davenport (1981) study. Moreover, studies in other social contexts (e.g., joining a social movement organization, selecting an academic major) have shown that measures of expectation play a part in predicting behavioral intentions (Feather, 1988a, 1988b; Feather & Newton, 1982). There is also plenty of evidence from laboratory studies that expectations make a difference as far as choice, performance, and persistence are concerned (e.g., Bandura, 1986; Feather, 1982c, in press).

In the published report (Feather & O'Brien, 1987), we provide a number of possible explanations for this failure to find the hypothesized relation between control-optimism and job-seeking behavior. Some of these explanations concern the level at which the variables were measured (e.g., whether it might have been more appropriate to develop more specific measures of the expectation variable). It may be the case, however, that relations between control-optimism and behavior are more complicated than we assumed, especially in the context of real-life events. In a recent review of studies on controllability and predictability, Mineka and Hendersen (1985) came to a similar view: "Recent work . . . forces the conclusion that the effects of prediction and control, while orderly, are extraordinarily complicated, requiring analysis at many different levels before they can be properly understood" (p. 521). Once one moves outside the laboratory to investigate the stream of behavior as it occurs in everyday life, variables such as control-optimism may be involved in complex ways with changes in other variables, such as coping styles, cognitive-affective appraisals, ways of explaining events, motivational forces, and the self-concept. Some variables that account for individual differences in responses in constrained and well-controlled laboratory settings may become much less important sources of variance in real-life contexts where there is a wide set of influences and where actions occur in relation to the realities of situational constraints, social norms, task requirements, and other imposed conditions.

Normative variables are taken into account in the theory of reasoned action developed by Fishbein and Ajzen (1975), a theory that also involves expectancy-value concepts. This theory relates actions to behavioral intentions that are assumed to depend not only on personal or attitudinal factors but also on social or normative considerations. Ajzen and Fishbein (1977, 1980) claim support for their approach when the variables in their model are appropriately measured and take account of the action itself, the target of the action, the context in which the action occurs, and the time at which the action is performed. We did not include normative variables when designing our study of job-seeking behavior but perhaps we should have. It is possible that various external pressures (e.g., from parents) may push young people to look for employment even when they have very low expectations of success and feel that they have little control over what happens. Any tendency for young unemployed people to scale down job-seeking behavior because of low expectations may then be counteracted by their compliance with normative pressures to look for a job.

It could also be the case that strong feelings of control and confidence about finding a job may in some cases represent a denial of reality, given the structural socioeconomic basis of much present-day unemployment. Excessive confidence and internality in the face of negative events might then signal failure to adapt and these coping mechanisms might bear little relation to actual job-seeking behavior. On the other hand, some unemployed people may genuinely believe that the economic situation may change and that they will ultimately get the sort of job that they really desire. Their resistance to accepting any kind of job may also be realistically based, given the fact that lowering their aspirations may result in accepting jobs that pay less, have less status, and require more accommodation in their lifestyle. As Liem and Liem (1988) point out, this kind of strategy in which there is resistance to settling for less presents an image of the unemployed person as, "retaining his/her priorities, acting creatively in their service, and contesting the redefinition of his/her status based solely on external conditions" (p. 102).

I have presented these possible explanations for our failure to find a positive relation between control-optimism and job-seeking behavior partly to make the point that the application of psychological models to real-life events is beset with difficulties but worth attempting. Such applications can often reveal gaps in conceptualization that need to be filled. They draw our attention to variables that may not have been fully appreciated. On the positive side, however, our results did support some of our predictions. Job valence emerged as an important predictor of job-seeking behavior. So did the measure of job applications, that is, more past activity in the form of job applications predicted to more current job-search activity. At some point, however, one might expect that a large number of unsuccessful job applications made over a long period of unemployment would reduce expectations to such an extent that some people withdraw from the search for a job. The results also showed that, while job-seeking behavior could be predicted from variables relating to current unemployment, that prediction was unsuccessful when it was attempted with a one or two-year time gap. Thus, in order to predict job-seeking behavior, one needs to focus upon current conditions and concerns rather than on variables measured at a distance (see also Ajzen & Fishbein, 1977, 1980). Finally, we were able to specify some of the determinants of the expectation and valence variables, supporting theoretically derived hypotheses.

There is one further qualification that should be added. I have assumed that frequency of job-seeking behavior can be predicted from measures of expectations and valences within a structural network containing other variables (one possible structure was presented in Figure 8.1). Some relations may, however, be interpreted in the reverse direction. For example, Shamir (1986b) reports positive correlations between a measure of job-search intensity and measures of anxiety and depressive affect and a negative correlation between job-search intensity and morale. We found that a measure of undifferentiated negative affect predicted job-seeking behavior (see Feather & O'Brien, 1987, for details). It is plausible to argue that unsuccessful job-seeking behavior that involves repeated frustration could determine levels of negative affect that become more intense the more frequently a person tries to get a job and that the results just described could be an outcome of this process. One could also argue that the affective variables (unemployment disappointment, unemployment depression) that partly defined the job valence variable were also influenced by this process and, therefore, that there should be reciprocal links in Figure 8.1 between job valence and job-seeking behavior. The complete picture probably does involve feedback loops with affect influencing the actions that are taken (via variables such as valences and attitudes) and the outcomes of the behavior in turn determining particular levels of affect.

There have been other recent attempts to model job-seeking behavior. One possible model has been presented by Ullah and Banks (1985) on the basis of data they obtained from a large-scale study that involved 1150 unemployed 17-year-olds drawn from 11 urban sites in England. The interview included measures of employment commitment, expectations of getting a job, current attitude toward looking for work, and three measure of job-search activity (current job-seeking activity, job applications made in the past four weeks, and number of job-search methods that were used).

Ullah and Banks (1985) related their hypotheses to the expectancy-value approach as discussed by Feather and Davenport (1981) and, following Fishbein and Ajzen (1975), they recognized that it would be important to assess the attitude toward performing a specific act (in this case, job-seeking) as an important predictor of behavioral intentions (see also Banks & Ullah, 1988). They found that lower expectations of getting a job, a less positive job-search attitude, and lower levels of employment commitment were significantly associated with lower levels of reported job-seeking activity for all of the three measures that they used. In addition, they found that long spells of unemployment were associated with lower expectations of getting a job and with a less positive job-search attitude but not with lower levels of employment commitment. So increasing duration of unemployment predicted decreases in an unemployed person's positive attitude toward looking for a job but attitudes towards having paid employment (employment commitment) were not affected by increasing duration of unemployment. Ullah and Banks (1985) also found that longer spells of unemployment were associated with fewer recent job applications and with fewer job-search methods (see also Shamir, 1986b). So, in contrast to our findings reported in Table 8.4, there was evidence of diminished job-search activity (or labor market withdrawal) with increasing length of unemployment. Finally, Ullah and Banks (1985) found that the number of recent job applications made by their unemployed respondents was positively related to current job-seeking activity and that there were some differences in job-seeking activity that related to ethnic background (black versus white respondents).

It will be observed that some of the findings from the Ullah and Banks (1985) study are similar to those of the Feather and O'Brien (1987) study reported in this section. Differences in the results may be due to differences in the populations sampled (Banks and Ullah studied underqualified young people), cultural differences, or other factors. Banks and Ullah (1985) presented a general model suggested by their results (see Figure 8.2). They acknowledged that it may be necessary to build feedback loops into this model. In general, however, their emphasis is consistent with our own in its recognition of the need to take account of the mediating role of values, expectations, and attitudes when predicting job-seeking behavior.

A study by Vinokur and Caplan (1987) with an unemployed adult sample recruited from nine state unemployment offices in southeast Michigan found support for predictions based upon the Fishbein and Ajzen (1975) attitude-behavior model. They found that intention to try hard to seek reemployment

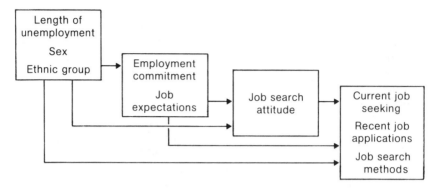

Figure 8.2. A proposed model of the relationship between unemployment, sex, ethnic group, labor market attitudes, and job-seeking activity. (From Ullah, P., & Banks, M.H. (1985), "Youth Unemployment and Labour Market Withdrawal," in *Journal of Economic Psychology, 6*, pp. 51–64. Copyright 1985 by Elsevíer Publications. Reprinted with permission.)

was the main significant predictor of job-seeking behavior in the four-month period they identified. The significant determinants of this intention were the attitude toward job-seeking and subjective norms (perceived social pressure to seek reemployment). Vinokur and Caplan (1987) also found that social support can counteract the negative effects of an unsuccessful job search on mental health, especially among the more highly motivated job seekers. It is evident that the Vinokur and Caplan (1987) study is also congruent with our own in its attempt to develop a motivational analysis of job-seeking behavior based upon expectancy-value (valence) concepts. In their case, however, an explicit attempt was made to apply the Fishbein and Ajzen (1975) theory of reasoned action, incorporating measures of attitude toward the act, subjective norms, and behavioral intentions.

Quality of Employment

The analyses of the longitudinal data that I have described so far concentrated on differences between young school-leavers who found jobs in contrast to those who did not and on variables that influence job-seeking behavior. None of the analyses addressed the question of whether or not the quality of the employment experience makes a difference as far as psychological well-being and other variables are concerned. Not all employment would be expected to enhance self-esteem, reduce stress and depression, increase life satisfaction, or positively affect other aspects of psychological well-being. Mundane, routine, and tiring jobs may have negative effects on well-being, especially where they provide low income, limited social contacts, and poor working conditions and where there is little opportunity to exercise one's skills, experience variety, or exert control in day-to-day activities in the workplace. This point has been recognized by most authors who have considered the nature of work. O'Brien (1986), for example, emphasizes the importance for workers of skill utilization, variety, influence, and control. Warr (1987a, 1987b) distinguishes between good employment and bad employment, and between good unemployment and bad unemployment. He applies his vitamin model, listing nine environmental features that affect mental health, both to the work situation and to the situation of those who are jobless. Jahoda (1982) also recognizes that work environments vary widely in their quality, but still function to fulfil manifest and latent needs. These various approaches were discussed in Chapter 3.

We have conducted analyses of the longitudinal data that distinguish between good employment and poor employment in terms of the degree to which jobs use employee skills. Subjects in our study who were employed were asked to rate the degree to which their jobs allowed them to learn new skills, permitted them to work in the way they thought best, enabled them to use their abilities and provided opportunities for using their skill and experience. Answers were coded 1 to 5 for each item and total skill-utilization scores could range from 4 to 20. This skill-utilization scale has been used in many previous studies (e.g., O'Brien, 1980, 1982, 1983; O'Brien & Dowling, 1980; O'Brien & Humphrys, 1982). Note that it measured actual skill utilization on the job rather than desired skill utilization. We used the median score for employed respondents in all groups as the criterion by which we allocated each individual to good (above-median) and poor (below-median) categories.

The analyses that we conducted were concerned with the relative effects of unemployment and the quality of employment on a selected list of variables (O'Brien & Feather, 1989). The main dependent variables were stress symptoms, depressive affect, life satisfaction, Protestant ethic values, desired skill utilization, desired variety, desired influence, external control, and self-rated competence. All of these variables and the methods for assessing them have been described previously.

The results of our new analyses showed clearly that the positive benefits of employment for young people depended upon the quality of their employment (O'Brien & Feather, 1989, for details). Table 8.7 reports a summary of these results based upon multiple regression analyses. Negative effects of unemployment were apparent when unemployed respondents were compared with those in good employment. The unemployed reported higher depressive affect, lower life satisfaction, lower scores on the Mirels and Garrett (1971) Protestant ethic scale, higher external control, and lower self-rated competence. But differences on these variables between those who were unemployed and those who were in poor employment were negligible. The only difference was in life satisfaction. The employed reported feeling significantly more positive about their lives even though they were similar in regard to the other variables. Those in good employment, when compared with those in

Table 8.7. Group differences on affect, work values, and personal control.

Dependent variable	Unemployed X_1 / Poor employment X_2	Unemployed X_1 / Good employment X_3	Poor employment X_2 / Good employment X_3
Affect			
Stress	No difference	No difference	No difference
Depressive affect	No difference	$X_1 > X_3$	$X_2 > X_3$
Life satisfaction	$X_2 > X_1$	$X_1 < X_3$	$X_2 < X_3$
Work Values			
Protestant ethic	No difference	$X_3 > X_1$	$X_3 > X_2$
Desired skill utilization	No difference	No difference	$X_3 > X_2$
Desired variety	No difference	No difference	No difference
Desired influence	No difference	No difference	No difference
Personal Control			
External control	No difference	$X_1 > X_3$	$X_2 > X_3$
Competence	No difference	$X_3 > X_1$	$X_3 > X_2$

Notes: Group differences were measured using Cohen's dummy variable regression procedure. Differences were estimated by comparison of group unstandardized regression coefficients. X_1 = unemployed; X_2 = poor employment; X_3 = good employment. Predictors are groups (student group as control), initial score on dependent variable, teachers' ratings of academic potential, age, and social class. Criterion of significant difference is $p < 0.01$.

Source: From O'Brien, G.E., & Feather, N.T. (1989). *Journal of Occupational Psychology*, in press.

poor employment, tended to report lower self-rated depressive affect, higher life satisfaction, higher Protestant ethic scores, higher desired skill utilization, lower external control, and higher self-rated competence.

In a related study, Winefield et al. (1988) found that employed young people who reported being dissatisfied with their jobs were significantly worse off in terms of self-esteem, depressive affect, and minor psychiatric disturbances when compared with employed young people who were satisfied with their jobs. Those in the dissatisfied employed subgroup were no better off in regard to these measures than a third subgroup who were unemployed.

The Winefield et al. (1988) findings as well as other results from their program (Tiggemann & Winefield, 1984; Winefield & Tiggemann, 1985) suggest that getting a job has positive effects on some variables (e.g., self-esteem). Winefield et al. (1988) emphasize the positive advantages of good employment for ego development and psychological functioning (see also Gurney, 1980b). They refer to Erikson's (1959) theory of ego development and the role that employment plays in assisting young people to develop their identity as individuals (see also Chapter 4). Not getting a job may mean missing out on a life experience that is important for identity formation and subsequent ego development. Stagnation may occur rather than regression. The young person remains on a sort of plateau instead of moving forward in regard to ego development.

These results contrast with those that emerged from the analyses that I have reported in this chapter. We found consistent evidence for the negative effects of unemployment on some variables but, in our longitudinal study, the effects of finding employment were somewhat inconsistent across the time periods that we investigated. These differences in the pattern of findings between the two longitudinal research programs are puzzling because both studies used school-leavers from Adelaide high schools and were conducted around the same time in the early 1980s.

One possible basis for these differences lies in the different measures that were used. For example, we used differentiated measures of the self-concept based on semantic differential ratings (i.e., self-rated competence, positive attitude, depressive affect, activity, and anger). Winefield and his colleagues used a global measure of self-esteem, the Rosenberg (1965) Self-Esteem Scale. Research has shown that scores on a modified version of this scale tend to increase with age. Thus, Bachman and O'Malley (1977) reported substantial increases in self-esteem (assessed by a modified version of the Rosenberg scale) in a longitudinal study of young American men between 1966 (when respondents were beginning 10th grade) and when they were retested in 1974. Rowley and Feather (1987) found that middle-aged unemployed men were higher in global self-esteem, also assessed by a modified version of the Rosenberg scale, when compared with a younger sample of unemployed males. The results of Winefield and his colleagues are also consistent with a general trend for global self-esteem, assessed by the Rosenberg scale, to increase with age (Tiggemann & Winefield, 1984; Winefield & Tiggemann, 1985; Winefield et al., 1988). Thus, for whatever reason, global self-esteem seems to increase as young people become older; this general trend may make it difficult to identify decrements in global self-esteem as a result of negative life experiences in longitudinal studies where age necessarily varies.

This discussion underlines the importance of having some theoretical understanding of the measures included in studies of the psychological impact of employment and unemployment and for research strategies that identify similarities and differences in these measures. Differentiated measures of self-esteem, for example, may provide better indicators of the effects of negative life experiences than more general and global measures. As I indicated in Chapter 3 there is a movement toward a more analytic treatment of different aspects of the self-concept.

Chapter 9

Studies with Older-Age Groups

The studies that I reviewed in the preceding three chapters were all concerned with youth unemployment because that has been the main focus of my research program. In this chapter I will describe two recent studies that involved older age groups. These investigations were conducted with a view to examining whether the relations found in the research on youth unemployment also occur for unemployed people who are older. I also wanted to study the role of variables such as financial stress and financial strain that were not a focus of interest in the research described so far and to obtain further information about duration effects, job-seeking behavior, and time use after job loss.

I have already observed that one would expect to find that unemployment has different effects depending upon whether a person is just entering the workforce, is middle-aged, or is close to retirement (Chapter 4; see also Spruit & Svensson, 1987; Warr, 1987a, 1987b). These different effects can be related to a whole constellation of age-related variables such as whether or not the person has just left school or has been in the workforce for some time, whether the person is still partly supported by parents or has his or her own family to support, the level of ego development that the person has attained, the financial strain that unemployment imposes on the person, the degree to which the person is familiar with employment and unemployment and has been able to develop ways of coping with negative life events, the extent to which the person has a circle of friends beyond the immediate family, the availability of welfare services and training schemes, and so forth. Many of these variables await detailed investigation for unemployed people at different parts of the life cycle. The two studies that I will describe provided relevant information about some of these effects.

Young Versus Middle-Aged Groups

The first study examined the possibility that age and duration of unemployment may interact so that duration has different consequences depending on the age of the unemployed person (Rowley & Feather, 1987). This kind of comparative research has been ignored in Australian studies. The cross-sectional investigation to be described was an attempt to redress this state of affairs by examining the effects of differing lengths of unemployment for young and middle-aged male respondents. Age and duration effects were studied in relation to the following variables: global self-esteem, psychological distress, employment commitment, perceived use of time, financial strain, and job-seeking behavior.

Much of our knowledge about age and duration effects comes from research into unemployment conducted by the Sheffield group. The findings from these studies indicate that unemployment during the middle years is especially likely to have negative effects on the psychological well-being of unemployed men compared with younger and older age groups and that any adverse effects of length of unemployment will also be more apparent in the middle-age range (Jackson & Warr, 1984; Warr & Jackson, 1985, 1987). Unemployed men in the middle years have different problems from young people who have recently left school and older people closer to retirement (Jackson & Warr, 1984). Their family responsibilities are much greater and so are their financial commitments (e.g., children to be supported, home loans requiring repayment). Paid work is therefore very important to them. Indeed, Estes and Wilensky (1978) characterize early middle-aged men as especially vulnerable to a family "life-cycle squeeze."

The evidence from the Sheffield studies further suggests that the negative effects of unemployment show their most rapid development within the first three months and stabilize after about six months and that these effects are greater among individuals who place more value on paid employment (i.e., higher employment commitment) and who suffer from more extreme financial stress (Jackson & Warr, 1984; Warr & Jackson, 1985, 1987). Warr and Jackson (1987) found that some adaptation occurred in regard to psychological ill-health and nonmoney problems after a long period of unemployment (an average of 25 months continuous unemployment) but that psychological ill-health assessed by the 30-item version of the General Health Questionnaire (GHQ; Goldberg, 1972) remained very high when compared with levels found in employed samples (Banks et al., 1980).

Our own studies of the effects of duration of unemployment have relied upon self-report measures of how many weeks a person has been without paid employment and they have been cross-sectional in nature. There are some methodological pitfalls in this kind of approach. The estimates provided by respondents may be inaccurate and in most cases they cannot be validated. Furthermore, the interpretation of relations between these estimates and measures of psychological well-being is ambiguous. At least two possible interpretations can be advanced for positive correlations between unemployment duration and psychological health in cross-sectional studies. First, there may be a genuine deterioration in well-being that goes on with time and that may stabilize at some point; second, there may be changes in the composition of the sample so that those who are more skilled and healthier obtain jobs earlier and those who are unskilled and less healthy remain in the sample. As Warr et al. (1982) observe, "... groups of people who have been unemployed for varying lengths of time will differ in the mix of 'stock' and 'flow' in a way which is likely to yield differences in important psychological variables" (p. 208). One can control for the latter possibility in longitudinal studies where the same sample of continuously unemployed subjects can be investigated at different time points (e.g., Jackson & Warr, 1984; Warr & Jackson, 1985, 1987). But findings from cross-sectional studies that correlate reported duration of unemployment with current well-being are open to the possibility that significant findings may be due to the changing composition of the sample.

Despite these problems we have examined relations between reported unemployment duration and other variables in a number of our studies. For example, Feather and Davenport (1981) found that measures of expectation, employment value, need, and unemployment disappointment were unrelated to subjects' reports of how many weeks they had been out of work. Reported length of unemployment was, however, negatively related both to the measure of initial effort ($r = -0.14$, $p < 0.05$; longer reported unemployment/ lower ratings of initial effort) and to the extent to which school qualifications were rated higher than those of other people of similar age who were looking for employment ($r = -0.15$, $p < 0.05$; longer reported unemployment/lower ratings of school qualifications). Reported length of unemployment was also positively related to the measure of external difficulty used in the Feather and Davenport (1981) study ($r = 0.14$, $p < 0.05$; longer reported unemployment/ higher ratings of external difficulty). Feather and Barber (1983) reported significant positive correlations between duration of unemployment and measures of perceived uncontrollability and internal attributions for unemployment (see Table 6.3). Feather (1982e) found that reported weeks out of paid employment was negatively correlated with global self-esteem scores and negatively correlated with a measure of job seeking (Chapter 7, pp. 145–146). As I reported in the last chapter, Feather and O'Brien (1987) obtained a significant negative correlation between reported weeks without a job and a measure of control-optimism but there were significant positive correlations between this duration measure and measures of job applications and job-seeking (see Table 8.4).

I noted other results involving duration measures in the preceding chapter (e.g., Shamir, 1986b; Ullah & Banks, 1985). In addition, Warr and Jackson (1985) found that job-search activity tended to decrease with increasing length of unemployment. Other recent findings have been reported by Warr et al. (1982) and Warr and Jackson (1987) for different samples—see Fryer and Payne (1986) for a review of some of these studies. Warr (1987a, pp.

232–233) has discussed the effects of duration of unemployment in relation to his vitamin model.

Considered as a whole, the results of cross-sectional studies using self-reported duration measures are not altogether consistent. One is on more secure ground when studies are longitudinal rather than cross-sectional and when they track the same group of continuously unemployed subjects over different time periods, as has been the case in the more recent Sheffield studies that I mentioned (Jackson & Warr, 1984; Warr & Jackson, 1985, 1987). As I indicated, findings from these studies indicate initial deterioration in affective well-being, followed by stabilization, followed by some adaptation in the long term. But the changes that occur may be restricted to particular kinds of measures (e.g., Warr & Jackson, 1987) and it is evident that more research is needed to examine possible effects over a wider range of variables that go beyond measures of psychological health.

Let us now turn to the hypotheses that were tested in the Rowley and Feather (1987) investigation. Based on the preceding discussion and results presented in previous chapters, we predicted that:

1. Unemployed men in the middle-age range will report more employment commitment, more financial strain, more job-search activity, and more psychological distress when compared with younger unemployed men.
2. Psychological distress and financial strain will increase with increasing length of unemployment for unemployed men in the middle-age range but there may be no relation between these variables for younger unemployed men.
3. Psychological distress will be positively related to employment commitment and financial strain for both age groups.
4. Self-esteem and job-search activity will decrease with increasing length of unemployment.
5. Increasing length of unemployment will be associated with a decreasing tendency for individuals to perceive their use of time as structured and purposive.
6. Higher employment commitment among the unemployed will be associated with a greater tendency for individuals to report their use of time as lacking in structure and purpose.
7. Reports that use of time lacks structure and purpose will be positively associated with psychological distress and negatively associated with self-esteem.

We investigated these hypotheses in a cross-sectional study that involved two groups: young unemployed men (15–24 years old) and middle-aged unemployed men (30–49 years old), with three different levels of reported unemployment duration (less than 6 months, 6 months to less than 18 months, 18 months or more). The boundary of the shortest category (less than 6 months) was chosen in view of the finding from the Sheffield group that psychological distress associated with unemployment seems to reach a plateau after about 3 to 6 months without a job (e.g., Warr & Jackson, 1984).

We obtained our total sample of 107 unemployed males through centers for unemployed people located in metropolitan Adelaide. All were contacted in June/July 1985 and all were without full-time employment (paid work of at least 35 hours per week) at the time of questionnaire completion. No unemployed males were included who had resigned from their last full-time job for reasons of illness. The mean age of the "young" group (15–24 years old) was 20.8; the mean age for the "mature" group (30–49 years old) was 38.9. The young group had been out of full-time employment for a mean of 75.9 weeks (median = 31 weeks); the mature group had been unemployed for a mean of 97.6 weeks (median = 59 weeks). Further details about the sample are provided in the published report (Rowley & Feather, 1987).

Subjects completed a questionnaire either individually or in small group settings in the unemployment centers. There were five sections in the questionnaire. The first section contained questions about duration of unemployment and job-search activity. Duration of unemployment was assessed by asking subjects how long they had been unemployed since their last full-time job (to the nearest week). Job-search activity was assessed by asking subjects to check how many job-search methods they had used (e.g., checking notice boards, examining the "vacancies" section in newspapers) and the number of times they had used each method in the previous two weeks. The number of different methods that subjects checked from the list that was provided to them defined a variable that we called *job-search methods*. The total frequency of use of the methods summed over the list defined a variable that we called *job-search frequency* (see Chapter 5).

The second section of the questionnaire contained an eight-item measure of employment commitment similar to the one used by Warr and Jackson (1984) but with minor modifications to suit the Australian context (see Chapter 5). The interitem reliability (alpha) was 0.85.

The third section consisted of the 10-item Rosenberg Self-Esteem Scale (Rosenberg, 1965) as used in our previous research (e.g., Feather, 1982e; Feather & Barber, 1983; Feather & Bond, 1983; see Chapter 5) to provide a measure of global self-esteem. The interitem reliability (alpha) was 0.82.

The fourth section consisted of the 12-item version of the General Health Questionnaire (GHQ-12), which was used to measure psychological distress (Goldberg, 1972, 1978). The interitem reliability (alpha) was 0.82.

The fifth section contained a five-item scale concerned with the use of time and based upon the Feather and Bond (1983) questionnaire and subsequent modifications to it (Bond & Feather, 1988). Subjects answered each item by using a 1–7 scale (Feather & Bond, 1983). Total scores could therefore range from 5 to 35, with higher scores indicating more structure and purpose in the use of time. The interitem reliability (alpha) was 0.65.

The remaining items in the questionnaire were designed to obtain background and demographic information. A final question was concerned with financial strain: "Thinking back over the past month, how often have you had serious financial worries?" Subjects circled a number on a five-point Likert scale (Never = 0, Hardly ever = 1, Frequently = 2, Nearly all the time = 3, All the time = 4). This item has previously been used by the Sheffield group to measure financial strain (e.g., Warr et al., 1985; Warr & Jackson, 1985).

Table 9.1 presents the results of a 2 × 3 analysis of variance for each of the major variables with age (young versus mature group) as the first factor in each analysis and unemployment duration (<6 months, 6–18 months, 18 months or more) as the second factor. Table 9.1 shows that the older group had significantly higher scores than the younger group for global self-esteem, psychological distress, and employment commitment. Mean scores for financial strain tended to increase with increasing duration of unemployment and reported financial strain was especially high for the older unemployed subjects who had been unemployed for 18 months or more (mean = 3.53). However, there were no statistically significant interaction effects.

The intercorrelations between the variables for the two age groups separately are presented in Table 9.2. The correlations for the younger group are above the diagonal; for the older group they are below the diagonal. In both groups statistically significant positive correlations were obtained between self-esteem and time structure, between psychological distress and financial strain, between employment commitment and job-search frequency, and between job-search frequency and job-search methods. Statistically significant negative correlations were obtained between self-esteem and psychological distress, and between time structure and financial strain in both samples.

When both samples were combined and when age was included as an additional variable, we found statistically significant positive correlations between age and self-esteem ($r = 0.35$, $p < 0.001$), between age and psychological distress ($r = 0.18$, $p < 0.05$), between age and employment commitment ($r = 0.23$, $p < 0.01$), between unemployment duration and psychological distress ($r = 0.19$, $p < 0.05$), between unemployment duration and financial strain ($r = 0.22$, $p < 0.05$), and between employment commitment and psychological distress ($r = 0.33$, $p < 0.001$). There were significant negative correlations between unemployment duration and self-esteem ($r = -0.18$, $p < 0.05$), between age and job-search methods ($r = -0.17$, $p < 0.05$), and between unemployment duration and time structure ($r = -0.18$, $p < 0.05$).

Significant differences were also obtained when the correlations between financial strain and unemployment duration were compared for the two samples (the positive correlation was significantly higher for the mature group) and when the correlations between job-search methods and unemployment duration were compared for the two samples (a negative correlation occurred for the mature group, a positive correlation for the young group)—see Table 9.2 and Rowley and Feather (1987) for details.

These results provide mixed support for our hypotheses. On the positive side, there was evidence of more psychological distress and more employ-

Table 9.1. Mean scores on major variables and results of analyses of variance.

Variable	Theoretical midpoint	YOUNG GROUP (15 to 24 years) Unemployment Duration			MATURE GROUP (30 to 49 years) Unemployment Duration			F Values		
		Less than 6 months ($n = 26$)	6 months to 18 months ($n = 13$)	18 months or more ($n = 20$)	Less than 6 months ($n = 12$)	6 months to 18 months ($n = 19$)	18 months or more ($n = 17$)	Age effect	Duration effect	Interaction effect
Self-esteem	30	40.00	39.77	37.65	43.00	42.95	42.53	12.41***	0.92	0.33
Psychological distress	18	12.23	10.23	13.70	15.33	13.32	16.12	4.90*	2.01	0.03
Employment commitment	24	30.08	26.46	26.85	34.42	29.95	30.53	6.37*	2.81	0.03
Job-search methods	—	3.12	3.23	3.55	3.50	2.42	2.06	4.16*	0.36	2.87
Job-search frequency	—	15.88	14.38	14.67	15.91	8.06	10.00	2.37	1.14	0.65
Time structure	20	23.73	24.69	23.45	26.67	25.58	24.18	1.68	0.49	0.38
Financial strain	2	2.56	2.62	2.70	2.50	2.21	3.53	0.44	3.38*	2.39

Note: ns varied from those listed for two variables, job-search activity and financial strain, due to a small number of missing cases.
*$p < 0.05$; **$p < 0.01$; ***$p < 0.001$.
Source: From Rowley, K.M., & Feather, N.T. (1987), "The Impact of Unemployment in Relation to Age and Length of Unemployment," in Journal of Occupational Psychology, 60, pp. 323–332. Copyright 1987 by the British Psychological Society. Reprinted with permission.

Table 9.2. Intercorrelations between variables for young and older age groups.

Variable	Variable							
	1	2	3	4	5	6	7	8
1. Unemployment duration (weeks)	—	−0.27*	0.15	−0.19	0.13	−0.08	−0.10	0.01
2. Self-esteem	−0.19	—	−0.53***	−0.04	0.05	0.06	0.26*	−0.05
3. Psychological distress	0.20	−0.44***	—	0.21	0.00	0.12	−0.36**	0.28*
4. Employment commitment	−0.11	0.01	0.40**	—	0.08	0.27*	−0.10	−0.05
5. Job-search methods	−0.27	0.05	0.29*	0.30*	—	0.71***	0.12	−0.09
6. Job-search frequency	−0.11	0.19	0.12	0.26*	0.73***	—	−0.15	−0.07
7. Time structure	−0.27*	0.42**	−0.55***	−0.02	0.00	0.25	—	−0.26*
8. Financial strain	0.40**	−0.19	0.41**	0.18	−0.03	−0.14	−0.44***	—

Note: Correlations for the young group are above the diagonal; correlations for the mature group are below the diagonal. *ns* for the correlations ranged from 55 to 59 for the young group and from 42 to 48 for the mature group. Tests of significance are one-tailed.
*$p < 0.05$; **$p < 0.01$; ***$p < 0.001$.
Source: From Rowley, K.M., & Feather, N.T. (1987), "The Impact of Unemployment in Relation to Age and Length of Unemployment," in *Journal of Occupational Psychology, 60,* pp. 323–332. Copyright 1987 by the British Psychological Society. Reprinted with permission.

ment commitment among subjects in the middle-age range than among the younger subjects (Hypothesis 1). Financial strain increased with increasing length of unemployment for this older group but these variables were uncorrelated for the younger group (Hypothesis 2). In both age groups psychological distress was positively related both to financial strain and to employment commitment, though the commitment/distress correlation fell short of statistical significance in the younger sample (Hypothesis 3). Self-esteem tended to decrease with increasing length of unemployment (Hypothesis 4). Respondents who had been out of a job longer were more likely to judge that their use of time lacked structure and purpose (Hypothesis 5). Reports of lack of time structure were more likely to occur among those subjects who reported higher psychological distress and among those whose self-esteem was lower (Hypothesis 7).

On the negative side, however, there was no evidence that unemployed men in the middle-age range were more active job-seekers or reported more financial strain, as had been predicted (Hypothesis 1). Instead, the evidence indicated that the young job-seekers reported using more job-search methods than did the older group. It might be the case that younger people with less experience of unemployment have to learn what methods to use and that they sample a wider range of methods before beginning to exclude some of them. Psychological distress tended to increase with increasing length of unemployment when data for all subjects were combined but there was no evidence to support the prediction that this relation would be more apparent in the older age group (Hypothesis 2). Job-search activity measured by either frequency or methods used did not decrease with increasing length of unemployment as was predicted (Hypothesis 4). Instead the evidence indicated a positive relation between these variables for the younger group and the predicted negative relation for the older group, neither relation being statistically significant. Finally, contrary to prediction (Hypothesis 6), we did not find a relation between reports of lack of time structure and employment commitment. These variables were unrelated in both samples.

The results of the Rowley and Feather (1987) study provided new comparative information about the psychological impact of unemployment on young and older unemployed men in the Australian context. Most of the results were consistent with those found by the Sheffield group and with results from other studies in our research program but there were some exceptions that are not easy to explain. For example, the lack of a significant negative correlation between time structure and employment commitment is surprising, given the Feather and Bond (1983) results. We were also surprised not to find evidence of more financial strain in the older group, given the additional responsiblities that middle-aged men usually have. These kinds of results may be due to sample characteristics, cultural factors, or other unknown variables. For example, our study covered a much wider unemployment duration range and it included a higher percentage of chronically unemployed men than has usually been the case. Also, as I have indicated previously, there is no guarantee when comparing results across cultures that results found in one culture (e.g., Great Britain) will automatically transfer to another culture (e.g., Australia), given the different ways in which governments deal with the problems of unemployment and given the many other differences that may occur (e.g., in cultural values and attitudes, social organization, resources, climate, leisure activities, social support, family structures, ethnic groups, and the legacy of a nation's history).

Finally, I should mention some methodological qualifications that relate to the present study. First, the investigation was cross-sectional in nature. Obviously we need longitudinal studies in Australia that follow mature unemployed people over time, as has occurred in the British studies (e.g., Jackson & Warr, 1984; Warr & Jackson, 1985, 1987) and in studies in Europe and North America (e.g., Brenner & Starrin, 1988; Brenner & Levi, 1987; Cobb & Kasl, 1977; Iverson & Sabroe, 1987, 1988; Linn et al., 1985; Pearlin et al., 1981). We already have longitudinal studies of unemployed young people (Chapter 8) but the mature age group has been neglected in Australian unemployment studies, as has the elderly age group close to retirement. Second, our use of the measure of reported unemployment duration should be viewed with caution, given the problems of interpretation discussed earlier in this chapter. Third, we need to determine whether the age effects that we found have anything to do with unemployment per se. It could be the case, for example, that people in the middle age range generally, whether employed or unemployed, report higher psychological distress, higher self-esteem, and more employment commitment when compared with much younger age groups. This question needs to be addressed in future studies by using employed as well as unemployed respondents in the research design. I noted in Chapter 8 that there is already evidence concerning age-related differences in global self-esteem measured by the Rosenberg (1965) Self-Esteem Scale (e.g., Bachman & O'Malley, 1977; Tiggemann & Winefield, 1984; Winefield & Tiggemann, 1985; Winefield et al., 1988).

I also believe that future studies of age-related differences in samples of employed and unemployed respondents could benefit by closer attention to the literature concerned with changes that occur across the life-span, especially in relation to the self-concept, ego development, and psychological well-being (Chapter 4). There would be value in forging links between research into the psychological impact of unemployment at different ages and the theoretical insights and research findings that are emerging from the area of life-span developmental psychology and life event research.

Reported Behavior Change in Older Men

The second study to be described was mainly concerned with behavioral changes following job loss but it also included a number of other variables, including financial stress and financial strain (Feather, 1989a). As I indicated in Chapter 2, behavioral changes were described in some detail in studies of the effects of unemployment during the Great Depression, and there was recognition that unemployment led to increases in the social isolation of the unemployed and to the withdrawal of the family from many social activities, especially those that required money (e.g., Bakke, 1933; Jahoda et al., 1933; Komarovsky, 1940). Thus, the classic study of life in the Austrian village of Marienthal (Jahoda et al., 1933) was concerned with quite specific activities such as loans from the library, engagement in political activity, and subscribing to newspapers, in addition to obtaining a wealth of other sociographic material.

In Chapter 7, I indicated that unemployment research in the 1980s has also been concerned with the question of time use, some of it fostered by Jahoda's (1982) analysis of the latent functions of paid employment. The general finding that emerges from these studies is that reported difficulty in occupying time increases with unemployment and is positively associated with psychological distress (e.g., Hepworth, 1980; Payne et al., 1984; Warr et al., 1985). In Chapter 7, I described the results of the Feather and Bond (1983) study with the Time Structure Questionnaire (TSQ) in which unemployed university graduates were found to report less structure and purpose in their use of time when compared with employed university graduates and where subjects who reported more structure and purpose in their use of time were found to have higher self-esteem and fewer depressive symptoms when compared with those who reported less structure and purpose (see also Bond & Feather, 1988).

These studies have focused on time use in general. However, some studies in the 1980s have investigated specific activities, either by asking unemployed subjects to keep time diaries (e.g., Kilpatrick & Trew, 1985; Miles, 1983; Miles, Howard, & Henwood, 1984) or by presenting them with lists of activities and asking them whether their involvement in each activity has increased, decreased, or remained the same since they became unemployed (Warr, 1984b; Warr & Payne, 1983). These studies have also examined relations between time use and psychological well-being. Thus, Kilpatrick and Trew (1985) found that there was a progressive decline in mental health (assessed by the GHQ; Goldberg, 1978), in a sample of 25- to 45-year-old unemployed men in Northern Ireland, with decreasing activity and withdrawal into the home.

I continued this focus on specific activities in the present study, using the procedure described by Warr (1984b) and Warr & Payne (1983). These investigators found reported increases in domestic activities and in other pastimes not requiring money for their samples of unemployed men, and decreases in activities that did require payment of money. I expected to find similar results in an Australian sample of unemployed men (Hypothesis 1).

I also predicted that psychological well-being would be positively associated with increases in activities that had clearly defined goals but negatively related to increases in activities that were passive in nature and not integrated into a goal structure (Hypothesis 2). This prediction follows from the results of our previous work on time structure that showed that the structured and purposive use of time is more beneficial to well-being than aimless activity (Bond & Feather, 1988, Feather & Bond, 1983).

Finally, I predicted that unemployed respondents who reported more financial stress and strain would also report lower psychological well-being (Hypothesis 3). Lack of money is a very important source of personal and family problems among the unemployed and this has been well-documented in many published reports (e.g., Fryer, 1988; Warr, 1987a, pp. 217–219). I indicated in Chapter 2 that poverty was also emphasized as an acute problem for the unemployed in the 1930s' literature (e.g., Bakke, 1933). An association between worries about money and being in debt and low levels of affective well-being among the unemployed has been reported in a number of recent studies (e.g., Finlay-Jones & Eckhardt, 1984; Jackson & Warr, 1984; Kessler et al., 1987, 1988; Payne et al., 1984; Ullah et al., 1985; Warr & Jackson, 1985), including the study described in the previous section (Rowley & Feather, 1987).

These hypotheses were tested by using a sample of 42 unemployed men in metropolitan Adelaide who were contacted via a helping organization late in 1986. The subjects ranged in age from 40 to 66 years of age with a mean age of 52.60 years ($SD = 8.03$). Further details of the sample are provided in the published report (Feather, 1989a). The mean duration of unemployment since the last paid job was 75.54 weeks (median = 42 weeks).

Subjects completed a questionnaire that was distributed by the helping organization. It consisted of a number of sections that contained both single items and multiitem scales, many of which have already been described in relation to our other studies. Thus, the 12-item General Health Questionnaire (GHQ-12) was again used to measure psychological distress, with item responses scored from 0 to 3 (Goldberg, 1972, 1978). The interitem reliability for the scale (Cronbach, 1951) was 0.95. The Rosenberg (1965) Self-Esteem Scale as modified by Bachman et al. (1978) was used to provide a measure of global self-esteem, but with a 1–7 rating scale for each item. The interreliability for the scale (Cronbach, 1951) was 0.74. The single-item measure of financial strain used in the Rowley and Feather (1987) study ("Thinking back over the past month, how often have you had serious financial worries?") was also included in the questionnaire.

The new variables were concerned with life satisfaction, quality of life, financial stress, and reported behavior changes. A single-item measure of life satisfaction was used. Subjects were asked: "To what extent are you satisfied with your present daily life?" They were required to circle a number from 1 to 7 on a rating scale that was labeled "very dissatisfied" at the low end (scored 1) and "very satisfied" at the high end (scored 7).

To measure quality of life I asked subjects: "To what extent does your present daily life provide you with (a) the chance to use your abilities and skills?; (b) change or variety in what you do?; (c) the opportunity to influence what happens to you?; (d) a sense of purpose in what you do?; and (e) a structure to the way you use your time during the day. Subjects answered each of these questions by using a five-point rating scale with the following categories: Not at all = 1, Very little = 2, Some = 3, A great deal = 4, and A very great deal = 5. The item scores were added to obtain a total quality of life score that could range from 5 to 25. The interitem reliability for the scale (Cronbach, 1951) was 0.89. It should be apparent that the five items used in the scale were based on the measures of work values used by Feather and O'Brien (1986b) and on our research into time structure (Bond & Feather, 1988; Feather & Bond, 1983).

Financial stress was measured by asking subjects to answer the following seven questions, using rating scales numbered from 1 to 7 with "Definitely not" = 1 and "Yes, definitely" = 7 as the end labels: (1) "Are you able to afford a home suitable for yourself/your family?"; (2) "Are you able to afford furniture or household equipment that needs to be replaced?"; (3) "Are you able to afford the kind of car you need?"; (4) "Do you have enough money for the kind of food you/your family should have?"; (5) "Do you have enough money for the kind of medical care you/your family should have?"; (6) "Do you have enough money for the kind of clothing you/your family should have?"; and (7) "Do you have enough money for the leisure activities you/your family want?" The items were reverse-coded so that higher item scores indicated higher financial stress and then were added to obtain a total financial stress score that could range from 7 to 49. The interitem reliability for the scale (Cronbach, 1951) was 0.92.

To measure reported changes in behavior after job loss I presented subjects with a list of 27 different behaviors with instructions that corresponded to those used by Warr (1984b) and Warr and Payne (1983). Subjects were told: "We would like to find if being unemployed has changed the way you spend your time. Listed below are a number of activities that people sometimes do and we would like to know whether you do more or less of the things on the list compared to when you were employed full-time. Please think back over the past month and indicate by ticking the box under the appropriate response." The response alternatives were: More than when I was employed, Same as when I was employed, Less than when I was employed, and I never do that. The 27 different behaviors were based on the list of activities used by Warr (1984b) and Warr and Payne (1983) and they were presented in unsystematic order. Following Warr (1984b) and Warr and Payne (1983) the items were subsequently grouped into seven categories: domestic work, domestic pastimes, other pastimes, book reading, recreations, entertainment through money, and social contacts (see Table 9.3).

The results that concern reported behavior change are presented in Table 9.3. Column 1 indicates the percentage of subjects who reported that they never undertake a specific behavior, Column 3 indicates the percentage of subjects who reported that they undertake the behavior the same amount as when they were employed, and Columns 2 and 4 present the percentages of subjects who reported decreases or increases in the behavior since job loss.

Table 9.3. Reports of stability or change in each of 27 behaviors following job loss.

Behavior	Never do (%)	Less (%)	Same (%)	More (%)	Significance of change (<)
Domestic Work					
1. Prepare meals for others	28	3	28	41	0.001
2. Prepare meals for yourself	8	5	29	58	0.001
3. Look after children	42	6	22	31	0.01
4. Do household chores	10	5	20	66	0.001
5. Go shopping	3	18	13	66	0.001
Domestic Pastimes					
6. Listen to radio	11	16	30	43	0.05
7. Sit around at home	15	15	26	44	0.05
8. Watch television	8	5	41	46	0.001
9. Sleep during the day	47	18	8	26	n.s.
Other Pastimes					
10. Window shopping (not actual shopping)	34	16	8	42	0.05
11. Read newspapers (other than job hunting)	10	5	31	54	0.001
Book Reading					
12. Read books and magazines	2	10	32	56	0.001
13. Go to classes or courses	37	13	29	21	n.s.
14. Visit the public library	38	5	27	30	0.05
Recreations					
15. Gardening	10	10	13	68	0.001
16. Do physical exercise (e.g., jog, aerobics)	32	24	21	24	n.s.
17. Do repairs and decorating around home	8	11	32	50	0.001
Entertainment Through Money					
18. Go for trips (e.g., country, beach)	15	36	18	31	n.s.
19. Go to the pub or a club	57	27	8	8	0.05
20. Go to the pictures or theater	45	37	16	3	0.001
21. Have a drink at home	29	34	24	13	n.s.
Social Contacts					
22. Attend trade union meetings	94	0	3	3	n.s.
23. Go to church	66	5	24	5	n.s.
24. Do jobs for friends and neighbors	26	5	31	39	0.001
25. Spend time with neighbors	35	14	38	14	n.s.
26. Spend time with friends	16	24	40	21	n.s.
27. Help with charities or do voluntary work	53	3	23	23	0.01

Source: From Feather, N.T. (1989a), "Reported Changes in Behaviour After Job Loss in a Sample of Older Unemployed Men," in *Australian Journal of Psychology* (in press). With permission of the author and by courtesy of the Australian Psychological Society.

The results of *t*-tests for the distribution of change scores for each of the activities are also presented in Table 9.3. For this analysis I combined the two forms of no change (i.e., "Never do" and "Same") and assigned a score of zero. An increase in the behavior was scored +1 and a decrease was scored −1. The mean of each distribution of scores was calculated for each item and the difference between the mean and zero was tested for statistical significance by using the *t*-test. The results of these analyses for the set of items are presented in Column 5.

The results in Table 9.3 are consistent with the first hypothesis and most of the results reported by Warr (1984b) and Warr and Payne (1983) for much larger samples. They show that there were increases in domestic activities and a wide range of other activities following job loss and decreases in activities that required spending money. In fact, all forms of domestic work (items 1 to 5) showed significant increases. Most of the domestic pastimes (items 6 to 8) also showed significant increases, except for sleep during the day which did not change (item 9). There were also significant increases in other pastimes (items 10 to 11), in book and magazine reading and visits to the public library (items 12 and 14), but no overall tendency to increase or decrease attendance at classes or courses (item 13). Recreations that involved upkeep of the house and property (gardening, home-repairs and maintenance, items 15 and 17) increased significantly but physical exercise (item 16) showed no significant change.

Significant decreases occurred for some activities that required spending money. Thus, there was a significant decline in visits to the pub or club (item 19) and in visits to the pictures or theatre (item 20), but going on trips (item 18) and home drinking (item 21) showed no significant change.

Social contacts that involved doing jobs for friends and neighbors (item 24) increased significantly. There was also a significant increase in helping with charities or doing voluntary work (item 27). The other activities that involved social contact, namely, going to trade union meetings (item 22), going to church (item 23), spending time with neighbors (item 25), and spending time with friends (item 26), showed no significant change.

Like the 1930s' studies, therefore, there was evidence that financial deprivation was setting limits to the sorts of activities that the jobless person could engage in but, unlike the 1930s' studies, there was no evidence that the unemployed subjects significantly reduced their social contacts beyond the family, as was reported to have occurred in some of the studies conducted during the Great Depression (e.g., Bakke, 1933; Jahoda et al., 1933). Comparisons between the 1930s' and the 1980s' studies of the psychological impact of unemployment are hazardous, however, given the many differences in social and economic conditions over the past 50 years, the different circumstances of unemployment during the Great Depression, and the increased sophistication that has occurred in research methodologies (Jahoda, 1982).

In order to investigate relations between reported behavior change, psychological well-being, and other variables, I computed aggregate change scores for each of the seven categories of behavior shown in Table 9.3 by adding the change scores (-1, 0, or $+1$) for each item in the category for each subject. The correlations between these aggregate change scores and psychological distress (GHQ), global self-esteem, life satisfaction, quality of life, financial stress, and financial strain are presented in Table 9.4.

It can be seen in Table 9.4 that higher levels of psychological distress were significantly associated with less time spent on each of the following activities: domestic work, entertainment through money, and social contacts. Higher levels of life satisfaction were significantly associated with less time spent on domestic pastimes and with more time spent on social contacts. Those subjects with higher quality of life scores were less likely to report increases in domestic pastimes.

Table 9.4 also shows that higher levels of financial stress were significantly associated with less time spent on recreations and entertainment through money. Note that the corresponding correlations for financial strain were also negative but they were not statistically significant.

Because domestic pastimes and other pastimes were similar in that both involved passive activities (e.g., sitting around at home, watching television, reading newspapers), I combined these categories and computed aggregate change scores for their combination. Aggregate change scores for the resultant category (passive activities) were positively correlated with psychological distress, $r = 0.31$, $p < 0.05$, and negatively correlated with both life satisfaction, $r = -0.28$, $p < 0.05$ and quality of life scores, $r = -0.41$, $p < 0.01$ (one-tailed tests were used to test for statistical significance). Thus, increased time spent in passive activities had negative implications for psychological well-being and quality of life.

These various results support the second hypothesis by showing that psychological well-being was positively related to increases in directed activities that fit into a goal structure (e.g., domestic work) but negatively related to increases in passive activities that were less structured and less goal-oriented. They are consistent with the results of our previous research on time structure (Bond & Feather, 1988; Feather & Bond, 1983; Rowley & Feather, 1987) in that they show that it is not activity per se that seems to be important for adjustment and psychological well-being but activity that is structured and directed toward personal goals relevant to the underlying needs of the individual. They add to the picture, however, by providing evidence based on specific behaviors. In this respect the findings are consistent with those of studies conducted in the United Kingdom (Kilpatrick & Trew, 1985; Warr, 1984b; Warr & Payne, 1983). For example, Warr and Payne (1983) found that for both middle-class and working-class respondents, increases in the more passive domestic and other pastimes had the highest positive correlations with both activity problems (i.e., problems with "Keeping myself from being bored"; "Finding enjoyable things to do"; and "Finding useful ways to spend my time") and with psychological distress assessed by the 12-item version of the GHQ (Goldberg, 1972, 1978).

Table 9.4. Correlations between behavior change in each area following job loss and other variables.

Behavior area	Psychological distress (GHQ)	Self-esteem	Life satisfaction	Quality of life	Financial stress	Financial strain
			Variables			
Domestic work	−0.36*	0.20	0.14	0.17	−0.24	−0.33
Domestic pastimes	0.31	−0.12	−0.33*	−0.45**	0.16	0.08
Other pastimes	0.31	−0.01	−0.19	−0.26	0.27	0.18
Book reading	−0.01	0.03	0.00	0.04	0.15	0.17
Recreations	−0.28	0.25	0.17	−0.01	−0.37*	−0.24
Entertainment through money	−0.35*	−0.05	0.29	0.13	−0.34*	−0.19
Social contacts	−0.54***	0.30	0.42*	0.27	−0.29	−0.02

Note: $N = 42$. Ns varied for the correlations due to a small number of missing cases on some variables. Tests of significance are two-tailed.
$*p < 0.05$; $**p < 0.01$; $***p < 0.001$.
Source: From Feather, N.T. (1989a), "Reported Changes in Behaviour After Job Loss in a Sample of Older Unemployed Men," in *Australian Journal of Psychology* (in press). With permission of the author and by courtesy of the Australian Psychological Society.

The findings in Table 9.4 that indicate that increases in social contacts were positively related to measures of psychological well-being and quality of life measures are consistent with those of other studies that have also reported positive associations between psychological health among unemployed subjects and social support and contact (see Warr, 1987a, pp. 220–228, for a summary). For example, Ullah et al. (1985) found in a sample of unemployed 17-year-olds that respondents who had someone to turn to for money had significantly lower scores on five measures of distress and those who reported having someone to turn to for suggestions about interesting things to do had significantly lower GHQ, depression, and anxiety scores. Warr et al. (1985) found with the same sample that time spent with friends correlated negatively with measures of psychological distress (GHQ), anxiety, and depression; and, in a North American study, Kessler et al. (1987, 1988) found that social support helped to reduce the negative impact of unemployment. We need to conduct further studies that examine the effects of more differentiated forms of social support on the psychological well-being of unemployed people. The results that I just mentioned suggest that financial support and support that helps the unemployed person to escape from boredom and establish goal direction in daily activities may be especially important forms of support.

Finally, Table 9.5 presents the intercorrelations between the measures of psychological well-being, financial stress, and financial strain. It is clear that, consistent with the third hypothesis, psychological distress increased with more financial stress and strain and both life satisfaction and quality of life decreased with more financial stress and strain. As would be expected, life satisfaction was negatively related to psychological distress and positively related to quality of life; psychological distress was negatively related to quality of life; and financial stress and financial strain were positively related. All of these correlations were statistically significant. These results indicate the importance of including economic measures in studies of the psychological impact of unemployment. The economic imperative sets limits to the extent to which individuals can satisfy their basic needs and thereby influences psychological health and adjustment.

I should recognize two limitations of the study being described. First, the sample was a small one when compared with samples used in other similar studies (e.g., Warr, 1984b; Warr & Payne, 1983). Had I been able to use a larger sample it would have been possible to analyze for the effects of such variables as age, gender, and social class. It has not so far proved to be easy, however, to gain access to large samples of unemployed adults in the Australian context, partly because of government restrictions on access to information and partly because some unemployed adults see little purpose in completing questionnaires unless the findings will help them to obtain jobs. Second, to return to a common theme that has been emphasized throughout this book, there is a need for longitudinal studies with unemployed people that include the sorts of measures of specific activities that I used in the present study. The results of longitudinal studies would provide clearer informa-

Table 9.5. Means, SDs, and intercorrelations between variables.

Variable	Midpoint of scale	Mean	SD	Correlations					
				Psychological distress (GHQ)	Self-esteem	Life satisfaction	Quality of life	Financial stress	Financial strain
Psychological distress (GHQ)	18	16.93	9.05	—					
Self-esteem	40	57.48	9.14	−0.11	—				
Life satisfaction	4	3.45	2.18	−0.70***	−0.07	—			
Quality of life	15	12.48	4.20	−0.58***	0.07	0.70***	—		
Financial stress	28	29.43	12.20	0.64***	−0.30	−0.38*	−0.34*	—	
Financial strain	3	2.88	1.15	0.55***	−0.22	−0.41**	−0.42**	0.69***	—

Note: $N = 42$. Ns varied for the correlations due to a small number of missing cases on some variables. Tests of significance are two-tailed.
*$p < 0.05$; **$p < 0.01$; ***$p < 0.001$.
Source: From Feather, N.T. (1989a), "Reported Changes in Behaviour After Job Loss in a Sample of Older Unemployed Men," in *Australian Journal of Psychology* (in press). With permission of the author and by courtesy of the Australian Psychological Society.

tion about cause-effect relations. The interpretation of results is ambiguous in cross-sectional studies such as the present one. For example, did subjects who increased their time spent on passive activities then become more psychologically distressed and less satisfied with their lives because they moved to activities that had little purpose or did they increase their time spent on these activities because they already had low levels of psychological well-being? The ambiguity is less when financial stress and financial strain are the variables of interest. It is much more plausible to argue that higher financial stress determined a reduction in activities involving entertainment through money than to argue the reverse, because such activities depend upon available financial resources.

Whatever may be the case, these results highlight the importance of the availability of money, social contacts, and goal-directed activities for unemployed people. They imply that a life that involves inadequate financial resources, limited social support, and low levels of structure and purpose in daily activities is one that is conductive to poor psychological well-being among the unemployed.

Job-Seeking Behavior: Further Findings

I also included measures of job-seeking behavior in the study just described that were based upon those used in previous studies (Feather & O'Brien, 1987; Rowley & Feather, 1987). Thus, I used the measures of job-search frequency and job-search methods that were employed in the Rowley and Feather (1987) study, that is, the frequency with which a range of job search methods was used in the last two weeks and the number of different methods that were used. I also included a measure of job-seeking behavior that was similar to the one used in the Feather and O'Brien (1987) study ("How frequently do you look for paid employment?"). The response categories were as follows: Not looking for a job (scored 1); Very infrequently = 2; Monthly = 3; Weekly = 4; Every couple of days = 5; Daily = 6. I will call this variable job-seeking activity. A further question asked subjects: "In the next four months, how hard do you intend to try to find a job where you would work over 20 hours per week?" They answered by circling a number from 1 to 7 on a rating scale with "Not hard at all" (scored 1) and "Extremely hard" (scored 7) as the end-labels. I will call this variable future job-seeking.

I examined relations between these four measures of job-seeking behavior and self-reports of how helpless subjects felt about being unemployed, how confident they were about finding the job that was really wanted in the near future, how confident they were about finding any kind of job at all, the extent to which they believed that it was beyond their power to change the cause of their unemployment (perceived uncontrollability), how much they needed a job, how depressed they felt about being unemployed, and how angry they felt about being unemployed. All of these measures have been described before (Chapter 5) and all of them were previously included in the Feather and O'Brien (1987) study of job-seeking behavior. Each measure involved the use of a rating scale numbered from 1 to 7, labeled at each end according to the variable that was being investigated. Duration of unemployment, measured in terms of the number of weeks the unemployed person reported that he had been without a job, was also included as a variable.

Table 9.6 presents the correlations between the four measures of job-seeking behavior, the variables just listed, and measures of psychological well-being described in the previous section. Also included in Table 9.6 are the correlations between the job-seeking measures and a measure of job valence obtained by adding scores for job need, unemployment depression, and unemployment anger; and the correlations between the job-seeking measures and a measure of control-optimism obtained by adding the scores for unemployment helplessness and perceived uncontrollability (after reversal or reflection of scores on these items) and the scores for confidence (desired job) and confidence (any job). These aggregate variables are very similar to the corresponding ones described in the Feather and O'Brien (1987) study of job-seeking behavior.

The results reported in Table 9.6 show that there were statistically significant positive intercorrelations between all four measures of job-seeking behavior (see bottom right-hand corner of Table 9.6). Thus there was reliable evidence relating to the validity of these measures. The results also indicate that the measures of job-seeking behavior were positively related to the measure of job valence, replicating the results of the earlier Feather and O'Brien (1987) study. As was the case in that study, however, job-seeking behavior (here assessed in four ways) was not significantly related to the measure of control-optimism. Finally, the pattern of findings indicated statistically significant positive correlations between the measures of job-seeking behavior and reported negative affect (financial strain, depression, anger, helplessness) and negative correlations when the reported affect was positive (life satisfaction). These results show that negative affective reactions predicted job-seeking behavior, in the sense that those whose feelings about not having a job were most negative were also those who were most likely to be looking for a job (see also Feather & O'Brien, 1987). However, feeling satisfied about one's present life had the reverse effect among unemployed subjects; they were less likely to look for jobs than those who were dissatisfied with their present life.

Were there any statistically significant correlations that involved duration of unemployment? Those who reported being out of paid employment longer tended to report higher levels of helplessness about being unemployed ($r = 0.34$, $p < 0.05$) and higher levels of financial strain ($r = 0.35$, $p < 0.05$). Control-optimism was negatively related to duration of unemployment ($r = -0.27$). Thus, as in the Feather and O'Brien (1987) study, lower levels of control-optimism were associated with longer periods of unemployment duration. This negative correlation would be statistically significant if a one-tailed

Table 9.6. Means, SDs, and correlations between variables and four measures of job-seeking behavior.

Variable	Mean	SD	Correlations with Job-Seeking Behavior			
			Job-search methods	Job-search frequency	Job-seeking activity	Future job seeking
Psychological distress (GHQ)	16.93	9.05	0.38*	0.14	0.21	0.15
Self-esteem	57.48	9.14	0.17	0.23	0.20	0.50***
Life satisfaction	3.45	2.18	−0.53***	−0.25	−0.42**	−0.35*
Quality of life	12.48	4.20	−0.42**	−0.17	−0.27	−0.06
Financial stress	29.43	12.20	0.25	0.01	0.05	−0.01
Financial strain	2.88	1.15	0.31*	0.06	−0.02	−0.08
Unemployment depression	4.60	2.18	0.43**	0.09	0.32*	0.23
Unemployment anger	4.95	2.32	0.52***	0.40*	0.35*	0.40**
Job need	5.75	1.55	0.45**	0.36*	0.19	0.37*
Job valence	15.30	5.31	0.54***	0.31	0.34*	0.38*
Perceived uncontrollability	5.03	2.08	0.18	−0.04	0.03	−0.31
Unemployment helplessness	5.05	2.12	0.33*	0.19	0.33*	0.13
Confidence, desired job	3.00	1.94	−0.03	−0.09	−0.18	0.16
Confidence, any job	3.63	1.96	0.04	−0.06	0.02	0.28
Control-optimism	12.53	6.04	−0.17	−0.10	−0.18	0.21
Unemployment duration (weeks)	75.54	75.94	−0.13	−0.21	−0.19	−0.13
Job-search methods	3.24	1.46	—	0.46**	0.65***	0.46**
Job-search frequency	17.90	13.52	0.46**	—	0.44**	0.34*
Job-seeking activity	4.93	1.35	0.65***	0.44**	—	0.53***
Future job seeking	5.15	2.21	0.46**	0.34*	0.53***	—

Note: $N = 42$. Ns for the correlations varied due to a small number of missing cases. Tests of significance are two-tailed.
*$p < 0.05$; **$p < 0.01$; ***$p < 0.001$.

test were used. The remaining correlations involving unemployment duration were nonsignificant.

Concluding Comments

The two studies described in the present chapter are useful extensions of the research that I discussed in previous chapters because they take us beyond the study of youth unemployment and they examine the psychological impact of unemployment in samples of older adults who have been out in the workforce for some time before losing their jobs. The studies also provide comparative information and they include important new variables such as financial stress, financial strain, and changes in specific behaviors. Though both studies were restricted to fairly small samples and were cross-sectional in nature, the results increase our understanding of unemployment effects in older groups and they also provide a replication of some of the previous findings. There is an obvious need to look more intensively at the effects of unemployment across the life span, using longitudinal designs and much larger samples.

Chapter 10

Epilogue

This chapter will review some of the main themes that have been presented in previous chapters in an attempt to bring them together and to indicate future directions for research. I will begin with a general summary and then conclude by considering a selection of issues that relate to research into the psychological impact of unemployment.

General Summary

My intention in writing this book was to report the results of a systematic series of studies concerned with the psychological effects of unemployment, to describe a number of theoretical approaches that are relevant to the unemployment area, and, where possible, to draw connections between theory and research. I have therefore tried to go beyond description of the unemployment experience to a more conceptual approach that attempts to show how selected aspects of reactions to unemployment can be related to psychological theories.

The first part of the book reviewed relevant research and theory, beginning with findings and interpretations that came both from studies of the impact of the Great Depression on the lives of the unemployed and from unemployment research conducted in the 1970s and 1980s. I then considered conceptual analyses that have emerged from this research background and that have been especially concerned with the areas of work, employment, and unemployment. Thus, I discussed stage theories, the latent functions analysis of Jahoda (1979, 1981, 1982), approaches that emphasize job content and internal versus external locus of control (O'Brien, 1986), agency theory where the person is seen as an active agent rather than as a passive object acted upon by external forces (Fryer & Payne, 1986), and the most fully developed approach at this time, namely, Warr's (1987a) vitamin model. It will be recalled that these various theoretical accounts are primarily concerned with the psychological well-being of those who have jobs and, looking at the reverse side of the coin, the well-being of those who are unemployed. The measures that have been used vary in their generality and range from context-free measures of mental health to job-related aspects of well-being (see Warr, 1987a).

However, theoretical analyses of unemployment effects are not limited to theories that have been specifically derived from research into work, employment, and unemployment. Nor are they restricted to theories that concern the determinants of different levels of psychological well-being. There are behavioral consequences of becoming unemployed (e.g., job-seeking behavior, changes in how the unemployed person uses time) that also require conceptual analysis. There are also questions about the effects of job loss that relate to how coping responses are influenced by variables such as a person's gender, location in the life cycle, financial stress, social support, commitment to paid employment, value priorities, and personality characteristics. We need a deeper theoretical understanding of how these variables influence reactions to unemployment. Chapter 4 dealt with some wider theoretical frameworks that were relevant to these issues. Thus, I described recent developments in self-concept theory, stress and coping research, expectancy-value theory, attribution theory, learned helplessness theory, self-efficacy theory, and life-span developmental psychology and I drew out some implications for unemployment research. My aim in presenting these various forms of analysis was to indicate that there are theoretical approaches already available from different areas of psychology that may help us to account for different aspects of the unemployment experience.

The remainder of the book was concerned with the program of research into the psychological impact of unemployment that I have been involved with since the late 1970s. My general aim was to present the main findings from this research, to show how the findings can be interpreted in terms of some of the theoretical approaches discussed in the first part of the book, and to relate the results to those of other recent studies. I do not claim that the set of studies that I have described represents a tightly integrated program, with one study inevitably leading on to the next. There is, however, a progression in the program from simpler to more sophisticated research designs and a movement into new areas of inquiry. I have also attempted, where possible, to build in replication checks on earlier findings from the program. Throughout this development I have tried to dig beneath the surface and to make theoretical sense of the results. It should be clear, however, that no single unified theory is being tested in the present research program. That is because I am dealing with a range of questions, each of which requires a different form of conceptual analysis.

I reviewed in Chapter 5 some of the main scales and measures used in the research program. Then, in Chapters 6, 7, and 8, I described studies of the psychological impact of unemployment on young people, progressing from single-group studies to comparison-group studies to a major multivariate, longitudinal study of school-leavers that provided a wealth of data for analysis.

Finally, in Chapter 9, I described two recent studies, each of which involved older groups of unemployed subjects, where the range of variables was again extended so as to encompass financial stress, financial strain, and social contacts.

Some General Conclusions

Where has this journey taken us? The evidence that I have presented from our research program and the results from other sources indicate that the experience of unemployment does have negative effects, though these effects vary across studies depending upon the population that is sampled (e.g., young unemployed versus middle-aged unemployed) and the ways in which variables are assessed. We found from our longitudinal study of school-leavers (Feather & O'Brien, 1986a, 1986b, 1987) that getting or not getting a job has effects on respondents' feelings and moods (e.g., life satisfaction, depressive affect), Protestant ethic values, perceived control, perceived activity, perceived competence, and beliefs about the causes of unemployment. In our cross-sectional studies, differences between employed and unemployed samples were also found in regard to other variables (e.g., global self-esteem, time structure, depressive symptoms) but, as noted many times throughout this book, such evidence is not sufficient to establish cause-effect relations in the absence of a longitudinal design.

Our results also showed that there were differences between employed and unemployed subjects that were present while these respondents were still at school and before they attempted to find a job. These preexisting differences (e.g., in perceived competence, perceived activity, positive attitude toward self, life satisfaction, and stress symptoms) may have influenced the likelihood of respondents obtaining employment. In some cases the initial differences were magnified as a result of respondents either finding or not finding a job (e.g., for perceived competence, perceived activity, life satisfaction). These predisposing factors need to be studied in more detail in regard to the movement of people into employment or unemployment.

Also important is the need to take account of the effects of good and bad employment, the effects of different forms of unemployment, and the effects of different patterns of employment and unemployment across time. These issues have been discussed in various sections of this book and they deserve more attention in future research. Thus, employment can be rewarding or nonrewarding in regard to a person's basic motives, unemployment can be continuous or intermittent, people can vary in the "stock" and "flow" of their employment experience across time and in the extent to which they are totally without paid jobs or have part-time or casual employment, and so forth.

Comparisons between groups labeled as employed or unemployed often neglect specific contextual features that are important at the individual level, although more recent survey studies have sought information about the effects of such variables as social support, financial stress, and a person's previous experience of employment and unemployment. The large-scale surveys that have been conducted need to be supplemented by intensive interviews of selected groups so as to obtain more detailed information about the unemployment experience and how individuals cope when they have no paid employment. In this way one can flesh out the results that emerge from questionnaire studies and obtain leads that help to guide future research. We find in the more recent literature a movement in the direction of more intensive investigation of selected groups so that the bare statistics of survey studies can be supplemented by information about specific cases (e.g., Fineman, 1987; Fryer & Ullah, 1987).

It would also be an obvious advantage to go beyond questionnaire measurement that depends upon verbal reports and to obtain reliable measures of actual behaviors that are associated with both employment and unemployment. Verbal reports are subject to consistency pressures that lead respondents to present a consistent view of how they feel and what they do, despite the fact that there may actually be inconsistencies in their thoughts and actions. Behavioral and other types of information can be obtained in carefully planned studies. By using different methods one can increase one's confidence that the conclusions reached do not depend on the specific method that is used to elicit information. The benefits of convergent validation achieved by sampling a range of different methods and variables are well-known by psychologists (e.g., Campbell & Fiske, 1959) and their advantages were evident in one of the earliest studies of the psychological impact of unemployment, namely, the Marienthal study (Jahoda et al., 1933).

It need hardly be emphasized that the measures used in unemployment research should be psychometrically respectable, with satisfactory levels of reliability and acceptable information about validity. Due to time limitations an investigator may sometimes be restricted to using a small number of questionnaire items, but well-planned research programs should allow for the inclusion of scales with known psychometric properties and the possibility of empirical and conceptual replication of results with new samples. The conceptual status of the measures that are used should also be closely examined. For example, is the measure a global one or does it involve a set of differentiated components? Does it measure a state of the person that currently exists but that can change from time to time (e.g., present life satisfaction, depressed mood), or a more stable aspect of the person (e.g., a trait) that is assumed to influence behavior over time and situations? If the latter, then it may be more difficult to detect change in the variable that is being assessed (see Warr, 1984a; Chapter 8).

The last point again reminds us that the selection of the variables and populations that are studied should be guided by conceptual as well as practical considerations. Variables that go by the same name are not necessarily equivalent and it would be simplistic to expect that samples drawn from different populations will yield the same kinds of results. For example, in previous chapters I have noted the differences in results obtained when global versus differentiated measures of self-esteem are used in unemployment studies and I drew attention to differences that one might expect when middle-aged unemployed men rather than unemployed school-leavers are the subject of investigation. Similar observations could be made for other variables and other kinds of samples. Inconsistent results emerging from different unemployment studies can usually be attributed to differences in the way variables were measured and differences in the populations that were studied.

To take the last point further, one would not expect to find the same effects of unemployment in different sectors of the general population or across different cultures or at different times in a culture's history. There may be some common effects, but the search for similarity should not obscure the recognition of differences. For example, societies differ in their cultural values, social welfare schemes, unemployment rates, climates, opportunities for leisure activities, and the way they administer unemployment benefits, etc. These kinds of contextual factors would be expected to influence psychological well-being.

Two examples will suffice to illustrate this point. The situation of a young unemployed Australian may be very different from that experienced by a young unemployed person in the United Kingdom, or in a large city in the United States, or in the Netherlands. Ullah (1988) has recently presented results from a comparative study of young unemployed English and Australian respondents indicating that scores on the General Health Questionnaire (GHQ; Goldberg, 1972, 1978), assessing negative aspects of psychological well-being, were more closely associated with commitment to paid employment in the English sample than in the Australian sample. However, the GHQ scores were more closely associated with financial strain in the Australian sample than in the English sample. These results imply that psychological well-being may be associated with different value priorities among the young people who were sampled in the two cultures, with affective well-being among the young Australians being determined more by the availability of money and the easy, comfortable life that money may bring and less by the work ethic and a commitment to paid employment than was the case with the young unemployed English subjects. As the second example, Schaufeli (1988b) notes that stronger negative effects of unemployment tend to be reported by English and German researchers than by Dutch researchers. He suggests that the difference may be due to the fact that disabled and unemployed people are classified and treated separately in the Netherlands. Because of this, Dutch unemployed workers as a group are probably relatively more healthy when compared with their British (and probably also their American and German) counterparts, where some of the unemployed who are studied may also be disabled. Moreover, Dutch unemployment benefits tend to be relatively high compared with the benefits offered in other countries so unemployed people there are less likely to be under financial strain. Hence they would be less subject to psychological distress. Schaufeli (1988b) also notes that his professional samples had opportunities to engage in unpaid work without penalty, enabling them to use their skills and develop some purpose and meaning in their lives.

The two examples just described indicate the importance of considering the context of unemployment in detail. Clearly, there is a need for further comparative studies of the psychological impact of unemployment both within and across cultures.

Theoretical Issues

Throughout this book I have emphasized the importance of grounding research on the psychological impact of unemployment within conceptual frameworks. In earlier chapters I presented various theoretical approaches that can be used as a basis for research into unemployment effects. The reader can probably think of others that could be added to the list.

My preference has been to use middle-range theories in the studies that I have conducted. For example, the study of job-seeking behavior described in Chapter 8 was developed within the general context of expectancy-value theory. To some extent this strategy has been successful, but not entirely. One problem is that psychological theories may not be sufficiently well articulated to meet the complex conditions of real-life situations and events. We found, for example, that our measure of control-optimism was not associated with differences in job-seeking behavior but the measures of job valence and affective concern did predict job-seeking behavior (Feather & O'Brien, 1987; Chapter 8). Research in applied contexts with some of our current theoretical models should help to indicate how well these models can be transferred in their application beyond laboratory settings to actual situations that involve important commitments and consequences. Research in applied areas can usefully suggest new variables that need to be taken into account and can question the extent to which theoretical concepts can easily be coordinated to the specific circumstances of real-life situations and behaviors.

I am not arguing that general models have no utility in applied contexts. It is clear that they serve an important function by identifying key variables and their relations, thereby providing a structure that can guide perceptions and research activity. I am asserting, however, that general models can be improved and refined by testing them against a range of empirical data from both laboratory and applied contexts. Such testing may indicate that a theory is too generally stated to be of much predictive usefulness in a particular situation; that the concepts are too loosely defined and require more detailed specification; that the model is incomplete and needs the addition of new concepts; that relations between the concepts are more complex than assumed and require more analysis; that the theory is useful for some domains but not for others; and so forth.

There is plenty of scope for using some of the more general theoretical approaches that I described in Chapter 4 in relation to future research in the employment and unemployment areas. Theories that deal with the self-concept, stress and coping, expectations and valences, causal attributions, learned helplessness, self-efficacy, and development across the life span can be used as a basis for framing hypotheses that concern the effects of having or not having paid employment. Generating research from some of these theoretical frameworks should help to broaden our horizons, taking us beyond theories from organizational/occupational psychology that deal with the specific functions of work. The wider perspective would open up new areas of investigation, some of which were alluded to earlier in this book.

These various theoretical approaches have their own appropriate range of application. Some deal with motivation, some with self processes, some with changing beliefs and expectations, some with adjustment, some with developmental changes, and so forth. They do not cover the same territory. It is clear that there are many key questions to be investigated in the general domain of work, employment, and unemployment and research directed toward answering these questions will not require one all-embracing theory. Instead one has recourse to a range of approaches, the selection from which depends upon the type of question that is posed. The analysis of job-seeking behavior provides a clear example of this point where theories from the areas of motivation and cognition (e.g., expectancy-value theory, self-efficacy theory, attribution theory) are probably the most appropriate ones to use at the present time. In contrast, research that compares different age groups or groups that differ in gender or social class characteristics would be based more appropriately on theories that concern socialization influences, social norms, gender roles, changes across the life span, social and personality development, and so forth.

We have seen that a major area of investigation in the literature has been the impact of unemployment on the psychological adjustment and mental health of the unemployed. I reviewed theories in Chapter 3 that were especially relevant to this question. The results of my own research program generally support Warr's (1987a) emphasis on certain environmental factors that are necessary for good psychological health. It will be recalled that Warr (1987a) identifies nine environmental features, namely, opportunity for control, opportunity for skill use, externally generated goals, variety, environmental clarity, availability of money, physical security, opportunity for interpersonal contact, and valued social position, that he considers are determinants of mental health in all kinds of environment. These features are assumed to enhance mental health up to a certain level after which some of them may be associated with decrements in mental health if they are at very high levels (e.g., the negative effects of too many goals, too much variety). The environmental features are assumed to function in a way analogous to vitamins in that deficiencies in vitamins cause ill health; there are no toxic consequences from high intakes of some vitamins, but other vitamins do have toxic consequences when taken at very high levels.

I have not investigated the effects of all of the environmental features that Warr (1987a) identifies in his vitamin model. Nor are our results relevant to the assumption in the vitamin model that there are negative effects on mental health when there is an overabundance of some of the environmental features. However, our research program does provide evidence about the negative effects of deficiencies in selected variables. In particular, results from our studies that relate to opportunities for skill utilization, the structured and purposive use of time, social support, perceived control over actions and outcomes, and financial stress and strain demonstrate that negative effects on psychological well-being occur when these variables are in short supply. Each of these variables can be coordinated to environmental features from the vitamin model (Warr, 1987a).

Note that one can study these variables as either independent or dependent variables, depending on the question asked. For example, differences in the degree to which individuals perceive their use of time to be structured and purposive predict differences in psychological well-being (e.g., Bond & Feather, 1988; Rowley & Feather, 1987) but perceptions of time use are also dependent on particular environmental conditions and can change as these conditions alter (e.g., Feather & Bond, 1983). The same point applies to other variables. Thus, self-esteem assessed globally or according to differentiated aspects can be treated as a variable that might moderate the impact of unemployment, with high self-esteem helping to buffer some of the negative effects of unemployment (e.g., Kessler et al., 1988; Shamir, 1986b), or self-esteem can be studied as a dependent variable that is affected by the experience of unemployment (e.g., Feather, 1982e; Feather & Bond, 1983; Feather & O'Brien, 1986b). Similarly, perceived control can be regarded as a dependent variable, as is the case in research that documents the effects of unemployment or different job environments on internal versus external locus of control (e.g., Feather, 1982e; Feather & Bond, 1983; Feather & O'Brien, 1986b; Kohn & Schooler, 1983; O'Brien, 1986; O'Brien & Feather, 1989) or as an independent variable that predicts job satisfaction and other psychological aspects of adjustment.

Warr (1987a) adopts a situation-centered enabling approach in his emphasis on environmental features, basing his terminology on a classification of psychological theories developed by Gergen and Gergen (1982). When I discussed the vitamin model in Chapter 3, I indicated that theories that single out environmental features that are deemed to be important for mental health have to deal with the question of why these features are important. An answer to this question requires analysis of the characteristics of people, especially their basic motives, needs, and values. Warr (1987a) recognizes this point in accepting the fact that a ". . . situation-centred model thus inevitably contains some person-centred assumptions . . ." (p. 17).

One can find lists of needs in the psychological literature that overlap with Warr's environmental features (e.g., McClelland, 1985; Murray, 1938). Indeed, Warr (1987a, p. 257) provides a list of possible matching characteristics for each of his environmental categories. He accepts the need to study both environmental and individual characteristics, and reviews the main attempts to do so especially in regard to contributions from organizational and industrial psychology. His discussion considers both the direct effects of personal characteristics on job-related mental health and the modifying (or moderating) effects of personal characteristics when considered in relation to particular job conditions. He also refers to various preference models of person-environment fit that begin with a focus on employees' needs, interests, or values and the degree to which these are met in specific kinds of jobs. In these approaches reactions to a particular environment are related to the degree to which the needs, interests, and values of the person are congruent with the environment (e.g., Dawis & Lofquist, 1984; Feather, 1975, 1979; French, Caplan, & Van Harrison, 1982; Holland, 1973, 1976; O'Brien, 1988; Pervin, 1968; Stern, 1970). I have suggested in previous discussions that models that focus upon the benefits of person-environment fit also need to acknowledge that people are usually not satisfied with a "lotus-land" existence where all their needs are met. They also seek a certain amount of novelty and challenge in their daily lives, selecting and modifying their environments so as to bring about new experiences that stimulate their interests and satisfy their curiosity (Feather, 1975).

One can only endorse this emphasis on the need to consider both personal characteristics and environmental features in psychological theorizing, whatever the area of enquiry. That emphasis has been a central part of my own theorizing over many years (e.g., Atkinson & Feather, 1966; Feather, 1975; Feather, 1982c) and it has also been acknowledged by many others (e.g., Cronbach, 1957, 1975; Endler & Magnusson, 1976; Lewin, 1936; Nygard, 1981).

There is a need to develop detailed studies of the psychological impact of unemployment that pay close attention to the actual environments in which unemployed people find themselves and the personal characteristics of the unemployed. Thus, unemployed people with different underlying needs, interests, and values would be expected to react differently when the environment that follows job loss is similar for all, and unemployed people with similar underlying needs, interests, and values would be expected to react differently when the environment that follows job loss differs in its salient features across groups and individuals. To illustrate this point, an unemployed person with a strong achievement need (or a high affiliation need) would be expected to respond differently to a jobless environment lacking in challenge (or social contacts) when compared with a person whose achievement (or affiliation) need is weaker in strength; jobless environments that differ in their provision of opportunities for control and skill utilization would be expected to have different consequences for people even when their needs, interests, and values are similar; these kinds of situation and person factors can interact to determine responses to the unemployed condition. So much appears to be obvious but there has been remarkably little detailed research

that teases out the interactive effects of environmental and personal characteristics on psychological reactions to unemployment in well-controlled
studies. This is a challenge for the future and one that has to be met.

Some final theoretical points need to be made. First, we need to move away
from relatively static conceptions about unemployment effects that take a
"one-shot" view of events (as if one were taking a single photograph with a
camera) to more dynamic views that examine the reactions of the jobless over
defined time periods (as if one were taking a movie version that captures the
changing process). It is not easy to construct theories that identify underlying
processes and the dynamics of change. Theories that allow for cognitive and
motivational changes (e.g., in beliefs, action tendencies, affective reactions)
are available, however, as are more formal models of the dynamics of action,
but these need to be wedded to the specific situation of the unemployed. We
tried to do this to a limited extent in our applications of the general framework
of expectancy-value (valence) theory to unemployment effects (e.g., Feather
& Barber, 1983; Feather & Davenport, 1981; Feather & O'Brien, 1987).
Thus, we found that respondents' expectations about finding a paid job
tended to decline with increasing duration of unemployment and that explanations of youth unemployment were modified depending upon whether
school-leavers found a job or became unemployed. There are other approaches from the cognitive and motivational domains that could also be
used as a basis for process-oriented research (see Chapter 4).

Second, we also need to recognize that people are active agents with the
power of shaping the content of their environments and not passive objects at
the mercy of environmental forces. They can affect their environments both
in the way they appraise and construe them and in the way they select and
create the situations in which they choose to exist. They actively develop ways
of coping with negative events and ways of adjusting to changing circumstances. Although the situation imposes limits on what can be done, people
usually have some scope for acting upon their environment and some can
even enhance and improve their lives despite adverse conditions. Research
into unemployment effects and in other areas is now recognizing the active
and constructive role of individuals (e.g., Feather & Volkmer, 1988; Fryer &
Payne, 1986; Smith & Anderson, 1986).

Third, following Jahoda (1982, 1988), we need to pay more attention to the
role of social institutions such as employment and the degree to which these
institutions fit individual needs. A wider focus on the context of institutional
arrangements within society should enable us to avoid a preoccupation with
theories that are concerned with individuals only.

Fourth, we need to develop more theoretical understanding of what it is
that makes some variables more important than others in determining how
people react to unemployment. It is unlikely, for example, that Warr's
(1987a) "vitamins" are all equally important influences on an individual's
reactions to employment and unemployment. Which are the more important
vitamins? To what extent does the relative importance of these different en-

vironmental features depend upon the strength of underlying needs, personality characteristics, gender, age, social context, and so forth. The results of our research point to two conditions that have an important influence on individual reactions to being without paid employment: lack of money and lack of structure and purpose in life. It is those people who suffer financial hardship and who feel that their lives have no purpose and structure who seem to be most affected by unemployment. The evidence from other studies also consistently points to the same conclusion (e.g., Fryer, 1988; Jahoda, 1988; Kessler et al., 1988; O'Brien, 1986). That is not to say that other factors are unimportant; only that these two factors seem to play a central role in regard to psychological distress.

Fifth, to repeat a point made throughout this book, we need to allow for the fact that unemployment has different effects depending on the group that is studied. It is clearly fallacious to treat the unemployed as a homogeneous mass. Though the psychological impact of unemployment tends to be negative, the nature of the impact varies. Young, unskilled individuals who have just left school react differently to a jobless environment when compared with older individuals with a history of employment; women without jobs react differently to unemployment when compared with unemployed men; children with families to support them react differently to lack of a job when compared with children who lack family support and who live from day to day on their own resources. Differences in cultural values, social class, and ethnic background may also affect the experience of unemployment. Future research should give more attention to these differences.

Sixth, we need to extend our inquiries to take account of a wider set of variables that may be influenced by unemployment. So far the major focus has been on mental health and adjustment, primarily indicated by measures of affective well-being and other aspects of health and coping behavior (Warr, 1987a). However, there are many other dependent variables that require more detailed investigation. For example, under what conditions is unemployment followed by a sense of injustice, alienation from society, anger and aggression, antisocial behavior such as crime and delinquency, drug-taking, and so forth. The study of some of these variables would shift the emphasis from a concern with individual reactions to more concern with the wider impact of unemployment on the community. Our studies have included measures of anger and potential social action (e.g., Feather & Bond, 1984; Feather & O'Brien, 1986a, 1986b) but much more could be done to broaden the focus of research.

Research with Larger Units

Recent contributions to research into the psychological impact of unemployment indicate an interest in going beyond the study of individuals to the investigation of how unemployment effects larger units such as the family and the community (e.g., Fineman, 1987; Fryer & Ullah, 1987). This wider focus was also present in the unemployment research from the 1930s, especially in the Marienthal study (Jahoda et al., 1933) and in studies of the effects of unemployment on family members (e.g., Komarovsky, 1940). The renewed interest in the wider impact of unemployment is a healthy development, opening up a range of important questions that deserve attention. The answers are not likely to be simple. For example, Liem and Liem (1988) reported significant increases in emotional strain for both husbands and their wives following involuntary unemployment (see also McKee & Bell, 1986). Changes may also occur within the family unit in regard to such factors as the quality of the marital relationship, the role performance of the partners, the family division of labor, traditional vs. egalitarian family norms, marital power, and the overall family climate (Atkinson, Liem, & Liem, 1986; Dew et al., 1987; Liem & Liem, 1988). The support provided by the family and the extent to which it can act as a buffer against stress may change over time. Initially the family may provide a source of social support but, with continuing unemployment, the marital relationship may be negatively affected. As Liem and Liem (1988) indicate in their discussion of the Atkinson et al. (1986) findings:

> the marital relationship both reacted to and moderated the emotional distress of workers. In cases displaying a very strong impact of unemployment on the marriage, however, there must surely be a point beyond which it would make little sense to treat the marital relationship as a potential source of stress moderation, regardless of what might happen under less stressful circumstances. The relevant concern then would be to identify interpersonal resources of the couple that might serve to moderate a stressed marital *relationship* rather than a stressed individual. (pp. 100–101)

Liem and Liem (1988) also argue for a movement away from a model of unemployment effects that emphasizes the passive, reactive aspect of the jobless experience to an approach that recognizes efficacy, resilience, assertiveness, and intentionality on the part of those workers who have lost their jobs. This shift in emphasis enables Liem and Liem to achieve a better understanding of how unemployed workers look for a new job, with some refusing at least for a time to significantly lower their aspirations (see Chapter 8, pp. 207–208), and why some unemployed workers resist seeking out and using professional human services, a response that Liem and Liem (1988) see as "dictated by the perception, often confirmed by past experience, that receiving help would require acquiescing to attributions of dependency and defeat" (p. 102).

Studies of the wider impact of unemployment on units such as the family have obvious social relevance. Again one would expect financial hardship to play a central role, not only by affecting the emotional climate in the home but also by determining structural changes. For example, in large families where the major bread-winner is unemployed, children may be forced to leave school at an early age, seek a job, or even leave the family and strike out on their own when they are ill-prepared to do so. The personal and social costs of these changes can be massive. They spread from the individual and the family to the entire community.

Note that unemployed children living at home can also affect family stress levels even though their own personal stress may be moderated or buffered by family support.

Final Comments

Does the research described in this book help us to devise ways of helping unemployed people? This is a question that most unemployment researchers must consider when they observe the destructive effects that unemployment often has on individual lives. Warr (1987a) argues that the environments of employment and unemployment can be described in terms of the same nine environmental features that are specified in his vitamin model. He believes that, in general, ". . . jobless environments are more adverse in these terms than employment settings, but there is likely to be a degree of overlap; some people's jobs are worse in terms of environmental 'vitamins' than are some settings of unemployment" (p. 291). Thus, just as there can be good and bad jobs that are distinguished in terms of their environmental features, so there can be good and bad conditions of unemployment. Some unemployed people, for example, may receive pensions and become involved in clubs and societies that provide social contact and opportunities for skill use and influence over the course of events. Others may not be so fortunate, existing in environments that are relatively devoid of positive features. Despite the fact that the environments of most unemployed people tend to be psychologically "bad," according to Warr (1987a) it should be possible to devise ways of shifting these environments toward conditions that are psychologically better. He considers two broad perspectives that have been adopted in an attempt to improve the position of unemployed people. The first involves interventions that reduce unemployment levels themselves and the second involves attempts to modify the principal environmental features of unemployed people so that their environments have more of the positive features that Warr (1987a) describes in his vitamin model.

At the most basic level, a nation can try to reduce unemployment levels by improving its economic performance. In difficult economic times, however, some approaches that specifically target unemployment levels can also be considered. First, there may be efforts to implement job creation schemes that provide jobs for those who would otherwise be unemployed (e.g., work with local councils, construction projects, expansion of self-employment opportunities). A second group of attempts to reduce overall levels of unemployment involves moves to restrict the total duration of the "working life." This may be achieved, for example, by the development of job-training schemes sponsored by the government, by expanding educational opportunities prior to a young person's entry into the labor market, or by lowering the retirement age. A third set of possible innovations involves developing ways of reducing the number of hours some employees spend in paid employment. This may be achieved, for example, by offering employees the possibility of permanent part-time employment, a shorter working week or working year, work-sharing, or a reduction in overtime hours. Some of these changes are resisted by those in paid employment, especially when incomes are at stake but, as Warr (1987a) notes, solutions that involve the possibility of opening up more part-time employment may be attractive to some members of the population (e.g., to women with young children, employees close to retirement, or school-leavers requiring some job experience).

The second broad approach to improving the position of the unemployed involves modifying the environment so that it contains more of the positive "vitamin" features listed by Warr (1987a). Governments, for example, may enact legislation that guarantees reasonable levels of unemployment benefits so that the unemployed are not under financial strain. They may also develop schemes that ensure physical security (e.g., by providing housing or other accommodation at low rentals for those who have difficulty finding jobs). Other important modifications would involve changes in the first four environmental features given the fact that "Unemployed people's lives are often diminished through limited opportunities for personal control and for skill utilization, the absence of externally generated goals, and a restricted variety of settings and activities" (Warr, 1987a, p. 300). Warr (1987a) argues that these changes would require additional or expanded formal and informal institutions in areas where there is high local unemployment. For example, special centers for the unemployed themselves might be created; centers that enable training and the exchange of skills might be established; or existing clubs, societies, and churches might expand their concerns so that they reach out to people who lack paid jobs. Intervention strategies may also be used to provide opportunities for the learning of skills in community settings (e.g., Cassell, Fitter, Fryer, & Smith, 1988). The creation and expansion of new kinds of institutions that provide more positive environments for the unemployed should also generate increased opportunities for social contact, assist in reducing the stigma that is often associated with being unemployed, and provide unemployed people with greater environmental clarity, enabling a more predictable and structured daily life.

At a national level there is also a need for the development of an overall policy in regard to unemployment and part-time employment. Governments often adopt shifting and short-term solutions when dealing with unemployment, depending upon the political climate of the day. Longer-term creative policies that are based on a concern for individuals rather than political expediency are needed. At the same time, it has to be acknowledged that the political dimension of the problem of unemployment is complex. Changes in the allocation of resources (e.g., increased welfare payments) have effects on other parts of the economy and what appears to be a benefit may end up as a larger social cost. Some of the political implications of unemployment have recently been discussed by Dooley and Catalano (1988) and by Kieselbach and Svensson (1988).

In addition to these broad approaches assistance can also be given by psychologists at the individual level in terms of advice, counseling, and other forms of intervention that aim to help unemployed people improve their prospects of obtaining paid employment. It may be the case, for example, that some unemployed people have limited information about where to find jobs, or need to improve their skills in various ways both in their chosen field of occupation and in their approach to the job interview, or are hampered by other personal problems in their efforts to obtain paid employment, or need to develop political skills at the group level that increase their bargaining power. Interventions of this kind need to be handled carefully and realistically with full information about employment prospects. False hopes raised by the intervention can easily be dashed when the person again tries to find employment in an unresponsive job market. The effects of failure to find a paid job could then be even more devastating than previously, leading to self-blame, diminution in self-esteem, and feelings of hopelessness and helplessness. Unemployed people may also resist professional counseling either because it is an admission of defeat or because they are already demoralized. Approaches that differ from traditional counseling may be necessary to overcome these problems. For example, use could be made of the resources, social support, and information that can be provided by self-help groups of unemployed people organized within particular settings (e.g., after a plant closure). Other kinds of interventions could also be tried that attempt to modify causal attributions for unemployment by informing unemployed individuals about the political and economic basis of current unemployment so as to counter self-blame and loss of self-esteem (see Catalano & Dooley, 1980; Deitch, 1984; Dooley et al., 1988; Kieselbach & Svensson, 1988; Liem & Liem, 1988; Schore, 1984). And unemployed groups might also be given lessons in political action and ways of influencing political decisions.

Questions about the future of work and about how the negative impact of unemployment might be reduced are basic questions that merit further study at a multidisciplinary level (e.g. Argyle, 1989, Clutterbuck & Hill, 1981; Frankel, 1987; Handy, 1984). The psychologist cannot lay sole claim to this territory; sociologists, economists, political scientists, and other social researchers all have contributions to make. However, paid employment, as Jahoda (1982) has argued, occupies a unique position in our society and it is not easy to replace it with alternative institutions that provide the same range of potentially positive features.

In general, the unemployed themselves do not appear to be very effective change agents. Many lack the power, skills, organization, and cohesion to alter events to their own advantage. They are also often the victims of conservative public opinion, being unfairly stigmatized as lazy and inefficient. That attitude is now changing as more people recognize that the major causes of present-day unemployment are basically structural and economic and are linked to technological changes and trends and events in the world's economies. Many people also now have direct experience with unemployed members of the community either from within their own families or among their friends. They learn that the unemployed cannot be regarded as a homogeneous mass that is easily stereotyped but instead should be seen as a differentiated sector of the population containing individuals who vary in their motives, abilities, and life circumstances.

We urgently need solutions to the problems raised by high unemployment rates so that all members of society are able to realize their potential and to develop a sense of structure and purpose, providing meaning to their existence. Though the problems of unemployment and poverty may sometimes appear to be intractable, it should be possible to develop creative approaches to solving them and to help the more unfortunate live productive and useful lives. We should all be guardians of the welfare of others and not islands unto ourselves.

References

Abramson, L.Y., Seligman, M.E.P., & Teasdale, J.D. (1978). Learned helplessness in humans: Critique and reformulation. *Journal of Abnormal Psychology*, *87*, 49–74.

Ach, N. (1910). *Uber den willensakt und das temperament*. Leipzig: Quelle & Meyer.

Ajzen, I., & Fishbein, M. (1977). Attitude-behavior relations: A theoretical analysis and review of empirical research. *Psychological Bulletin*, *84*, 888–918.

Ajzen, I., & Fishbein, M. (1980). *Understanding attitudes and predicting social behavior*. Englewood-Cliffs, NJ: Prentice-Hall.

Anderson, J.R. (1985). *Cognitive psychology and its implications* (2d ed.). New York: Freeman.

Antill, J.K., Bussey, K., & Cunningham, J.D. (1985). Sex roles: A psychological perspective. In N.T. Feather (Ed.), *Australian psychology: Review of research* (pp. 330–363). Sydney: Allen & Unwin.

Argyle, M. (1989). *The social psychology of work* (rev. ed.). Harmondsworth: Penguin.

Arnold, M.B. (1960). Perennial problems in the field of emotion. In M.B. Arnold (Ed.), *Feelings and emotions* (pp. 169–185). New York: Academic Press.

Atkinson, J.W. (1957). Motivational determinants of risk-taking behavior. *Psychological Review*, *64*, 359–372.

Atkinson, J.W. (1982). Old and new conceptions of how expected consequences influence actions. In N.T. Feather (Ed.), *Expectations and actions: Expectancy-value models in psychology* (pp. 17–52). Hillsdale, NJ: Erlbaum.

Atkinson, J.W., & Feather, N.T. (Eds.). (1966). *A theory of achievement motivation*. New York: Wiley.

Atkinson, T., Liem, T., & Liem, J. (1986). The social costs of unemployment: Implications for social support. *Journal of Health and Social Behavior*, *27*, 317–331.

Bachman, J.G., & O'Malley, P.M. (1977). Self-esteem in young men: A longitudinal analysis of the impact of educational and occupational attainment. *Journal of Personality and Social Psychology*, *35*, 365–380

Bachman, J.G., & O'Malley, P.M., & Johnston, J. (1978). *Adolescence to adulthood*. Ann Arbor, MI: Institute for Social Research.

Bakke, E.W. (1933). *The unemployed man*. London: Nisbet.

Bakke, E.W. (1940a). *Citizens without work*. New Haven: Yale University Press.

Bakke, E.W. (1940b). The unemployed worker. New Haven: Yale University Press.

Baltes, P.B., Reese, H.W., & Lipsitt, L.P. (1980). Life-span developmental psychology. *Annual Review of Psychology*, *31*, 65–110.

Baltes, P.B., Reese, H.W., & Nesselroade, J.R. (Eds.). (1977). *Life-span develop-mental psychology: Introduction to research methods*. Monterey, CA: Brooks/Cole.

Bandura, A. (1977). Self-efficacy: Toward a unifying theory of behavioral change. *Psychological Review, 84*, 191–215.

Bandura, A. (1982). Self-efficacy mechanism in human agency. *American Psychologist, 37*, 122–147.

Bandura, A. (1986). *Social foundations of thought and action: A social cognitive theory*. Englewood Cliffs, NJ: Prentice-Hall.

Bandura, A. (1988). Self-regulation of motivation and action through goal systems. In V. Hamilton, G.H. Bower, & N.H. Frijda (Eds.), *Cognitive perspectives on emotion and motivation* (pp. 37–61). Dordrecht: Kluwer Academic Publishers.

Bandura, A., & Cervone, D. (1983). Self-evaluative and self-efficacy mechanisms governing the motivational effects of goal systems. *Journal of Personality and Social Psychology, 45*, 1017–1028.

Bandura, A., & Cervone, D. (1986). Differential engagement of self-reactive influences in cognitive motivation. *Organizational Behavior and Human Decision Processes, 38*, 92–113.

Banks, M.H., Clegg, C.W., Jackson, P.R., Kemp, N.J., Stafford, E.M., & Wall, T.D. (1980). The use of the General Health Questionnaire as an indicator of mental health in occupational studies. *Journal of Occupational Psychology, 53*, 187–194.

Banks, M.H., & Jackson, P.R. (1982). Unemployment and risk of minor psychiatric disorder in young people: Cross-sectional and longitudinal evidence. *Psychological Medicine, 12*, 789–798.

Banks, M.H., & Ullah, P. (1985). *Youth unemployment: Social and psychological perspectives*. MRC/ESRC Social and Applied Psychology Unit, University of Sheffield.

Banks, M.H., & Ullah, P. (1987). Political attitudes and voting among unemployed and employed youth. *Journal of Adolescence, 10*, 201–216.

Banks, M.H., & Ullah, P. (1988). *Youth unemployment in the 1980s: Its psychological effects*. London: Croom Helm.

Bartley, M. (1987). Research on unemployment and health in Great Britain. In D. Schwefel, P-G. Svensson, & H. Zöllner (Eds.), *Unemployment, social vulnerability, and health in Europe* (pp. 90–91). New York: Springer-Verlag.

Beales, H.L., & Lambert, R.S. (1934). *Memoirs of the unemployed*. London: Gollanz.

Beck, A.T. (1967). *Depression: Clinical, experimental and theoretical aspects*. New York: Harper.

Beck, A.T. (1976). *Cognitive therapy and the emotional disorders*. New York: International Universities Press.

Beck, A.T., & Beck, R.W. (1972). Screening depressed patients in family practice: A rapid technic. *Postgraduate Medicine, 52*, 81–85.

Beck, A.T., Rush, A.J., Shaw, B.F., & Emery, G. (1979). *Cognitive therapy of depression*. New York: Guilford Press.

Beck, A.T., Weissman, A., Lester, D., & Trexler, L. (1974). The measurement of pessimism: The hopelessness scale. *Journal of Consulting and Clinical Psychology, 42*, 861–865.

Bengtson, V.L., & Starr, J.M. (1975). Contrast and consensus: A generational analysis of youth in the 1970s. In R.J. Havighurst & P.H. Dreyer (Eds.), *Youth* (74th Yearbook, National Society for the Study of Education). Chicago: University of Chicago Press.

Blakers, C. (1987). *Youth and society: The two transitions*. Hawthorn, Vic.: Australian Council for Educational Research.

Bond, M.J., & Feather, N.T. (1988). Some correlates of structure and purpose in the use of time. *Journal of Personality and Social Psychology, 55*, 321–329.

Bostyn, A.M., & Wight, D. (1987). Inside a community: Values associated with money and time. In S. Fineman (Ed.), *Unemployment: Personal and social consequences* (pp. 138–154). London: Tavistock.

Breakwell, G.M. (1986). Political and attributional responses to the young short-term unemployed. *Political Psychology, 7*, 265–278.

Breakwell, G.M., Collie, A., Harrison, B., & Propper, C. (1984). Attitudes towards the unemployed: Effects of threatened identity. *British Journal of Social Psychology, 23*, 87–88.

Brenner, M.H. (1973). *Mental illness and the economy*. Cambridge, MA: Harvard University Press.

Brenner, M.H. (1980). Importance of the economy to the nation's health. In L. Eisenberg & A. Kleinman (Eds.), *The relevance of social science for medicine* (pp. 371–395). New York: Reidel.

Brenner, M.H. (1983). Mortality and economic instability: Detailed analyses for Britain and comparative analyses for selected industrialized countries. *International Journal of Health Services, 13*, 563–620.

Brenner, S-O., & Levi, L. (1987). Vulnerability among long-term unemployed: A longitudinal study of mental and physical health among Swedish women at different phases of unemployment—some preliminary results. In D. Schwefel, P-G. Svensson, & H. Zöllner (Eds.), *Unemployment, social vulnerability, and health in Europe* (pp. 239–254). New York: Springer-Verlag.

Brenner, S-O., & Starrin, B. (1988). Unemployment and health in Sweden: Public issues and private troubles. *Journal of Social Issues, 44*, 125–140.

Briar, K.H. (1977). The effect of long term unemployment on workers and their families. *Dissertation Abstracts International, 37*, 6062.

Brotherton, P.L., Kotler, T., & Hammond, S.B. (1979). Development of an Australian index of social class. *Australian Psychologist, 14*, 77–83.

Brown, G.W., & Harris, T.O. (1978). *Social origins of depression*. London: Tavistock.

Buss, T.F., & Redburn, F.S. (1983). *Mass unemployment: Plant closings and community mental health*. Beverly Hills, CA: Sage.

Byrne, B.M., & Shavelson, R.J. (1987). Adolescent self-concept: Testing the assumption of equivalent structure across gender. *American Educational Research Journal, 24*, 365–385.

Campbell, D.T., & Fiske, D.W. (1959). Convergent and discriminant validation by the multitrait-multimethod matrix. *Psychological Bulletin, 56*, 81–105.

Carnegie Trust. (1943). *Disinherited youth: A survey 1936–1939*. London: T. & A. Constable.

Carver, C.S., & Scheier, M.F. (1981). *Attention and self-regulation: A control-theory approach to human behavior*. New York: Springer-Verlag.

Cassell, C., Fitter, M., Fryer, D., & Smith, L. (1988). The development of computer applications by non-employed people in community settings. *Journal of Occupational Psychology, 61*, 89–102.

Catalano, R.A., & Dooley, C.D. (1980). Economic change in primary prevention. In R.H. Price, R.F. Ketterer, B.C. Bader, & J. Monahan (Eds.), *Prevention in mental health: Research, policy and practice* (pp. 21–40). Beverly Hills, CA: Sage.

Catalano, R.A., & Dooley, C.D. (1983). Health effects of economic instability: A test of economic stress hypothesis. *Journal of Health and Social Behavior, 24*, 46–60.

Catalano, R.A., Dooley, C.D., & Jackson, R.L. (1981). Economic predictors of admissions to mental health facilities in a nonmetropolitan community. *Journal of Health and Social Behavior, 22*, 284–297.

Catalano, R.A., Dooley, C.D., & Jackson, R.L. (1985). Economic antecedents of help seeking: Reformulation of time-series tests. *Journal of Health and Social Behavior, 26*, 141–152.

Clark, A.W. (1985). The effects of unemployment on political attitude. *Australian and New Zealand Journal of Sociology*, *21*, 100–108.

Clutterbuck, D., & Hill, R. (1981). *The re-making of work*. London: McGraw-Hill.

Cobb, S. (1976). Social support as a moderator of life stress. *Psychosomatic Medicine*, *38*, 300–314.

Cobb, S., & Kasl, S.V. (1977). *Termination: The consequences of job loss*. Cincinatti: U.S. Department of Health, Education, & Welfare.

Cochrane, C.M. (1983). *Unemployment: Its relationship to self-esteem and depression in applicants for general enlistment in the Australian army*. Unpublished master's thesis, The Flinders University of South Australia, Bedford Park, South Australia.

Cohen, J., & Cohen, P. (1975). *Applied multiple regression/correlation analysis for the behavioral sciences*. Hillsdale, NJ: Erlbaum.

Cohen, S., & Syme, L. (Eds.). (1985). *Social support and health*. New York: Academic Press.

Cohn, R.M. (1978). The effect of employment status change on self attitudes. *Social Psychology*, *41*, 81–93.

Cook, T.D., & Campbell, D.T. (1979). *Quasi-Experimentation: Design and analysis issues for field settings*. Chicago: Rand McNally.

Cook, T.D., Crosby, F., & Hennigan, K.M. (1977). The construct validity of relative deprivation. In J.M. Suls & R.L. Miller (Eds.), *Social comparison processes: Theoretical and empirical perspectives* (pp. 307–333). New York: Wiley.

Cooley, C.H. (1902). *Human nature and the social order* (Reprinted 1964). New York: Scribner's.

Cronbach, L.J. (1951). Coefficient alpha and the internal structure of tests. *Psychometrika*, *16*, 297–334.

Cronbach, L.J. (1957). The two disciplines of scientific psychology. *American Psychologist*, *12*, 671–684.

Cronbach, L.J. (1975). Beyond the two disciplines of scientific psychology. *American Psychologist*, *30*, 116–127.

Crosby, F. (1976). A model of egoistical relative deprivation. *Psychological Review*, *83*, 85–113.

Crosby, F. (1982). *Relative deprivation and working women*. New York: Oxford University Press.

Crosby, F., & Gonzales-Intal, A.M. (1984). Relative deprivation and equity theories: Felt injustice and undeserved benefits of others. In R. Folger (Ed.), *The sense of injustice: Social psychological perspectives* (pp. 141–166). New York: Plenum Press.

Cullen, J.H., Ronayne, T., Cullen, K., Ryan, G., & Wynne, R. (1987). Long term unemployment: Its role in complex vulnerabilities and their health consequences. In D. Schwefel, P-G. Svensson, & H. Zöllner (Eds.), *Unemployment, social vulnerability, and health in Europe* (pp. 211–238). New York: Springer-Verlag.

Cutrona, C.E. (1986). Behavioral manifestations of social support: A microanalytic investigation. *Journal of Personality and Social Psychology*, *51*, 201–208.

Damstrup, V.L. (1987). The effects of youth unemployment: A review of the literature. In D. Schwefel, P-G. Svensson, & H. Zöllner (Eds.), *Unemployment, social vulnerability, and health in Europe* (pp. 167–183). New York: Springer-Verlag.

Daniel, W.W. (1974). *A national survey of the unemployed*. London: Political and Economic Planning Institute.

Dawis, R.V., & Lofquist, L.H. (1984). *A psychological theory of work and adjustment*. Minneapolis: University of Minnesota Press.

DeFrank, R.S., & Ivancevich, J.M. (1986). Job loss: An individual level review and model. *Journal of Vocational Behavior*, *28*, 1–20.

Deitch, C. (1984). Collective action and unemployment: Responses to job loss by workers and community groups. *International Journal of Mental Health*, *13*, 139–153.

Demo, D.H. (1985). The measurement of self-esteem: Refining our methods. *Journal of Personality and Social Psychology, 48*, 1490–1502.

Depue, R.A., & Monroe, S.M. (1978). Learned helplessness in the perspective of the depressive disorders: Conceptual and definitional issues. *Journal of Abnormal Psychology, 87*, 3–20.

De Volder, M.L., & Lens, W. (1982). Academic achievement and future time perspective as a cognitive-motivational concept. *Journal of Personality and Social Psychology, 42*, 566–571.

Dew, M.A., Bromet, E.J., & Schulberg, H. C. (1987). A comparative analysis of two community stressors: Long-term mental health effects. *American Journal of Community Psychology, 15*, 167–184.

Dobson, C., Goudy, W.J., Keith, P.M., & Powers, E. (1979). Further analysis of Rosenberg's Self-Esteem Scale. *Psychological Reports, 44*, 639–641.

Dohrenwend, B.P., & Dohrenwend, B.S. (Eds.). (1974). *Stressful life events: Their nature and their effects.* New York: Wiley.

Donovan, A., & Oddy, M. (1982). Psychological aspects of unemployment: An investigation into the emotional and social adjustment of school leavers. *Journal of Adolescence, 5*, 15–30.

Dooley, C.D., & Catalano, R. (1980). Economic change as a cause of behavioral disorder. *Psychological Bulletin, 87*, 450–468.

Dooley, C.D., & Catalano, R.A. (1984a). The epidemiology of economic stress. *American Journal of Community Psychology, 12*, 387–409.

Dooley, C.D., & Catalano, R.A. (1984b). Why the economy predicts help-seeking: A test of competing explanations. *Journal of Health and Social Behavior, 25*, 160–176.

Dooley, C.D., & Catalano, R. (1988). Recent research on the psychological effects of unemployment. *Journal of Social Issues, 44*, 1–12.

Dooley, C.D., & Catalano, R.A. (Eds.). (1988). Psychological effects of unemployment. *Journal of Social Issues, 44*(4).

Dooley, C.D., Catalano, R., & Rook, K.S. (1988). Personal and aggregate unemployment and psychological symptoms. *Journal of Social Issues, 44*, 107–123.

Duval, S., & Wicklund, R. A. (1972). *A theory of objective self-awareness.* New York: Academic Press.

Edwards, W. (1954). The theory of decision making. *Psychological Bulletin, 51*, 380–417.

Eisenberg, P., & Lazarsfeld, P.F. (1938). The psychological effects of unemployment. *Psychological Bulletin, 35*, 358–390.

Elder, G.H. (1974). *Children of the Great Depression.* Chicago: University of Chicago Press.

Elder, G.H. (1978). Family history and the life course. In T. Hareven (Ed.), *Transitions: The family and the life course in historical perspective* (pp. 17–64). New York: Academic Press.

Elder, G.H. (1980). Adolescence in historical perspective. In J. Adelson (Ed.), *Handbook of adolescent psychology* (pp. 3–46). New York: Wiley.

Elder, G.H., & Caspi, A. (1988). Economic stress in lives: Developmental perspectives. *Journal of Social Issues, 44*, 25–45.

Endler, N.S., & Magnusson, D. (1976). Toward an interactional psychology of personality. *Psychological Bulletin, 83*, 956–974.

Erikson, E.H. (1950). *Childhood and society.* New York: Norton.

Erikson, E.H. (1959). Identity and the life cycle. *Psychological Issues, 1*, 50–100.

Erikson, E.H. (1968). *Identity: Youth and crisis.* New York: Norton.

Erikson, E.H. (1980). *Identity and the life cycle.* New York: Norton.

Erikson, E.H. (1982). *The life cycle completed.* New York: Norton.

Estes, R.J., & Wilensky, H.L. (1978). Life cycle squeeze and the morale curve. *Social Problems, 25*, 277–292.

Eyer, J. (1977). Does unemployment cause the death rate peak in each business cycle? *International Journal of Health Services*, *7*, 625–662.

Fagin, L., & Little, M. (1984). *The forsaken families*. Harmondsworth: Penguin.

Feagin, J.R. (1972). Poverty: We still believe that God helps those who help themselves. *Psychology Today*, *6*, 101–129.

Feather, N.T. (1959a). Subjective probability and decision under uncertainty. *Psychological Review*, *66*, 150–164.

Feather, N.T. (1959b). Success probability and choice behavior. *Journal of Experimental Psychology*, *58*, 257–266.

Feather, N.T. (1963). Mowrer's revised two-factor theory and the motive-expectancy-value model. *Psychological Review, 70*, 500–515.

Feather, N.T. (1969). Attribution of responsibility and valence of success and failure in relation to initial confidence and task performance. *Journal of Personality and Social Psychology*, *39*, 129–144.

Feather, N.T. (1971). Organization and discrepancy in cognitive structures. *Psychological Review*, *78*, 355–379.

Feather N.T. (1972). Value similarity and value systems in state and independent secondary schools. *Australian Journal of Psychology*, *24*, 305–315.

Feather, N.T. (1974). Explanations of poverty in Australian and American samples: The person, society, or fate? *Australian Journal of Psychology*, *26*, 199–216.

Feather, N.T. (1975). *Values in education and society*. New York: Free Press.

Feather, N.T. (1979). Human values and the work situation: Two studies. *Australian Psychologist*, *14*, 131–141.

Feather, N.T. (1980). Values in adolescence. In J. Adelson (Ed.), *Handbook of adolescent psychology* (pp. 247–294). New York: Wiley.

Feather, N.T. (1982a). Actions in relation to expected consequences: An overview of a research program. In N.T. Feather (Ed.), *Expectations and actions: Expectancy-value models in psychology* (pp. 53–95). Hillsdale, NJ: Erlbaum.

Feather, N.T. (1982b). Expectancy-value approaches: Present status and future directions. In N.T. Feather (Ed.), *Expectations and actions: Expectancy-value models in psychology* (pp. 395–420). Hillsdale, NJ: Erlbaum.

Feather, N.T. (Ed.). (1982c). *Expectations and actions: Expectancy-value models in psychology*. Hillsdale, NJ: Erlbaum.

Feather, N.T. (1982d). Human values and the prediction of action: An expectancy-valence analysis. In N.T. Feather (Ed.), *Expectations and actions: Expectancy-value models in psychology* (pp. 263–289). Hillsdale, NJ: Erlbaum.

Feather, N.T. (1982e). Unemployment and its psychological correlates: A study of depressive symptoms, self-esteem, Protestant ethic values, attributional style, and apathy. *Australian Journal of Psychology*, *34*, 309–323.

Feather, N.T. (1983a). Causal attributions and beliefs about work and unemployment among adolescents in state and independent secondary schools. *Australian Journal of Psychology*, *35*, 211–232.

Feather, N.T. (1983b). Causal attributions for good and bad outcomes in achievement and affiliation situations. *Australian Journal of Psychology*, *35*, 37–48.

Feather, N.T. (1983c). Some correlates of attributional style: Depressive symptoms, self-esteem, and Protestant ethic values. *Personality and Social Psychology Bulletin*, *9*, 125–135.

Feather, N.T. (1984a). Masculinity, femininity, psychological androgyny, and the structure of values. *Journal of Personality and Social Psychology*, *47*, 604–620.

Feather, N.T. (1984b). Protestant ethic, conservatism, and values. *Journal of Personality and Social Psychology*, *46*, 1132–1141.

Feather, N.T. (1985a). Attitudes, values, and attributions: Explanations of unemployment. *Journal of Personality and Social Psychology*, *48*, 876–889.

Feather, N.T. (1985b). Masculinity, femininity, self-esteem, and subclinical depression. *Sex Roles, 12*, 491–500.

Feather, N.T. (1985c). The psychological impact of unemployment: Empirical findings and theoretical approaches. In N.T. Feather (Ed.), *Australian psychology: Review of research* (pp. 265–295). Sydney: Allen & Unwin.

Feather, N.T. (1986a). Employment importance and helplessness about potential unemployment among students in secondary schools. *Australian Journal of Psychology, 38*, 33–44.

Feather, N.T. (1986b). Human values, valences, expectations, and affect: Theoretical issues emerging from recent applications of the expectancy-value model. In D.R. Brown & J. Veroff (Eds.), *Frontiers of motivational psychology: Essays in honor of John W. Atkinson* (pp. 146–172). New York: Springer-Verlag.

Feather, N.T. (1987a). Gender differences in values. In F. Halisch & J. Kuhl (Eds.), *Motivation, intention, and volition* (pp. 31–45). New York: Springer-Verlag.

Feather, N.T. (1987b). The rosy glow of self-esteem. *Australian Journal of Psychology, 39*, 25–41.

Feather, N.T. (1988a). From values to actions: Recent applications of the expectancy-value model. *Australian Journal of Psychology, 40*, 105–124.

Feather, N.T. (1988b). Values, valences, and course enrollment: Testing the role of personal values within an expectancy-valence framework. *Journal of Educational Psychology, 80*, 381–391.

Feather, N.T. (1989a). Reported changes in behaviour after job loss in a sample of older unemployed men. *Australian Journal of Psychology*.

Feather, N.T. (1989b). The effects of unemployment on work values and motivation. In U.W. Kleinbeck, H.H. Quast, H. Thierry, & H. Hacker (Eds.), *Work motivation* (pp. 201–229). Hillsdale, NJ: Erlbaum.

Feather, N.T. (in press). Bridging the gap between values and actions: Recent applications of the expectancy-value model. To appear in R. Sorrentino & E.T. Higgins (Eds.), *Handbook of motivation and cognition* (Vol. 2). New York: Guilford Press.

Feather, N.T., & Barber, J.G. (1983). Depressive reactions and unemployment. *Journal of Abnormal Psychology, 92*, 185–195.

Feather, N.T., & Bond, M.J. (1983). Time structure and purposeful activity among employed and unemployed university graduates. *Journal of Occupational Psychology, 56*, 241–254.

Feather, N.T., & Bond, M.J. (1984). Potential social action as a function of expectation-outcome discrepancies among employed and unemployed university graduates. *Australian Journal of Psychology, 36*, 205–217.

Feather, N.T., & Davenport, P.R. (1981). Unemployment and depressive affect: A motivational and attributional analysis. *Journal of Personality and Social Psychology, 41*, 422–436.

Feather, N.T., & Newton, J.W. (1982). Values, expectations, and the prediction of social action: An expectancy-valence analysis. *Motivation and Emotion, 6*, 217–244.

Feather, N.T., & O'Brien, G.E. (1986a). A longitudinal analysis of the effects of different patterns of employment and unemployment on school-leavers. *British Journal of Psychology, 77*, 459–479.

Feather, N.T., & O'Brien G.E. (1986b). A longitudinal study of the effects of employment and unemployment on school-leavers. *Journal of Occupational Psychology, 59*, 121–144.

Feather, N.T. & O'Brien, G.E. (1987). Looking for employment: An expectancy-valence analysis of job-seeking behaviour among young people. *Journal of Occupational Psychology, 78*, 251–272.

Feather, N.T., & Said, J.A. (1983). Preference for occupations in relation to masculinity, femininity, and gender. *British Journal of Social Psychology, 22*, 113–127.

Feather, N.T., & Tiggemann, M. (1984). A balanced measure of attributional style. *Australian Journal of Psychology, 36*, 267–283.

Feather, N.T., & Volkmer, R.E. (1988). Preference for situations involving effort, time pressure, and feedback in relation to Type A behavior, locus of control, and test anxiety. *Journal of Personality and Social Psychology, 55*, 266–271.

Fenigstein, A., Scheier, M.F., & Buss, A.H. (1975). Public and private self-consciousness: Assessment and theory. *Journal of Consulting and Clinical Psychology, 43*, 522–527.

Fineman, S. (1983). *White collar unemployment: Impact and stress.* Chichester: Wiley.

Fineman, S. (Ed.). (1987). *Unemployment: Personal and social consequences.* London: Tavistock.

Fink, S.L. (1967). Crisis and motivation—A theoretical model. *Archives of Physical Medicine and Rehabilitation, 43*, 592–597.

Finlay-Jones, R.A., & Eckhardt, B. (1984). A social and psychiatric survey of unemployment among young people. *Australian and New Zealand Journal of Psychiatry, 18*, 135–143.

Fishbein, M., & Ajzen, I. (1975). *Belief, attitude, intention, and behavior: An introduction to theory and research.* Reading, MA: Addison-Wesley.

Fisher, S., & Reason, J. (Eds.) (1988). *Handbook of life stress, cognition and health.* Chichester: Wiley.

Frankel, B. (1987). *The post-industrial utopias.* Oxford: Blackwell.

Fraser, C. (1981). The social psychology of unemployment. In M. Jeeves (Ed.), *Psychology survey No. 3* (pp. 172–186). London: George Allen & Unwin.

French, J.R.P., Caplan, R.D., & Van Harrison, R. (1982). *The mechanisms of job stress and strain.* New York: Wiley.

Frese, M., & Sabini, J. (Eds.). (1985). *Goal directed behavior: On the concept of action in psychology.* Hillsdale, NJ: Erlbaum.

Frese, M., Stewart, J., & Hannover, B. (1987). Goal orientation and planfulness: Action styles as personality concepts. *Journal of Personality and Social Psychology, 52*, 1182–1194.

Freud, S. (1930). *Civilization and its discontents.* London: Hogarth.

Fryer, D. (1985). Stages in the psychological response to unemployment: A (dis)integrative review article. *Current Psychological Research and Reviews, 4*, 257–273.

Fryer, D. (1986). Employment deprivation and personal agency during unemployment: A critical discussion of Jahoda's explanation of the psychological effects of unemployment. *Social Behaviour, 1*, 3–23.

Fryer, D. (1987). Monmouthshire and Marienthal: Sociographies of two unemployed communities. In D. Fryer & P. Ullah (Eds.), *Unemployed people: Social and psychological perspectives* (pp. 74–93). Milton Keynes: Open University Press.

Fryer, D. (1988). The experience of unemployment in social context. In S. Fisher & J. Reason (Eds.), *Handbook of life stress, cognition and health* (pp. 211–238). Chichester: Wiley.

Fryer, D.M., & McKenna, S.P. (1987). The laying off of hands—Unemployment and the experience of time. In S. Fineman (Ed.), *Unemployment: Personal and social consequences* (pp. 47–73). London: Tavistock.

Fryer, D.M., & Payne, R.L. (1984). Pro-active behaviour in unemployment: Findings and implications. *Leisure Studies, 3*, 273–295.

Fryer, D., & Payne, R. (1986). Being unemployed: A review of the literature on the psychological experience of unemployment. In C.L. Cooper & I. Robertson (Eds.), *International review of industrial and organizational psychology* (pp. 235–278). Chichester: Wiley.

Fryer, D., & Ullah, P. (Eds.), (1987). *Unemployed people: Social and psychological perspectives.* Milton Keynes: Open University Press.

Furnham, A. (1982a). Explanations for unemployment in Britain. *European Journal of Social Psychology*, *12*, 335–352.

Furnham, A. (1982b). The protestant work ethic and attitudes towards unemployment. *Journal of Occupational Psychology*, *55*, 277–286.

Furnham, A. (1982c). Why are the poor always with us? Explanations of poverty in Britain. *British Journal of Social Psychology*, *21*, 311–322.

Furnham, A. (1985). Youth unemployment: A review of the literature. *Journal of Adolescence*, *8*, 109–124.

Furnham, A. (1988). *Lay theories: Everyday understandings of problems in the social sciences.* Oxford: Pergamon Press.

Garraty, J.A. (1978). *Unemployment in history: Economic thought and public policy.* New York: Harper & Row.

Gaskell, G., & Smith, P. (1985). An investigation of youth's attributions for unemployment and their political attitudes. *Journal of Economic Psychology*, *6*, 65–80.

Gergen, K.J., & Gergen, M.M. (1982). Explaining human conduct: Form and function. In P. Secord (Ed.), *Explaining human behavior: Consciousness, human action, and social structure* (pp. 127–154). Beverly Hills, CA: Sage.

Gjesme, T. (1981). Is there any future in achievement motivation? *Motivation and Emotion*, *5*, 115–138.

Glick, I.O., Weiss, R.S., & Parkes, C.M. (1974). *The first year of bereavement.* New York: Wiley.

Goffman, E. (1968). *Stigma: Notes on the management of spoiled identity.* Harmondsworth: Penguin.

Goldberg, D.P. (1972). *The detection of psychiatric illness by questionnaire.* London: Oxford University Press.

Goldberg, D.P. (1978). *Manual for the General Health Questionnaire.* Windsor: National Foundation for Educational Research.

Goldberger, L., & Breznitz, S. (Ed.). (1982). *Handbook of stress: Theoretical and clinical aspects.* New York: Free Press.

Gould, T., & Kenyon, J. (1972). *Stories from the dole queue.* Published in association with *New Society.* London: Temple Smith.

Grayson, J.P. (1985). The closure of a factory and its impact on health. *International Journal of Health Services*, *15*, 69–93.

Greenwald, A.G., & Pratkanis, A.R. (1984). The self. In R.S. Wyer & T.K. Srull (Eds.), *Handbook of social cognition* (pp. 129–178). Hillsdale, NJ: Erlbaum.

Gurney, R.M. (1980a). Does unemployment affect the self-esteem of school-leavers? *Australian Journal of Psychology*, *32*, 175–182.

Gurney, R.M. (1980b). The effects of unemployment on the psycho-social development of school leavers. *Journal of Occupational Psychology*, *53*, 205–213.

Gurney, R.M. (1981). Leaving school, facing unemployment, and making attributions about the causes of unemployment. *Journal of Vocational Behavior*, *18*, 79–91.

Gurr, T.R. (1970). *Why men rebel.* Princeton, NJ: Princeton University Press.

Hackman, J.R., & Oldham, G.R. (1975). Development of the Job Diagnostic Survey. *Journal of Applied Psychology*, *60*, 159–170.

Hackman, J.R., & Oldham, G.R. (1980). *Work redesign.* Reading, MA: Addison-Wesley.

Handy, C. (1984). *The future of work.* Oxford: Blackwell.

Hansson, R.O., Stroebe, M.S., & Stroebe, W. (Eds.). (1988). Bereavement and widowhood. *Journal of Social Issues, 44*(3).

Harré, R., & Secord, P.F. (1972). *The explanation of social behaviour.* Oxford. Blackwell.

Harrison, R. (1976). The demoralizing experience of prolonged unemployment. *Department of Education Gazette*, *84*, 339–348.

Hartley, J. (1980). The impact of unemployment upon the self-esteem of managers. *Journal of Occupational Psychology*, *53*, 147–155.

Hartley, J., & Fryer, D. (1984). The psychology of unemployment: A critical appraisal. In G.M. Stephenson (Ed.), *Progress in applied social psychology* (Vol. 2, pp. 3–30). Chichester: Wiley.

Harvey, J.H., & Weary, G. (1984). Current issues in attribution theory and research. *Annual Review of Psychology*, *35*, 427–459.

Harvey, J.H., & Weary, G. (1985). *Attribution: Basic issues and applications.* Orlando, FL: Academic Press.

Havighurst, R.J. (1973). History of developmental psychology: Socialization and personality development across the life span. In P.B. Baltes & K.W. Schaie (Eds.), *Life-span developmental psychology: Personality and socialization* (pp. 4–24). New York: Academic Press.

Hayes, J., & Nutman, P. (1981). *Understanding the unemployed.* London: Tavistock.

Heckhausen, H. (1977). Achievement motivation and its constructs: A cognitive model. *Motivation and Emotion*, *1*, 329–335.

Heckhausen, H. (1986). Why some time out might benefit achievement motivation research. In J.H.L. van den Bercken, Th.C.M. Bergen, & E.E.J. De Bruyn (Eds.), *Achievement and task motivation* (pp. 7–39). Lisse: Swets & Zeitlinger.

Heider, F. (1958). *The psychology of interpersonal relations.* New York: Wiley.

Hepworth, S.J. (1980). Moderating effects of the psychological impact of unemployment. *Journal of Occupational Psychology*, *53*, 139–145.

Higgins, E.T. (1987). Self-discrepancy: A theory relating self and affect. *Psychological Review*, *94*, 319–340.

Higgins, E.T., Strauman, T., & Klein, R. (1986). Standards and the process of self-evaluation: Multiple affects from multiple stages. In R.M. Sorrentino & E.T. Higgins (Eds.), *Handbook of motivation and cognition: Foundations of social behavior* (23–63). New York: Guilford Press.

Hill, J.M.M. (1977). *The social and psychological impact of unemployment.* London: Tavistock.

Hill, J.M.M. (1978). The psychological impact of unemployment. *New Society*, Jan. 118–120.

Holland, J.L. (1973). *Making vocational choices: A theory of careers.* Englewood Cliffs, NJ: Prentice-Hall.

Holland, J.L. (1976). Vocational preferences. In M.D. Dunnette (Ed.), *Handbook of industrial and organizational psychology.* (pp. 521–570) Chicago: Rand McNally.

Holmes, T., & Rahe, R.H. (1967). The social readjustment rating scale. *Journal of Psychosomatic Research*, *11*, 213–218.

House, J.S. (1981). *Work stress and social support.* Reading, MA: Addison-Wesley.

Howard, A., & Scott, R.A. (1965). A proposed framework for the analysis of stress in the human organism. *Behavioral Science*, *10*, 141–166.

Hull, C.L. (1943). *Principles of behavior.* New York: Appleton-Century-Crofts.

Hunt, S.M., McEwen, J., & McKenna, S.P. (1985). Measuring health status: A new tool for clinicians and epidemiologists. *Journal of the Royal College of General Practitioners*, *35*, 185–188.

Israeli, N. (1935). Distress in the outlook of Lancashire and Scottish unemployed. *Journal of Applied Psychology*, *19*, 67–69.

Iverson, L., & Sabroe, S. (1988). Psychological well-being among unemployed and employed people after a company closedown: A longitudinal study. *Journal of Social Issues*, *44*, 141–152.

Jackson, M.P. (1985). *Youth unemployment.* London: Croom Helm.

Jackson, P.R., Stafford, E.M., Banks, M.H., & Warr, P.B. (1983). Unemployment and psychological distress in young people: The moderating role of employment commitment. *Journal of Applied Psychology*, *68*, 525–535.

Jackson, P.R., & Warr, P.B. (1984). Unemployment and psychological ill-health: The moderating role of duration and age. *Psychological Medicine*, *14*, 605–614.

Jackson, P.R., & Warr, P.B. (1987). Mental health of unemployed men in different parts of England and Wales. *British Medical Journal*, *295*, 525.

Jacobson, E. (1971). Normal and pathological moods: Their nature and function. In E. Jacobson (Ed.), *Depression: Comparative studies of normal, neurotic, and psychotic conditions* (pp. 66–106). New York: International Universities Press.

Jahoda, M. (1979). The impact of unemployment in the 1930s and 1970s. *Bulletin of the British Psychological Society*, *32*, 309–314.

Jahoda, M. (1981). Work, employment, and unemployment: Values, theories, and approaches in social research. *American Psychologist*, *36*, 184–191.

Jahoda, M. (1982). *Employment and unemployment: A social-psychological analysis*. Cambridge: Cambridge University Press.

Jahoda, M. (1987). Unemployed men at work. In D. Fryer & P. Ullah (Eds.), *Unemployed people: Social and psychological perspectives* (pp. 1–73). Milton Keynes: Open University Press.

Jahoda, M. (1988). Economic recession and mental health: Some conceptual issues. *Journal of Social Issues*, *44*, 13–23.

Jahoda, M., Lazarsfeld, P.F., & Zeisel, H. (1933). *Marienthal: The sociography of an unemployed community* (English translation, 1971). Chicago: Aldine.

Jahoda, M., & Rush, J. (1980). *Work, employment, and unemployment*. Occasional Paper Series, No. 12, Science Policy Research Unit, Sussex University.

James, W. (1890). *The principles of psychology*. New York: Holt.

Janoff-Bulman, R. (1979). Characterological versus behavioral self-blame: Inquiries into depression and rape. *Journal of Personality and Social Psychology*, *37*, 1798–1809.

Jaspars, J., Fincham, F.D., & Hewstone, M. (1983). *Attribution theory and research: Conceptual, developmental and social dimensions*. London: Academic Press.

Jennings, M.K., & Niemi, R.G. (1975). Continuity and change in political orientations: A longitudinal study of two generations. *American Political Science Review*, *69*, 1316–1335.

John, J. (1987). Health effects of unemployment: Approaches and results of empirical research in the Federal Republic of Germany. In D. Schwefel, P-G. Svensson, & H. Zöllner (Eds.), *Unemployment, social vulnerability, and health in Europe* (pp. 48–89). New York: Springer-Verlag.

Jones, E.E., & Davis, K.E. (1965). From acts to dispositions: The attribution process in person perception. In L. Berkowitz (Ed.), *Advances in experimental social psychology* (Vol. 2, pp. 220–266). New York: Academic Press.

Jones, E.E., & Nisbett, R.E. (1972). The actor and the observer: Divergent perceptions of the causes of behavior. In E.E. Jones, D.E. Kanouse, H.H. Kelley, R.E. Nisbett, S. Valins, & B. Weiner (Eds.), *Attribution: Perceiving the causes of behavior* (pp. 79–94). Morristown, NJ: General Learning Press.

Jones, W. (1981). *Education and unemployment*. Hawthorn, Vic.: Australian Council for Educational Research.

Kahneman, D., Slovic, P., & Tversky, A. (Eds.). (1982) *Judgment under uncertainty: Heuristics and biases*. New York: Cambridge University Press.

Karasek, R.A. (1979). Job demands, job decision latitude, and mental strain: Implications for job redesign. *Administrative Science Quarterly*, *24*, 285–308.

Karasek, R.A. (1981). Job socialization and job strain: The implications of two related psychosocial mechanisms for job design. In B. Gardell & G. Johansson (Eds.), *Working life*. Chichester: Wiley.

Kasl, S.V. (1979). Changes in mental health status associated with job loss and retirement. In M.E. Barrett, R.M. Rose, & G.L. Klerman (Eds.), *Stress and mental disorder*. New York: Raven Press.

Kasl, S.V. (1982). Strategies of research on economic instability and health. *Psychological Medicine*, *12*, 637–649.

Kasl, S.V., & Cobb, S. (1982). Variability of stress effects among men experiencing job loss. In L. Goldberger & S. Breznitz (Ed.), *Handbook of stress: Theoretical and clinical aspects* (pp. 445–465). New York: Free Press.

Kaufman, H.G. (1982). *Professionals in search of work: Coping with the stress of job loss and underemployment.* New York: Wiley.

Kelley, H.H. (1967). Attribution theory in social psychology. In D. Levine (Ed.), *Nebraska symposium on motivation* (Vol. 15, pp. 192–238). Lincoln: University of Nebraska Press.

Kelley, H.H., & Michela, J. (1980). Attribution theory and research. *Annual Review of Psychology*, *31*, 457–501.

Kelvin, P. (1980). Social psychology 2001: The social psychological bases and implications of structural unemployment. In R. Gilmour and S. Duck (Eds.), *The development of social psychology* (pp. 293–316). New York: Academic Press.

Kelvin, P., & Jarrett, J.E. (1985). *Unemployment: Its social psychological effects.* Cambridge: Cambridge University Press.

Kessler, R.C. (1987). The interplay of research design strategies and data analysis procedures in evaluating the effects of stress on health. In S. Kasl & C. Cooper (Eds.), *Stress and health: Issues in research methodology* (pp. 113–140). New York: Wiley.

Kessler, R.C., House, J.S., & Turner, J.B. (1987). Unemployment and health in a community sample. *Journal of Health and Social Behavior*, *28*, 51–59.

Kessler, R.C., Price, R.H., & Wortman, C.B. (1985). Social factors in psychopathology: Stress, social support, and coping process. *Annual Review of Psychology*, *36*, 531–572.

Kessler, R.C., Turner, J.B., & House, J.S. (1987). Intervening processes in the relationship between unemployment and health. *Psychological Medicine*, *17*, 949–961.

Kessler, R.C., Turner, J.B., & House, J.S. (1988). The effects of unemployment on health in a community survey: Main, modifying, and mediating effects. *Journal of Social Issues*.

Kieselbach, T., & Svensson, P-G. (1988). Health and social policy responses to unemployment in Europe. *Journal of Social Issues*, *44*, 173–191.

Kilpatrick, R., & Trew, K. (1985). Life-styles and psychological well-being among unemployed men in Northern Ireland. *Journal of Occupational Psychology*, *58*, 207–216.

Klinger, E. (1975). Consequences of commitment to and disengagement from incentives. *Psychological Review*, *82*, 1–25.

Klinger, E. (1977). *Meaning and void: Inner experience and the incentives in people's lives.* Minneapolis: University of Minnesota Press.

Kluckhohn, C., Murray, H.A., & Schneider, D.M. (Eds.). (1955). *Personality in nature, society, and culture.* New York: Knopf.

Kobasa, S.C., Maddi, S.R., & Courington, S. (1981). Personality and constitution as mediators in the stress-illness relationship. *Journal of Health and Social Behavior*, *22*, 368–378.

Kobasa, S.C., Maddi, S.R., & Kahn, S. (1982). Hardiness and health: A prospective study. *Journal of Personality and Social Psychology*, *42*, 168–177.

Kohlberg, L. (1984). *The psychology of moral development: The nature and validity of moral stages.* San Francisco: Harper & Row.

Kohn, M.L. (1977). *Class and conformity: A study in values* (2d ed.). Chicago: University of Chicago Press.

Kohn, M.L., & Schooler, C. (1983). *Work and personality: An inquiry into the effect of social stratification.* Norwood, NJ: Ablex Publishing Co.

Komarovsky, M. (1940). *The unemployed man and his family. The effect of unemployment upon the status of the man in 59 families.* New York: Dryden.

Kubler-Ross, E. (1969). *On death and dying.* New York: Macmillan.

Kuhl, J. (1985). Volitional mediators of cognition-behavior consistency: Self-regulatory processes and action versus state orientation. In J. Kuhl & J. Beckmann (Eds.), *Action control: From cognition to behavior* (101–128). New York: Springer-Verlag.

Kuhl, J. (1987). Action control: The maintenance of motivational states. In F. Halisch & J. Kuhl (Eds.), *Motivation, intention and volition* (279–291). New York: Springer-Verlag.

Kuhl, J., & Beckmann, J. (Eds.) (1985). *Action control: From cognition to behavior.* New York: Springer-Verlag.

Lazarsfeld, P.F. (1971). Introduction. In M. Jahoda, P.F. Lazarsfeld, & H. Zeisel, *Marienthal: The sociography of an unemployed community* (English translation, 1971, by Aldine-Atherton, New York).

Lazarus, R.S. (1966). *Psychological stress and the coping process.* New York: McGraw-Hill.

Lazarus, R.S., & Folkman, S. (1984). *Stress, appraisal, and coping.* New York: Springer-Verlag.

Lazarus, R.S., & Launier, R. (1978). Stress-related transactions between person and environment. In L. A. Pervin & M. Lewis (Eds.), *Perspectives in interactional psychology* (287–327). New York: Plenum.

Lehman, D.R., Wortman, C.B., & Williams, A.F. (1987). Long-term effects of losing a spouse or child in a motor vehicle crash. *Journal of Personality and Social Psychology, 52,* 218–231.

Lenney, E. (1977). Women's self-confidence in achievement settings. *Psychological Bulletin, 84,* 1–13.

Lens, W. (1986). Future time perspective: A cognitive-motivational concept. In D.R. Brown & J. Veroff (Eds.), *Frontiers of motivational psychology: Essays in honor of John W. Atkinson* (pp. 173–190). New York: Springer-Verlag.

Lerner, M.J. (1980). *The belief in a just world: A fundamental delusion.* New York: Plenum Press.

Leventhman, P.G. (1981). *Professionals out of work.* New York: Free Press.

Levinson, D.J., Darrow, C.N., Klein, E.B., Levinson, M.H., & McKee, B. (1978). *The seasons of a man's life.* New York: Knopf.

Lewin, K. (1936). *Principles of topological psychology.* New York: McGraw-Hill.

Lewin, K. (1938). The conceptual representation and the measurement of psychological forces. *Contributions to Psychological Theory, 1.* New York: Johnson Reprint Corporation.

Lewin, K (1951). *Field theory in social science.* New York: Harper.

Lewin, K., Dembo, T., Festinger, L., & Sears, P.S. (1944). Level of aspiration. In J. McV. Hunt (Ed.), *Personality and the behavior disorders* (Vol. 1, pp. 333–378). New York: Ronald.

Liem, R., & Liem, J.H. (1988). Psychological effects of unemployment on workers and their families. *Journal of Social Issues, 44,* 87–105.

Liker, J.K., & Elder, G.H. (1983). Economic hardship and marital relations in the 1930s. *American Sociological Review, 48,* 343–359.

Linn, M.W., Sandifer, R., & Stein, S. (1985). Effects of unemployment on mental and physical health. *American Journal of Public Health, 75,* 502–506.

Lipset, S.M. (1972). *Rebellion in the university.* Boston: Little, Brown & Co.

Locke, E.A., Motowildo, S.J., & Bobko, P. (1986). Using self-efficacy theory to resolve the conflict between goal-setting theory and expectancy theory in organizational behavior and industrial/organizational psychology. *Journal of Social and Cli-*

nical Psychology, *4*, 328–338.

Locke, E.A., Shaw, K.N., Saari, L.M., & Latham, G.P. (1981). Goal setting and task performance: 1969–1980. *Psychological Bulletin*, *90*, 125–152.

Markus, H., & Nurius, P. (1986). Possible selves. *American Psychologist*, *41*, 954–969.

Marsden, D., & Duff, E. (1975). *Workless: Some unemployed men and their families*. Harmondsworth: Penguin.

Marsh, C., Fraser, C., & Jobling, R. (1985). Political responses to unemployment. In B. Roberts, R. Finnegan, & D. Gallie (Eds.), *New approaches to economic life: Economic restructuring, unemployment and the social division of labour*. Manchester: Manchester University Press.

Marsh, H.W., & O'Neill, R. (1984). Self-description Questionnaire III (SDQIII): The construct validity of multidimensional self-concept ratings by late adolescents. *Journal of Educational Measurement*, *21*, 153–174.

McClelland, D.C. (1985). *Human motivation*. Glenview, Ill: Scott, Foresman & Company.

McKee, L., & Bell, C. (1986). His unemployment, her problem: The domestic and marital consequences of male unemployment. In S. Allen, A. Waton, K. Purcell, & S. Wood (Eds.), *The experience of unemployment* (pp. 134–149). London: Macmillan.

McKenna, S.P., & Fryer, D.M. (1984). Perceived health during lay-off and early unemployment. *Occupational Health*, *36*, 201–206.

Mead, G.H. (1934). *Mind, self and society*. Chicago: University of Chicago Press.

Miles, I. (1983). *Adaptation to unemployment?* Occasional Paper Series, No. 20, Science Policy Research Unit, University of Sussex.

Miles, I., Howard, J., & Henwood, F. (1984). *Dependence, interdependence and changing work roles*. University of Sussex, Science Policy Research Unit Report.

Miller, G.A., Galanter, E., & Pribram, K.H. (1960). *Plans and the structure of behavior*. New York: Holt, Rinehart, & Winston.

Mineka, S., & Hendersen, R.W. (1985). Controllability and predictability in acquired motivation. *Annual Review of Psychology*, *36*, 495–529.

Mirels, H.L., & Garrett, J.B. (1971). The Protestant ethic as a personality variable. *Journal of Consulting and Clinical Psychology*, *36*, 40–44.

Mitchell, T.R. (1982). Expectancy-value models in organizational psychology. In N.T. Feather (Ed.), *Expectations and actions: Expectancy-value models in psychology* (pp. 293–312). Hillsdale, NJ: Erlbaum.

Muller, E.N. (1980). The psychology of political protest and violence. In T.R. Gurr (Ed.), *Handbook of political conflict: Theory and research* (pp. 69–99). New York: Free Press.

Murray, H.A. (1938). *Explorations in personality*. New York: Oxford University Press.

Nie, N.H., Hull, C.H., Jenkins, J.G., Steinbrenner, K., & Bent, D.H. (1975). *SPSS: Statistical package for the social sciences*. New York: McGraw Hill.

Nisbett, R., & Ross L. (1980). *Human inference: Strategies and shortcomings of social judgment*. Englewood Cliffs, NJ: Prentice-Hall.

Nuttin, J. (1985). *Future time perspective and motivation*. Hillsdale, NJ: Erlbaum.

Nygard, R. (1981). Toward an interactional psychology: Models from achievement motivation research. *Journal of Personality*, *49*, 363–387.

O'Brien, G.E. (1980). The centrality of skill-utilization for job design. In K. Duncan, M. Gruneberg, & D. Wallis (Eds.), *Changes in working life* (pp. 167–187). Chichester: Wiley.

O'Brien, G.E. (1981). Locus of control, previous occupation and satisfaction with retirement. *Australian Journal of Psychology*, *33*, 305–318.

O'Brien, G.E. (1982). The relative contribution of perceived skill-utilization and other perceived job attitudes to the prediction of job satisfaction: A cross validation study. *Human Relations*, *35*, 219–237.

O'Brien, G.E. (1983). Skill-utilization, skill-variety and the job characteristics model. *Australian Journal of Psychology*, *35*, 461–468.

O'Brien, G.E. (1984). Locus of control, work, and retirement. In H.M. Lefcourt (Ed.), *Research with the locus of control construct* (Vol. 3, pp. 7–72). New York: Academic Press.

O'Brien, G.E. (1985). Distortion in unemployment research: The early studies of Bakke and their implications for current research on employment and unemployment. *Human Relations*, *38*, 877–894.

O'Brien, G.E. (1986). *Psychology of work and unemployment.* Chichester: Wiley.

O'Brien, G.E. (1988, August). *A theory about the psychological functions of work.* Paper presented at 24th International Congress of Psychology, Sydney, Australia.

O'Brien, G.E., & Dowling, P. (1980). The effects of congruency between perceived and desired job attributes upon job satisfaction. *Journal of Occupational Psychology*, *53*, 121–130.

O'Brien, G.E., Dowling, P., & Kabanoff, B. (1978). *Work, health, and leisure.* Working paper 28, National Institute of Labour Studies, Flinders University of South Australia.

O'Brien, G.E., & Feather, N.T. (1989). The relative effects of unemployment and quality of employment on the affect, work values and personal control of adolescents. *Journal of Occupational Psychology*, in press.

O'Brien, G.E., & Humphrys, P. (1982). The effects of congruency between work values and perceived attributes upon job satisfaction of pharmacists. *Australian Journal of Psychology*, *34*, 91–101.

O'Brien, G.E., & Kabanoff, B. (1981). Australian norms and factor analysis of Rotter's internal-external control scale. *Australian Psychologist*, *16*, 184–202.

Parkes, C.M., & Weiss, R.S. (1983). *Recovery from bereavement.* New York: Basic Books.

Parnes, H.S., & King, R. (1977). Middle-aged job loser. *Industrial Gerontology*, *4*, 77–95.

Patton, W., & Noller, P. (1984). Unemployment and youth: A longitudinal study. *Australian Journal of Psychology*, *36*, 399–413.

Payne, R.L. (1979). Demands, supports, constraints and psychological health. In C.J. McKay & I. Cox (Eds.), *Response to stress: Occupational aspects.* London: International Publishing Corporation.

Payne, R.L., & Hartley, J. (1984). *Financial situation, health, and personal attributes as predictors of psychological experience amongst unemployed men.* MRC/ESRC Social and Applied Psychology Unit Memo. No. 727, University of Sheffield.

Payne, R., & Hartley, J. (1987). A test of a model for explaining the affective experience of unemployed men. *Journal of Occupational Psychology*, *60*, 31–47.

Payne, R.L., Warr, P.B., & Hartley, J. (1984). Social class and psychological ill-health during unemployment. *Sociology of Health and Illness*, *6*, 152–174.

Pearlin, L.J., Lieberman, M.A., Menaghan, E.S., & Mullan, J.T. (1981). The stress process. *Journal of Health and Social Behavior*, *22*, 337–356.

Pearlin, L.J., & Schooler, C. (1978). The structure of coping. *Journal of Health and Social Behavior*, *19*, 2–21.

Perlmutter, M., & Hall, E. (1985). *Adult development and aging.* New York: Wiley.

Perloff, J.M., & Persons, J.B. (1988). Biases resulting from the use of indexes: An application to attributional style and depression. *Psychological Bulletin*, *103*, 95–104.

Pervin, L.A. (1968). Performance and satisfaction as a function of individual-environment fit. *Psychological Bulletin, 69,* 56–68.

Pervin, L.A., & Lewis, M. (Eds.). (1978). *Perspectives in interactional psychology.* New York: Plenum.

Peterson, C., Schwartz, S.M., & Seligman, M.E.P. (1981). Self-blame and depressive symptoms. *Journal of Personality and Social Psychology, 41,* 253–259.

Peterson, C., & Seligman, M.E.P. (1984). Causal explanations as a risk factor for depression: Theory and evidence. *Psychological Review, 91,* 347–374.

Peterson, C., Semmel, A., von Baeyer, C., Abramson, L.Y., Metalsky, G.I., & Seligman, M.E.P. (1982). The attributional style questionnaire. *Cognitive Therapy and Research, 6,* 287–299.

Piers, G., & Singer, M.B. (1971). *Shame and guilt.* New York: Norton.

Pilgrim Trust. (1938). *Men without work.* Cambridge: Cambridge University Press.

Powell, D.H., & Driscoll, S.P.F. (1973). Middle class professionals face unemployment. *Society, 10,* 18–26.

Quinn, R., & Shepard, L. (1974). *The 1972–3 quality of employment survey.* Ann Arbor, MI: Survey Research Center, University of Michigan.

Raynor, J.O., & Entin, E. (Eds.) (1982). *Motivation, career striving, and aging.* Washington, DC: Hemisphere.

Rogers, C.R. (1961). *On becoming a person.* Boston: Houghton Mifflin.

Rokeach, M. (1973). *The nature of human values.* New York: Free Press.

Rosenberg, M. (1957). *Occupations and values.* Glencoe, IL: Free Press.

Rosenberg, M. (1965). *Society and the adolescent self-image.* Princeton, NJ: Princeton University Press.

Rosenberg, M. (1979). *Conceiving the self.* New York: Basic Books.

Rosenberg, M. (1981). The self-concept: Social product and social force. In M. Rosenberg & R.H. Turner (Eds.), *Social psychology: Sociological perspectives* (pp. 593–624). New York: Basic Books.

Rosenthal, R., & Rosnow, R.L. (1975). *The volunteer subject.* New York: Wiley.

Rotter, J.B. (1954). *Social learning and clinical psychology.* Englewood Cliffs, NJ: Prentice-Hall.

Rotter, J.B. (1966). Generalized expectancies for internal versus external control of reinforcement. *Psychological Monographs, 80,* 1–28.

Rowley, K.M., & Feather, N.T. (1987). The impact of unemployment in relation to age and length of unemployment. *Journal of Occupational Psychology, 60,* 323–332.

Russell, D.W. (1982). The causal dimension scale: A measure of how individuals perceive causes. *Journal of Personality and Social Psychology, 42,* 1137–1145.

Sarason, I.G., & Sarason, B.R. (Eds.). (1985). *Social support: Theory, research, and applications.* Boston: Martinus Nijhoff.

Schaefer, C., Coyne, J.C., & Lazarus, R.S. (1982). The health-related functions of social support. *Journal of Behavioral Medicine, 4,* 381–406.

Schafer, R. (1967). Ideals, the ego ideal, and the ideal self. In R.R. Holt (Ed.), Motives and thought: Psychoanalytic essays in honor of David Rapaport [Special issue]. *Psychological Issues, 5,* 131–174.

Schaie, K.W. (Ed.). (1983). *Longitudinal studies of adult psychological development.* New York: Guilford Press.

Schaufeli, W.B. (1988a). Perceiving the causes of unemployment: An evaluation of the causal dimensions scale in a real-life situation. *Journal of Personality and Social Psychology, 54,* 347–356.

Schaufeli, W.B. (1988b). *Unemployment and psychological health: An investigation among Dutch professionals.* Unpublished doctoral dissertation. Ryksuniversiteit Groningen.

Schore, L. (1984). The Fremont experience: A counseling program for dislocated workers. *International Journal of Mental Health, 13,* 154–167.

Schwefel, D., Svensson, P-G., & Zöllner, H. (Eds.). (1987). *Unemployment, social vulnerability, and health in Europe.* New York: Springer-Verlag.

Seligman, M.E.P. (1975). *Helplessness: On depression, development, and death.* San Francisco: Freeman.

Seligman, M.E.P., Abramson, L.Y., Semmel, A., & von Baeyer, C. (1979). Depressive attributional style. *Journal of Abnormal Psychology, 88,* 242–247.

Shamir, B. (1986a). Protestant work ethic, work involvement and the psychological impact of unemployment. *Journal of Occupational Behaviour, 7,* 25–38.

Shamir, B. (1986b). Self-esteem and the psychological impact of unemployment. *Social Psychology Quarterly, 49,* 61–72.

Shaver, K. (1985). *The attribution of blame: Causality, responsibility, and blameworthiness.* New York: Springer-Verlag.

Shontz, F.C. (1975). *The psychological aspects of physical illness and disability.* New York: Macmillan.

Silver, R.L., & Wortman, C.B. (1980). Coping with undesirable life events. In J. Garber & M.E.P. Seligman (Eds.), *Human helplessness: Theory and applications* (pp. 279–340). New York: Academic Press.

Sinfield, A. (1968). *The long term unemployed.* Paris: OECD.

Sinfield, A. (1970). Poor and out-of-work in Shields. In P. Townsend (Ed.), *The concept of poverty* (pp. 220–235). London: Heinemann.

Sinfield, A. (1981). *What unemployment means.* Oxford: Martin Robertson.

Smith, T.W., & Anderson, N.B. (1986). Models of personality and disease: An interactional approach to Type A behavior and cardiovascular risk. *Journal of Personality and Social Psychology, 50,* 1166–1173.

Spence, J.T., Helmreich, R.L. (1978). *Masculinity and feminity: Their psychological dimensions, correlates, and antecedents.* Austin: University of Texas Press.

Spence, K.W. (1956). *Behavior theory and conditioning.* New Haven: Yale University Press.

Spruit, I.P., Bastiaansen, J., Verkley, H., van Niewenhuijzen, M.G., & Stolk, J. (1985). *Experiencing unemployment, financial constraints and health.* Leiden: Institute of Social Medicine.

Spruit, I.P., & Svensson, P-G. (1987). Young and unemployed: Special problems? In D. Schwefel, P-G. Svensson, & H. Zöllner (Eds.), *Unemployment, social vulnerability, and health in Europe* (pp. 196–208). New York: Springer-Verlag.

Stafford, E.M., Jackson, P.R., & Banks, M.H. (1980). Employment, work involvement and mental health in less qualified young people. *Journal of Occupational Psychology, 53,* 291–304.

Stern, G.G. (1970). *People in context: Measuring person-environment congruence in education and industry.* New York: Wiley.

Stokes, G., & Cochrane, R. (1984). A study of the psychological effects of redundancy and unemployment. *Journal of Occupational Psychology, 57,* 309–322.

Super, D.E., & Hall, D.T. (1978). Career development: Exploration and planning. *Annual Review of Psychology, 29,* 333–372.

Taylor, F.I. (1909). *A bibliography of unemployment and the unemployed.* London: P.S. King & Son.

Taylor, M.C. (1982). Improved conditions, rising expectations, and dissatisfaction: A test of the past/present relative deprivation hypothesis. *Social Psychology Quarterly, 45,* 24–33.

Taylor, S.E. (1983). Adjustment to threatening events: A theory of cognitive adaptation. *American Psychologist, 38,* 1161–1173.

Taylor, S.E. (1986). *Health psychology.* New York: Random House.

Thoits, P. (1983). Dimensions of life events that influence psychological distress: An evaluation and synthesis of the literature. In H.B. Kaplan (Ed.), *Psychosocial stress: Trends in theory and research* (pp. 33–103). New York: Academic Press.

Thomae, H., & Lehr, U. (1986). Stages, crises, conflicts, and life-span development. In A.B. Sorensen, F.E. Weinert, & L.R. Sherrod (Eds.), *Human development and the life course* (pp. 429–444). Hillsdale, NJ: Erlbaum.

Tiffany, D.W., Cowan, J.R., & Tiffany, P.M. (1970). *The unemployed: A social psychological portrait.* Englewood Cliffs, NJ: Prentice-Hall.

Tiggemann, M., & Winefield, A.H. (1984). The effects of employment on the mood, self-esteem, locus of control and depressive affect of school-leavers. *Journal of Occupational Psychology, 57*, 33–42.

Tolman, E.C. (1955). Principles of performance. *Psychological Review, 62*, 315–326.

Turner, R.L. (1983). Direct, indirect, and moderating effects of support on psychological distress and associated conditions. In H.B. Kaplan (Ed.), *Psychosocial stress: Trends in theory and research* (pp. 105–155). New York: Academic Press.

Ullah, P. (1988). *Cross-cultural differences between English and Australian youths in the psychological experience of unemployment.* Paper presented at 24th International Congress of Psychology, Sydney, Australia.

Ullah, P., & Banks, M.H. (1985). Youth unemployment and labour market withdrawal. *Journal of Economic Psychology, 6*, 51–64.

Ullah, P., Banks, M.H., & Warr, P.B. (1985). Social support, social pressures and psychological distress during unemployment. *Psychological Medicine, 15*, 283–295.

Van Calster, K., Lens, W., & Nuttin, J.R. (1987). Affective attitude toward the personal future: Impact on motivation in high school boys. *American Journal of Psychology, 100*, 1–13.

Vaux, A. (1985). Variations in social support associated with gender, ethnicity, and age. *Journal of Social Issues, 41*, 89–110.

Vinokur, A., & Caplan, R.D. (1987). Attitudes and social support: Determinants of job-seeking behavior and well-being among the unemployed. *Journal of Applied Social Psychology, 17*, 1007–1024.

Vroom, V.H. (1964). *Work and motivation.* New York: Wiley.

Walker, I., & Mann, L. (1987). Unemployment, relative deprivation, and social protest. *Personality and Social Psychology Bulletin, 13*, 275–283.

Walker, I., & Pettigrew, T.F. (1984). Relative deprivation theory: An overview and conceptual critique. *British Journal of Social Psychology, 23*, 301–310.

Warr, P.B. (1983). Work, jobs and unemployment. *Bulletin of the British Psychological Society, 36*, 305–311.

Warr, P.B. (1984a). Job loss, unemployment and psychological well-being. In V. Allen & E. van de Vliert (Eds.), *Role transitions* (pp. 263–285). New York: Plenum.

Warr, P.B. (1984b). Reported behaviour changes after job loss. *British Journal of Social Psychology, 23*, 271–275.

Warr, P.B. (1984c). Work and unemployment. In P.J.D. Drenth, H. Thierry, P.J. Willems, & C.J. de Wolff (Eds.), *Handbook of work and organization psychology* (pp. 413–443). Chichester: Wiley.

Warr, P.B. (1985). Twelve questions about unemployment and health. In B. Roberts, R. Finnegan, & D. Gallie (Eds.), *New approaches to economic life.* Manchester: Manchester University Press.

Warr, P.B. (1987a). *Work, unemployment, and mental health.* Oxford: Clarendon Press.

Warr, P.B. (1987b). Workers without a job. In P.B. Warr (Ed.), *Psychology at work* (pp. 335–356). Harmondsworth: Penguin.

Warr, P.B., Banks, M.H., & Ullah, P. (1985). The experience of unemployment among black and white urban teenagers. *British Journal of Psychology, 76*, 75–87.

Warr, P.B., Cook, J.D., & Wall, T.D. (1979). Scales for the measurement of some work attitudes and aspects of psychological well-being. *Journal of Occupational Psychology, 52,* 129–148.

Warr, P.B., & Jackson, P.R. (1983). Self-esteem and unemployment among young workers. *Le Travail Humain, 46,* 355–366.

Warr, P.B., & Jackson, P.R. (1984) Men without jobs: Some correlates of age and length of unemployment. *Journal of Occupational Psychology, 57,* 77–85.

Warr, P.B., & Jackson, P.R. (1985). Factors influencing the psychological impact of prolonged unemployment and of re-employment. *Psychological Medicine, 15,* 795–807.

Warr, P.B., & Jackson, P.R. (1987). Adapting to the unemployed role: A longitudinal investigation. *Social Science and Medicine, 24,* 1–6.

Warr, P.B., Jackson, P.R., & Banks, M.H. (1982). Duration of unemployment and psychological well-being in young men and women. *Current Psychological Research, 2,* 207–214.

Warr, P.B., Jackson, P.R., & Banks, M.H. (1988). Unemployment and mental health: Some British studies. *Journal of Social Issues, 44,* 47–68.

Warr, P.B., & Parry, G. (1982). Paid employment and women's psychological well-being. *Psychological Bulletin, 91,* 498–516.

Warr, P.B., & Payne, R. (1982). Experiences of strain and pleasure among British adults. *Social Science and Medicine, 16,* 1691–1697.

Warr, P.B., & Payne, R.L. (1983). Social class and reported changes in behavior after job loss. *Journal of Applied Social Psychology, 13,* 206–222.

Watson, D. (1982). The actor and the observer: How are their perceptions of causality divergent? *Psychological Bulletin, 92,* 682–700.

Webb, E.J., Campbell, D.T., Schwartz, R.D., & Sechrest, L. (1966). *Unobtrusive measures: Nonreactive research in the social sciences.* Chicago: Rand McNally.

Weber, M. (1976). *The Protestant ethic and the spirit of capitalism* (T. Parsons, Trans.). London: George Allen & Unwin. (Original work published 1904–1905).

Wedderburn, D. (1964). *White collar redundancy.* Department of Applied Economics Occasional Papers, No. 1, University of Cambridge.

Weiner, B. (1980). *Human motivation.* New York: Holt, Rinehart & Winston.

Weiner, B. (1986). *An attributional theory of motivation and emotion.* New York: Springer-Verlag.

Weiner, B., Russell, D., & Lerman, D. (1978). Affective consequences of causal ascriptions. In J.H. Harvey, W.J. Ickes, & R.F. Kidd (Eds.), *New directions in attribution research* (Vol. 2, pp. 59–88). Hillsdale, NJ: Erlbaum.

Weiner, B., Russell, D., & Lerman, D. (1979). The cognition-emotion process in achievement-related contexts. *Journal of Personality and Social Psychology, 37,* 1211–1220.

Wells, L.E., & Marwell, G. (1976). *Self-esteem: Its conceptualization and measurement.* Beverly HIlls, CA: Sage.

White, M. (1983). *Long-term unemployment and labour markets.* London: Policy Studies Institute.

Wilson, G.D. (Ed.). (1973). *The psychology of conservatism.* New York: Academic Press.

Wilson, G.D., & Patterson, J.R. (1968). A new measure of conservatism. *British Journal of Social and Clinical Psychology, 7,* 264–269.

Windschuttle, K. (1979). *Unemployment: A social and political analysis of the economic crisis in Australia.* Melbourne: Penguin.

Winefield, A.H., & Tiggemann, M. (1985). Psychological correlates of employment and unemployment: Effects, predisposing factors and sex differences. *Journal of Occupational Psychology, 58,* 229–242.

Winefield, A.H., Tiggemann, M., & Goldney, R.D. (1988). Psychological concomitants of satisfactory employment and unemployment in young people. *Social Psychiatry and Psychiatric Epidemiology, 23*, 149–157.

Wortman, C.B., & Brehm, J.W. (1975). Responses to uncontrollable outcomes: An integration of reactance theory and the learned helplessness model. In L. Berkowitz (Ed.), *Advances in experimental social psychology* (Vol. 8, pp. 278–336). New York: Academic Press.

Wylie, R. (1979). *The self-concept* (Vols. 1 and 2, rev. ed.). Lincoln: University of Nebraska Press.

Zawadski, B., & Lazarsfeld, P.F. (1935). The psychological consequences of unemployment. *Journal of Social Psychology, 6*, 224–251.

Author Index

Subject Index

Springer Series in Social Psychology
Recent Titles

Springer Series in Social Psychology
Recent Titles